COST-BENEFIT ANALYSIS

New Directions in Management and Economics

. . . a series of authoritative books for more effective decision-making . . .

COST-BENEFIT ANALYSIS

AN INTRODUCTION

E. J. MISHAN

PRAEGER PUBLISHERS

New York • Washington

BOOKS THAT MATTER

Published in the United States of America in 1971
by Praeger Publishers, Inc.
111 Fourth Avenue, New York, N.Y. 10003

Library of Congress Catalog Card Number: 70–150700

Printed in the United States of America

TO
DAVID AND FREDA

Contents

Preface

There is very little in this volume beyond the grasp of any person who has absorbed the contents of a good introductory economics textbook. Other than the occasional resort to some elementary algebra, no mathematics are used in the text, and the diagrams are of the kind familiar to all economics students. I am aware that in certain sections of the book, especially those to be found in Parts IV and V, recourse to mathematical formulation would have appeared more elegant and saved many pages. But the student's time is a lot scarcer than printed paper, and the chief concern of an introductory textbook ought to be the digestibility of its contents. With this in mind I have sought to avoid abstraction and develop the more important parts of the arguments by working through simple examples. My guiding aim, in writing each Part, has been to convey to the interested reader with a smattering of economics some of the crucial notions and procedures that lie behind the techniques used in cost-benefit studies. There should be enough in this volume to make him become more critical of the proposals of government officials and the reports of committees of 'experts'—enough, at any rate, to enable him to ask sensible questions of an official body, and possibly embarrassing ones also.

There is some additional warrant for this pedagogic device of working through examples in a treatment of cost-benefit analysis. First, the advantages of elegance, generality, and compactness of statement lie with those branches of the subject that have already passed through a phase of controversy and development and appear to be settling down to a more pedestrian existence. Such is not the state of cost-benefit analysis which is—as readers will soon recognize —an application of welfare economics. Like the parent subject, cost-benefit can be made to look deceptively simple, whereas there are everywhere pitfalls for the unwary. If, therefore, a writer on this subject is vain enough to believe that he has useful advice to offer, he has every incentive to make his meaning clear.

Secondly, there is not at present, so far as I am aware, any intro-

1

ductory textbook wholly devoted to cost-benefit analysis. There are some well-known works on public investment, such as that by R. N. McKean, *Efficiency in Government through Systems Analysis*, or that by Krutilla and Eckstein on *Multiple Purpose River Development*, which cover an important part of the subject matter. Also there are several weighty volumes of case studies with valuable introductions such as the *Measurement of Benefits of Government Investments*, edited by Robert Dorfman, or the studies put out by the Brookings Institute, written by Arthus Maass and others, entitled *Design of Water Resource Systems*. Finally, there are any number of excellent treatises on decision theory with particular reference to problems of uncertainty, to say nothing of the number of works on mathematical programming, operations research, game theory, and the like, that have something to offer in the way of ideas or techniques to cost-benefit analysis. On the subject proper, however, there are, apart from the individual case studies throughout the more technical literature, only some short surveys, the best known being that of Prest and Turvey in the *Economic Journal* for 1965, and an excellent introduction by G. H. Peters put out as a sixty-page Eaton Paper by the Institute of Economic Affairs in 1968.

Without reliable antecedents in the form of a *Principles* of the subject, one is obviously more exposed. All the more is the temptation to retreat into abstract generality about which there is always some penumbra of ambiguity and some latitude of interpretation. But the growing popularity of cost-benefit studies in an age imbued with the notion of efficiency is a sobering thought. The influence on our daily lives of vast investment projects need hardly be stressed. Nor, consequently, need the required appreciation of its scope and limitations by those trained to apply its techniques. If, then, there are critical errors of omission and commission, it is important that the exposition be such that they stand out starkly enough to attract the strictures of competent critics. Any success I have in making the arguments explicit and unequivocal will increase the relevance and the particularity of the criticisms of professional colleagues, as a result of which I, and others, may become the better equipped to produce more suitable cost-benefit treatises.

Notwithstanding these expressions of brave intent, I have had recourse to some form of self-insurance by placing two of the more controversial aspects in Part VI, which carries the noncommittal

2

title of 'Further Notes Relating to Cost-Benefit Analysis'. Logically, Note A, 'The Welfare Basis of Cost-Benefit Analysis', should have appeared at the beginning of the book. Pedagogic reasons could be always found, however, for placing it at the end: for one can pick up a lot about the applications of a subject while remaining untroubled about its 'foundations'. But, as suggested above, my own view concerning the basis of cost-benefit analysis is very particular. It is as well, then, to keep it apart from the text which, though it has occasional pretensions to novelty, ought to go over well enough—apart from possible errors—with the profession. Like considerations impelled me to place Note C, on 'Allocation, Distribution, and Equity', in the same place of refuge. Note B, 'More Accurate Measures of Economic Surplus', however, was relegated to Part VI for the very simple reason that it was, perhaps, too exacting for the ordinary reader. And though it will, I hope, be of interest to some, it is obviously more of a refinement than a requisite.

. . . . . .

The sophisticated practitioner may observe that the analytic structure erected in this volume is somewhat monolithic. I state explicitly that cost-benefit analysis is an application of welfare economics and, more particularly, that the rationale of cost-benefit analysis is based on that of a potential Pareto improvement. This thesis runs through the book, and what is valid and what is relevant is consistently determined by reference to it.

There can be two possible objections to this procedure. First, it can be said that it ignores considerations of distribution and equity; second, that it ignores indices of merit other than Pareto-based ones.

The first objection is not a strong one. In the first place, there is an overt concern with distribution and equity in Part III on external effects, and also in Note C, on 'Allocation, Distribution, and Equity'. In addition, it is pointed out in several places, and especially in Note A, on 'The Welfare Basis of Cost-Benefit Analysis', that although the outcome, or magnitude, of a cost-benefit evaluation is independent of its potential distribution effects, a project which meets an adopted cost-benefit test can properly be rejected on grounds of distribution or equity. Moreover, the economist has a duty to point up all relevant effects that do not enter the cost-benefit computation.

3

But having said all this, the cost-benefit calculation remains a thing apart. Notwithstanding attempts made from time to time in the literature to integrate the distributional effects with the 'efficiency' effects—usually by weighting with, say, utility indices the dollar value of net benefits enjoyed by the various income groups—the tradition of separating the cost-benefit calculation from the distributional effects continues in practice, and is unlikely to change in the foreseeable future. I might add in passing that even if a system of distributional weights could be agreed upon, a concern with distributional justice would continue to require reference to the expected effects on distribution. For allowing that a dollar of net benefit to the 'poor' is more heavily weighted than a dollar of net benefit to the 'rich', a project which (using the system of agreed weights) qualifies for admission on some adopted criterion may still be one that makes the rich richer and the poor poorer.

As to the second objection, I again defer to tradition and current practice, though not without recognizing the scope for innovation in the choice of other social merit indicators which—though not having quite the same sanction as a Pareto-based indicator—may yet become acknowledged as revealing and pertinent for particular sorts of projects. But until such social merit indicators have become more widely established, an introductory text may be justified in disregarding them.

Current applications of cost-benefit analysis do not, as it happens, require fastidious equipment in the way of statistical methods or simulation techniques, though obviously familiarity with them will extend the reach and the versatility of the practitioner. There is, however, no advantage in including sections on curve-fitting and identification, and so on, not only because there are already quite a number of competent textbooks devoted to the problems they give rise to, but also because such techniques have a wide range of applications that are not peculiar to cost-benefit methods. The present volume has concentrated wholly on the concepts underlying the applications: on the interpretation to be given to the magnitudes. In short, the volume can be regarded as an essay on what is and what is not agenda; on what is to count and what is not to count in a cost-benefit evaluation. And if the reader ever becomes master of this difficult craft, he need not worry too much if his knowledge of statistics remains somewhat skimpy. There is no lack of good statisticians among economists. But there is, at present, an acute shortage of economists skilled in the design of cost-benefit studies.

. . . . . .

Like yesterday's lovers, today's textbook writers act in haste and repent at leisure. Before the War, the practice among academic authors was to mull over a script for several years before offering one's work, with some diffidence if not trepidation, to a more limited community of scholars. The profession was then both more learned and more fastidious. Style and proportion were qualities valued and cultivated. Yet, the fact is that they could afford to move at a more leisurely pace. The numbers in any academic discipline were a small fraction of those today. And the sheer output and pace of development were not there to goad them into indecent haste. These things will be in the mind of the charitable critic as he detects occasional parochialisms and superficialities.

The task of revising a first draft was made easier by the generous response of a couple of my colleagues, and friends, at the London School of Economics. Mr Kurt Klappholz scrutinized Part III, on External Effects, and brought to light a number of errors and ambiguities. Mr Lucien Foldes undertook to vet Parts IV and V—on Investment Criteria and Uncertainty, respectively—in the course of which he made many valuable suggestions. While making the conventional disclaimer on behalf of both, I wish to record my gratitude to them.

I wish to acknowledge the kindness of the Editors of *The American Economic Review, The Canadian Journal of Economics, The Economic Journal, The Journal of Political Economy* and *Oxford Economic Papers,* for permission to make use of the ideas and exposition in a number of my papers that appeared in these journals between 1960 and 1970.

E. J. M.

Foreword

Why Cost-Benefit analysis? Why not plain honest-to-goodness profit and loss accounting?

The simple answer is provided by the familiar thesis, that what counts as a benefit or a loss to a part of the economy—to one or more persons, or groups—does not necessarily count as a benefit or loss to the economy as a whole. And in cost-benefit analysis we are concerned with the economy as a whole; with the welfare of a defined society, and not any smaller part of it.

A private, or even a public, enterprise comprises only a segment of the economy, often a very small segment. More important, whatever the means it employs in pursuing its objectives—whether rules of thumb or more formalized techniques, such as mathematical programming or operations research—the private enterprise, at least, is guided by the ordinary commercial criterion requiring its revenues to equal to or to exceed its costs. The fact that its activities are guided by the profit motive, however, is not to deny that it confers benefits on a large number of people other than its shareholders. It confers benefits on its employees, on consumers, and—through the taxes it pays—on the general public. Yet the benefits enjoyed by others continue only in so far as they issue ultimately in profits to the enterprise. Without a public subsidy, the enterprise will not survive if it makes losses. If it is to survive as a private concern, and to expand, it must, over a period of time, produce profits large enough either to attract investors or to finance its expansion.

There is, of course, the metaphor of the Invisible Hand—the *deus ex machina* discovered by Adam Smith which directs the forces of private greed so as to issue in social beneficence. And one can, indeed, lay down the simple and sufficient conditions under which the uncompromising pursuit of profits acts to serve the public interest. They are, that all effects relevant to the welfare of individuals be priced through the market, and that perfect competition prevail in all economic activities.[1]

---

1 Exception being made for the economic activity that concerns itself with the production of money. Unless the economy is on a full gold standard, the creation of money has to be a (government) monopoly if continuous inflation is to be avoided.

Once we depart from this ideal economic scene, however, the set of outputs and prices to which the economy tends may not serve the public as well as some other set of outputs and prices. In addition to a possible misallocation of resources among the goods being produced, it is possible also that certain goods which can be economically justified do not get produced, while others which cannot be economically justified do get produced. If, for instance, technical conditions and the size of the market are such that a number of goods can be produced only under increasing returns to scale (or decreasing average costs), it is possible that, although some of these goods will be produced by monopolies charging prices above marginal cost,[2] others will not be produced at all. If they are not produced, it will be because—although benefits would accrue to potential customers if they were produced—a non-discriminating monopolist could not transfer enough of these benefits to himself to make the venture worth while. Again, certain goods having beneficial, though unpriced, spillover effects ought, economically, to be produced even though they cannot be produced at a profit. The reverse is also true: profitable commercial activities sometimes produce noxious spillover effects, and would be declared uneconomic on a more comprehensive pricing scheme.

The economist engaged in the cost-benefit appraisal of a project is not then, in essence, asking a different sort of question than the accountant of a private enterprise. Rather, the same sort of question is asked about a wider group, society as a whole, and is asked more searchingly. Instead of asking whether the owners of the enterprise will be made better off by the firm's engaging in one activity rather than another, the economist asks whether society as a whole will be made better off by undertaking this project rather than not undertaking it, or by undertaking, instead, any of a number of other projects. Broadly speaking, for the more precise concept of the revenue of the private concern, the economist substitutes the less

---

2 Increasing returns to scale do not rule out perfect competition as a logical possibility. As Marshall (1924) pointed out, external economies internal to the industry allow each firm to produce at constant average cost in long-period equilibrium while, at the same time, a particular process, one which they all make use of and has been taken over by a particular firm, yields increasing returns to scale.

7

precise, yet meaningful, concept of the social benefit. For the costs of the private concern, the economist will substitute the concept of opportunity cost—or social value forgone elsewhere in moving factors into a projected economic activity. For the profit of the private concern, the economist will substitute the concept of excess social benefit over cost, or some related investment criterion.

It transpires that the realization of practically all proposed cost-benefit criteria—often cast as investment criteria in order to take account of costs and benefits through time—implies a concept of social betterment that amounts to a *potential* Pareto improvement (sometimes referred to in the older literature as a 'test of hypothetical overcompensation'). The project in question, to be considered as economically feasible, must, that is, be capable of producing an excess of benefits such that everyone in society could, by a costless redistribution of the gains, be made better off.[3]

The essential idea is straightforward enough. But once the net is thrown wider, and the repercussions over the economy at large are brought into the calculus, a number of problems arise which require extended treatment. Chief among them are the concepts and measurements of consumers' surplus and rents, the distinction between benefits and transfer payments, the concept of shadow pricing, external economies and diseconomies, the choice of investment criteria, and the problems of uncertainty. They are dealt with in that order in the following chapters.

---

3   The reader who is impatient to pursue this theme further may turn to Part VI, Note A, on 'The Welfare Basis of Cost-Benefit Analysis'.

PART I. SOME SIMPLIFIED EXAMPLES OF COST-BENEFIT STUDIES

Chapter 1
INTRODUCTORY

Each of the following chapters contains brief notes on a particular cost-benefit study that has been undertaken within the last few years. They are not intended to be summaries of these studies. If they were, there would have to be reference to some of the statistical problems encountered, and some mention also of the variety of assumptions behind the calculation of the benefits over the future. Without mention of these things, a judgement about the usefulness of any of the studies would not be possible. They are not important, however, if the purpose of presenting these notes is to bring to the reader's attention some of the ideas which determine the shape these benefits and costs will take in particular cases. The ideas themselves are rooted, ultimately, in that branch of the subject known as welfare economics, yet no more than an elementary knowledge of economic principles is required for their appreciation.

If the reader does not, at first, fully understand the significance of some of the ways of calculating costs or benefits, both of which are briefly described in the following chapters, he is urged not to worry about it at this stage, but to read on. It is enough if these crude and partial reconstructions convey a rough picture of what a cost-benefit study is about and so, perhaps, whet his appetite for a more detailed discussion of the principles that follows. They were placed here with· no other purpose in mind and, indeed, could be omitted on a first reading. Once he has worked through the book, the reader can always return to these chapters which will then, I trust, seem to him straightforward enough.

Chapter 2

AN UNDERGROUND RAILWAY

1. The 'Victoria Line' is a recent extension of London's underground railway system. It runs currently from Victoria Station to Walthamstow in North East London, and passes through Oxford Circus and Euston Station. First proposed in 1949, its construction was authorized by the government in 1962 following a cost-benefit study by Foster and Beesley.[1]

2. The calculation of the initial capital and operating costs presented no difficulty. The estimate of the social benefits did, however, pose a problem. On ordinary financial calculations based on the existing (and projected) fare structures, an annual loss of about £2 million from operating the Victoria Line was confidently predicted. On the underground system as a whole, moreover, the annual loss resulting from its construction was put at £3 million—a consequence simply of the expected reduction in revenues arising from passengers changing from longer routes to the shorter ones to be provided by the Victoria Line.

However, social returns were deemed to diverge from financial returns in this instance for two main reasons: (1) because of the pricing policy of the London underground system, and (2) because of the relative prices of road and rail transport.

With respect to (1), London underground fares are set so as to equal average costs: there is no rise in fares when marginal costs rise during 'rush hours'. Moreover, there is no attempt to 'exploit' the demand curve for underground travel. Thus, the consumers' surplus remains as an obvious measure of unexploited benefit, but one that is not included in the financial returns.

With respect to (2), the maximum sums that people will pay for the service offered by the Victoria Line, indeed for underground

---

1 The study is summarized in their 1963 paper given before the Royal Statistical Society.

railway services generally, will vary with road prices. The higher are road prices the greater will be the demand for the services of London's underground railway services. In fact, road vehicle users pay less than their true marginal cost of travel. Once a vehicle is bought, the only relevant cost to the owner is the cost of its operation, largely the cost of fuel (including, of course, the fuel tax). But the marginal cost of operating a car, additional to the resource cost of the fuel used, is not merely the additional wear and tear on the roads. More importantly, it is the costs of the additional congestion imposed by any particular vehicle on all other existing vehicles currently using the same route. And these so-called *social* marginal costs are believed to be much greater than the fuel tax. Indeed, if the surface traffic were correctly priced, the authors did not doubt that the Victoria Line would pay its way financially.

3. Nevertheless, Foster and Beesley accepted as a political constraint, the existing road taxes, and the fare structure of the London underground railway, and went on to estimate the social benefits arising from the construction of the Victoria Line.

The kinds of social benefit they attempted to estimate are of three sorts:

A. Cost-savings (which include the saving in fares) by using the more direct routes to be offered by the Victoria Line.

B. Time-savings, which include the saving in time by underground passengers switching to the Victoria Line, and the time saved by hitherto surface travellers changing to the Victoria Line. In so far as road-users also changed to the Victoria Line, the congestion on the roads would be relieved and time would be saved in surface travel. There would also be some saving in time by underground passengers not using the Victoria Line—a consequence of the easing of traffic on all other lines from the switch to the Victoria Line.

C. Other benefits, such as increased comfort, or reduced stress, brought about by the new arrangement.

In addition to the benefits to be enjoyed by the existing number of people who would travel across London in the absence of the Victoria Line, the operation of the Victoria Line will induce additional numbers of people to travel. Some estimate of the benefit to be attributed to this generated traffic was also made.[2]

4. Each of the component estimates of benefits has a time trend attached to it; transforming it into a series of such benefits over a fifty-year period (increasing the period beyond fifty years made practically no difference).

As for costs, only capital costs are relevant. Operating costs are not required simply because one of the benefits is estimated as *savings* in cost—the excess of the operating costs incurred on the existing underground routes over the costs of the underground when the Victoria Line is included.

The costs of construction were spread over 5½ years. Compounded at 6 per cent per annum to the finishing date, the end of 1968, the capital outlay was reckoned at £55 million. The stream of social benefits, fitted to the trends, over the following fifty years and discounted at 6 per cent, came to £86 million.

The benefit-cost ratio is, therefore, 86/55, and the *net* benefit-cost ratio is (86 − 55)/55, or 35/55. Given that the rate of discount of 6 per cent is acceptable, a benefit-cost ratio greater than unity, or a *net* benefit-cost ratio greater than zero, is necessary if the project is to be regarded as economically feasible. The obvious comparison that might then be made is that between the Victoria Line project and the cost-benefit ratios of alternative investment projects. But this was beyond the scope of the study.

---

2 In the longer run, people might be induced to change the location of their homes and that of their work, but the authors estimate the benefit only from the increased traffic generated for the Victoria Line. Changes in land and in property values are excluded also, on grounds (a) that the rise in the values in one area can be at the expense of a decline in values in other areas, and (b) that the rise in values as a result of transport improvement reflects the value of the prospective reduction in cost over the future. To include the rise in land values also would be to engage in double-counting.

Chapter 3
DISEASE CONTROL

1. Investment in human capital is one of the most popular themes to be found in the postwar economic literature. Such investment is not confined to higher education or vocational training however. It is extended to housing, hospitals, public health and amenity, all of which can be conceived as contributing to the efficiency of men's productive capacities. Measurability of any one of a number of complementary types of investment poses problems, in particular when it is recognized that the benefits to be reaped by the community are not only in the form of higher outputs but also in the form of a direct improvement of health and spirits. It is the task of the economist to bring such benefits into the calculus along with the more mundane, albeit more measurable, benefits.

Proceeding from investment in human productivity to investment in health, we can narrow our sights further to the prevention of certain diseases. In this chapter we shall indicate the methods used by Klarman (1965) in calculating the potential benefits of syphilis eradication in the United States.

2. The interest in syphilis springs partly from reports that it is rising again, after its dramatic postwar decline, and partly from its being a highly communicable disease, one, moreover, carrying a social stigma.

The benefits of a particular disease-control programme are simply those current costs of the disease which are averted by the programme, such benefits being compared with the resource-costs of the programme. Such benefits, or averted costs, can be split into three broad categories: (1) expenditures on medical care, (2) losses of current production, and (3) the pain and discomforts accompanying, and following, the disease.

(1) The expenditures on medical care include the costs of the services of physicians and other personnel, drugs, hospital facilities and equipment. (2) The losses of current production—at the stage

where complications set in are reckoned (a) as the loss of gross earnings,[1] the result of a loss of working hours in order to have diagnosis and treatment, and (b) a reduction in gross earnings in consequence of the social stigma which renders a person less employable—at any rate less mobile, once the fact of his having suffered from syphilis is entered into his records. (3) The pain and discomforts associated with the disease, like social stigmas, are not easy to evaluate, and the procedure was clearly arbitrary.

3. The public health literature in 1962 stated that 1.2 million Americans had syphilis, that 60,000 acquired it every year, and that 120,000 cases were reported annually, most of them years after the onset of the infection. For the calculation of benefits from eradicating the disease, it is the latter figure—the numbers reporting in the year 1962—that is used.

An estimate of the three sorts of cost mentioned were made for each of five groups of cases: (A) cases reported in the infectious (primary or secondary) stages (about 20,000); (B) cases treated in the infectious (primary and secondary) stages but not reported (33,400); (C) cases treated in the early latent stage (17,000); (D) cases treated in the late latent stage (48,200); and (E) cases treated in the late complications stage (about 800). Each of these groups was broken down into Male and Female, and White and Non-White, and for each of these sub-groups an average figure for all the three items of cost was estimated. Finally, a 4 per cent per annum discount rate was employed in order to reduce to a present, 1962, value all the future expenditures on medical treatment and associated losses of output, allowance being made both for the expected annual rise in physician's fees and for increased annual productivity.

So calculated, the total costs incurred by all these cases in 1962 were estimated at $117.5 million. The value of the benefits accruing from the total eradication of the disease would, therefore, be equal to this annual sum realized in perpetuity. Employing a 4 per cent discount rate this future stream of benefits has a present capital value $f $2.95 billion. If, in addition, the existing control and surveillance mechanisms were abandoned, an extra $6 million per

---

1 The earnings of housewives were calculated by reference to the earnings of domestic servants.

annum would be saved, yielding a present value at 4 per cent of $150 million. The total present value of eradicating the disease can, therefore, be put at $3.1 billion.

More than 40 per cent of this, $1.3 billion, however, was attributed to 'stigma' which was, somewhat arbitrarily, evaluated at 1 per cent or 0·5 per cent of earnings subsequent to the discovery of syphilis. Roughly one-third of the total was due to averting future losses of output, and one-sixth to the saving of future medical expenses.

Although the approach to the benefit side is interesting, and the items are broken down as to make rough calculations possible, the study was not perhaps an ideal model of cost-benefit analysis. Moreover, as was pointed out at the time,[2] no attempt was made to estimate the benefits flowing from a defined control programme which could achieve a reduction of the incidence of the disease to some specified level.

---

2   By Selma Mushkin in commenting on Klarman's paper (1965).

Chapter 4
RESERVOIR CONSTRUCTION

1. One of the most popular applications of cost-benefit techniques is that of water-control, involving the construction of a reservoir or a dam, and the machinery for electricity-generation, flood-control, or irrigation. There is already some very specialized literature on the methods of estimating costs and benefits for such projects,[1] possibly because the range of practicable schemes for any one or multiple-purpose project is much larger than it is for other common applications of cost-benefit techniques, such as tunnels, highways, bridges, and airports.

2. The following highly simplified example[2] provides the reader with an idea of a possible cost-benefit approach to reservoir construction. A reservoir is to be built on each, or on either, of two tributaries to a river in order to reduce flood damage beyond the point of confluence.

From the data collected over, say, fifty years, it is possible to construct a frequency, or probability, curve of the flood damage to be expected. If, for instance, flood damage valued at $75,000 occurred in four out of the fifty years, we may be able to judge whether climatic and other conditions are likely to change little enough to warrant our using a frequency of 4/50 or 8 per cent for this amount of damage over the future. If we decide that we can accept the events over the past fifty years as a fair sample, then the expected benefit of any construction designed to prevent damage above a certain figure is the value of the damage it can prevent times the probability of its occurrence.

The distribution shown in Figure I.1 reveals that the maximum damage which can be eliminated by a specific construction, $100,000 within a year, has a 4 per cent probability of occurring in any year.

---

1   A good introduction to investment in water resource projects is to be found in Maass (1962), from which this example is taken.
2   Taken from Hufschmidt, in Maass (1962).

If, then, either a single reservoir or two reservoirs can be constructed so as to eliminate this maximum damage completely, but no smaller damage, the benefit, say B_1, is to be reckoned as $100,000 times 4 per cent, or $4,000 per annum.

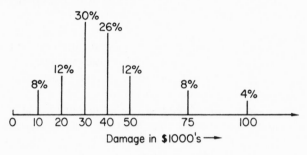

Fig I.1

There will be some larger construction of one, or of two, reservoirs which will, in addition, completely eliminate any possibility of a $75,000 damage within the year. Since the probability of this lesser damage occuring is 8 per cent, the expected benefit, B_2, from this construction is reckoned as ($75,000 × 8%) + ($100,000 × 4%), a total of $10,000 per annum.

A larger construction yet would be needed to eliminate the possibility of the yearly damage of $50,000 as well. The benefit accruing to this construction is reckoned as ($50,000 × 12%) + ($75,000 × 8%) + ($100,000 × 4%), a total expected benefit of $16,000 per annum. A yet larger construction, removing the possibility of any $40,000 damage, would secure an annual expected benefit, B_4, of $26,400, and so on.

It should be clear that the expected value of the damage caused, and therefore the value of the expected benefit from eliminating the damage, depends upon the prices expected for the crops which can be destroyed by flood. The probability distribution depicted in Figure I.1 may be accurate enough with respect to the physical damage over the area, but the expected value of such damage must depend also on the expected price of the crops and the extent and intensity of the farming in the region. If the output of the crops is expected to increase year by year, and/or if the prices of the crops are expected to rise relative to the prices of other goods over time,

17

then the value of potential damage has to be increased in successive years. In that case, the B_1 expected benefit for instance, would not be a stream of benefits of \$4,000 per annum over the future, but a stream of benefits beginning with \$4,000 and increasing over time. Whatever the ultimate shape of the expected B_1 benefit stream, we can discount it to a present value using a chosen rate of discount.

3. Having got a present discounted value for each of the expected streams of benefits $B_1, B_2, \ldots, B_7$ (each of such streams corresponding, successively, to a more expensive reservoir construction), the cost of these reservoirs has to be estimated.

Now, in general, the elimination of flood damage which corresponds to some given benefit stream, say B_1, can be effected by a variety of reservoir systems. In our simple instance of a maximum of two reservoirs, we have the choice of building a single reservoir

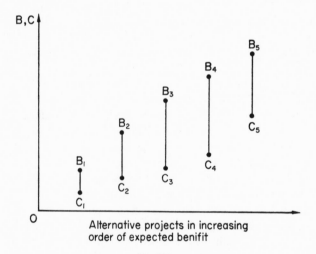

Alternative projects in increasing
order of expected benifit

Fig I.2

on one tributary to the river, or a single reservoir on the other tributary, or a reservoir across the river itself, or some combination of these. The costs over the future of constructing each of these alternative reservoir systems are compared, and the alternative having the lowest discounted present value, say C_1, is selected as the appropriate one for preventing the expected damage associated with

18

B_1. Exactly the same procedure is gone through for each of the other expected benefit streams, B_2, B_3, . ., B_7, in order to produce them at the lowest cost constructions, C_2, C_3, . ., C_7, respectively.

These alternative cost-benefit magnitudes are plotted vertically in Figure I.2 for each of B_1, B_2, . . ., B_7, in that order. The reservoir system chosen is that giving the largest excess benefit over cost, here $B_4 - C_4$, provided that there are no constraints on the funds available.[3]

If the variations in benefit and cost were conceived as continuous, and a continuous B-curve and C-curve were drawn, the reader would perceive the analogy between Figure I.2 and the total cost and total revenue curves of the firm, measured against output along the horizontal axis. Given the conventional shape of the total cost and total revenue curves, maximum net revenue (revenue less cost) is at the output for which the tangents to the two curves are parallel.

---

3 If, on the other hand, a choice had to be made subject to a limited capital budget, we should want to get as close to the optimum B_4-C_4 as the budget allows. But if, moreover, there were a number of such projects to be undertaken simultaneously in different areas, we should do best by using the limited funds among projects yielding the highest B/C ratio. These alternative criteria are discussed in some detail in Part IV.

Chapter 5
CHANNEL TUNNEL

1. In 1963 the result of a study jointly undertaken by British and French officials was published in the United Kingdom with the title, *Proposals for a Fixed Channel Link* (Cmnd. 2137). The study compared both a Tunnel and a Bridge with the existing means of cross-channel travel, predicted over a fifty-year period, between 1969 and 2018. In selecting some features of this study, we can ignore estimates for the Bridge project which, in any case, revealed a net loss.[1]

2. The impression given by the *Proposals* was that of limited variability in the type of tunnel. After much description of the physical details of the constructions possible, and the type, time and frequency of services, an upper and lower estimate of capital and operating costs were estimated. The difference between the upper and lower estimate for operating costs was not large, however, and was non-existent for capital costs.

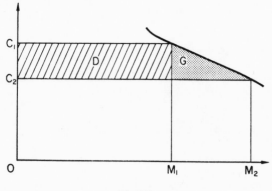

Fig I.3

1 The estimates of future traffic were crude; no more in fact than projections of the average growth of cross-channel traffic for periods 1951–62 and 1950–7.

20

For the purpose of estimating benefits, the traffic expected over the future was broken down into three types, passengers, vehicles (including the private cars of passengers), and goods. A division was then made between (1) traffic *diverted* from the existing means of travel, and (2) additional traffic that would be *generated* only in virtue of the construction of the tunnel. An impression of the significance of this distinction is afforded by the areas D and G respectively in Figure I.3, along the horizontal axis of which is measured number of journeys per period, and along the vertical axis of which is measured the cost per journey.

If the cost of the journey falls from C_1 to C_2 the number of people who had previously made OM_1 journeys would be better off by the saving in cost equal to the shaded rectangular area D. If, in consequence of the lower cost of the journey, the price was lowered proportionally, M_1M_2 additional journeys would be made. The extra gain from these additional journeys is equal to the dotted triangular area G. This is explained as follows.

The unit cost of the existing means of travel can be taken as OC_1, and the number of journeys by this means OM_1. A fall in the unit cost from OC_1 to OC_2, when the journey is undertaken by tunnel, implies a cost-saving of C_2C_1 for each of the OM_1 journeys, now diverted from the existing means of travel to the tunnel. The area of rectangle D represents, therefore, the gain from the *diverted* traffic. But, at a lower unit cost of the journey, OC_2, M_1M_2 journeys are undertaken that would not otherwise take place. These additional journeys are the *generated* traffic, and the gain they offer is measured by the consumers' surplus triangle G.

3. Following this distinction, the benefits over the 50-year period were calculated as follows:

(1) for *diverted* traffic which, as it happened, provided by far the greater part of the benefits, there would be a saving in both capital costs (of the existing means—ships and planes) and operating costs over time as a result of the tunnel construction. For instance, in the year 1963 it was expected that x_1 million passengers would make the channel crossing by the existing means, so also would x_2 million vehicles and x_3 million tons of freight. In the *absence* of the tunnel project, each of these figures was expected to increase at a figure between some upper and lower percentage per annum over the future.

If, on the other hand, the tunnel were to be built, at a cost of £141 million in 1969, the upper estimate of the diversion of traffic to it would release resources used by the existing means to an adjusted 1969 value of £308 million. Ships and planes might be scrapped the sooner. But, more important, additional ships and planes which would have been built in the absence of the tunnel, would then no longer be built. The resources (men and materials) which would have been used in their operation, would also be released for other economic activities.

Against this saving of £308 million in capital expenditures we should have to place the costs of operating the tunnel transport, which were reckoned at an adjusted 1969 value of £68 million. The net saving in capital and other costs is, therefore, £308 million *less* £68 million, or £240 million.

(2) For *generated* traffic, the estimate was of a profit on additional freight, which would not otherwise have been undertaken, of £47 million. To this figure was added an estimate of consumers' surplus of additional passengers, who would not otherwise have made the journey, of £7 million, a total of £54 million when adjusted to 1969.

The total benefits, on the upper estimates, were, therefore, £240 million from the diverted traffic *plus* £54 million for the generated traffic, a total of £294 million to be compared with the initial capital outlay of £141 million. If the criterion adopted was that of a Benefit-Cost ratio greater than unity, then certainly it would be met by the upper estimates of the project. The calculation based on the lower traffic estimates produced a benefit cost ratio of 215/141, which is also acceptable.

4. The costs and benefits were, as state d, spread over a long period It was estimated that it would take six years, 1962–8 inclusive, to construct the tunnel, over which period the costs would fall most heavily in the last two years. The 1969 figure of £141 million, therefore, represented a compounding of the earlier capital outlays (at 7 per cent per annum) to that date. Moreover, the figure represents the initial capital sum only. Beginning with the year 1973, and from then on, capital costs were expected to be incurred in almost every year down to 2018. These future capital costs, along with the annual operating costs, from 1969 to 2018, were discounted to 1969 to yield the upper estimate of £68 million already referred to. The saving

of capital and the saving of operating expenses by the existing means were also expected to be distributed over a large number of years beginning from 1969. They were discounted at 7 per cent to the year 1969 to yield the £308 million figure also referred to above.

The resulting stream of benefits and costs were used also to work out the internal rate of return over cost,[2] which was 13·3 per cent for the higher estimate, and 10·4 per cent for the lower estimate— both being higher than the 7 per cent discount rate adopted.

5. The study mentioned other economic factors which were not quantified; for instance, (a) the fact that passengers are *not* indifferent as between different modes of travel. If the tunnel-journey fare were the same as, or even lower than, that of the sea or air journey, passengers might still prefer to travel by sea or air. In that case a fare low enough to attract their custom from the existing means of travel would have to be credited with conferring a benefit smaller than the full saving in the fares. And (b) other repercussions on the economies of the Continental countries and Britain were mentioned, though without being specific. One can think of a number of unwanted effects in this connection, such as traffic congestion near the vicinity of the tunnel entrances, and what is now known as 'tourist blight' resulting from the increased traffic.

---

2 For a definition and description of the internal rate of return over cost, the reader is referred to Chapter 28 in Part IV.

Chapter 6
COST-BENEFIT CAPACITY ADJUSTMENTS

1. Cost-benefit techniques are not confined to appraising complete investment projects but are employed, also, to determine whether the capacity of existing projects should be extended and, if so, by how much. In so far as the question is one of estimating the optimal amount of new capacity, or the optimal use of the existing capacity, the economist is explicitly concerned with conventional marginal analysis.

2. A popular example of the latter would be the taxing of vehicles on some existing road in order to realize an optimal traffic flow. As the flow of vehicles increases over a given stretch of highway there comes a point after which the average speed falls as the flow, or volume, of traffic increases. Simplifying some of the ideas put forward by Walters (1961), and thinking in terms of a uniform type of vehicle, we can separate two sorts of costs which motorists, as a group, impose on themselves, and which grow as the volume of traffic grows: (a) the time of the trip and, therefore, since we can attribute a value to people's time, the cost of the trip, and (b) the direct costs of operating a vehicle, chiefly fuel.

Volume of traffic is measured along the horizontal axis of Figure I.4, and cost per vehicle trip is measured vertically. The vertical distance between the horizontal axis and the A curve at any point, therefore, measures the average cost per vehicle trip for that volume of traffic—cost including (a) time and (b) fuel. The sum of these costs are represented as being constant up to traffic volume OQ_0, but increasing beyond that volume. Thus beyond OQ_0 not only does every additional motorist raise the composite cost to himself, by raising the average cost he also causes each of the motorists already using the road—the 'intra-marginal' motorists—to bear this additional cost. The sum of the *additional* costs borne by all the intra-marginal motorists, *plus* his own total cost, makes up the increment of total cost attributable to the additional motorist. At any volume of traffic, the relation between the average cost per motorist and this corresponding increment of total cost caused by an additional vehicle is given, as every economics student knows, by the respective heights of the average curve and the curve marginal to it.

In Figure I.4, the marginal cost curve M appears as a dotted line that is marginal to the average cost curve A. Once the A curve begins

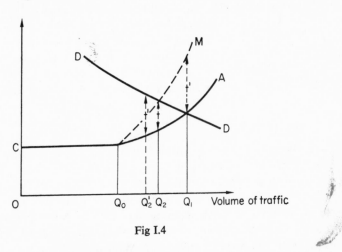

Fig I.4

to rise, as it does after traffic volume OQ_0, the marginal cost curve M also rises, but more steeply. The DD curve is the demand curve for trips along this stretch of highway, and can usefully be thought of as indicating, at any volume of traffic, the marginal value of the trip to the existing number of motorists. In the absence of any restriction the volume of traffic would tend to settle[1] at OQ_1. At this volume of traffic, each motorist finds the marginal value of his trip to be equal to, or no lower than, the cost (in terms of time and fuel) of his trip. Once the cost of his trip is revised to include the additional cost the motorist imposes on the intra-marginal vehicles, we have to be guided by the marginal cost curve M. Employing the marginal cost

---

1 Strictly speaking, a statement about 'tending to settle' implies that the equilibrium volume of traffic at OQ_1 is stable. Since we are interested with optimality questions here, and not with stability conditions, we shall continue to assume stability conditions are met unless otherwise indicated.

principle of choosing as optimum the volume at which marginal cost is equal to marginal value, or price, volume OQ_2 is chosen—the point at which the M curve intersects the DD curve. This optimal flow of traffic, OQ_2, can be brought about by levying an optimal tax, t, on each vehicle using this highway—t being equal to the difference, at Q_2 between the average and the marginal cost curve.

3.   In order to calculate this tax it might seem necessary (1) to make some statistical estimate of the average cost curve in Figure I.4 and, therefore, of the cost of its two main components, time and fuel, and (2) to make some estimate of the demand curve DD for trips along this stretch of highway. With respect to (1), however, estimating the full range of the average cost curve is not necessary; only the portion of it between Q_2 and Q_1. Indeed, if one has estimates of the average cost in the vicinity of Q_2, there is enough information to calculate the 'point elasticity' of the A curve at Q_2—point elasticity being here defined, conventionally, as the per cent increase in the volume of traffic for a one per cent increase in average cost—which enables us to calculate the marginal cost at Q_2.

We could further simplify things by assuming that this point elasticity remains constant along the relevant range between Q_1 and Q_2—though Q_2 cannot be discovered until we have made an estimate of the demand curve DD. With respect to (2), and if we declare ourselves satisfied with a rough calculation of the optimal tax t, we could either assume the demand curve to have a unit elasticity at all points or we can omit consideration of the demand curve, at least provisionally. Let us follow this latter alternative. Provided we have the average cost, and its corresponding point elasticity, for the existing volume of traffic at Q_1, the marginal cost at Q_1 can be derived by the familiar formula $M = A(1 + 1/E)$, where E is the point elasticity at Q_1 of the A curve, and M and A respectively are marginal and average cost.[2]

Now the tax per vehicle trip, or toll, t, must be set equal to the difference between average and marginal cost; i.e. $t = M - A$, or

---

2   Let total cost be $T = AQ$, where A is average cost and Q is total quantity. Define dT/dQ as marginal cost M, which $= d\ (AQ)/dQ = A + Q\ (dA/dQ)$. Therefore $M = A\ [1 + (Q/A)\ (dA/dQ)]$. But, by definition $(dQ/dA)\ (A/Q)$ is point elasticity, E, of the average cost curve. Hence, $M = A\ (1 + 1/E)$.

$t = (1 + 1/E)A - A$, or $t = (1/E)A$. Thus the required toll is got by multiplying the average cost of the journey at Q_1 by the inverse of the elasticity. If, for example, the average cost of the trip at Q_1 is $2.50, and E is equal to 5, the toll is set at $2.50 × 1/5, or at $0.50.

This toll, equal to t_1 in Figure I.4, is clearly estimated for the existing volume of traffic OQ_1, which is somewhat greater than the toll t in the Figure that realizes the optimal traffic volume at OQ_2. If this toll t_1, somewhat larger than the 'ideal' toll t, were imposed, the volume of traffic would in fact be reduced to OQ_2', somewhat below the optimal traffic volume OQ_2. It is manifest that the steeper is the demand curve DD the smaller is the difference between Q_2 and Q_2'. If the cost of estimating the relevant portion of the demand curve about $Q_0 Q_1$ was high, and the error likely to be high also, the calculated toll t_1, and the output OQ_2' resulting from its imposition may be judged satisfactory.

This toll can easily be converted to a fuel tax. By dividing the fifty cents toll by the number of miles of highway, say twenty-five we obtain a tax of two cents per mile. If, on the average, there are fifteen miles to the gallon with the calculated optimal volume of traffic, the optimal fuel tax becomes thirty cents per gallon.

The complications we have avoided—traffic composition, variety of highway systems, daily patterns of traffic flow—are obvious enough. But this has enabled us to make the concept clear. A more complete calculation, even for the simple case we have been considering, would have required that the spillover-effects of additional traffic on persons other than motorists be brought into the calculation.

4.   The cost-benefit analysis of a road-widening scheme fits in well with the preceding construction. The relevant comparison is that between the optimal traffic volume OQ_1' with the existing road system, at which, in Figure I.5, the marginal cost curve M_1 cuts the demand curve DD, on the one hand, and the optimal traffic volume OQ_2', on the other, for some added width to the road.

If, for example, we double the width of the existing road—which allows the maximum volume of traffic at constant cost to double, let us say, from OQ_1 to OQ_2—we can compare the average and marginal curves, and the respective optimal volumes, OQ_1' and OQ_2'. The shaded area represents the excess benefit; the excess of additional motorists valuations over the additional operational and congestion costs of moving from OQ'_1 optimal volume to OQ'_2 optimal volume. This measure of excess benefit over all currently incurred costs would have to be projected over the future as a stream of benefits. The benefit stream may then be discounted to the present and compared with the initial capital costs of road-widening.

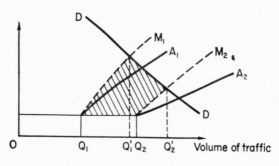

Fig I.5

If this investment were the only one available, we should—provided the rate of discount used was equal to the rate of return on investment in the private sector[3]—continue investing in road widening until the discounted benefit–cost ratio were unity, or until the investible funds were exhausted, which ever took place first. If however, a large number of roads could be widened to some extent and the funds available were limited, these funds should be spread among them as to maximize the total benefit–cost ratio.

5. A similar sort of analysis is at the base of the decision to increase the capacity of an electricity generating plant. Simplifying Williamson's (1966) treatment, we can suppose that additional electricity plant can be effectively supplied only in indivisible units.

In Figure I.6 we assume an unchanged demand over the period, with existing capacity equal to OQ_1. Thus marginal cost is constant up to output OQ_1 after which it becomes vertical. It therefore traces the reverse-L shaped line $C_1F_1M_1$. The overhead costs for the output OQ_1 is given by the rectangle $C_1C_2F_2F_1$. If the demand curve were

---

3 See Chapter 32 in Part IV.

to pass through F_2 (which it does *not* do in the Figure), it would not pay to install the additional indivisible unit of capacity generating an additional output Q_1Q_2; for the value of each additional unit of electricity, from Q_1 onwards, would be below the average inclusive cost (current cost plus overhead cost), OC_2. But with the demand curve DD, as shown in the Figure, it just pays to do so, since the social gain measured by the triangle A for the first Q_1M additional units exactly offsets the social loss measured by triangle B on the remaining MQ_2 units. If the demand curve were higher than DD shown in the Figure, the A triangle would exceed in area the B triangle, and there would be an excess of benefit over cost in extending generating capacity from OQ_1 to OQ_2.

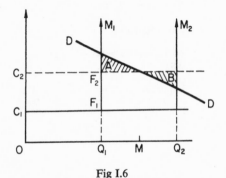

Fig I.6

No difference in principle arises if the demand for electricity fluctuates over the period in question, but the demand curve has to be shaped accordingly by an appropriate weighting system. If the highest price the community will pay for a given unit of electricity is $1 per hour for eight hours of the day (a maximum daily price of $24), and only fifty cents per hour (a maximum daily price of $12) for the remaining sixteen hours of the day, then over the twenty-four hours it would average $66\frac{2}{3}$ cents.

In this simple case of a division of the day into an 8-hour peak and a 16-hour off-peak period, the daily demand curve for the calculation would be the vertical sum of the two prices, each weighted by its fraction of the day. In general, if the peak price was p_1, the off-peak price p_2, the fraction of the day for peak usage w_1, and the fraction for off-peak usage w_2, then the composite daily price is

$p_1w_1 + p_2w_2$. In the above case, therefore, it is $(\frac{1}{3} \times 1.0) + (\frac{2}{3} \times 0.50)$ or $66\frac{2}{3}$ cents, as stated.

Having derived the weighted demand curve by such methods, it is again necessary that the area of triangle A exceed that of B in order to justify the introduction of an additional generating plant.

REFERENCES AND BIBLIOGRAPHY FOR PART I

Foster, C. D. and Beesley, M. E. 'Estimating the Social Benefit of Constructing an Underground Railway in London', *Journal of The Royal Statistical Society*, 1963.

Hufschmidt, M. M. 'Application of Basic Concepts: Graphic Techniques', in Maass, A. and others, *Design of Water-Resource Systems*, London; Macmillan, 1962.

Klarman, H. E. 'Syphilis Control Problems', R. Dorfman (ed.) *Measuring Benefits of Government Investments*, Washington D.C.; Brookings Institution, 1965.

Ministry of Transport, U.K. *Proposals for a Fixed Channel Link*, Cmnd. 6137. 1963.

Mushkin, S. 'Comment' on Klarman's paper (cited above).

Walters, A. A. 'The Theory and Measurement of Private and Social Cost of Highway Congestion', *Econometrica*, 1961.

Warford, J. J. 'Water Requirements: The Investment Decision in the Water Supply Industry' (with appendix by W. Peters), *The Manchester School*, 1966.

Williamson, O. E. 'Peak-Load Pricing and Optimal Capacity under Indivisibility Constraints', *American Economic Review*, 1966.

PART II. CONCEPTS OF BENEFITS AND COSTS

Chapter 7

CONSUMERS' SURPLUS

1. In economics, in 'normative economics' at least, the worth, or value, of a thing is determined simply by what a person is willing to pay for it. If a man is ready to pay $5 for a gallon of cider, it may be inferred that it is worth to him (in his own estimation) no less than $5.[1] If the gallon of cider is priced at $2 then the purchase of one gallon of it provides him with a 'consumer's surplus' of $5 (or more) *less* $2; or at least $3. Following Marshall (1924), we could define this consumer's surplus as the maximum a consumer will pay for a given amount of a good, less the amount he actually pays. We may extend the idea by thinking about asking a consumer the maximum sum per week he would be willing to pay for only one pint of milk; the maximum sum he will then pay for a second; the maximum for a third, and so on. These sums, which we can speak of as 'marginal valuations', are plotted as the heights of successive columns in Figure II.1. If a price per pint of milk is fixed at, say, twenty cents, he continues to buy additional pints of milk until his marginal valuation is equal to or below the price. Figure II.1 illustrates a case in which the man buys seven pints of milk at twenty cents, so spending $1.40 per week on milk. The area contained in the shaded parts of the columns above the price line is a sum of money equal to the man's consumer's surplus.

---

1 Although this simple view of the matter will suffice for the analysis in the following chapters, the reader might be interested in the theoretical refinements explained in Note B of Part VI. These refinements can be important, as will be indicated later, in the treatment of External Effects in Part III.

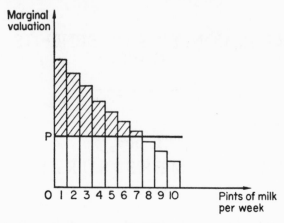

Fig II.1

2. Once perfect divisibility is assumed, the stepped outline of the columns gives way to a smooth demand curve. From a point on the vertical, or price, axis, the horizontal distance to the curve measures the maximum amount he will buy at that price. The *market* demand curve, being a horizontal summation of all the individual demand

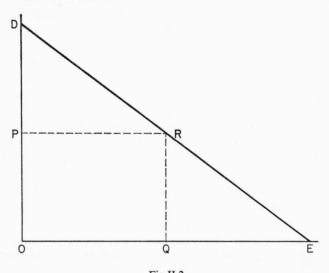

Fig II.2

32

curves, can be regarded as the marginal valuation curve for society. For example, the height QR in Figure II. 2, corresponding to output OQ, gives the maximum value some person in society is willing to pay for the Qth unit of the good—which, for that person, may be the first, second, or nth unit of the good bought. But to each of the total number of units purchased, which total is measured as a distance along the quantity axis, there corresponds some individual's maximum valuation. The whole area under the demand curve, therefore, corresponds to society's maximum valuation for the quantity in question. If, say, OQ is bought, the maximum worth of OQ units to society is given by the trapezoid area $ODRQ$. Now the quantity OQ is bought by the market at price OP. Total expenditure by the buyers is, therefore, represented by the area $OPRQ$ (price OP *times* quantity OQ). Subtracting the maximum worth to buyers ($ODRQ$) from what they have to pay ($OPRQ$) leaves us with a total consumers' surplus equal to triangle DRP.

If an entirely new good x is introduced into the economy, and is made available to all and sundry free of charge, the area under the resulting demand curve, ODE, (given that prices of all other goods are unaffected) is a good enough measure of the gain to the community in its capacity as consumer. The services provided by a new bridge, or a new park, would be familiar examples. Again, however, if a price, OP, for the service is introduced, the amount OQ will be bought, leaving the triangular area PDR in Figure II. 2 as the consumers' surplus. Estimates of consumers' surplus, it need hardly be said, are to be entered as benefits in all cost-benefit calculations.

3. Any investment having the object of reducing the cost of a product or service is deemed to confer a benefit on the community, which benefit is often referred to as a 'cost-difference', or a 'cost-saving'. The benefit of a new motorway, or flyover, is estimated by reference to the expected savings of time, and of the cost of fuel, by all motorists who will make use of the new road or flyover. The concept of cost-saving, however, is derived directly from the concept of consumers' surplus, as can be shown by reference to Figure II. 3. Thus, prior to the introduction of, say, the new flyover in question, the consumers' surplus from using this particular route (being the maximum sum motorists are willing to pay above the amount they currently spend on the journey—an average of OP per journey) is the

triangle PDR. If the flyover halves the cost of the journey to them, from OP to OP_1, at which lower cost the number of journeys undertaken is increased from OQ to OQ_1, the consumers' surplus increases from PDR to P_1DR_1, an increase equal to the shaded strip PP_1R_1R. This increment of consumers' surplus can be split up into two parts.

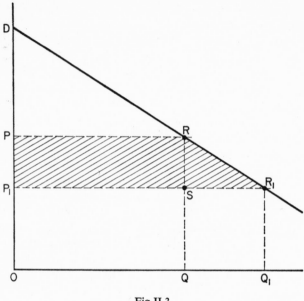

Fig II.3

There is, first, the cost-saving component, the rectangle PP_1SR, which is calculated as the saving per journey, PP_1, multiplied by the original number of journeys made, OQ. The other component, represented by the triangle SRR_1, is the consumers' surplus made on the additional journeys undertaken, QQ_1, either by the same motorists or by additional motorists. The cost-saving item that often enters into a cost-benefit calculation, is, in fact, no more than a portion, often the main portion, of the increment of consumers' surplus from a fall in the cost of the good. Since it takes no account of the additional goods that will be bought in response to the fall in cost, the cost-saving rectangle can be accepted as a *minimum* estimate of the benefit.

We might call this explanation a casual account of the matter, though not a misleading one. Nothing need be said about *utility* since we are not going to translate our money magnitudes into utility terms: the area under the market demand curve, that is, does not become translated into a sum of individual utilities, but remains simply as a sum of their valuations. The extent of the collective improvement from the introduction of a good is, then, expressed in terms of a sum of money which is measured by a triangle of consumers' surplus, such as PDR in Figure II. 2. Its interpretation is simply the maximum amount of money the group as a whole would offer in order to be able to buy OQ of this new good at price P. The extent of the collective improvement from a reduction in its price, however, is expressed as an increment of consumers' surplus, as for example the strip PP_1R_1R in Figure II. 3. The strip can be interpreted as the maximum amount of money the group as a whole would offer in order to have the price reduced from OP to OP_1.

4. Something more, however, has to be said about this relationship between price and quantity. Beginning from a general equilibrium system, we could deduce that the amount of a good x that is bought depends not only on its own price, but, in general, on the prices of all other goods and factors. In statistical estimates of the price-demand curve for x, the relationship is much more restricted. We might, for example, try to gather enough data so as to derive a specific equation from the relationship $X = F(P_x, P_y, P_z, M)$, X being the maximum amount of good x demanded, P_x, P_y, P_z, being the prices respectively of the goods x, y, and z, and M being aggregate real income. Goods y and z could be chosen as being close and important substitutes for x, or else y could be a close substitute and z a close complement of x, the relative prices of all other goods being ignored. Sometimes the price of one or more factors are to be included in the function. If, for example, the good x is taken as being farm tractors, the income of the farm population would obviously be a significant variable in the demand for tractors. In any statistical estimate of the price-demand curve for X, the *ceteris paribus* clause will operate to hold constant only those variables, other than P_x, that are included in the function F. All those variables that are not included in the function F—an almost unlimited number of goods and factor prices— are assumed, provisionally at least, to be of negligible importance.

Although this procedure is fairly general, there has been some recent controversy about the M term.[2] If aggregate *real* income is held constant in constructing this *ceteris paribus* demand curve, we are left with a curve which summarizes the pure substitution effect of, say, a declining price. No income-effects are included, and the measure of consumers' surplus derived therefrom will be conceptually accurate.[3] If, on the other hand, aggregate *money* income is held constant, any fall in the price of x raises the real value of an unchanged aggregate money income and—if the income-effect on x is positive—results in some further increases in the amount of x bought (along with changes in the amounts bought of all other goods).[4] The resultant demand curve is a compound of substitution and income effects. In consequence, the measure of consumers' surplus derived from such a demand curve can be no more than an approximation to the ideal measure based on a pure substitution-effect demand curve, as proposed by Friedman (1949). It will be less accurate according as the income effect is more important.

However, the difference that arises from using constant *real* income, as against constant *money* income, in the statistical derivation of a demand curve for a single good, is likely to be too slight relative to the usual order of statistical error to make the distinction significant in any cost-benefit study. The emphasis in the *ceteris paribus* pound of the market price-demand curve for x is to be placed, instead, on the constancy of the prices of the goods closely related to x. Thus, the *amounts* bought of all other goods in the economy, including those of y and z, may alter as they please in response, say, to a decline in the price of x. The measure of the

---

2 A controversy started by Friedman (1949).
3 Moving along a demand curve for which real income is constant entails an unchanged welfare—no shifting, that is, of the marginal valuation curve because of changes in welfare (or real income). For further elaboration, the reader is referred to Note B in Part VI.
4 If a person is willing to pay, say, $5 for the first pint of milk per week, and, after paying $5 for the first pint is willing to pay $4 for a second pint, then he would be willing to pay more than $4 for the second pint if he did *not* have to pay as much as $5 for the first pint, but some smaller sum, say $3. For in that case he would be making a consumer's surplus of $2 on the first pint of milk bought, and to the extent that this makes him better off he is willing to pay more (assuming his income-effect with respect to milk is positive) for the second pint. See Note B in Part VI.

consumers' surplus is not thereby affected. Only if alterations take place in the *prices* of the closely related goods, y and z, following a fall, say, in the price of x, does the measure of x's consumers' surplus have to be qualified. For the area under the demand curve for x is a valid measure of the gain to consumers only when the introduction of x, or a decline in its price, is accompanied by access to all other goods at unchanged prices. Before elaborating this latter proposition, which is the subject matter of the following chapter, let us dispose of a possible fallacy, one arising from the fact that the amounts bought of other goods will alter, in general, when a new good x is introduced, or the price of good x is reduced. For this purpose we shall assume, provisionally, that all goods are produced at constant costs.

5.   Let us suppose, first, that a new good, x, is introduced into the economy since this necessarily implies smaller expenditures on other goods.[5] Now the reader may suspect that if expenditure is withdrawn from other goods in the economy, losses are incurred there, and that these losses ought to be offset against the consumers' surplus for x as conventionally measured. Such a suspicion is, in general, unwarranted—at least, under the usual assumption of maximizing behaviour. In order to convince the reader that this is so, we shall cook up an example which, at first, seems to bear out the belief that losses will be incurred elsewhere. We shall take as our example, then, an existing ferry service across a river that is to be replaced by a railway bridge. The ferry charges $2 per person, and manages to break even when carrying the existing number of passengers. The average cost of labour and maintenance is $1.50, the remaining fifty cents being the return on capital (the capital expenditure on the ferry-boat).

For simplicity we can suppose that people are quite indifferent as between the two ways of crossing the river. If the *inclusive* unit cost of the rail service (total variable cost plus total overheads *divided* by number of journeys) is expected to be also $2, no profit could be made above the normal return on capital. There would then be no incentive to undertake the building of the bridge. Indeed, there would

---

5   If an existing good x were reduced in price, expenditure on it may remain constant—which is a necessary (though not sufficient) condition for the amounts bought of all other goods to remain unchanged.

be a negative incentive in view of the fact that capital had already been invested in the ferry service. For rather than lose passengers to the rail service, the ferry-owners would be ready to reduce fares below $2; any fare above $1.50 is in the nature of a quasi-rent, and contributes something to the owners of the ferry-boat who cannot extricate their investment.[6] If, however, the inclusive unit cost of the rail service is expected to be $1.20, it could introduce the service at, say, $1.40, make a profit (above normal return on capital), and put the ferry out of business. Now if we reckon the annual benefit of the investment in the bridge as consisting of this profit and, also, the consumer's surplus from reducing the fare from $2 to $1.40, then indeed, we should have to set against it the loss to the ferry-boat owners of fifty cents per unit. But this way of reckoning things is unnecessary: it offsets a gain of fifty cents to the passengers against a loss of fifty cents to the ferry-boat owners, which is only a transfer as between one group and another. It is simpler to reckon the benefits as a straight-forward cost-saving; the savings effected from reducing per unit current resource cost of $1.50 to per unit resource cost of $1.20, *plus* some area of surplus for any additional number of journeys taken in response to a reduction in the price from $1.50 to $1.40. Let us be quite clear about the reduction in unit resource costs.

The relevant current cost of the ferry journey is, in total, $1.50, for the capital invested in the boat is irrecoverable (bygones are bygones in economics). The full costs of the resources required to maintain the ferry service are therefore $1.50, these being only the variable costs of operating the service. The relevant current cost of the rail-bridge service is, however, only $1.20. Since capital costs have not yet been incurred, this $1.20 per unit includes the capital cost (the return that capital would fetch if placed, instead, in some other use). It is the difference between these current resource costs of providing the existing service which is a measure of the minimum gain—any additional services, in consequence of setting the price lower than $2, adding some area of surplus as indicated in Figure II. 4.

---

6 On the assumption that there is no alternative use, and no scrap value, for the ferry-boat. If there is, the minimum contemplated by the owners will be above $1.50.

Let C_1 ($1.50) be the current cost of the ferry service, and P_1 ($2) the price it charges. Let C_2 ($1.20) be the expected current cost of the rail service, and P_2 the price contemplated ($1.40). With the ferry service, the consumers' surplus is equal to the triangle $P_1 D R_1$, and the quasi-rent to the ferry-boat owners is the rectangle $P_1 R_1 S_1 C_1$.

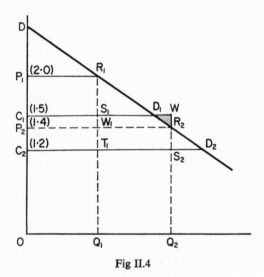

Fig II.4

With the rail service, the consumers' surplus will equal the triangle $P_2 D R_2$, and profit (above normal return) equal to the rectangle $C_2 P_2 R_2 S_2$. The difference in social benefit as between the two services, therefore, amounts to the cost difference on the *original* number of journeys, this being a sum equal to the rectangle $C_1 C_2 T_1 S_1$ *plus* the additional gains to consumers from a reduction in the price from P_1 to P_2, which gains are equal to the triangle $R_1 W_1 R_2$, *plus* the profit ($C_2 P_2$ per unit) on the additional number of journeys, $Q_1 Q_2$, which is equal to $T_1 W_1 R_2 S_2$.[7]

---

7 This is equal to the cost-difference on the amount of the service that will be taken at the P_2 price, which is equal to the rectangle $C_1 C_2 S_2 W$, *less* the small dotted triangle $D_1 W R_2$ *plus* the triangle $R_1 S_1 D_1$.

Clearly, if the price P_2 were reduced to the cost C_2, there would be an additional benefit equal to the triangle $R_2 S_2 D_2$, consumers thereby gaining an area $P_2 C_2 D_2 R_2$, which exceeds by that triangle the loss to capital-owners (equal to the rectangle $C_2 P_2 R_2 S_2$).

What is significant is that—assuming the variable resources to be perfectly mobile—the loss of quasi-rents by the ferry-boat owners will be wholly offset by the gains to consumers when the price falls from P_1 to P_2. Moreover, an estimate of the saving in costs as between the two services, when reckoned over the original amount demanded, will always be an underestimate of the benefit.

Moreover, in a perfectly competitive economy, where market prices can be taken to equal their average costs, we should need to compare only C_1 and C_2, which is much simpler. The benefit would be equal to the strip $C_1C_2D_2D_1$, which area can be broken into the cost-difference *times* the original amount sold, plus the triangle of consumers' surplus on the additional amount sold as a result of the reduction in price (equal cost).

Even if the new good that is introduced is not identical with the old good, whose sales are now reduced, the general conclusion follows. The strip of consumers' surplus may be taken as an estimate of the benefit in disregard of the reduction in sales of the old good. Similarly if x and y are substitutes a decline in the price of x, with the price of y remaining unchanged, will produce a benefit that is equal to the gain of consumers' surplus when this is measured with respect to the *ceteris paribus* demand curve for x. Problems of adjustment arise only when the price of y changes simultaneously either exogenously, or as a direct consequence of the reduction in the price of x, and to these problems we now turn.

Chapter 8

ADDING CONSUMERS' SURPLUSES

1. Consider the case where two goods x and y are close, though imperfect, substitutes. In Figures II. 5 (x) and 5 (y) the *ceteris paribus* demand curves for each are the solid lines. D_xE_x is the demand curve for x given that the price of y, p_y, is held constant, and D_yE_y is the demand curve for y given that the price p_{x_1} is held constant. If, now, as a result of some improved method of production, the price of x falls from p_{x_1} to p_{x_2}, the demand curve for y falls from D_yE_y to $D'_yE'_y$ as shown in II. 5 (y). At the unchanged price p_y, the smaller quantity OB is demanded (rather than OC, which was demanded before the fall in the price of x).

With a lower price of x, consumers are obviously better off. They would, of course, be better off even if they continued to buy exactly the same amounts of x and y as they did before the fall in the price of x. Assume, as a first stage in the argument, that they are constrained to buy the same quantities as before. Then, by removing this constraint, they further improve their welfare by buying more of x, and buying less of y. Having made these changes, and buying now OQ of x and OB of y, how do we interpret consumers' surpluses?

First, the measure of the gain in consumers' surplus is represented wholly by the shaded strip in Figure II. 5 (x) between the original price p_{x_1} and the new price p_{x_2}. Provided all other goods prices remain unchanged—and, in particular, that of its close substitute y remains unchanged at p_y—this shaded strip measures the most that consumers will pay to have the reduction in the price of x. As for the factors of production that are no longer needed to produce BC of y, they may be supposed to spread themselves among other uses for a negligible change in their prices.[1] This is a long-run assumption

---

[1] If the demand for x has an elasticity greater than unity, the factor costs of producing OQ units will be greater than those necessary to produce OM units. Some of the factors discharged from y will then move into the production of x. If, however, the elasticity for x is less than unity, factors will move out of x as well as out of y. Provided total consumers' expenditure remains unchanged, factors moving out of x and/or y will find employment elsewhere.

41

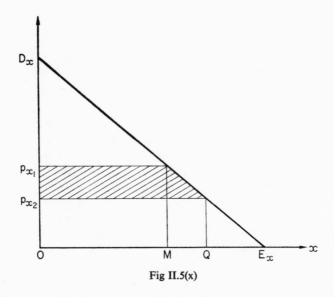

Fig II.5(x)

that the economist is free to make, but if there are perceptible costs of factor movements they should obviously enter into the calculus.

Secondly, the dotted triangle shown in Figure II. 5 (y) represents the consumers' surplus in having a price p_y when the price of x is

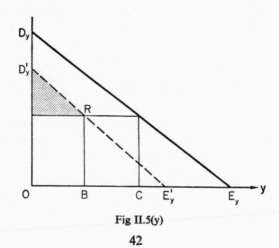

Fig II.5(y)

now p_{x_2}. This triangle is the difference between the most they would pay for OB of y (OD_yRB), when x is priced at p_{x_2}, and what they have to pay for OB of y (OP_yRB).

2. Let us turn now to the more general case in which the cost curves of the firms, or the supply curves of the industry, are not all constant, some being upward- or downward-sloping. Suppose only the supply curve for y is no longer constant, but instead is upward-sloping. In that case a reduction in the price of x from p_{x_1} to p_{x_2}, that causes the amount of y demanded to fall from OC to OB, also causes the supply price of y to decline. This decline in the price of good y, which is a substitute for good x, results, therefore, in a leftward shift of the demand curve for x. In the new equilibrium, then, both the measure of x's total consumers' surplus and that of the increment of consumers' surplus given by the shaded strip will appear somewhat smaller than they do when, instead, the price of y is held constant. But though the incremental measure of consumers' surplus is now smaller than before, consumers are not worse off. On the contrary, the are now better off than they would be if the supply price of y had remained constant. For, in addition to the exogenous fall in the price of x, from p_{x_1} to p_{x_2}, they benefit also from some endogenous reduction in the price of y.

We may conclude that if the supply curves of goods that are close substitutes with x are upward-sloping then, once the new equilibrium is established, the shaded strip in Figure II. 5 (x) *underestimates* the increment of consumers' surplus from a fall in the price of x. The reverse conclusion holds for a downward-sloping supply curve of y: as a result of a higher cost of y when less of it is bought, the demand curve for x is shifted outward, giving an appearance of greater gain when, in fact, consumers are made worse off in consequence of this rise in the cost of y. Thus, when supply curves of goods that are close substitutes for x are downward-sloping then, once the new equilibrium is established, the shaded strip in Figure II. 5 (x) *overestimates* the increment of consumers' surplus from a fall in the price of y.

Similar remarks would apply if the project in question is directed, not to reducing the cost of an existing good x, but to introducing into the economy some new product, or service, x. If water-powered electricity-generating plant is being introduced into an area which hitherto depended entirely on coal for warmth and industrial fuel, and, as a result, the fall in the demand for coal brings about a fall in its price, we can be confident that the area under the resulting demand curve for electricity will understate the consumers' gain. We can, however, say more than this. Given the resulting fall in the price of the substitute good, say coal, we can make more accurate estimates of the actual consumers' gain.

3. Hicks (1958) has shown how the consumers' surplus on two or more substitute goods, say gas and electricity, that are introduced simultaneously, or in succession, can be measured. Suppose that gas is introduced at a given price p_g into an area which has no electricity. The shaded triangle of Figure II. 6 (g) can be taken as a measure of the resulting consumers' surplus. If, following this event, electricity is introduced at a price p_e, the demand curve for electricity D_eE_e is obviously smaller when gas is available at a fixed price p_g than it would be in the absence of gas. For already the consumers derive much benefit from gas, and the introduction of a fairly close substitute is not so great a boon as it would be if, instead, there had been no gas in the first place. The additional gain to consumers from introducing electricity into a gas-using area is given by the dotted triangle in Figure II. 6 (e). The sum of these two

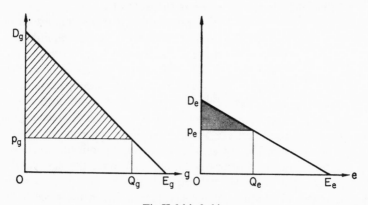

Fig II.6 (g) & (e)

triangles together measure the consumers' surplus from providing both gas and electricity at prices p_g and p_e respectively. It need hardly be said that if electricity had been introduced at price p_e first, followed by gas priced at p_g, or had both electricity and gas been introduced simultaneously at these prices, the resulting gain to the consumers would be the same.[2]

The consumers benefit from introducing electricity at price p_e, when gas is already available at p_g, has been measured as the dotted triangle in Figure II. 6 (e). Let gas now have an upward-sloping supply curve as shown by SS in Figure II. 7. On the introduction of

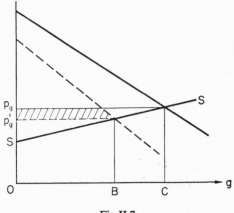

Fig II.7

electricity, the demand curve for gas contracts from the solid line to the broken line, the amount of gas taken being reduced from OC to OB, and the equilibrium supply price falling from p_g to p'_g. By a small extension of the logic of the preceding paragraph, the total increment of benefit to the consumers of (i) the introduction of electricity at price p_e, plus (ii) an induced fall in the supply price of gas from p_g to p'_g may be calculated by taking them in sequence. First, the shaded triangle in Figure II. 6 (e) gives (i), the increment of consumers' surplus from introducing electricity at price p_e *with the price of gas at p_g*. Secondly, the shaded area in Figure II. 7 gives (ii), the further increment of consumers' surplus for a fall in the price of gas from p_g to p'_g, *with the price of electricity remaining at p_e*. The sum of the two areas, then, is a measure of the consumers

---

2 Thus, when the demand curves for both gas and electricity are drawn, each on the assumption that the price of the other is fixed, the sum of the areas under the two demand curves can be much smaller than the area under the demand curve for either in the absence of the other good.

benefit from (interpreted as the most they are willing to pay for) introducing electricity at price p_e when, as a result the price of gas to them will fall from p_g to p'_g.[3] An extension of the analysis reveals that if gas has, instead, a downward-sloping supply curve, the leftward shift in its demand curve, following the introduction of electricity, results in a higher price for gas, and therefore entails a further *subtraction* of consumers' surplus.

Symmetrical reasoning applies to goods that are *complements*. If, for example, an existing good x is complementary with a newly introduced good y then (a) if x has an upward-sloping supply curve, the resulting rightward shift in its demand curve raises its price. The adjustment requires a further subtraction of consumers' surplus. If (b) x has a downward-sloping supply curve, the adjustment entails an additional increment of consumers' surplus.

4. There is, of course, more to be said about the measurement of consumers' surplus, which concept is crucial to cost-benefit analysis, and further observations will be made in later chapters. A final remark here concerns the question of political constraints.

Increments of consumers' surplus are to be regarded as measures of *changes* in consumers' welfare taken from any initial level of their welfare. If the price of a substitute good, y, is raised as a result of an excise tax levied on it, the demand for the good x is thereby raised. Conversely, if the price of y is lowered as a result of an excise subsidy, the demand for x is thereby lowered. The economist can properly argue that, in the absence of government intervention, the increment of consumers' surplus from a fall in the price of x would have appeared smaller, or larger, respectively if the government had not intervened in the price of y. But if the excise tax or excise subsidy on y is to be maintained over the foreseeable future, the economist will accept the resulting price of y, along with all other prices, and, taking the existing level of consumers' welfare as his starting point, measure

---

3   If electricity were also an upward-sloping supply curve industry, there would, following the fall in the price of gas, be a further reduction of any initial cut in the cost of electricity. In the newly established equilibrium we should have to take into account this further increment of gain. I leave this as an exercise for the reader, rather than clutter up the text with refinements of this order. For practical problems, economists would be satisfied if the two calculations in the text could be made with tolerable accuracy.

the resulting increment of consumers' surplus of a fall in the price of x.

The same argument applies if the government introduces a substitute for x, or withdraws a substitute for x. The economist is always at liberty to point out that the lack of economic justification for such government actions, and the consequences that follow therefrom. But, on the assumption that this policy is to prevail, he will still measure changes of consumers' welfare, as a result say of changes in the price of x, from the level established by the government's policy. Such changes in consumers' welfare are, of course, to be measured as increments, or decrements, in consumers' surplus, as illustrated in Figure II. 5 (x).

What the economist must be on guard against, however, is interpreting as a net increase of consumers' total benefit, the enlarged area under the demand curve for x, arising from *an outward shift* of the demand curve for x that may follow from such government action as the taxing of y, or the withdrawal of y (regarded as a substitute for x). This is a simple point, but its neglect is a potent source of error.[4] It should be obvious that government action in raising the price of y, or withdrawing y from the market, will make consumers as a whole worse off, notwithstanding that the rightward shift of the demand curve for x produces a larger area between the demand curve and price. The only valid interpretation of this larger area under the demand curve for x is that, having accepted the results of the government's action (which lowers consumers' welfare), the consumers' surplus from their being able to buy x at the same price, p_x, is greater than it was before the price of y was raised, or before y was withdrawn. Put otherwise, now that y is dearer, or is no longer available, the *loss* of consumers' surplus in withdrawing the opportunity to buy x at p_x, will be greater than it was before.

---

4 For an important example of this misuse of consumers' surplus to justify investment in private transport, see Mishan (1967).

Chapter 9
RENT AND PRODUCERS' SURPLUS

1. Conventionally, a person's price-demand curve is drawn as sloping downward to the right, his price-supply curve as sloping upward to the right. If income effects are zero, the individual's demand curve must slope downward: it can slope upward—the characteristic of a so-called 'Giffen good'—only if the income effect is negative, and large relative to the substitution effect. Analogous remarks apply to the individual's supply curve. If the income-effect, or rather the 'welfare effect',[1] is zero, the individual supply curve must slope upward: it can slope downward, or become 'backward-bending', only if the welfare effect is *positive* and large relative to the substitution effect.[2]

In general, the smaller are these welfare effects that accompany

---

1 Assuming his *money* income constant, a fall in the price of a good, which makes a person better off, can be regarded as an increase in his real income. For there is some rise in his money income which (given all other prices constant) will be accepted by him as equivalent to a fall in the price of that good. Here, no difficulty arises in identifying the increase in his welfare with the income effect so measured.

In the case of his supplying a service to the market, however, his money income cannot be assumed constant, since, obviously, it varies with the amount of the service he elects to supply at the price offered. What is more, a rise or fall in the *resulting* money income does not necessarily correspond with a rise or fall in his welfare (or 'real' income). A rise in the wage-rate, for instance, may result in workers choosing so to reduce hours as to maintain money income constant, notwithstanding which his welfare has increased: for his income is the same while he enjoys additional leisure. A positive welfare effect, that is, can be associated with no change in his money income, or even with a reduction of his money income. For this reason, it is more sensible to talk of the 'welfare effect' resulting from a change in the supply price.

2 An increase of welfare has a 'normal', or positive, welfare effect if the person offers *less* at any given price—if, that is, he keeps more of the good he is offering for himself. A worker who came into an inheritance would supply less labour (or take more leisure). Hence, if the price of the good a person supplies is raised, the substitution effect induces him to supply more while a positive welfare effect causes him to supply less. As distinct, then, from the income effect on the demand side, the 'welfare effect' on the supply side, if it is positive, or 'normal', works *against* the substitution effect.

price changes, the more accurate as an estimate of consumer's surplus, or rent, will be the relevant area derived, respectively, from the individual's demand, or supply, schedule. In the case of a person's demand curves, there is a presumption that the welfare effects are small. For a man's current expenditure, at least in the West, is commonly spread over a wide variety of goods each of which—with, perhaps, the exception of housing—absorbs only a small proportion of his total income. Indeed, as living standards rise, the variety of goods offered by the market increases along with the increase in a man's real income. One might surmise, therefore, that the welfare effect will become less important an ingredient in his price-demand curve for any single good.

The case is otherwise for the individual's supply curves, in particular for his supply of productive services, say the supply of labour, skilled or unskilled. If he supplies to the market only one sort of labour, the welfare effect arising from a change in the price of this labour falls entirely on this quantity. It then exerts a preponderant effect. Backward-bending supply curves for individual workers are not regarded as curiosa, a fact which would seem to make the measurement of economic rent rather awkward.

But there is a countervailing feature in connection with individual supply curves, which tends to restore measurability. Notwithstanding the mathematical convenience in postulating an economy in which each individual contributes, in general, to all goods in the economy, spreading his total effort among them—as he spreads his income among all goods—on the equi-marginal principle, this postulate is recognized as unrealistic. Nor is it a necessary condition for the model of perfect competition, which model is quite consistent with the more realistic assumption that the worker is constrained in his chosen employment to work a given number of hours, and between stated times. (He may, of course, be offered overtime work, though again it will be subject to constraints on the days and times.) For this reason, there is little point in conceiving of the worker's rent from his employment in precisely analogous terms as his consumer's surplus.

2. In picturing consumer's surplus, we think of the excess marginal valuation over price of the first unit bought, of the second unit bought, of the third, and so on until, with the purchase of the nth

unit, the excess is zero. Ignoring welfare effects, the analogous procedure for rent would be the excess of the supply price over the marginal valuations, or minimal sums acceptable to the worker, for each of a number of successive units of labour offered until, again, for some m^{th} unit of labour offered, the excess became zero. But, as we have indicated in the preceding paragraph, the worker is not permitted to choose his hours of work on the equi-marginal principle. If, on the contrary, he were allowed, his rising marginal curve VV, in Figure II. 8, would intersect the wage-rate line, W, at, say, 32

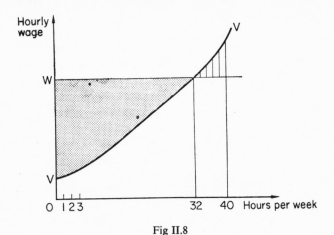

Fig II.8

hours. His rent would then be the dotted area above VV and below the W line. If, however, the job offered a forty-hour week, and no less, he would be constrained to work eight hours longer than the thirty-two hours that he would choose in the absence of any constraint; and for these eight hours the wage offered is below his successive marginal valuations. On these eight unwanted hours extra he suffers a loss equal to the shaded triangle. His net rent is therefore the dotted area *minus* the shaded area. And, since he is offered the job as an all-or-nothing proposition, he will accept the job only if the difference between these two areas is positive.

Since all workers finding employment in this occupation will be obliged to work the forty-hour week, irrespective of whether they would prefer to work fewer or more hours, the net rent from working the forty-hour week is, for any one of them, the first area less the second area (if any). Letting the worker's weekly (disposable) pay be represented as the area of a unit column with height equal to this weekly wage, as in Figure II. 9, the rent is the dotted rectangle

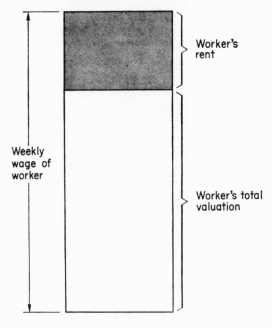

Fig II.9

measured from the top of the column. By gradually raising the weekly wage and observing the numbers that enter the industry, in response to the higher wage, a supply curve of labour to the industry is generated, and from this we are able to identify the rent of those employed. Thus in Figure II. 10, if at the lowest wage, W_1, seven men just agreed to work, they make no rent. If now the wage rises to W_2 and, in response, another ten men are just willing to enter the industry, the first seven enjoy between them a rent equal to the dotted rectangle (W_2-W_1) *times* the distance 0 –7. If the wage rises to W_3, and four more men enter, the first seven men between them make a rent equal to (W_3-W_1) *times* the distance 0 –7, and the next ten men between them make a rent equal to (W_3-W_2) *times* the

51

distance 7–17, and so we could go on. We are enabled to do this simply because no worker is allowed to alter the number of hours he gives to the industry in response to changes in the wage.

Once large numbers of men are involved the stepped supply curve gives way to a smooth supply curve. The corresponding

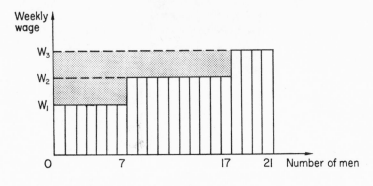

Fig II.10

dotted area above this supply curve can then be used as an approximate measure of the aggregate rent enjoyed by those employed in the industry. Its magnitude can be interpreted as the largest sum they would be willing to pay to be in this occupation at the existing wage, given all the other opportunites open to them. An estimation of such rents would always be entered into a cost-benefit analysis of a project if it were known that a wage lower than the existing wage (necessary to attract enough workers to operate the enterprise) would yet suffice to attract *some* workers.[3]

3. This area above the industry, or project, supply curve of a factor, which may be used as a measure of the rent of the factors employed there, is to be distinguished, in general, from the area above the supply curve of a firm or industry.

---

3 In estimating the rent of the industry's workers by such a supply curve of labour, it is not necessary that labour offered be equally efficient. If, as the industry expanded, the subsequent workers were less efficient than the original ones, costs to the industry would indeed rise. But the measure of workers rent remains unaffected.

There are, nonetheless, particular circumstances in which the area above the supply curve for an industry, or firm, can be properly interpreted as a measure of rent. First, there is Ricardian rent in which labour and capital, both of them available in any amounts at constant prices, are applied in fixed proportions to a given quantity of land. The supply curve of the resulting product, say corn, rises, not because of any changes in the supply prices of the variable factors, labour and capital, since, as just stated, their supply prices remain unchanged. The supply curve of corn rises simply because the best land is limited in supply, and, as the price of corn rises with an expanding demand, it becomes worth while to bring inferior lands into cultivation. Even if there is only one quality of land, though limited in amount relative to demand, rent will accrue to it once the marginal cost of a bushel of corn rises above its average cost—as it eventually will, because of diminishing average returns to additional 'doses' of labour and capital. In these circumstances, the area between such a supply curve and the price of the product provides a measure of the rent accruing to the owner of the fixed factor, land, which rent is accordingly entered on the benefit side of the analysis.

Secondly, there is the case in which the area above the supply, or cost, curve has to be identified as, what Marshall (1924) called, *quasi-rent*. For over a short period, during which the capital employed by the industry, or firm, is in the specific form of plant or machinery, it is deemed to be fixed in amount, and to have no alternative use. In this short period, then, it partakes of the nature of land, and all its earnings above those necessary to induce it to remain in the occupation (zero in the strict Marshallian quasi-rent concept) are to be regarded as rent. In this short period, then, if the price of the product rises above the per unit variable cost of the product, the resulting excess receipts over the total of these variable costs, are quasi-rents; such positive sums making a contribution to the industry's, or firm's, overheads or capital costs.

The above two instances are clear examples of economic rent to a scarce factor. They enter as part of the benefit of producing a given amount of goods during either a short or a long period. Thus, if a given piece of land is used to grow a new crop, or to site some new project, a rise in its rent is part of the benefit of the scheme. If, within a short period, some investment in the industry, or firm, causes its variable costs to fall, the additional quasi-rents that result are to be counted as benefits.

4. The case is quite different, however, when the long run supply curve of a good is produced by two or more factors, that are imperfect substitutes and may, indeed, be used in varying proportions. To appreciate the difference with the minimum of effort, let us follow the standard textbook procedure and, first, assume that all firms in the industry are of equal size and efficiency. In that case the rise in the supply price of the good reflects the growing scarcity of the factor that is intensive to the product. With only two factors, say labour and capital, the production of a larger amount of a good x will entail a rise in the price of capital relative to labour, where capital is used more intensively in x than it is in the production of other goods. Owing to the greater weight of capital used in x as compared with its weight, on the average, in other goods, the per unit cost of x rises relative to the unit costs of other goods.[4]

Two things are to be noticed about this rising supply price for the product. First, any point along it indicates the *minimum average cost* for each of the firms in the industry and, therefore, the minimum average cost for that output. Thus, at output Ox_1 in Figure II. 11, the minimum average inclusive cost for all firms is given by x_1m_1, and a typical long-period envelope curve for such a firm is represented as S_1S_1. At the larger output Ox_2, the minimum average inclusive cost for the industry is x_2m_2, a typical long-period envelope curve for the firm being represented as S_2S_2.

Second, as the output of the industry expands, the rent of one factor, say that of capital, rises *relative* to that of the other factor, labour—and, unless there are increasing returns to scale, the price of capital will rise in real terms and the price of labour will fall in real terms. Yet neither the shape of the curve, nor the area above it, can be associated with a net gain for both factors taken together. Nor can it be interpreted as a net gain by the producers, or entre-

---

4 Put otherwise, if there are more than two goods in the economy, the expenditure on capital, as a per cent of total factor expenditure, is, for x, above the average per cent for the economy as a whole. x's increased proportional expenditure on the higher-priced factor, capital, results therefore in a higher-than-average rise in (relative) cost.

preneurs, each of which makes zero (Knightian) profit[5] in long-period equilibrium.

The long-period industry supply curve which, given constant returns to scale, rises only because factor proportions differ as

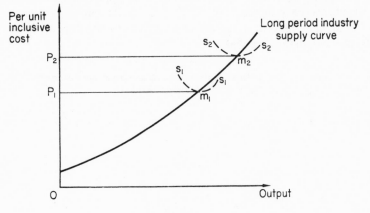

Fig II.11

between industries, has to be conceived of as an *average* supply curve for the product. There is no welfare significance attaching to the area above the supply curve.

5. The reader will, perhaps, have noted that no mention has been made of the concept of 'producers' surplus', of which we used to hear a lot of until recently. There is no call for it. The concept that is symmetric with consumers' surplus is that which is known as economic rent, and which we examined in the earlier part of this chapter.

There is, then, no third concept to which a 'producers' surplus' can apply: certainly not the area above the long-period industry supply curve which, as we have just pointed out, carries no welfare significance. True, some instances of economic rent—Ricardian

---

5 Normal return on capital is not profit, any more than normal return on labour. In the long-period equilibrium, at any point on the industry supply curve, expenditure on factors (both labour and capital) is deemed to be just covered by revenue, leaving no profit, positive or negative, to induce firms to move into, or out of, the industry respectively.

rent and Marshallian quasi-rent—have occasionally been referred to as 'producers' surpluses'. But the use of the term in this connection, or in any connection, has served only to confuse issues,[6] and we shall continue to use only the more generic term economic rent—either (a) *consumers'* rent, or *consumers'* surplus, in so far as the benefits accrue to members of society from a fall in product prices, or else (b) *factor* rents in so far as benefits accrue to members of society from a rise in factor prices.

---

6   For a more detailed critique of the notion of producers' surplus the reader is referred to my 1968 paper, *American Economic Review*.

Chapter 10

GROWTH AND CHANGE INDUCED BENEFITS

1. Economic growth comprises both population growth and growth of per capita real income. Together they contribute to the growth of benefits over time arising from any investment today. The faster the rate of economic growth, then the swifter, in general, will be the rate of growth of future benefits. In cost-benefit studies the likelihood of such growth-induced benefits has to be taken into account.

Throughout the analysis we shall assume no change in the level of prices over time—growth in income being interpreted as equivalent to growth in real output. We shall also ignore, though only for the present, population movements within the country. Alternatively, we may confine our observations to the economic growth that takes place within a particular locality.

2. In the absence of any expected growth in the economy, a hypothetical investment of 100 is expected to yield an annual stream of benefits of, say, 10, 10, 10, ..., 10—at least, if we disregard uncertainty. Allowing for an annual growth rate of 4 per cent, and assuming an income elasticity of unity for the goods produced by the investment, there is a case for revising the annual stream of benefits to something like 10.4, 10.8, .., 10 $(1.04)^n$. Indeed, the investment may prove to be economically unacceptable in the absence of such a rate of growth. It behoves the economist, therefore, to declare explicitly the average annual rate of growth on which the cost-benefit study is predicated. Having done this, he will discuss the way in which this expected rate of growth will affect the benefits of the goods produced by the investment project.

This appears to be straightforward, wherever a single project is in issue, such as a tunnel under the Severn, a bridge over the Channel, a unique national park. For such projects will not, in the foreseeable future, be 'threatened' by rival projects of a like nature. In such cases (a) growth in population alone (ignoring, that is, any increase in per capita income) will tend to increase the demand for the services of such projects. The value of the social benefits will grow simply because the same service is being provided to more people. The bridge, or national park, for instance, will accommodate an increase in the number of travellers or visitors per annum—presumably without much increase in current costs.[1] As for (b) growth in per capita income alone, the increase in the usage of such things is less certain; the average individual's income effect on the demand for park visits, or cross-channel journeys, may not be positive. Nonetheless, if a person pays no more visits to a national park as he becomes richer, it is likely—and unless his tastes change, more than likely—that his valuation of such goods will become higher.[2] This is not because, say, his annual visit to a park, or zoo, provides him with any more *utility* than it did when he was poorer, but simply because the maximum sum he would be willing to pay for such a visit is higher when his real income, or welfare, is higher. And if, at a constant price level, we make our calculations on the basis of money values, any rise in the value of benefits over time, for all such reasons must be entered into the calculations.

3.   Consider now the building of a bridge A, one to be built in anticipation that in, say, five years time another bridge B will be built. If this later bridge, B, will be built wholly in response to the growth in traffic—itself a result of growth in population and in per capita income—there may be no reduction in the traffic using the A bridge. But a problem will arise if the B bridge is competitive with the A bridge. The questions in issue are two: whether the A bridge should be built at all if it is known that a competitive, possibly a superior, B bridge will be built at a later date? And, if the A bridge is built, when should the B bridge be introduced?

A private firm having built the A bridge would not also build a B bridge unless the (discounted value of) future expected revenues it could collect on the B bridge would not only cover the capital costs

---

1   We are ignoring the costs of congestion which can be looked at as spillover effects, or external diseconomies falling on the users themselves of bridges, roads, tunnels, national parks, and so on.

2   If a person's income effect, or welfare effect, is positive, a rise in his real income, or in his welfare, will imply that he will pay more for some given amount of a good.

of the B bridge but, in addition, would cover any loss of revenues it would have to sustain on the old A bridge. If, on the other hand, the B bridge were to be built by some other private company, the private company building the A bridge would have to take into account that the revenues they would be able to collect would become much smaller once the B bridge were built. In these circumstances it may not be profitable to build the A bridge.

If, instead, the government decides to go in for bridge-building, the calculation is quite different. We can assume for simplicity that current costs of bridge-maintenance are zero, and that no charge is therefore levied on the traffic. Given the existence of the A bridge, the building of the B bridge is justified simply if the future benefits—as measured by expected consumers' surplus from use of the B bridge—exceeds the capital costs. It would not matter, even, if the traffic that is expected to use the B bridge, and to generate benefits sufficient to cover its capital costs, had the incidental effect of leaving the A bridge devoid of all traffic. The A bridge has already been built: the capital sunk into it irrecoverable. We need then consider only the new costs of building the B bridge, and the new benefits. The demand schedule for the services of the B bridge provides us then with a measure of the *additional* benefits to be reaped from an *additional* capital expenditure. The area under this demand curve, that is, provides us with a rough measure of the consumers' surplus, which is to be interpreted as the maximum sum that the users of the bridge are willing to pay *when already they have the A bridge at their disposal.*

In the decision to build A, therefore, the magnitude of the annual benefits will not have to be written down after, say, five years, when the B bridge is expected to be opened for traffic. For the benefits, as measured, for the services of the B bridge are additional to thos~ currently anticipated for the A bridge. Again, and for the same reason, in determining the point of time at which the B bridge is to be built, no account is to be taken of the consequent fall in the demand for the services of the A bridge.

4. If we now suppose a spontaneous movement of population, say, from London to Brighton, that takes place over a number of years, and ignore economic growth for the present, investment in social capital will be required in Brighton at the same time as existing social

capital in London becomes unused. If, for example, prior to the exodus, the amount of social capital was just right in both places, a prospective shortage of 100,000 houses in Brighton would be matched by a prospective vacancy of 100,000 houses in London. There would be a need also to extend schools, build roads, invest more in transport, electricity, gas, water, telephones, and provide additional distributional services in Brighton, all of which would require additional capital, while the equivalent capital investment in London would become superfluous. Clearly, it would have been more economical of society's scarce resources if the desire to move to Brighton had not occurred, for then the existing social capital stock would have sufficed. But, once this change has occurred, the economist is concerned only with ways of meeting it efficiently.

The losses in moving are to some extent borne directly by householders, since each householder has to buy a new house while being unable to sell his old (London) house, except at a price low enough to induce some London family, or society, to take an additional house But other financial losses have to be borne by others—by landlords (in the case of rented rooms), by private companies, by ratepayers in the London areas affected. The losses to these people take the form of a loss of quasi-rents on existing social capital (or of the less of the excess receipts above current costs), of providing these 100,000 families with the usual range of public services.

The question arises: are such losses to be set against the apparent benefits that would otherwise cover the costs of establishing new plant and facilities in Brighton? The answer would seem to be no, on the grounds that once capital is irretrievably sunk (in London areas) all that matters is whether the additional benefits are expected to be in excess of additional capital outlays in Brighton. But what people are willing to pay in Brighton depends on what they are compelled to pay in London. Only if they had to pay no more than the marginal costs of public services in London, could the amounts they would be willing to pay in Brighton be accepted as a correct measure of the benefits there. Indeed, an ideal allocative procedure would require that managers of these service industries (public utilities, and the like) be ready at all times to reduce the charges for such services to no more than the current marginal costs of providing them, rather than lose a customer. If the economy actually worked in this way, the services of the economist could be dispensed with in such circumstances. But since it is difficult to discriminate as between customers in this way, and since extending a reduction in charges made on behalf of one customer to all other customers, involves the company in losses of revenue—such losses being, in effect, transfer payments from the company to its customers—the customary charges are generally maintained.

If this is so, however, it follows that the choice of moving from London to Brighton is being made on the wrong terms. For if, by lowering the charges of one or more of such public services closer to the marginal cost of its provision, a number of such 'emigrant' families can be induced to stay on in London, then a potential Pareto improvement can be effected: everyone concerned can be made better off as compared with the alternative situation in which such families move to Brighton.[3] The ideal experiment is to allow no family to move from London to Brighton without first offering him the option of buying all such existing services at their marginal running costs. If, when such terms are offered to potential migrants and they are still willing to move, and to pay for all newly required public services prices which cover their inclusive costs, well and good.

Unless marginal cost pricing is already established in the public utility sector, such an ideal experiment—call it option 1—is likely to run into administrative and political objections. For the costs of discovering potential migrants, and of offering them special marginal cost terms without arousing the suspicion and hostility of other households can be prohibitive. If, however, option 1 is adopted, and all potential emigrants from the London area are presented with special permits enabling them buy public utility services at their marginal costs, their demand schedules for any such service, say electricity, in Brighton will be based on a *ceteris paribus* clause that includes a price for electricity in London equal to its marginal cost. In order to determine, in advance, whether there can be an excess of benefit over cost from installing an electricity-generating plant in Brighton to meet the requirements of potential migrants,

---

3 If the annual excess over the variable current costs of providing family A with electricity is $100,, an effective bribe of $60 would leave the electricity company with $40 more revenue than it would earn if the A family moved. Both the A family and the company are therefore better off than if the A family moved to Brighton.

the optimal output of such a plant must first be estimated by reference to this option 1 demand schedule. At this optimal output, it is necessary that the total revenue from the sale of electricity plus the consumers' surplus (on, say, an annual basis) together exceed the total operating and overhead costs. (It should be evident that the *apparent* losses of quasi-rent suffered by the London electricity authority, in consequence of its being obliged to offer to sell electricity to all potential emigrants at marginal cost, are in fact no more than transfers of benefit. Those potential emigrants that now decide to stay on will enjoy the transfer directly. Those that, notwithstanding the marginal cost offer, move to Brighton, make allowance for this potential bonus in their valuation of the worth of electricity in Brighton.) Such calculations do, indeed, pose statistical difficulties. But unless there is reason to believe that there is an excess of social benefit over cost under the hypothetical conditions of option 1, there can be no presumption that a potential Pareto improvement is realized by such an investment simply because there is an excess of benefit estimated by reference to the *uncorrected* demand schedule.

Option 2 consists of offering marginal cost prices for London's public utilities only *after* the migrant families have incurred expenses in moving to Brighton. Since they will now have to incur the additional expenses of returning to London in order to avail themselves of these privileges, their demand schedule for Brighton electricity will be somewhat higher than that under option 1. Yet if they have, indeed, already moved to Brighton, this option 2 demand schedule is the correct one to use in evaluating the electricity project. Clearly, if excess benefits are assured under the 1 option, they are *a fortiori* assured under the 2 option. On the other hand, if excess benefits are not possible under the 1 option, they may be possible under the 2 option. In that case, it may be inferred that although the potential migrants would not be willing fully to finance the additional electricity-generating capacity in Brighton if they were offered marginal cost prices *before* they left London, once they moved to Brighton (without knowing of the special offer) they might be prepared to cover the total costs of the additional capacity rather than incur the expenses of returning to London.

Finally, the economist may have to accept the administrative and political constraints that prevent option 1 or option 2 being implemented. Even if there are low-cost ways of obtaining reliable answers to hypothetical questions, which enable the economist to form an estimate of the option 1 demand curve and which, in turn, enables him to declare that the electricity project is uneconomic in that a potential Pareto improvement will not ensue, there may be nothing he can do to persuade families not to move to Brighton. In such circumstances, the avoidable losses of quasi-rents by the London electricity authority which have to be borne because of the 'unnecessary' emigration from London (of those families which, if offered marginal cost prices, would have stayed in the London area), and which may not be covered by the excess benefits of the Brighton electricity project when calculated by reference to an uncorrected demand schedule, have to be accepted as an inevitable consequence of the institutional constraints. In other words, since people are constrained to choose whether to stay on or to move to Brighton on the 'wrong' terms, the possible losses are inevitable, and the economist has to regard them as bygones. By accepting a demand curve for electricity based on a *ceteris paribus* clause that includes the prevailing London prices, he concludes that the project is economically feasible if his calculation reveals an excess of benefits over cost—that is, if benefits exceed costs after ignoring losses of quasi-rent arising from the institutional, or political, constraints (which, in this instance, serve to present the potential migrant with the 'wrong' terms).

5. So far nothing has been said directly about the increase of land values which results from economic growth or from population movements, either arising spontaneously or following the construction of a railroad, or highway, between two towns.

It is sometimes alleged that a rise in rents paid by restaurants, shops, gasoline stations, etc., in some new locality, or along some new route—which rents reflect the increased benefit derived from such facilities by migrating families, or by additional drivers or passengers—may be ignored inasmuch as rents elsewhere will have fallen. There is, it is argued, simply a shift in rents, a result of a shift in demand from one area to another, or from one route to another.

In the absence of economic growth, this can be true. But where it is true, it is a reflection of the belief that the *flow* of additional benefits in some areas is equal to the *flow* of additional losses in other areas.

If economic growth is supposed, the flow of some additional benefits will exceed the corresponding flow of losses. What one has to guard against, is that of counting the same benefit or loss twice; once as a flow, and again, later, as a change in asset-valuation derived from the flow.

The annual rent of a particular site is, in the first instance, a transfer to the landowner of the annual excess profits made by the owner of the business established on it. And these excess profits are, themselves, nothing more than a transfer to the owner of consumers' benefits from the services that are sold on the site. Provided, that in the case of people who transfer their custom to this business, the transfer was made on the proper terms[4] (the services of the business from which they transferred their custom being offered at their marginal cost) any excess valuation above costs of these additional services furnished by this business should, in any case, be entered into the relevant cost-benefit calculation. If this site were to be sold, its market price would be the capitalized value of the now higher expected stream of rents. However, the rise in the stream of rents to this particular site—the result of the excess profit, arising from the increased demand (and increased consumer valuation) of such services—has been, or should have been entered into the calculation of the flow of benefits. Since in any case such benefit streams are to be discounted to the present in a cost-benefit calculation, in order to compare them with capital costs, we must not, in addition, include increased site valuations.

To illustrate, if the construction of a railroad from A to B raises the market value of those houses that are situated near the new railroad station in A, these capital gains are not to be brought separately into the calculation of benefits. The value of such houses rises simply because, once the railroad is built, their occupants have additional advantages either for job opportunities, shopping opportunities, or outings. The estimate of these advantages already have, or should have, been entered into the cost-benefit analysis of the railroad on an annual basis. Therefore to add, also, their capital gains would amount to a clear case of double-counting. Needless to say, the same remarks apply to the capitalized stream of the value of

---

4 Otherwise, if the old services were offered at prices above marginal cost, the estimate of additional benefit is overstated, as explained above.

any disadvantages that arise from the siting of the stations, or from the construction of the railroad.

6. Economic growth is not necessarily associated with changes in tastes, though in the world as we know it the association is strong. Part, at least, of the enterprise of advertising agencies is directed toward attempts to alter existing patterns of taste so as to favour the goods of the clients they represent. The question arises as to the benefit, if any, to society of resources used expressly for this purpose.

A spontaneous change in taste, from some existing good x to another existing good y, would appear to involve society in a waste of resources—unavoidable, perhaps, but waste for all that. A part, at least, of the capital invested in the production of x is, for no 'sensible' reason[5] rendered useless, and additional capital has to be built to meet the additional demand for y; additional capital which could have otherwise been used in raising real income. In that sense society is worse off than it would have been had its tastes remained unchanged. This conclusion emerges with greater force, if we suppose first, a change from x to y followed, after an interval, by a change in tastes back from y to x again, with the cycle, perhaps, repeating itself. In this way capital is used up which could otherwise—had tastes remained unchanged—have been invested as useful additions to the capital stock.

If, however, under its existing political institutions, society permits the use of scarce resources for the express purpose of inducing these changes in taste—including attempts to shift tastes from x to y, and later from y to x—the social waste can no longer be held to be unavoidable, a consequence only of exogenous factors. Even if the attempts to alter existing tastes are not always successful, one can point to a social loss of those resources that are used up by advertising agencies.[6]

---

5 Unless economists make judgments about tastes which, up to the present, they have been very wary of doing.

6 I am concerned only with resources used to persuade people to change their tastes, not with resources used to provide information. I am aware that advertisers have long sought to convince the public that advertising is also entertaining and informative, and even (priced at zero) demanded by the public as a joint product. But there is no great difficulty in maintaining a distinction between the aim of providing partial information (as offered by commercial advertisers) and the aim of providing impartial information (as offered, say, by consumers' associations). Nor is much imagination needed to surmise that if all commercial advertising were to cease, newspapers, and other media, would give more space, and time, to providing information on the goods offered by industry.

Moreover, if we are thinking in terms of a more dynamic economy, and the induced changes of tastes are from x to y, from y to z, from z to w, and so on, where y, z, w, are new sorts of goods which, without persuasion, would not have been wanted (or, at least, not in those quantities), then idle capacity is prematurely brought about in the production of each of these goods, and an unnecessary rate of obsolescence is 'artificially' induced. So long as the economist remains neutral as between tastes, avoidable waste can be said to be taking place. Such losses, if unexpectedly introduced, are borne by the owners of capital. But once the risk of rapid changes in taste are recognized, they are passed on to the country at large (along with the factor costs of advertising) through the higher prices needed to cover the higher costs of 'artificial' obsolescence.

An investment for the express purpose of changing tastes—as distinct from expenditures necessary to provide impartial information—such as that undertaken by an advertising agency, may be expected to generate a future stream of additional revenues to the producers. The factor costs of the investment in advertising are, of course, paid ultimately by the consumers of the advertised products. But whether this investment creates additional demand for existing or new goods, the additional revenues cannot be interpreted as social benefits. Furthermore, the resulting obsolescence of the plant and machinery, used in the production of these goods from which demand has been removed, can be interpreted as an avoidable social loss. Thus, so long as the economist has no means of ranking tastes, he cannot place any additional social value on the demand for goods generated in this way. The economist's calculations are based on the assumption that existing tastes remain unchanged for the period covered by the calculation. Only on such a condition can he make comparisons between alternative economic organizations.[7]

---

7 Supposing that the problem of scarcity still exists (a moot point with respect to Western countries), there is a case for society's making provision for using resources in order to avoid spontaneous changes in tastes, and to maintain existing tastes; a better case, I should think, than could be made for the use of scarce resources in order to induce changes in tastes, so effectively reducing the available stock of capital, or its rate of growth.

Chapter 11
TRANSFER PAYMENTS

1. So far we have omitted to identify the group which, in a cost-benefit analysis, is taken as coterminous with society. If the economist is working for a corporation, or a local authority, it could be argued that his allegiance is primarily to the corporation, or to the local authority, and that he can therefore rightly ignore any gains and losses that fall on persons or businesses outside the jurisdiction of the corporation, or local authority. There is nothing to prevent the economist from confining his calculation in this way, though if he does so it behoves him to make his decision explicit. For the generally accepted view is that a cost-benefit analysis is undertaken on behalf of the nation at large, and is designed to capture the benefits and losses accruing to all groups in the nation. A tariff on foreign imports may then be held to benefit the nation, even though it inflicts a loss on foreigners which exceeds that gain.

Although the convention is plain enough, political decisions can cause problems. To illustrate, the central government may have agreed to give a bounty to any local authority undertaking to build a hospital, or a road, to certain specifications. In the absence of the bounty, we can suppose, none of the projects would be admitted as economically feasible, whereas each of them would be if the bounty were entered into the calculation as a net benefit, or as a contribution to the costs—as undoubtedly it would be by the local authority.

It may, of course, be argued that the bounty offered by the central government is, at least, equal to the net benefits enjoyed by the rest of the nation—which includes all those people other than the local citizens having direct access to the hospital, or road, and whose expected benefits have been entered into the calculation. But since the cost-benefit calculation should, in any case, take account of the benefits to be experienced by everyone in the nation, there is no economic justification for separately including the amount of the bounty also on the benefit side. On a strict interpretation of the Pareto principle there is no warrant, then, for admitting a project that would, in the absence of the bounty, be regarded as economically unfeasible.

The bounty, it may then be alleged, is granted in consideration of some benefit to the nation at large that is difficult to quantify. A broader, or longer, highway than would otherwise be undertaken, or a hospital having underground facilities, may have a military value for the nation which the economist, or any one for that matter, will find difficulty in appraising. The economist may be able to salve his professional conscience by entering the value of the bounty as equal to the additional security provided to the nation by the project— leaving it open to experts, however, to argue that the same additional amount of security could be provided at smaller cost.

If, on the other hand, no such consideration is present, the bounty is no more than a transfer from the nation's taxpayers to the present and future inhabitants within the locality—notwithstanding which, government authorities may insist that the bounty be entered as a cost-saving item in evaluating the project. In such cases, the economist, as a practical matter at least, may have to comply: his calculations are, in effect, being subjected to political constraints. For all that, he should make it quite clear in his report that the calculation is subject to this political element; and that, on a strictly economic calculation, the bounty cannot be treated as a benefit, or cost-saving, item.

This is not the first occasion in this volume, nor will it be the last, that political, or institutional, constraints will have to be considered. Wherever such constraints affect the outcome of the evaluation, in particular where, in their absence, the investment decision would be otherwise, the economist has the duty of making the fact abundantly clear. Not even majority opinion is to be treated by him as the considered opinion of the nation, the voice of the people in council. Political decisions may be poor decisions for a large number of reasons too tedious to recount. The further information and economic analysis the economist can offer are the materials of a more informed debate which can reverse preceding political decisions. Moreover, the economic criterion he employs is quite independent of the outcome of current political debate or current voting procedures.[1]

---

[1] For a further discussion of this allegation the reader is referred to Note A in Part VI.

2. Although corporations will assess the profits of their enterprises net of all taxes, the economist interested in *social* cost-benefit analysis—which is tacitly understood by the term cost-benefit analysis, unless prefixed by the word *private*—values all benefits gross of tax. If, out of a $100,000 per annum benefit resulting from the construction of a dam, $35,000 is paid from the revenues as direct taxes to the government, this transfer of $35,000 to other nationals, via the central government, does not of itself entail a loss for society. If a number of people benefit from the dam to the tune of $100,000, after all costs are incurred, the fact that between them they transfer $35,000 to other members of society entails a spreading, a redistribution of the benefit of $100,000, but not a reduction of it. In contrast, however, accepting the conventional nationalistic scope of cost-benefit analysis, the benefits arising from the overseas projects of domestic corporations will exclude all taxes levied on the proceeds of such projects by foreign governments for their own benefit. Not only are the revenues from overseas investments reckoned net of all foreign taxes, it should be clear that the calculation of the initial gross benefits are taken to be equal to the untaxed excess gross revenues. They are not to be estimated by reference to consumers' surpluses inasmuch as the products of these overseas investments are sold abroad, and the consumers' surplus above price accrues to foreign, not domestic, customers. Finally, the gross benefits of a particular foreign investment can be reckoned as being the gross revenues (before foreign taxes) only if this particular investment has no effect on the sales of goods produced by plant and equipment established abroad by previous investment from the home country. If, for example, a new investment in the foreign country B, by the nationals of the home country, A produces goods which are substitutes for those already being produced in B from previous investments there made by country A, any loss of profits sustained on these previous investments have to enter as part of the costs of the new investment.[2]

---

2 In the limiting case of a continuous demand curve in country B for a good x produced there as a result of previous investment goods from country A, the same investor in country A reckons his revenues not by reference to the price of x but by reference to x's marginal revenue. In such a case, the economist follows suit.

If, on the other hand, the new goods are complementary with those produced by plant and machinery already invested in country B by the nationals of country A, the additional profits earned by these older investments have to be added to the expected gross revenues of the new investment.

Reverting to purely domestic projects, the reader will recall the statement that a cost-benefit calculation cannot remove tax payment made by the enterprise since these tax payments are, in effect, benefits that are transferred to other nationals through the machinery of government. The obverse error is to include as additional benefits those already comprehended in some initial calculation of the benefit. The obverse error, in other words, is a double counting of some items in the flow of benefits.

If, for example, a new railroad so reduces the time and increases the convenience of travel as to offer new job oppportunities to a number of men, we ought *not* to include the measure of these new rents (a measure of the increase in their welfare from switching to the new jobs, as given by the compensating variation) as *additional* benefits. For such benefits are already subsumed in the (potential) consumers' surplus of the new railroad. Such a measure of consumers' surplus—approximated, say, by an estimate of the potential demand schedule for train journeys per annum—reveals the maximum sum each person will pay for a number of train journeys. And in determining this maximum sum, he will take account of the rents of the new job and, indeed, all other incidental utilities and disutilities accruing to him from the new railroad service.

The same *caveat* also applies where the consumers' surplus measure of benefit that arises from reducing the cost of a good comprehends the additional profits enjoyed by a number of intermediate agents that handle the good.

Consider, for example, an irrigation project that reduces the cost of grain production over an area. The benefit, to be placed against the costs of the project, is to be reckoned as the saving in costs of production on the existing output *plus* the area of the triangle of surplus (representing the excess of value over cost of the additional output demanded at a lower price, equal to the new and lower cost). Once more, however, any rise in the profits of farmers, or of grain merchants, or of bankers, and so on, is *not* to be entered as benefits additional to this full cost-saving of the irrigation project. Such items are to be seen as transfers of part of this benefit from consumers to farmers and middle-men—at least during some period of adjustment in a competitive economy. Put more generally, the calculated benefit arising from the lower resource cost of grain is distributed among consumers, farmers, and middlemen, according to market forces and institutions.[3]

3. Within a fully employed and perfectly competitive economy, in the absence of all spillover effects,[4] the cost to an industry of using any of its factors, say an hour of labour type A, is taken to equal the market price of that factor which, in overall equilibrium, is deemed equal to its marginal opportunity cost (or the value the factor could add if employed elsewhere, producing some other market good). If, however, the economy is not fully employed, and some project under consideration will have the effect of bringing into employment factors that are involuntarily unemployed, the cost to the economy of using such factors is, in general, smaller than their existing market price. How much less depends upon the period of idleness of such factors expected in the absence of the opportunity provided by the project, and the worth of 'idleness' to the factor-owner. If the unemployed type A labourer, who could be brought into employment by the project, would otherwise remain unemployed for an average period of about a year, then a special price for such A labour used—just enough to compensate the labourer to forgo the 'enjoyment', if any, of his idleness—is to be entered as its cost only for the one year. After that year, it is supposed, this type A labourer can be employed elsewhere, and the cost therefore of continuing to use it in this project is equal to its marginal product elsewhere—which, in a competitive economy, is equal to the market price of that type A labour.

---

3 It may be thought that additional sales, or processing, of grain should raise the profits of middlemen and millers since, at an unchanged mark-up, they handle a larger volume of grain. Yet inasmuch as it requires some additional services to handle an additional volume of grain, the rise in profits is to some extent a private rather than a social gain. For existing workers may have to work harder without a commensurate rise in earnings. To the extent this is not so, there can be short-period quasi-rents which disappear in the long period when additional factors are brought into grain distribution and processing as to restore normal profits there.

4 These are treated in Part III.

Idle land provides another familiar example. If the owner has no personal use for it—neither hunting on it, strolling on it, or getting any pleasure at all from merely gazing at it in its unused state—its opportunity cost to him is nil. If a project can now make use of this piece of land in the production of a good x, and (by discriminating exploitation of its demand curve[5] for x) could offer, at most $10,000 for its use, the whole of this $10,000 would be the measure of additional social benefit from bringing the land into economic use. Whether, after some bargaining by the landlord, the price he is paid is much less, say $2,000, and whether the price is set so that consumers have a surplus of, say, $5,000, the remaining $3,000 going initially to the owners of the business as excess profits, makes no difference to the measure of this additional benefit of $10,000. It affects only the distribution of the $10,000 of benefit.

The case is no different if the landowner had entered into a contract with a private corporation, or government agency, giving it full rights over the land for a fixed period. If, after a number of years, the private corporation or government agency, finding no use for the land, is ready to transfer the rights at the rent specified in the contract, or even at a lower rent, the mere fact that the newly negotiated rent (between the government agency, or corporation, and the owners of the new project) enters into the annual expenses of the project activity, does not admit them as costs in the cost-benefit calculation. The opportunity cost of this piece of land to the economy is still nil, and as such it must be entered.[6] Only if an alternative use for this land is discovered, say that of growing potatoes, will its opportunity cost become positive, and equal to the additional value it confers in the potato growing activity.

4. We may recognize that the land and the landowner are separate entities, while, in the case of labour, the services of the labourer and

---

5 The perfectly discriminating monopolist is, of course, a fictional character who, by discriminating among each of his consumers, and charging each the maximum for successive units, manages to appropriate to himself the whole of the consumers' surplus.

The revenue of the discriminating monopolist can be taken as equal to the consumers' surplus of the quantity he sells if it were all priced at zero.

6 Exactly the same argument applies to any other asset, plant, equipment or piece of property, that contributes nothing, outside its contemplated use, to anybody's satisfaction.

the labourer himself are inseparable. This difference may have important philosophical and social implications. But in economics the distinction is not of itself significant. It may, however, produce a difference of degree. For there is a likelihood that workers attach greater value to the 'idleness'—or, more precisely, to the 'non-market activities'—of their factors than do landowners.

Indeed, the value attached by factor-owners to the non-market activities of their factors can bear yet more emphasis in this connection. The fact that the marginal product of labour in agriculture, in some parts of Asia, is nil does not warrant its being costed at nil in the evaluation of any industrial project. It may be true that labour in the fields may be used until its marginal physical product is nil. It is true therefore that if the labour were transferred elsewhere, its apparent opportunity cost *in terms of the physical output or market value it produces in agriculture* is also nil. Indeed, we are to suppose it is nil. But guided by the Pareto principle, which admits only those changes that can make everyone better off, the opportunity cost of employing this labour elsewhere is equal, in this case, to the value the worker himself places on his employment in agriculture. More precisely, and ignoring costs of movement, it is equal to the minimal sum that would induce him to leave agricultural employment and take up employment elsewhere.[7] And this sum can be a small or a large fraction of the going industrial wage in such regions, according to the value the worker places on his leisure, on the stigma (if any) of being unemployed, and on the non-market opportunities open

---

7 In certain areas of Asia many small holdings are large family affairs, and though the marginal product of a person working on a holding is nil, each person (or each family) is paid a share of the proceeds, equal, say, to the average product. If a person is indifferent to all but the pecuniary aspects of the job, he would consider his opportunity cost as equal to his share, or average product. If, then, he were moved elsewhere agricultural product would not diminish, and the remaining members of the farm could afford to pay him the same share without their being any worse off. Anything he could produce elsewhere now adds to aggregate product, and any earnings he receives makes him better off than before. But once we admit that he is not indifferent to non-pecuniary factors, that he prefers to be with the larger family, and that the larger family prefer his presence among them, the value of any additional goods he produces elsewhere must be enough to compensate him and the remaining members, among others, if there is to be a Pareto improvement.

to him. In the absence of restrictions imposed by labour unions, and in the absence of transfer payments such as unemployment benefits, the costs of drawing labour into industry from an existing pool of unemployment, or a pool of agriculturally 'superfluous' labourers, would appear in a competitive economy simply as the supply price of the additional labour required by industry.[8]

It is to be noticed, however, that we are no longer dealing with a specific (type A) sort of labourer, one who can either be employed in a specific occupation or else remain unemployed. Rather, we are dealing with a more general, unskilled or semi-skilled, labourer; one who can turn his hand to a number of different jobs among which, presumably, he has preferences. For this reason it follows, contrary to what is sometimes assumed, that the opportunity cost of his labour, even though fully employed, can be determined only in relation to some new occupation. Properly conceived, the opportunity cost of, say, a labour-week employed in industry y is the value of this labour-week when employed instead in, say, industry x *plus* the (weekly) compensating variation which would just induce the worker to transfer his labour from x to y[9]. These two sums together make up the total value forgone in moving the labourer from x to y. Unless the weekly value added by the labourer in y exceeds this total value forgone, or opportunity cost, the Pareto criterion is not met. Clearly, if the worker were, instead, moved from x to z, or from x to w, his compensating variation could alter and, therefore, in relation to a contemplated movement to z and w, the opportunity cost of his labour is also altered.

We have ignored the costs of movement so far, simply because there is nothing to be said about it, other than the costs (the subjective costs to the worker, that is, which may be more than the

---

8 As the reader may know, schemes for moving unemployed labour, or agriculturally 'superfluous' labour, in economically backward countries, into industry have occasionally proposed that such labour be valued at zero; equal, that is, to its marginal product. At the same time, it is also admitted that a positive wage would be necessary to attract such 'idle' labourers from their wonted pursuits. Schemes that would appear feasible on this logic (contrary to that in the text) might not be justified on the Pareto principle.

9 If in moving from x to y the worker is paid more than his compensating variation, he earns an economic rent.

objective costs) should be entered into the costs of the scheme that requires his labour.

5. The practice is not much different once we introduce unemployment benefits in the economy. What matters, again, is simply that the additional value added by the hitherto unemployed worker exceed his opportunity cost in his new occupation. Where he has no preference, given any level of expenditure, as between being employed and being unemployed, the opportunity cost of his moving into employment can be taken as equal to zero. It follows that if his labour can now be used to produce no more than $1 worth of output, society is to that extent better off. In such circumstances, his labour, wherever used, enters a cost-benefit calculation priced at zero.

If, as will be the case in general, the worker is not indifferent to non-pecuniary factors,[10] his opportunity cost to industry is not equal to zero. It is the compensating variation necessary to induce him to move from his 'unemployment activities' to a particular industry and, therefore, once more, it will vary according to his preference for working in the particular industry in question. Moreover, the compensating variation may be a negative sum if, on the whole, he resents being unemployed. For this means that, if necessary, he will pay up to some maximum weekly amount, say $10 from his savings rather than remain unemployed. In that case, the opportunity cost of his labour to the particular industry is *minus* $10.[11] If, on the contrary, he attaches some positive utility to his being unemployed, the compensating variation will be a positive sum. He must then be paid some minimum sum, say $20, before he will agree to move to

---

10 It is common in advanced Western economies to put the accent on *non-pecuniary* activities, as against the accent on *non-market* activities in less advanced economies. The distinction is of no importance for a cost-benefit analysis that is consistent in regarding the worker's compensating variation (for moving from his current occupation) as a necessary component of the opportunity cost of his labour in some new industry.

11 If his wage in that industry is $50 and the value he adds to its product is $80, we can infer (i) the remaining members of society are better off by $30 ($80 of value added less the $50 paid to him), and (ii) the worker is better off by $60 (his $50 wage plus the $10 he is willing, but does not have, to give up). The total social gain is therefore $90. And this $90 is the excess of the value he creates over the opportunity cost; $80 *less* (− $10).

some specific employment opportunity. In that case, the opportunity cost of his weekly labour to that industry is $20. Unless, then, he adds at least $20 worth of value by his efforts there, society is better off, on the Pareto principle, leaving him unemployed.

This bit of argument is straightforward enough. The only excuse for presenting it is that the financial aspects of unemployed benefit have been known to confuse matters.

Unemployment benefit, whether it is collected by the worker 'as of right' from an insurance scheme, or whether it is wholly or partly government relief, is to be regarded, in a cost-benefit analysis, as a transfer from the earning members of society to the non-earning beneficiary. Nor does it matter whether the money paid to the unemployed worker is from taxes, from loans, or from an issue of new money. For, during the period in question, the worker does not add to the value of the aggregate product, this being the result of the contributions of other members of society. Yet he is entitled to, and does consume, a part of that product. It follows that no part of this transfer payment to him should enter as the opportunity cost of his being employed in some industry.

Nevertheless, although this transfer of money to him is not itself the opportunity cost of his labour, the amount of the transfer does affect the level of his welfare and, therefore, also does affect the magnitude of the opportunity cost. If, for instance, there were no unemployment benefits, he might overcome his dislike of taking on a certain job for a weekly sum of $8, whereas if his unemployment benefit were $25 a week, it might require a weekly sum of $40 at least—an excess of $15 above his unemployment benefit—to induce him to accept the work. In the former case, the opportunity cost of his labour is $8. In the latter case it is $15—the *excess* above his unemployment benefit he would require to agree to do the job. If, therefore, his marginal product in this employment were above $15, say it was $17, he should be given the job. For the worker, when paid $40, will be as well off as before, and the remainder of society will be better off by $2. (The rest of society gains the $25 it no longer has to transfer to the worker, and instead gives up only $23 as a subsidy needed to make up the difference between his marginal product

($17), and his wage ($40).)[12]

If, on the other hand, being employed of itself had a positive utility for the worker, an excess of earnings above unemployment benefit would be unnecessary. Indeed, he would be willing to take the job for as little as, say, $20; that is, to give up $5 a week in order to have the job. In that case, the opportunity cost to the industry which employs him is *minus* $5. If his marginal product in that industry is, as before, $17, the social gain is $22.

In sum, accepting the initial distribution of welfare as determined by the *status quo*, which involves, also, an acceptance of the existing rates of unemployment benefits to those currently unemployed, the compensating variation required by any unemployed worker to move him to a particular occupation—measured as the minimum wage he will accept for that job *less* the unemployment benefit—has to be regarded as the opportunity cost of his labour to that industry. In order to realize a potential Pareto improvement it is necessary only that the value of his product in that industry exceeds this opportunity cost.

Finally, unemployment benefit that runs for a limited period, or falls way gradually, or precipitately, after a certain length of time, introduces only an obvious qualification. If, for example, unemployment benefit runs for exactly six months, a man is liiely to accept a lower wage after the elapse of five months than after the elapse of only five days. This eventuality, however, poses no conceptual

---

12 The unemployment benefit, being contingent upon his remaining unemployed, results in the worker's comparing the desirability of a specific job with the *excess* earnings it offers; i.e. the wage offered, *less* the unemployment benefit. But it is by reference to his level of welfare that he determines his compensating variation; and only if his compensating variation is less than his *excess* earnings does he accept the job (ignoring labour union restrictions). Since his compensating variation for moving into the job is also the relevant opportunity cost to society, it follows that if his excess earnings were set equal to his marginal product, his choice of whether or not to move into that employment would accord with the social interest.

In the latter example, above, his compensating variation to move into the job was $15, and his excess earnings were also $15 (a wage of $40 less unemployment benefit of $25). His marginal product, however, was $17. If his excess earnings were set equal to $17—if, that is, he were offered $42 rather than the $40—he would certainly have taken the job, and society would therefore have been made better off by $2.

problem. Economists have to accept the decision of any factor-owner concerning the minimum worth of his factors, and therefore his compensating variation, in whatever circumstances the factor-owner finds himself.[13]

13　In the case of capital, however, occupational preferences can be disregarded, leaving opportunity costs to be determined by earning differentials alone. If, in a short period, existing machines are specific to their existing function, their value elsewhere is nil and, therefore, their opportunity costs are nil. If, on the other hand, the machines have a range of uses, (as, for instance, lathes) they can, at some cost of conversion, produce a value in other uses. In that case opportunity costs are positive. In any cost-benefit calculation, an existing machine has to be valued at this opportunity cost. Where such a machine has a number of alternative uses, it is clearly to be valued at the highest of the alternative opportunity costs. Earnings above this *highest* opportunity cost (sometimes known as its transfer price) are defined as quasi-rents, and accrue to the owners of the machine. In a cost-benefit analysis, however, we need consider only the benefits in excess of these, and other, opportunity costs.

Chapter 12

THE USE OF SHADOW PRICES

1. A 'shadow' or 'accounting' price—the terms are interchangeable—is the price the economist attributes to a good or factor on the argument that it is more appropriate for the purpose of economic calculation than its existing price, if any. There is nothing very special about the notion of a shadow price. In evaluating any project, the economist may effectively 'correct' a number of market prices and, also, attribute prices to unpriced gains and losses that it is expected to generate. He will, for example, add to the cost of a factor, or subtract from the cost of a good, in making allowance for some external diseconomy. Wherever the amounts of a good, to be added to or subtracted from the existing consumption, are large enough, the economist will substitute for price the more discriminating measure of benefit, consumers' surplus. Certain gains, or losses, to an enterprise he will value as zero, since for the economy at large they are only transfer payments. The cost of labour that would otherwise remain idle, he must value at its opportunity cost; not at its wage; and so on.

Nonetheless, the term has been used more specifically in a number of connections,[1] and it will, perhaps, avoid confusion if these are briefly indicated.

2. First, the term has long been used in mathematical programming, a technique in which the value, at given prices, of an 'objective function' is, say, maximized, subject to certain amounts of inputs and a number of technologically feasible factor-combinations. From this 'primal' problem, a 'dual' problem can be derived having a corresponding objective function which is to be minimized. It transpires that, for a wide class of problems, the variables in the dual solution can be interpreted as shadow prices, or accounting prices,

---

1   The interested reader is referred to Roland McKean's excellent article, 'The Use of Shadow Prices' (1968).

inasmuch as they are the 'correct' input prices—being consistent with the maximum value of the primal objective function.[2] We shall not, however, be using the term shadow price in connection with this technique.

Secondly, the term has been extended to estimates of social benefits, or social losses, that are either unpriced or not satisfactorily priced. Unpriced, or inadequately priced, benefits or losses may be valued either (a) by adopting the prices of similar things elsewhere, or (b) by calculating the price for a good, or a 'bad', that is *implicit* in government decisions to undertake particular projects, or (c) by calculating the spillover effects by reference to market prices, or by some other method.

(a) The price adopted for some public good, or service, may be based on that at which it is sold in some other region of the country. Thus, the value of a public amenity such as a beach, a park, or a museum, to be established, say, in New York may be estimated by reference to the prices charged for similar beaches, parks, or museums, in other parts of the United States. Such prices, even when attempts are made to allow for differences in circumstances, are not very satisfactory. The prices that are set elsewhere for such things are not likely to be optimal prices, and are sometimes set arbitrarily or, rather, by reference only to political considerations. Since a correct measure of the benefit is the maximum that people would pay for the service rather than go without, one cannot hope for much from this device. At any rate, no generalization that is useful, and also not obvious, can be made with respect to this practice, and we need say no more about it here.

(b) Wherever there is an unpriced benefit, G, arising from some government authorized project which, on a cost-benefit calculation confined to measurable benefits, reveals an excess of cost over benefits, ΔK, it may be said that the implicit, or shadow, price of G is

---

2 When these shadow prices are imputed to the given inputs, the value of the dual objective function is minimized. It can then be interpreted as the minimum input cost, subject to the constraints, and to the requirement that no profits (excess revenues) be made. These shadow prices are, therefore, no different from the factor prices that would emerge in a perfectly competitive equilibrium in which product prices are exogenously determined. An unusually clear introduction to the uses of mathematical programming is provided in Throsby's book (1970).

ΔK — or, rather, that it is *at least* equal to ΔK.[3] One of the difficulties of this argument is that one cannot hope for a deliberate and systematic criterion to be invoked in such cases. There can be, and there are, the widest discrepancies between these implicit valuations. Yet even if this were not the case, the validity of the procedure is open to question[4] and we need not discuss it further at this point.

(c) The existence of spillover effects requires that market prices be corrected, *inter alia*, for incidental losses and gains falling on persons other than the producers or users of goods. These incidental social losses or gains can sometimes be valued by reference to market prices, though not without difficulties. Prices of such goods, once corrected for spillover effects they produce, are also spoken of as shadow prices. However we defer discussion of spillover effects to Part III.

Finally, and most commonly perhaps, shadow prices are associated with economic calculation in countries, often poor countries, in which domestic prices do not properly reflect relative scarcity, whether of finished goods or of materials, and whether these are produced at home or imported. The inadequacy of prices (as indicators of relative scarcity) arises from a number of factors that interfere with the working of markets, both domestic and foreign. The domestic currency in such countries is commonly over-valued, and maintained through exchange controls, import quotas, and other trade restrictions. The analysis in this chapter is restricted to the use of shadow prices on this interpretation.

3. Since we shall be particularly interested in the shadow, or accounting, prices of imported goods, we shall assume that the official exchange rate of the domestic currency is set at a level other than that which would prevail in conditions of free international trade. If such countries intend to maintain their over-valued currencies through trade and exchange restrictions, in addition to short and long term foreign borrowing, shadow prices are, indeed, indispensable in evaluating projects there. In this connection, some of the

---

3 If, instead, there is an unpriced social loss, D, arising from a government project which shows an excess of measured benefit over cost, ΔB, then, on the same argument, the implicit, or shadow, price of the social loss D is taken as ΔB — or, rather, it is taken as *not greater than* ΔB.

4 For arguments tending to reject the validity of this method of implicit valuation, the reader is referred to the chapters on 'Loss of Life and Limb' in Part III.

largest poor countries come to mind: India, Pakistan, Brazil—although, under a system of fixed exchange rates, West European countries are occasionally prone to periods of trade imbalance which might warrant the introduction of shadow prices.

Assuming full employment and international free trade equilibrium there is no problem of calculating the accounting price of traded goods. Ignoring transport costs etc., the foreign price of a ton of manganese imported into India is equal to its domestic price there which, in turn, is equal to the value of Indian exports necessary to pay for it. Given perfectly competitive factor and product markets, and in the absence of external effects, Indian exports are priced at the opportunity cost of the factors used in their production. In that case the domestic price of a ton of imported manganese (or a unit of any other import) is equal, ultimately, to the opportunity cost of the Indian factors used in producing the goods to pay for it.

Removing the assumption of international free trade, the domestic costs of imports rise with the degree of protection provided. If there is say, a 200 per cent *ad valorem* tariff on manganese the domestic price will be three times the foreign or world price (assuming constant world supply price). The question arises, which price do we use—the domestic or the world price—as the relevant opportunity cost of the manganese imports to the Indian economy. The accounting price for Indian exports poses a similar problem. Do we use the world price of such exports,[5] or do we use the value of these exports to the domestic economy?

In disclosing the analysis by which the question can be answered, it will simplify matters if we confine ourselves to small changes. We then avoid the need to invoke consumers' surpluses, and rents, and take the market prices (in the absence of spillovers) as indicators of per unit social valuation. One might think, first, to come down in favour of using foreign, or world, prices—*not* domestic market prices—on the grounds, (a) that everything produced and consumed domestically has an effect (via the availabilities argument) on the balance of payments; (b) that, because of substitution possibilities, we can compare one thing with another and, in particular, it is

---

5 The use of world prices in evaluating projects has been recommended most recently by Little and Mirlees (1969). Some of their reasons, which are summarized below, are given on pp. 91–92 of their book.

convenient to compare any good with foreign exchange; (c) because world prices express their real cost, or benefit, to the country in terms of foreign exchange; and (d) free foreign exchange is a good yardstick because it can be used to satisfy almost any need.

4. These considerations are not very compelling. There is no question but that if $1 million of foreign exchange can be used to purchase x tons of foreign steel, or y tons of foreign nickel, then, *in terms of exchange reserves*, x tons of foreign steel and y tons of foreign nickel are equally costly irrespective of the duties on each. The revenues from the tariffs can, of course, be regarded simply as transfer payments, the cost (in terms of foreign exchange) to the country, as a consumer in the world economy, being simply the world price—assuming, always, it is constant.[6]

One may concede all this, however, without concluding, that in any cost-benefit study, traded goods should be valued at world prices. On the contrary, there may be a stronger case to be made for valuing traded goods at domestic prices. We shall be in a better position to say so after some analysis of the conditions under which either sort pf valuation is allocatively correct.

In general, the question of valuation depends on the relevant political constraints. The economist, as a rule, will accept the rate of exchange as a datum over the foreseeable future, and he will do so in full knowledge of the restrictions on trade and payments that the government deems necessary to maintain it. If, therefore, within the foreseeable future there is small expectation of any change in existing policy, the economist does the best he can only by working within these apparently irremovable restrictions.[7]

---

6 If the foreign supply price is upward-sloping, the marginal import cost is above the foreign price. (Similarly, if the foreign demand for the country's exports is downward sloping the country's marginal export revenue is below the foreign demand price.) But since we are concerned here with more fundamental issues, we may assume that over the relevant range world supply prices are constant, unless otherwise stated.

7 The economist may, indeed he should, urge on the authorities the need for a change to more 'rational' economic policies. But once he comes to making cost-benefit estimates, they are to be made by reference to those economic policies that are likely to prevail, not those that 'ought to' prevail.

We shall now compare the effects, on the prices of traded goods, of quotas and tariffs under two main assumptions; first that the government cannot further increase its imports by exporting additional goods, but can do so only by reducing other imports; and secondly, that it can increase its imports by increasing its exports, though at increasing cost.

5. (a) Suppose, then, a rigid quota system for manganese imports, having the result that the domestic market price is $3,000 a ton whereas the foreign purchase price is $1,000 a ton.[8] Since existing private firms value the manganese, at $3,000 a ton, a public enterprise, requiring annually 100 tons of manganese, that could not make a profit at this price of $3,000 per ton might yet be able to make a profit if it costed the imported manganese at only $1,000 per ton. If this is the case, the manganese allocated by the government to this public project could well be at the expense of that used in the private sector. But the resulting movement of a scarce material from existing uses to one where it has a lower value is a retrograde move: potential welfare is reduced.

It is possible, of course, for the government to reduce some other kind of imports in order to make available this 100 tons of manganese to the public project in question. In that event, the value to the domestic economy of those imports which the government chooses to reduce is the opportunity cost of this additional 100 tons of manganese. The economist, if asked to advise, would suggest that the government offset the additional payment of $100,000, in exchange for the 100 tons of foreign manganese, by reducing the purchase of $100,000 worth of imports having the lowest domestic value. But in the last resort, he must estimate the opportunity cost by the reduction in the domestic value resulting simply from the government's choice of what imports to sacrifice.[9] If, therefore, the government chooses to import $100,000 less of cutlery having a value on the domestic market of $200,000, then the opportunity cost of the 100 tons of manganese to the public project is $200,000. It may well be the case that the manager of the public project could make a greater

---

8 Since the exchange rate is taken to be fixed, dollar prices can be used in lieu of rupee prices.

9 The immediate reduction of $100,000 of foreign exchange reserves is not here regarded as an alternative policy. Sooner or later either other imports must be reduced or exports must be increased.

profit by selling the annual 100 tons of manganese to the private sector than by using them to manufacture goods he had planned, though it may also be the case that the government forbids such transactions, so sacrificing some potential gain. But whatever the outcome, the opportunity cost of this additional 100 tons of manganese is still $200,000.

(b) Consideration of a flexible quota scheme enables us to introduce the alternative possibility: in any year included in the project's cost-benefit period, India may increase its exports in order to pay for the additional 100 tons of manganese. The only conditions under which we can now justify using, as the opporutnity cost of manganese, its world price of $1,000 a ton are: (1) that the world demand for one or more of India's exports is infinitely elastic, and (2) that there is no purely domestic tax on the exported good.

Now, as the reader will recognize, the prices of exportables can be forced down if more is offered on the world market, so that, in general, marginal export revenue, rather than existing export price, should be used. Apart from bilateral dealings, it may be possible to confine an export subsidy to additional sales only. If so, the additional export revenue will be greater than if prices are reduced on all exports of a particular good.

If we use such information to determine the accounting price of *the additional import* of 100 tons of manganese—supposing for the moment that the second condition, no domestic tax on exported goods, is met—we have to ask: what is the reduction in domestic value necessary to fetch an additional $100,000 of foreign exchange in order to pay for the 100 tons of manganese? If the domestic price of jute is $1 per pound but, because of inelasticity of foreign demand, 250,000 pounds of it has to be exported to fetch $100,000, then the accounting price of the 100 tons of manganese is (at least) $250,000.

Of no less importance is the second condition. If, now, the first condition is met (constant export demand price), and the $100,000 can be obtained simply by exporting 100,000 pounds of jute, the accounting price of the manganese will be $100,000 only if there is no domestic excise tax on jute. If, however, there is, say, a 60 per cent *ad valorem* tax on domestic use of jute, the accounting price of the manganese is $160,000. Once neither condition is met, recourse to the above hypothetical figures would result in an accounting price for manganese of $250,000 plus 60 per cent, or $400,000—this being (at least) the loss of value to the domestic economy experienced by the withdrawal of 250,000 pounds of jute which are needed to pay for the 100 tons of manganese.

Finally, if we remove the assumption about constancy of the world supply price of manganese to India the resulting accounting price of the 100 tons of imported manganese is still higher. For instance, let the elasticity of foreign supplies of manganese be such that additional imports of 100 tons per annum involve additional payment of $200,000 or twice as much foreign exchange as with a constant world supply price, and therefore twice the volume (at least) of Indian exports. The accounting price of the 100 tons of manganese is then (at least) $800,000; being the value to the domestic economy of (at least) an additional 500,000 pounds of jute exported in exchange for the 100 tons of manganese.[10]

6. If we now shift our attention from quota schemes, or exchange controls (that directly ration either particular categories of imported goods or else imported goods in general), toward tariff schemes that ration imports by price, the essential arguments are unchanged. If there is a 200 per cent *ad valorem* tariff on manganese, a ton of manganese bought at $1,000 on the world market sells at a domestic price of $3,000. True, in the tariff case the government collects the revenue of $2,000 on each imported ton of manganese, whereas in the quota case this $2,000 becomes a windfall to the initial recipient of the quota who might well (if the government allows it) sell his quota-permit to others at a maximum price of $2,000 per permitted ton. But whether this 'monopoly rent' is received by the government, or by private persons or firms, is merely a distributional aspect which, of itself, provides no guidance in the determination of the accounting

---

10 I have made no allowance in these proposals for the degree of monopoly in the production of the chosen exported good, say, jute. In so far as the domestic price (without tax) of jute is above the export price the argument in the text applies, the relevant price being the domestic price.

It is true that the greater the degree of monopoly (as measured say, by the ratio of price to marginal cost) in the production of jute as compared with the production of other goods in the economy the greater the scope for allocative improvements. Again, however, though the economist can recommend such improvements, in undertaking a cost-benefit study he has to accept the present and future prices of goods (corrected for spillover effects) as indicative of their value, at the margin, to the community.

price of imported manganese. What is significant however, is again, the potential sacrifice of domestic value entailed in using an additional ton of manganese for this project. Where the country cannot, or will not, increase its exports, the opportunity cost of 100 tons of manganese is, as before, the domestic value of these imported goods that are to be withdrawn from the economy in order to make available the foreign exchange for the manganese imports. Where the country is able, and chooses, to pay for the additional manganese by additional exports, its opportunity cost is the domestic value subtracted from the economy by exporting goods in order to meet the additional foreign payments.

More generally, the import of an additional 100 tons of manganese, presents the country with a choice of reducing other imports, or increasing exports, or a combination of both.

It goes without saying that, accepting the existing trade restrictions, economic efficiency is promoted by keeping the opportunity costs of either method in line with one another. If the smallest loss of domestic value from reducing other kinds of imports were $300,000, and the smallest loss of domestic value from increasing exports were $350,000, the first method—import-reduction—is to be preferred each time until both methods (or any combination of the two methods) yield the same result. Again, however, the economist can only recommend such policies to the government. In so far as the government fails to implement them, the economist must derive his social costing from the actual, or expected, responses. If the government elects to pay for an additional 100 tons of manganese by exports of jute, which subtracts from the economy a domestic value of $400,000, when it might instead have raised the necessary foreign exchange by exports of raw cotton, which would subtract a domestic value of $300,000, the actual accounting cost of the manganese continues to be $400,000 until such time as the government changes its policy and makes payment through cotton exports.

7. So much for the calculation of accounting prices for *imports* used in public projects. What of the calculation of accounting prices for the *exported* outputs of these projects? It will be conceded that goods produced by the project, and exported, should be evaluated by reference to the same conceptual framework used in determining

the accounting prices of imports. But whereas the accounting prices of the project's imports, being an alternative to the domestic inputs, are to be reckoned as *opportunity costs* in terms of domestic value forgone,[11] the accounting prices of the project's exports, being an alternative to their domestic consumption, are to be regarded as conferring *benefits* on the economy. The measure of such benefits is the value to the domestic economy of the imports they make available to it.[12] In particular, the benefit measure of the project's exports is the domestic value of the specific goods that will be imported from the additional foreign exchange made available. A rational procedure, in this connection, would be one that used the additional exchange reserves in purchasing imports having the largest domestic value—account being taken of external effects, if any. But, again, in any project evaluations the calculation of the expected benefits, arising from the project's exports, must depend on the economist's judgment of the additional imports the government will actually allow; if one million yards of cloth exported by a new textile project adds $1 million to the foreign exchange reserves, they should not be priced at $1 million but at the domestic value of the additional imports that are to be bought for the $1 million. Given, say, a rising foreign supply price of the imports in question (which reduces the buying power of the extra $1 million foreign exchange) and a high tariff on those imports, the domestic value of the additional imports, now made possible by these exports, could be, say, $2,500,000, which is then the social benefit, or accounting price, of the additional exports of cloth.[13]

11   The costs of these imports can, if necessary, be compared directly with the benefit to be imputed to them from the sale of the outputs of the project—ultimately the addition to domestic social value.

12   The benefits of the exports, so calculated, can also be compared directly with the costs of their production—ultimately their opportunity cost in terms of domestic value forgone.

13   It might seem reasonable to argue that the exportable part of the output of the project *also* has an *opportunity cost*, in that it could have been sold instead on the home market and added, therefore to domestic value. Again, however, the resolution of the problem depends upon the constraints postulated. If the economist is to decide where all the project's outputs are to go, in particular which parts are to be exported and which retained for home use, he will regard them as alternative opportunities and, therefore, choose to place any output where it adds most to domestic value. In the text, however, we are assuming that the decision to export certain portions of the project's annual output is one that has already been made either by authority or custom, or possibly by the economist working within certain constraints.

In sum, the accounting prices of both additional imports and exports involved in any investment project—or the social opportunity cost of imports and the social benefits of exports—are to be calculated by reference respectively to the subtraction from, and addition to, the country's domestic value; not by reference to world prices of traded goods.

Admittedly the implementing of these proposals will present more difficulty than the use of world prices as accounting prices. For one thing, the practicing economist cannot always be sure, in evaluating a project involving traded goods, which particular imports will be displaced, or which particular imports or exports will be increased. He has perforce to engage in some guesswork. But he is at least guessing at the magnitudes of the right things. And wherever the calculations that arise from using two alternative methods can be significantly different—as they certainly can be wherever substantial trade restrictions exist—it is advisable to place reliance upon rough estimates of the relevant concepts than on more exact estimates of irrelevant ones.

Though this topic is far from exhausted, enough has been said to start the reader thinking along the right lines.

Chapter 13

THE PROBLEM OF SECOND BEST

1.   Wherever the familiar optimum conditions are not met in the rest of the economy, one *cannot*, in general, justify employing the marginal cost pricing rule to determine ideal outputs in the remaining sectors. As for evaluating a particular project, it is no longer possible, in these circumstances, to enter the prices of factors as costs in the usual way. The problem of what is then to be done, what rules to employ, is the problem posed by the theory of second best.[1] Although account has been taken of a number of special cases in the preceding chapters, the subject warrants more explicit treatment for two reasons: first, because familiarity with allocative economics pre-supposes an understanding of the context in which the second best theorem is pertinent. In particular, the economist, tendering advice on investment projects, has to be aware of the limited conditions under which the usual allocative propositions are valid. Secondly, because cost-benefit analysis is specifically concerned with the proper pricing of factors, which prices enter into the costs of the projects. To an increasing extent, also, cost-benefit analysis is invoked to determine the optimal size of the plant to be established and, in a 'short period' the size of the optimal output of the existing plant.

2.   It is a commonplace that optimal conditions are no more than first order, or necessary, conditions in maximizing a social welfare function subject to a production constraint.[2] The second best theorem

---

1   Although this problem had been recognized and discussed previously, the attempt to formulate it explicitly, and in full generality, was first made by Lipsey and Lancaster (1957).

2   The reader may wish to consult my *Survey* paper (1960), section II, which interprets and examines these optimal conditions.

does no more than point out that, if one or more additional constraints are imposed on this welfare function, the necessary conditions for a maximum are different from the usual ones and, in general, are more complex.[3] The obvious corollary follows that, in order to identify a maximum welfare position under these circumstances, it may be necessary to forsake those familiar optimal conditions that are strictly relevant to the simple case of a single constraint, the boundary of production possibilities.

Now in the simple case of no constraint additional to the production boundary, the more relevant set of necessary conditions is cast in the familiar form of setting the price of each good proportional to its corresponding marginal cost. Put otherwise, the ratio of the prices of any pair of goods has to be made equal to the ratio of their corresponding marginal costs. It follows, therefore, that if there is but one constraint additional to the production boundary, which takes the form, say, of the price in sector X being 40 per cent above its marginal cost, the above condition is met—and a general optimal position attained—simply by setting the prices in all the remaining

---

3 The more general proof proceeds as follows: in order to maximize some function,

$$F(x_1, x_2, \ldots, x_m)$$

subject to a single constraint

$$\phi(x_1, x_2, \ldots, x_m),$$

using the Langrangian method, maximize $W = F - \lambda\phi$. The necessary conditions will include $F_i = \lambda\phi_i$, or . . . .

$$F_i/F_j = \phi_i/\phi_j \ (i = 1, 2, \ldots, m).$$

However, if now an additional constraint is introduced, say $F_l/F_m = k\phi_l/\phi_m$, where $k \neq 1$, the Langrange method requires that we maximize the function

$$W' = F - \lambda\phi - \mu (F_l/F_m - k\phi_l/\phi_m),$$

and the necessary conditions become much more complex. See Lipsey and Lancaster (1957).

sectors 40 per cent above their corresponding marginal costs.[4]

One cannot depend on the problem being that simple, however, and the economist has to face the question of determining a price and output for one or more industries in circumstances where he cannot hope to influence price and output policies in the rest of the economy. Since there is not the slightest prospect of his being able to obtain the necessary data to calculate an exact second best solution for the industry, or industries, in question, it is necessary to consider conditions under which he can, with some assurance, recommend either marginal cost pricing or some other simple rule.

The existence of varying degrees of monopoly in the economy at large does not, of itself, justify much concern over misallocation. Enterprises that continue to survive are able to cover their full costs and, in a fairly competitive economy, not many enterprises are

---

4 It is occasionally asserted that the stricter condition, price *equals* marginal cost is required, since it meets a further optimum condition which is not met in equi-proportional case, as in the 40 per cent above cost instance in the text. This further condition is then identified as that ensuring equality between the marginal product of the factor in that use and the marginal (subjective) valuation to the factor-owner in alternative non-market uses (say leisure). If, for example, the hourly wage of a specific type of labour is $5, and the market value of its marginal product is 40 per cent more, or $7 then, it is argued, by allowing the worker to increase his number of hours, a net social gain will obtain. The worker, for instance, may agree to work an hour longer for $5.50, a further hour for $6, and so on. At the same time, as he produces more, the market value of the good declines. By allowing workers to extend their outputs until the market value of an hour's work is equal to the workers' subjective value of the hour, both worker and consumer can be made better off, or rather, as well off as possible.

This argument would be valid if, in perfect competition, each worker separately determines the number of hours he works in each job in each industry by reference to the wage offered to him. But whether he is paid by the hour or by what he accomplishes, this condition is never met in modern industry, no matter how competitive. Given the wage, or the rate for the job, he cannot adjust the number of hours to his own preferences. The worker has to accept, as a constraint, the hours of work per week (plus the specific overtime opportunities, if any) that go with the job. The modern worker is then faced with an all-or-nothing weekly agreement. He measures the wage offered against the full forty-hour week, say, and accepts or rejects. Marginal adjustments to output are, even in the absence of all intervention by labour unions, not by the hour, or by the piece, but only by the entrance, or exit, of additional workers; the marginal worker having zero rent.

Given these constraints, full employment and universal perfect competition imply that, in equilibrium, the opportunity cost of moving a worker from x to y is the same as his value in x; and no reshuffling of factors can result in a potential Pareto improvement. The economy is then in an optimal over all position, with the prices of all goods set m per cent above their corresponding marginal costs.

likely to make revenues that vastly exceed their costs for any length of time. Thus, although it is not to be expected that the economy, at any moment of time, attains an optimum position, in its continuous adjustment to changes in the conditions of demand and supply, it may not be too far from an overall optimal position for any prolonged period.[5]

The one factor that diminishes such hopes, however, even in a highly competitive economy is the existence of significant spillover effects, since there is no necessary tendency here toward self-correction. The larger the spillover effects and the less uniform is their incidence throughout the economy, the smaller is the confidence that can be reposed in the presumption that a competitive economy tends to a tolerably good allocation.[6]

3. The above remarks do not afford much consolation, but, in certain circumstances, the economist can say something more definite. For what matters in determining the price and output of the good in question, say X, are the price or output policies followed in the production of closely related goods, say Y and Z, that are identified as the constrained sectors. If, in an otherwise perfectly competitive economy, the constrained Y and Z sectors were 'deviant', Y's price being 50 per cent above its marginal cost and Z's price being 10 per cent above its marginal cost then—provided Y and Z were substitutes for X—the mark-up for the free sector, X, should obviously be something between 10 per cent and 50 per cent. This is intuitively plausible. For if, instead, we had set the mark-up for X at below 10 per cent or above 50 per cent, we should have widened the price-marginal cost ratios between the three substitute goods, thereby removing them further from an ideal position of equal price-marginal cost ratios.

---

5 The scope for improvement in productive, or technological, efficiency may, however, be far more important than allocative efficiency of this overall sort. And if so, the question of whether to spend a given sum of money in seeking such allocative improvements or in seeking advances in productive efficiency is easily answered. But whether attempts at increasing productive efficiency are successful or not, the allocative problem still remains.

For the arguments that productivity improvements are, at present, more profitable than the usual allocative improvements, the reader is referred to Leibenstein's 1966 paper.

6 Allocative and other aspects of spillovers, and their treatment in a cost-benefit analysis are discussed at length in Part II which follows.

Nor need we stop here. We could surmise that the excess price-marginal cost ratio, EPR, to be adopted in determining X's output, would not be far removed from a correct second-best ratio if it were calculated as an average of the EPRs of Y and Z, when these EPRs are weighted by their respective total values. Clearly if the value of Y with its 50 per cent EPR were large relative to the value of Z with its 10 per cent EPR, this rule would provide an EPR for X closer to 50 per cent than to 10 per cent.

This rule, however, does assume that goods Y and Z are about equally good substitutes for X. If Y happens to be a closer substitute for X than Z is, the response of X's demand is more sensitive to a proportional change in the price of Y than it is to a proportional change in the price of Z. In consequence Y's weight, in determining the average EPR for X, has to be more than proportional to its total value. For the more sensitive is the demand for X to the price of a particular substitute, the greater is the departure from the correct second-best amount of X in response to a given movement from the correct second-best price of X. If we are concerned, as we are, with the second-best optimal *outputs* of the goods, it is more important to set the price of X, or rather the EPR of X, closer to that of the more sensitive substitute Y than to that of Z, other things equal.

If, however, either or both of Y and Z are complementary with X, the reasoning, though analogous, gives opposite results. Suppose X is bread and Y is butter, and imagine a situation in which both have the same price-marginal cost ratio of unity—an EPR of zero. Ignoring all other goods for the moment, there is then, as between X and Y, a correct allocation of factors. Now suppose a rise in the price of butter, Y, by 50 per cent. This does not raise the demand curve for X, and the value of X, as it would if X were a substitute. Being a complement, the demand curve for bread, X, and its value to people, fall. Its equilibrium output falls also. It follows that, comparing the X and Y outputs with their initially correct outputs, they are both too small relative to the outputs of all other goods. Clearly, an attempt to redress this subsequent 'allocative distortion' by responding to the exogenous rise in price of Y with a proportional rise in the price of X only aggravates the situation by reducing both outputs further. *Per contra*, responding to the exogenous rise in the price of y by a reduction in the initial price of X—in this instance *below* its marginal cost—increases the outputs of both X and Y:

the demand for X will increase directly following a reduction in its price, and, with a lower price of X, the marginal value of Y, and the demand curve for Y, the complementary good, will shift upward. The outputs of both X and Y are thereby increased by a lowering of X's price and the initial optimal position approached once more. If the only goods closely related to the free sector, X, are all complements, the required EPR for X would approximate a weighted average of their EPRs prefixed by a negative sign—with, again, those goods more closely complementary with X carrying more weight relative to their value.

The rule for setting the EPR for X when its related goods comprise both substitutes and complements follows accordingly. If the EPRs of all related goods are positive—which is very likely if the goods are produced by private enterprise—the EPR for X by this weighting rule, will be positive for a predominance of substitutes, and negative for a predominance of complements.[7]

If the general belief, that the predominating relationship between goods is that of substitutes, is accepted, it is also possible to justify, in a rough and ready way, marginal cost pricing of the free sectors irrespective of the deviations from marginal cost pricing in the constrained sectors. Or, rather, the rule to be adopted in the free sectors is that prices should be set, as suggested by Farrel (1958), *no lower than* their corresponding marginal costs. They, may, of course, be set a little higher: how much exactly can be roughly calculated or guessed at. But, in general, such prices are not to be set lower than marginal costs.

4. In addition to such guiding rules, one can visualize circumstances in which one can go ahead and use straightforward marginal cost pricing for a group of industries, or for all industries, within a geographical area, in disregard of what is happening in the constrained remainder of the economy. Thus, if changes in the prices, or outputs, of the industries within this area have negligible repercussions on the demand for goods outside this area of the economy,

---

7 The mathematically exact rules for setting the prices of the free sector goods, given the price-marginal cost ratios of the constrained sectors, have been derived by Green (1961).

we can set the prices of the goods within this area equal to their corresponding marginal costs without fear of making things worse. For maximizing the value of the outputs within the area, by equalizing (through the marginal cost rule) the value of the marginal products there of each factor class, does not very much effect the value of the collection of goods produced in the remainder of the economy. Thus without doing any worse in the constrained rest of the economy, we do the best we can for this area by reshuffling factors as to maximize the value of the resulting product-mix there.

This last mentioned proposition, however, is not of much use to the economist unless he is required to offer advice to all industries within such a geographical area. For a single project, such a restrictive condition, enabling one to ignore the effects of the price to be set on the outputs of other goods, is not likely to be met. Nevertheless, the economist may occasionally find that an alternative condition can be met: that the factors used in the project in question are *specific* to that project. Such factors that spring to mind, a specific site, or specific machine, or a highly specialized type of labour, have been discussed in a previous chapter, and the reader will appreciate that a factor that is strictly specific in the production of X implies that it has a zero value in any alternative production over some period, long or short. The price of X should therefore be set low enough as to employ all of such specific factors. True, the lower the price of X is set the smaller will be the demand and outputs of the substitute goods for X in the constrained sector, and the larger, therefore, will be the outputs of other goods. But since the opportunity cost of the specific factors is nil, it is better that X be expanded at zero opportunity cost to the economy at the expense of its substitutes, letting the non-specific factors (which have a *positive* opportunity cost) move out of these substitute goods in order to add value elsewhere.

Finally, if the economist confines himself to estimating the cost of some specific project that is technically feasible, he need not be too inhibited by the second-best theorem. For no matter what the allocative condition of the economy at large, a Pareto improvement is effected if a factor is transferred from its existing employment to one where its value is higher—or, put more generally, if the value of the marginal product of the factor to be employed in X exceeds its opportunity cost.[8]

5. Returning, finally, to the question of marginal cost pricing—either in the long run, which determines the size of the plant, or in the short run, which determines the output produced by the existing plant—the reader is reminded that the question has been discussed under the tacit assumption that any necessary changes in the tax structure do not, of themselves, have any allocative effects.

In the long period the optimal size of the plant is determined by the condition that demand price equals long period marginal cost. If, therefore, the demand curve cuts the long-period marginal cost curve at an output in the range of declining average cost—marginal cost, and therefore price, being below average cost—the plant size will be one for which average (inclusive) cost is below price. And if there is only one price, set to equal marginal cost, the enterprise cannot meet its total cost from its revenues. Similarly, if, in the short period, the demand is such that the output for which price equals marginal cost is one for which marginal cost is below average cost, the marginal cost pricing rule specifies an output at which, so priced, total revenues fall short of total factor costs.[9]

By discriminating monopoly pricing or, more practically, by the use of two- or multi-part tariffs, the marginal cost-pricing rule can, however, be made consistent with the aim of covering the full costs

---

8   In general, any transfer of factors from one product to another affects the distribution of real earnings in the economy, and also the relative prices of the goods as between which factors are transferred, both of these consequences affecting the general pattern of demand, and, therefore, of the existing price-marginal cost ratios. The first feature in particular implies that the optimal position itself—uniquely determined only if there is a uniquely specified welfare function (which, in fact, is usually assumed in the treatment of second best theory) —alters in response to the factor movements which one would want to recommend by reference to the marginal cost price ratios of the existing situation. Nonetheless, in so far as the magnitudes of the factor movements are those pertinent to cost-benefits studies, the assumptions of partial analysis may be adopted. For the secondary repercussions on product prices arising from such relatively limited factor movements are likely to be negligible.

9   The reader is reminded that the marginal cost pricing condition is a necessary, but not sufficient condition. Confining ourselves to a partial analysis, it is required also that total benefit from the output exceeds total costs.

of the enterprise.[10] There may, however, be political or other constraints that rule out the possibility of two- or multi-part tariffs. If so, the alternative is either (a) that of producing a smaller than optimal output in order to cover costs—setting price equal, at least, to average cost (and, therefore, above marginal cost)—or else (b) that of subsidizing the enterprise so as to enable it to meet its factor payments when it sets a price equal to marginal cost (and, therefore, below average cost).

If there are no 'distortions' involved in raising taxes—as, in principle, there would not be if lump-sum taxes could be levied[11]—there can be no purely allocative objections to the (b) alternative, and, therefore, to financing a falling-cost service by means of a public subsidy. But raising additional taxes of the usual sort does involve the community in costs. Apart from additional administrative costs of altering the tax structure, and of collecting the taxes, the raising of taxes, other than lump-sum taxes, has incidental allocative effects. Income taxes, in particular, can have effects on effort, and can reduce the incentive to produce marketable goods or services while increasing the incentive to spend more time and effort evading taxes. In view of these income tax effects, there may be a case, after all, for setting price above marginal cost and equal to average cost. The consequent misallocation need not be serious if the prices of substitutes for this good are already set somewhat above their corresponding marginal costs and/or the demand for this good has a low elasticity.

There may, also, be political or social objections, which the economist has to accept, to pricing a good at its marginal cost in the long or

---

10 A two-part tariff is usually one which exacts a fixed charge from the buyer unrelated to the amount of the good he takes at the price. The commonest examples are quarterly charges for telephone service and for electricity service, which charges are set independently of the consumption of the services. Such charges have the effect of transferring a portion of what would otherwise be the consumers' surplus to the service enterprises.

11 Lump sum taxes are taken to mean taxes that are invariant to a person's earnings. Although, as a result of the wealth effect, such taxes will in general alter the supply of a person's productive services, they will not 'distort' the objective rate of substitution between factor and product. If, therefore, there are no other taxes in the economy, the introduction of lump-sum taxes does not infringe the factor-product optimal condition.

short period, and financing the loss through public subsidies. If the good was consumed predominantly by wealthier groups, distributive arguments could be brought against the proposal to price at marginal cost and cover the losses from public revenues. On the other hand, even if the revenues raised by marginal cost pricing sufficed, or more than sufficed, to meet factor payments, there may also be objections to it on distributive grounds. It is not, for example, impractical to charge public transit passengers different fares for travelling at different times of the day. During peak-traffic hours, at least, higher fares could be charged to meet the higher marginal (congestion) costs. But, it may be objected, the passengers during peak hours have little choice in view of traditional business hours. In the circumstances, charging according to marginal costs would be charging lower income groups more for having to travel in discomfort, compared with those who have the choice and the leisure to travel more comfortably at other hours. This is so manifestly inequitable[12] that it has not been seriously contemplated. In such cases then, political constraints translate marginal cost pricing into 'average' marginal cost pricing.[13] And if public subsidy is not forthcoming, there may be no choice but to resort to 'average' average cost pricing.

REFERENCES AND BIBLIOGRAPHY FOR PART II

Blaug, M. 'The Rate of Return on Investment in Education in Great Britain'' *The Manchester School*, 1965.
Borus, M. E. 'A Benefit Cost Analysis of the Economic Effectiveness of Retraining the Unemployed', *Yale Economic Essays*, 1964.
Bos, H. C. and Koyck, L. M. 'The Appraisal of Road Construction Projects', *Review of Economics and Statistics*, 1961.
Dorfman, R. (ed.). *Measuring the Benefit of Government Investments*, Washington D.C.: Brookings Institution, 1965.
Eckstein, O. *Water Resource Development*, Cambridge, Mass.; Harvard University Press, 1958.
Farrell, M. J. 'In Defence of Public-Utility Price Theory', *Oxford Economic Papers*, 1958.
Friedman, M. 'The Marshallian Demand Curve', *Journal of Political Economy*, 1949.

---

12 For a useful discussion of the role and feasibility of marginal cost pricing, the reader should consult Vickrey's 1955 paper.
13 If vehicular traffic is believed to be subsidized, inasmuch as its current operational marginal costs do not include the spillover effects it generates, there is a case for setting the public transit fares below marginal costs.

Green, H. A. J. 'The Social Optimum in the Presence of Monopoly and Taxation', *Review of Economic Studies*, 1961.

Griliches. 'Research Costs and Social Returns: Hybrid Corn and Related Innovations', *Journal of Political Economy*, 1956.

Hammond, R. J. *Benefit-Cost Analysis and Water Pollution Control*, Stanford; University Press, 1958.

Hansen, W. L. 'Total and Private Rates of Return to Investment in Schooling', *Journal of Political Economy*, 1963.

Haveman, R. H. and Krutilla, J. V. *Unemployment, Idle Capacity, and The Evaluations of Public Expenditures*, Washington, D.C.; Resources for the Future, Inc., 1968.

Hicks, J. R. *A Revision of Demand Theory*, Oxford: Clarendon Press, 1956.

Leibenstein, H. 'Allocative Efficiency versus X-Efficiency', *American Economic Review*, 1966.

Lipsey, R. and Lancaster, K. 'The General Theory of Second Best', *Review of Economic Studies*, 1957.

Little, I. M. D. and Mirrlees, J. *Social Cost Benefit Analysis*.

McKean, R. N. *Efficiency in Government Through Systems Analysis*, New York; John Wiley & Sons, 1958.

Mishan, E. J. 'Survey of Welfare Economics, 1939-1959', *Economic Journal*, 1960.

——'Interpretation of the Benefits of Private Transport', *Journal of Transport Economics and Policy*, 1967.

——'What is Producer's Surplus?', *American Economic Review*, 1968.

Mohring, H. 'Land Values and the Measurement of Highway Benefits', *Journal of Political Economy*, 1961.

Mushkin, Selma J. 'Health as an Investment', *Journal of Political Economy*, 1962.

Peters, G. H. *Cost-Benefit Analysis and Public Expenditure*, London; Institute of Economic Affairs, 1968.

Prest, A. R. and Turvey, R. 'Cost-Benefit Analysis: A Survey', *Economic Journal*, 1965.

Rothenberg, J. 'Urban Renewal Programs' in R. Dorfman (ed.), *Measuring the Benefits of Government Investment*, Washington D. C.; Brookings Institution, 1965.

Throsby, D. *An Introduction to Mathematical Programming*, New York; Random House. 1970.

Vickrey, W. 'Some Implications of Marginal Cost Pricing for Public Utilities', *American Economic Review* (Supplement), 1955.

Weisbrod, B. A. *Economics of Public Health: Measuring the Impact of Diseases*, Philadelphia; University of Philadelphia Press, 1960.

Winch, D. M. *The Economics of Highway Planning*, Toronto; Toronto University Press, 1963.

Wiseman, J. 'The Theory of Public Utility Price—An Empty Box', *Oxford Economic Papers*, 1957.

PART III. EXTERNAL EFFECTS

Chapter 14
INTRODUCTION

1. External Effects, an abbreviation for External Economies and Diseconomies—sometimes referred to as 'externalities', more picturesquely as 'neighbourhood effects', somewhat vapidly as 'side effects', and more suggestively as 'spillover effects', or, briefly, 'spillovers'—first appear as 'external economies' in Alfred Marshall's *Principles* in connection with a competitive industry's downward-sloping supply curve. Marshall's argument is that, as industry expands by, say, an additional firm, any resulting reduction in the average costs of production accrues to *all* the firms in the industry. The total reduction of costs experienced by all the intra-marginal firms is to be attributed to the entry of the additional firm. The true or 'social' cost of the additional output produced by this marginal firm is not the total cost of it as calculated by that firm, but this cost *less* the total saving in costs by all the intra-marginal firms. This proposition is important in determining the 'correct' or 'optimal' output of the industry. For in practice the additional firm makes no allowance for the saving in costs it contributes to the rest of the industry. If, therefore, firms continue to enter the competitive industry until, at the going price of the product, the total cost of the firm is equal to its total revenue, the equilibrium size of the industry will be that at which the market demand price is equal to the average (inclusive) cost of the good in question. But the marginal cost, or total cost of the incremental firm, will be below average cost by the amount of the total cost-savings it confers on the intra-marginal firms. Therefore marginal cost will, to the same extent, be below the market price and, abiding by the marginal-cost pricing rule, output should be extended beyond the competitive equilibrium

until marginal cost is equal to price. The existence of external economies in a competitive industry, Marshall concludes, entails an equilibrium output that is below optimal.

Constructing a curve marginal to the industry's supply curve, the point at which this marginal curve cuts the demand curve identifies the 'ideal', or optimal, output. This concept, and its corresponding construction, was extended in a symmetrical manner to external diseconomies, to reveal that the optimal output of a competitive industry was below the equilibrium output. These external effects were later remarked to have wide application, not only as between firms in determining the optimal size of the industry, but as between industries themselves. Nor are such effects confined to industry. They operate as between persons and groups, and as between firms and industries and persons.

2. Fairly standard examples of spillovers include the adverse effects on flora, fauna, rainfall, and soil, in cutting down the trees of a forest; or the effects on the mosquito population of creating artificial lakes, and other ecological repercussions that ultimately enter into the welfare of people. The pleasure given by the erection of a beautiful building or, more commonly alas, the offence given by the erection of a tasteless or incongruous structure, is an external effect. So also is the congestion suffered by all the traffic from additional vehicles coming onto the roads; or the noise and pollution arising from the operation of industry or of its products; or the loss of life consequent upon the increase in air or ground traffic.

From a little reflection on examples such as these, it emerges that one characteristic common to all of them is the incidental, or unintentional, nature of the effect produced. The person or industrial concern engaged, say, in logging may, or may not, have any idea of the consequences on the profits or welfare of others. But it is certain that they do not enter into his calculations. The factory owners, whose plant produces smoke as well as other things, are concerned only to produce the other things that can be sold on the market. They have no interest in producing the smoke, even though they may be fully aware of it. But so long as their own productivity does not suffer thereby, and they themselves are not penalized in any way, they will regard the smoke as an unfortunate by-product.

If these external effects are not deliberately produced however, neither are they deliberately absorbed by others. Such effects may add to the enjoyment of life, as does the smell of fresh-cut grass, or else add to life's vexations as does the noise, stench, and danger of mounting automobile traffic. But they are not within the control of the persons who are absorbing them—at least not without their incurring expenses.[1] However, a definition of external effects that gives prominence to these aspects—that a person's welfare, or a firm's profits, depends upon things that are initially outside his control, which things are incidental to the activity of others—is by itself insufficient and may, indeed, lead to confusion. Let us see how.

3. The statement that a firm's or industry's outputs or profits, or a person's welfare, can be influenced by the activities of others is true, apparently, within the context of any general equilibrium system. In particular, it is true within a general equilibrium system that has no external effects of the sort illustrated above.[2] The familiar inter-dependent system of Leon Walras is a case in point. Among the set of equations posited are those for individuals regarded as consumers and owners of productive services. All the *variables* in each person's utility function—whether they refer to the amounts of finished goods bought or the amounts of productive services offered—are deemed to be entirely within his control. The parameters within each person's utility function, however, are the set of prices; and these are determined by the system as a whole.

Thus for each person, the quantities of the things that he is willing to buy or to sell depends, *inter alia*, on the set of market prices of these things. The amounts of goods supplied by perfectly competing firms also depend upon the market prices. These set of market prices can, in general, be altered by any changes in technology, in people's tastes, or in the accumulation and redistribution of assets. It follows that the activities of persons and firms, in response to these sorts of changes, have incidental effects on the welfare of others. If, to take a humble example, people start changing from tea to

---

1 If an adverse spillover effect could be avoided without incurring any costs, it could hardly be called an adverse spillover. Certainly no problem would arise.
2 The system is, of course, a *theoretical* construct only. Engineers affirm that in all input-output activities there is wastage, and therefore waste material is absorbed into the air, the earth or its waters, so creating the potential for external effects.

coffee, the price of tea will at first tend to fall and that of coffee to rise. The producers of tea will initially suffer and those of coffee benefit, while the consumers of tea will be better off and the consumers of coffee worse off.

But in this general equilibrium system, in the absence of all external effects as commonly understood, such interdependence operates indirectly, and through changes in market prices. Each and every exogenous change mentioned—a change in techniques, in tastes, or in factor endowment—entails a corresponding change in the equilibrium set of prices. Since, in general, every price is affected, every person's welfare is affected also, and this can be very important.[3] Nevertheless, given perfectly competitive markets and no external effects, each general equilibrium position meets the requirement of a Pareto optimum, viz. one in which it is not possible to make one or more persons better off without making at least one person worse off.[4] In contrast, the concern with external effects arises just because their existence implies that—unless special arrangements are made—the equilibrium solutions attainable may *not* be Pareto optimal.

We may, then, infer that external effects are effects on others that are conveyed directly, and not indirectly through prices. If we allow that these effects on people's welfare matter in principle no less than do the priced products and services, it follows that it is just because these external effects, these by-products of the activities of others, are not properly priced or not priced at all, that the equilibrium solution is not Pareto optimal. To illustrate, the competitive equilibrium price of steel spades is $10, price being equal to long-run average, and marginal cost. In their production, however, noise is produced, this being the only external effect in the economy. The noise created in producing the marginal spade would be tolerated without complaint only on receipt of, say, $7 by those disturbed by the noise. The net valuation of the marginal spade is, therefore, $10 minus $7, or $3 altogether. The marginal cost however is $10, and the equilibrium is not optimal. For if we produced one spade

---

3 For instance in appraising welfare criteria. See my 1957 paper.
4 If every relevant effect in the economy is properly priced, the economy is in an optimal position. The reverse however is not true, since optimality can be consistent with unpriced spillovers. See the example in Chapter 19.

less to start with, the factors released would—assuming universal perfect competition—create $10 of goods elsewhere. The accompanying loss in social value, however, is $3, as above. Society is better off to the extent of $7: some can be made better off (to the extent of $7) without any one else being made worse off. As stated, therefore, the original position could not have been optimal.

If external effects could somehow be 'properly' priced like the other goods and 'bads' of the economic system—where the term 'bads' is occasionally used as an alternative expression to disutility, or 'diswelfare', or 'discommodity', of which, say, the provision of labour services could be taken as an example—then indeed any perfectly competitive equilibrium would, again, be optimal. One can go further: if each external effect were to be priced in a competitive market, along with other goods and bads, it would cease to be an external effect. Before elaborating this point, however, let us attempt a definition.

4. Write the equation

$$U^1 = U^1(x_1^1, x_2^1, x_3^1, \ldots, x_n^1) \tag{1}$$

where U^1 is the utility, or welfare, of person 1, and x_1^1, x_2^1, x_3^1, are the amounts he has (flows, or stocks, according to the problem) of three of the goods, x_1, x_2, x_3, on which his utility, or welfare, depends. Equation (1) is no more than the statement that person 1's utility, or welfare, depends on the quantities he has of those goods. No external effects are implied by the equation. If, instead, we write his equation as

$$U^1 = U^1(x_i^2; x_1^1, x_2^1, x_3^1, \ldots, x_n^1) \tag{1a}$$

the possibility of an external effect is implied. The term x_i^2 gives the additional information that person 1's utility, U', depends, not only on his own quantities of a number of goods, but also on x_i^2, on person 2's quantities of x_i. If x_i were flowers, then person 1's welfare is affected not only by the flowers in his own garden but also by those in his neighbour's garden. We could also interpret equation (1a) as a production function, U^1 being the output of good 1, and the x's as the inputs used in the production of good 1. The equation (1a) is now interpreted as saying that the amount of good 1 depends directly on the inputs x_1, x_2, x_3, etc., used directly in the production of good 1, and depends also on the amount of input i used in the production of good 2. The amount of the ith input used in the production of good 2 (this amount being under the control of the producers of good 2—*not* of the producers of good 1) is therefore regarded as imposing external effects on the output of good 1, and also, therefore, on the price of good 1 and the profits of the producers of good 1.

Such notational definitions are common enough in the literature. Another would be $\partial U^1/\partial x_i^2 \neq 0$, which can be interpreted as saying that a small change in person 2's quantity of good i will not leave person 1's utility unchanged. For the external effect to *exist*, however, we should have to add the information that $x_i^2 \neq 0$. Thus $x_i^2 > 0$ implies that person 2 purchases some of the ith good; $x_i^2 < 0$ implies that he sells some of the ith good. If we write $\partial U^1/\partial x_i^2 > 0$, then person 2's external effect is one that raises person 1's welfare, the converse being true for a reversal of the inequality sign. Notation of this sort is helpful, but there are limitations. Thus, if x_i^2 refers to person 2's purchase of, say, a lawn-mower, it is not possible to infer from the notation alone whether person 1's welfare is reduced (a) by his envy of person 2's new lawn-mower, (b) by its being a noise-nuisance, (c) by the extra smoke suffered by person 1 among others (including person 2) in consequence of the factory's production of an extra lawn-mower, or (d) by a combination of any or all of these. We return to these possibilities in the following section.

Again, the fact that person 1 reacts to the amount of good i taken, or produced, by person 2, without his being able to control person 2's consumption or production of good i—which information is imparted by the notation above—does not suffice to define an external effect in the economist's sense. My wealthy aunt's welfare (as well as my own) depends unambiguously on the amount of arsenic I put into her tea. If it was discovered that in my impatience to inherit her fortune I had used arsenic to accelerate the natural process of aging, the coroner would be unlikely to refer to the results of my enterprise as an external effect. Yet, if person 1 be my aunt, person 2 be myself, x_i^2 be the amount of arsenic that I use, $\partial U^1/\partial x_i^2 < 0$ expresses the proposition that my aunt's welfare varies inversely with the amount of arsenic that I use. It would therefore fit the situation just depicted. In contrast, the conventional interpretation of the external effect indicated by the term $\partial U^1/\partial x_i^2 < 0$ would be that of my good aunt suffering at my injudicious consumption of arsenic, in small doses, as a stimulant. In order, therefore, to comply with the conventional meaning of external effect, the x_i^2 notation is to be interpreted strictly as person 2's consumption, or production, of good x_i which is determined solely by reference to his own immediate interest, and in disregard of the effects it may have on the welfare of others.

5. Once the reader has a clear idea of what an external effect is,[5] a little reflection will convince him that the number of external effects in the real world are virtually unlimited. If my wife is envious of her friend's new fur coat, her friend's wearing it in my wife's presence has an adverse external effect on at least one person. A cigar smoked in the presence of non-smokers has adverse external effects. Attractive short-skirted women may generate adverse external effects on other women and favourable external effects on men. A's promotion causes B to rejoice, and C to curse. And so one could go on.

Now if all the administrative costs, and all the associated expenses and efforts, involved in reaching mutually satisfactory arrangements were zero, the possibilities for mutual gain would be completely exhausted and, by definition, a Pareto optimum would prevail. Thinking along such lines, the utilitarian (in the narrow sense) would approve of measures designed to reduce the costs of reaching

---

5   There are quite a number of economic phenomena—all, perhaps, relevant to considerations of optimality—masquerading in the literature as external effects which cannot be admitted on the interpretation in the text. Common among these are such developments as better information (especially about the investment plans of others), the pooling of risks, improved training facilities, and other cost-saving arrangements. Such arbitrary extensions of the original concept, and the consequent ambiguity generated, are discussed in my 1965 paper. A recent misapprehension arises in the case of a person who cannot be admitted into an already packed theatre, or who has to queue without certainty of entry. The consequent decline in his welfare, certainly related to the welfare of others, is not, however, an instance of external effects, but of non-optimal pricing. An ideal mechanism would choose a set of prices as to fill the theatre exactly (ignoring discontinuities), with no one left out who would be willing to pay the price to get in. There are, of course, obvious practical difficulties in implementing such an 'optimal' set of prices; and these, not external effects, account for these frustrations.

mutual agreements about external effects. If, for example, negligible time and effort are required for the non-smoker to bribe the smoker to desist from lighting his cigarette, both can be made better off by the arrangement. However, the potential gains of a vast number of such mutual arrangements are likely to be smaller than the minimal costs and efforts needed for such arrangements. They are uneconomic in the sense that once these costs and efforts enter the calculus the net potential benefits are negative.

But this is not all. Among those external effects for which some arrangements would reveal net potential benefits that are positive, not all are socially acceptable. Economists, and society at large, might wish to distinguish, and in practice do distinguish, between external effects that are a source of 'legitimate' satisfaction or grievance, and those that are not. Among the latter are the resentment or envy felt by some people at the achievement or possessions of others.[6] But though such reactions may elicit sympathy, and qualify for psychiatry, they are unlikely to command moral approval. Once ethics are brought into external effects in this way, the question of which effects are to count and which not, must, in the last resort, depend upon a consensus in the particular society. Though such ethical distinctions will confine the application of Pareto improvements to 'legitimate' external effects, the economist would appear justified in accepting a distinction that society consistently makes. Though perhaps not formally embodied in legal documents, no economic policy that caters to these 'negative feelings' of people has ever been announced. In contrast, there is no lack of evidence that society does take seriously all tangible damage inflicted on people in the pursuit by others of pleasure or profit. Since adverse environmental effects provide, today, the most important instances of damage inadvertently inflicted on other people, they will feature prominently in our discussion of methods of evaluating them.

---

6 These are sometimes referred to as 'interdependence effects', since they are conceived of as the utility of one person being dependent upon the utility of another person—either directly, or via the goods that enter into the other's utility function.

Chapter 15

INTERNALIZING EXTERNAL EFFECTS

1. The verbal description of an external effect—that is, a direct effect on another's profit or welfare arising as an incidental by-product of some other person's or firm's activity—would seem adequate to convey its meaning. Its nature is made yet clearer, however, by examining the notion of 'internalizing' the external effect. The basic idea is that of transforming the incidental by-product into a joint product. I have been told by a number of Argentinians that before the turn of the century, cattle were slain on the ranches for their leather only. Their flayed carcasses were left to rot, but if found in time they could be used as fresh meat by the poor peasants. Apparently only the leather had a market price, the meat being a by-product, or external effect, of leather production —a favourable spillover of the leather industry for those peasants who happened to be in the vicinity.[1]

Suppose, however, that the human population began to multiply more rapidly than the cattle population, that the taste for meat grew, that meat began to be stored in refrigerators, and that, most important of all perhaps, the meat could be exported to distant markets. Domestic meat would become scarce and, therefore, a market for it would come into being. It would then cease to be a spillover, an unintended by-product in the process of obtaining hides for leather. It would take its place as a good in its own right, a joint product with leather. Whatever the separate demands for meat and leather are like, the long run competitive equilibrium output is optimal since the cattle population is expanded to the point at which the sum of the market prices are equal to the marginal cost of cattle production.

---

1 Notwithstanding which the number of cattle slain could be optimal if, at the margin, the value of the meat was zero. We discuss this point further in the next chapter in terms of 'allocative significance'.

The external effect has been internalized into the pricing system.[2]

Internalizing spillover effects arises also in the case of external diseconomies that are internal to the industry. Common examples of the latter category are deep-sea fishing, in which any additional fishing boat above a certain number reduces the catch of each of the existing fishing boats in the fishing grounds; or traffic congestion, in which every additional vehicle above a certain number causes delay to each of the existing number of vehicles using a given highway system. Internalizing this sort of spillover would require that a positive market price be imputed to the currently unpriced though scarce resource—the area of the sea in the first case, the highway in the second. Once such a resource is priced, it will be used more economically. The analogy of scarce land used in the production of, say, corn is exact. If priced correctly, which implies that in a competitive industry the rent of this scarce resource be maximized, the competitive equilibrium output that emerges is also the optimal output.[3]

Another example, though one in which internal accounting prices are substituted for market prices, is that of two separately owned but adjacent factories, A and B. Factory A produces shoes and is powered by an old-fashioned coal engine which emits so much smoke as to seriously affect the output of the B factory, which produces chocolate bars. The manager of the B factory remonstrates with the A manager, but to no effect. The daughter of the owner of

2　It may seem unnecessary to remark that the possibility of internalizing an external effect (or, in the absence of internalization, correcting for optimal outputs), does not mean that the creation of an adverse external effect need not make things worse. Yet students do sometimes argue as though this is so; as though, so long as optimizing by one method or another takes place, the creation of adverse external effects may be viewed with equanimity. The introduction of an adverse external effect into the economy is a bad thing no matter how the economy adapts to it. By internalizing the bad, or by optimizing the output that produces the bad, we are doing no more than making the best of a bad job. We are certainly not as well off as we should be if this bad had not appeared on the economic scene.

3　Assuming a period during which there is one scarce fixed factor and one factor that is variable in supply at a constant price, the average cost curve eventually slopes upward. A curve drawn marginal to this average cost curve cuts the demand curve at the optimal output. At this output, the difference between average cost and marginal cost *times* output gives the amount of the rent to the fixed factor—the maximum rent possible in a perfectly competitive market in which the price of the product is treated as a parameter.

the A factory and the son of the owner of the B factory decide to get married, in consequence of which the two factories come under common ownership and control, and the couple live together happily ever after. The cost of the smoke, reckoned in terms of the damage inflicted on the output of the B factory, is no longer a spillover generated by A and suffered by B. It is now unambiguously a cost to the joint A-B enterprise, and as such ways and means of reducing it will be sought. Either anti-smoke devices will be installed in the A factory, or else, if cheaper (and assuming the smoke-damage to B's output varies directly with A's output) A's output will be reduced to the point at which the value of the marginal damage to B's output, added to the marginal cost of shoe-production in A, is equal to the market price of A's shoes. Thus the smoke ceases to become a spillover effect, but a properly costed item that is internalized into the costing system of the A-B merger.

2. The number of spillover effects that can be internalized into the pricing mechanism, or into the costing systems of firms, is, however, limited. Among those that cannot be internalized are many of the by-products of modern industry and of the hardware it produces. One thinks, in this connection, of noise and various forms of pollution arising from the spread of sewage and garbage and radioactive wastes; also of the postwar phenomenal growth of diseases of the nerves, heart, and stomach, caused by high-tension living, the most ubiquitous by-product of sustained technological advance. Why cannot such spillovers be internalized? The answer is simple: in order for a competitive market for such spillovers to emerge, certain conditions have to be met which, in the nature of the physical universe, cannot be met. First, the potential victim of these adverse spillover effects must have legal 'property rights' in, say, their ownership of some quantum of quiet and clean air which, if such rights were enjoyed, they could choose to sell to others. Secondly, in order for such rights to be enforceable, it would be necessary to demarcate a three-dimensional 'territory' about the person of each potential victim in order to identify the intrusions of others and take appropriate legal action. Thirdly, in order for a monopsonistic situation not to arise, each of these three-dimensional properties within a given area, which can be rented for particular purposes (say, to accommodate the noise or pollution of someone's activity), must be a close substitute for the others.

The first condition could, of course, be met in the sense that all forms of pollution could be outlawed in the absence of specific agreements between the parties concerned. But because the second condition cannot be met in the world we inhabit, there is difficulty in demarcating each person's property, and a consequent difficulty in identifying the trespasser and the extent of the trespass. Nor can the third condition be met, for in this hypothetical scheme of things the right to use one man's 'territory', within some given area, is no substitute for that of another man. Each man within the area has his own three-dimensional territory and, since the noise to be created by the new activity, enters in some degree into all of such territories, the enterprise has to reach agreement with each one of them. None can substitute for the other. Unless all agree, the permission of those who do is worthless.

If it were otherwise, if one territory could be substituted freely for another, as could plots of land in an agricultural area, an appropriate market price would arise from the competition of the sellers. The physical universe being what it is however, each potential seller is in a completely monopolistic position. For without his particular consent the necessary arrangement for the whole of the affected area cannot be concluded. The reader will detect a similarity between this hypothetical problem, posed by the third condition, and that facing a railroad company having to buy every mile of land through which the track has to run. The cost of acquiring rights where a large number of landowners are involved could be prohibitive were it not for legislation compelling the sale of rights on terms which the courts will decide are reasonable. Another instance, occasionally reported by the press, is that of a single householder, or small business, holding out against a property company that is attempting to buy up a specific area of land as part of some new development scheme.

We must, then, resign ourselves to the prospect of never being able to internalize these important environmental spillovers within the economy: that is, of not being able to create a market for them— which is, of course, one of the reasons why cost-benefit methods are required to evaluate them.

3. Some further light is cast on the nature of spillover effects by briefly observing the connection between them and collective, or

public, goods. Environmental spillovers usually affect a large number of people within an area. If the spillover effect is favourable, it can be regarded as a form of collective good; if unfavourable, as a form of collective bad. If the favourable spillover effect is to be distinguished from a collective good, it is simply on the grounds (1) that the spillover is only a by-product of some other market-oriented activity, whereas the collective good is itself the intended product, and (2) that an adverse spillover effect, at least, is commonly thought of as *unavoidable*, or avoidable only at a cost, whereas the collective good may well be avoidable. To illustrate (2), consider an instance of an avoidable collective good; each person living within a neighbourhood is free to spend his time gazing at the public fountain, or walking in the municipal park.[4] In contrast, a downfall of artificial rain, caused by seeding the clouds above a certain area of farmland, would be an example of an *unavoidable* collective good (or avoidable only at a cost). If, on the other hand, too much rain water was one of the *by-products* of the destruction of a forest by a lumber company, this adverse spillover could also be regarded as an unavoidable collective bad.

In connection with the deliberately produced collective project whose effects are unavoidable, or non-optional, it must be realized that some persons may, indeed, receive too much of it—which is to say that their marginal valuation of the benefit is negative. Too much artificial rain, for example, might damage the particular crops of certain farmers. One may, nevertheless, call it a collective good if the sum of the maximum amounts of those who, on balance, benefit from the unavoidable collective effect exceeds the minimum payments necessary to compensate those who, on balance, suffer losses.[5] As indicated, one has only to think of this rainfall as one of the incidental effects of some other deliberate activity (the felling of the trees of a forest, or regular airline flights) to place it within the category of spillover effects.

---

4 There can, however, be a problem of congestion if the number of people increase relative to the number, or the size, of the facilities provided.
5 Among those who *on balance* gain from the given artificial rainfall, there can be those farmers whose crops receive too much rain in the sense that the benefit to them of the marginal inch of rain is negative. The optimal condition, however, requires that rain be increased until the sum of the benefits and losses of the marginal inch of rain is equal to the cost of producing it.

Chapter 16
ON THE VALUATION OF SPILLOVERS

1. In principle, the method of valuing spillover effects for a cost-benefit analysis is straightforward. Any particular spillover effect associated with a given project is but one among any number of consequences affecting the welfare of different people in the community. We must consider, therefore, only the *difference* made to their welfare by the spillover effect in question. Any i^{th} person made better off on balance by the spillover effect would offer a maximum positive sum, V_i, rather than go without it. Any i^{th} person made worse off on balance would require some minimum sum V_i to induce him to put up with the spillover, such sum to be received being prefixed by a negative sign. These sums are known as compensating variations; for if paid by the former individual, or if received by the latter individual, his welfare will remain unchanged.

Assuming n persons are affected, if the condition $\sum_{i=1}^{n} V_i > 0$ is met—if, that is, the algebraic sum of the individual compensating variations is positive—we conclude that gainers can more than compensate losers, and the value of the excess gain over loss is the value to be attributed to the spillover effect in question. Wherever $\sum_{i=1}^{n} V_i < 0$, however, an excess of loss over gain is to be attributed to the spillover. There may well be cases where part, or all, of these compensatory variations are determined directly by reference to market prices. The cost of the extra laundry bills arising from industrial smoke is a popular example. Crop damage done by straying cattle is another. But, in the last resort, the value individually attributed to the spillover effect is subjective, and is to be conceived as the exact sum of money, to be paid or to be received, that restores a person's welfare to its original pre-spillover level.

In establishing a new project, any single associated spillover effect for which $\sum_{i=1}^{n} V_i \neq 0$ has allocative significance, and must be considered in that project's evaluation. Wherever the type and size of the project is given to us by technology, the question of whether or not the project should be undertaken can be properly answered only by taking into account *all* the effects arising from the construction and operation of the project, all the costs and all the benefits and, therefore, all the spillover effects also. If, for example, building a dam for irrigational purposes has the following incidental consequences: (1) it creates an artificial lake in which people can swim or boat; (2) it spoils the fishing; (3) it provides a body of stagnant water which causes a rapid increase in the insect populations in the vicinity, the first is a positive spillover, the latter two are negative spillovers. Each is to be evaluated in the manner stated above, and added together algebraically to the excess benefits (positive or negative) of the project.

2. There will be occasions, however, when the economist is presented with a number of alternative projects that differ only in size of plant, and, therefore, in the volume of outputs produced. He then compares successively larger sizes of plant in order to discover the difference made to benefits and costs. Starting with some size of plant that yields excess benefits over costs, it should be obvious that so long as further increments of plant size confer more benefit than cost there is an advantage in increasing the plant size. And it goes without saying that the associated increments of spillover, positive or negative, should be added algebraically to the benefit side of the calculation. Some spillovers, however, may or may not vary with the size of the project. A small dam, for example, may destroy the fishing just as much as a large dam.

The size of these increments, in the limiting case, could be so small that for all practical purposes the changes in the plant size can be regarded as continuous. In this limiting case we are then in the familiar textbook world of continuous curves, comparing long-run marginal cost with long-run marginal benefit—except of course that for private goods each person's marginal benefit is coterminous with demand price, whereas for collective goods the marginal benefit is the aggregate of benefits conferred simultaneously on all persons by the marginal unit of the collective good.

It is not to be supposed for a moment, however, that cost-benefit analysis confines itself to evaluating collective goods. A railroad or hospital is not, strictly speaking, a collective good; the services produced by either can be separately allocated to each of a number of persons just as a loaf of bread can be allocated to a person for his own particular consumption. And for that matter, the construction of a bakery might warrant a cost-benefit analysis, with the initial size of the plant and, later on, the output to be produced, determined on the marginal cost pricing rule.

3. In the absence of all spillovers, the necessary rule requiring marginal valuation to the community to be equal to marginal cost of the good in question[1] is valid both for collective goods and single goods. For a single good, as distinct from a collective good, however, each person separately enjoys the amount of the good that he chooses: the consumption by person A of five loaves of bread a week is deemed to provide no satisfaction whatsoever to any one else. Thus, as distinct from a collective good, the single good has to meet a stricter condition: namely, that the amounts chosen by each person are such that the marginal valuation of bread for each one of them is exactly the same.[2] This is not, in general, true of collective goods: the last foot of width to a bridge, or the last acre to a national park, being valued differently by different people. This stricter condition for single goods is met in perfectly competitive equilibrium since each person equates his own marginal valuation to the price

---

1 Although this marginal-cost rule rolls easily from the tongue, care must be exercised in its interpretation. Although each consumer equates his marginal valuation of a loaf to the market price of a loaf and, in perfect competition, therefore, to the marginal cost of a loaf, it does not follow that *each* of, say, n consumers has a marginal valuation equal to the marginal cost of producing loaves of bread. Supposing the marginal cost curve of producing loaves of bread to rise smoothly, the marginal *cost* is below the marginal valuation of each of the consumers save the nth (where any of the n consumers could be the nth consumer). For the remaining n-1 consumers, the incremental unit cost of a loaf is, in varying degrees, below their marginal valuation of a loaf.

2 If there is only one price for each single good on the market then the so-called exchange optimum condition is also met: advantageous exchange of such goods as between persons is not possible.

of the good, which price is of course equal to marginal cost.[3]

This necessary rule, stated above, and valid both for collective and single goods, has to be modified in an obvious way, if, now, spillover effects accompany the production or consumption of the goods in question. Consider first a single good. If the bakery emits smoke which irritates people in the vicinity, and this irritating smoke varies directly with the number of loaves produced, smoke will be allocatively significant in determining the optimal output. The marginal valuation to society of the existing output of loaves is no longer just equal to the price that each and any of the n consumers is prepared to pay for his own marginal loaf of bread. For in order to meet the demand for any additional loaf the bakery must emit some additional smoke. From the value to society of an additional loaf one has therefore to subtract the sum of minimal compensatory payments, $\sum_{i=1}^{n} V_i$, which sum would be necessary to restore the welfare of the n smoke victims. Prior to any correction, the competitive equilibrium output would be one where the marginal valuation of loaves alone was equal to marginal cost, but where the marginal valuation of the joint loaf-and-smoke product was below its marginal cost. In order to meet the optimal condition for this joint product, the output has to be reduced below the competitive equilibrium (so raising the marginal valuation of loaves) until the marginal *social* valuation—that of the loaf and its associated spillovers—is positive, and equal to, marginal cost.[4] The alternative statement, that optimal output is determined at the point where the price of the good is set equal to its marginal *social* cost, is the result simply of transferring the calculated value of the associated spillovers to the other side of the equation. In this loaf example, instead of subtracting the calculated loss of the smoke damage from the value of the marginal loaf, the sum is added instead to the marginal cost of the loaf. Positive spillover effects, or, to be more precise, spillover effects that are on balance advantageous to society, are treated in the same manner, a positive sign for the compensatory sum sub-

3 This is a necessary though not sufficient condition for optimal output in a partial setting. It is further required (1) that total conditions be met, i.e. that there be an excess of total benefit over total cost, and (2) that there be no other output which has a greater excess benefit over cost. (If these conditions are met, 'second order' conditions must also be met.)

4 [See next page.]

stituting for the negative one above. Optimal output is therefore, in such cases, greater than competitive equilibrium output.

The same adjustment is required for collective goods. If some collective good, say a dam, has both positive and negative spillovers, say it provides boating but spoils the fishing, the net sums for all persons in the community are added algebraically, and the resulting total added algebraically to the marginal benefit of the collective good—or else subtracted, algebraically, from the marginal cost of the good.

4. A conscientious cost-benefit study, it is hardly necessary to remark, cannot ignore any spillover effect, positive or negative, that is of social concern. Although the value of some spillovers will be harder to estimate than others, the principle of evaluation indicated in this chapter may not be abandoned as a guide to the methods of calculation to be adopted. To adopt some other principle, such as deriving a value from the outcome of the political decision-making process, is to adopt a principle that is inconsistent with the Pareto criterion on which the estimates of the other, more measurable, items are based—on which, indeed, all allocative judgments are made in economics. A harsher judgment of this practice would regard it as tantamount to deception. For the economist is given his brief by a political authority in order to make an estimate according to independent *economic* principles; not in order to rationalize the political process. We shall have more to say about the tendency of economists to resort occasionally to this sort of subterfuge in the later chapter on estimating the value to society of loss of life and limb.

---

4   In this calculation there is a tacit but plausible assumption: that the individual consumer of loaves is not himself aware of the connection between his own purchases of loaves and the smoke irritation he suffers in consequence of his own purchases. If this is granted, his resulting loss of welfare can be included with those of the remaining n-1 consumers whose welfares decline with the purchase of his loaves. If, on the other hand, the spillover effect arises from his direct use of some good, say the noise from operating his lawn-mower, he can be assumed to subtract from his own satisfaction the value of any discomfort borne in operating the machine. In that case the uncosted spillovers, for which an adjustment has to be made, are those experienced by the remaining n-1 people in the vicinity.

Where n is a large number, we lose little accuracy but much work by calculating the spillover effects for n people rather than for a different $(n - 1)$ set of people for each person's purchases.

Chapter 17

ENVIRONMENTAL SPILLOVERS

1. We now turn to a more detailed consideration of adverse environmental spillovers. The warrant for doing so does not derive simply from their rapid growth, especially in the postwar period, nor simply from their frequent neglect, but from the evaluative problems that arise whenever an adverse spillover effect has a *large* effect on the welfare of a number of people. If the judgment, that adverse environmental spillovers have become more important, since the war, than favourable spillovers, is questioned by the reader, he need not complain of bias. The analysis of favourable spillovers is quite symmetrical, and economy in exposition suggests that a thorough treatment of either type of spillover alone, favourable or unfavourable, will suffice to demonstrate the principles.

2. We have taken it for granted that spillovers have to be evaluated, ultimately, by reference to the subjective estimates of the victims of spillover effects. One can go further. One can argue for these compensatory sums being actually paid to the victims in the event of a project being introduced that generates adverse spillovers. Indeed, this view of the matter would seem to follow from the classical liberal doctrines as expounded by John Stuart Mill, in contradistinction to a Pareto economic decision based simply on the determination of a net balance of gain or loss, one in which the question of actual compensation is disregarded. *A fortiori*, the liberal doctrine would reject the 'social engineering' approach to the spillover problem, an approach that seeks to formulate 'tolerance levels' for society. True, the upper limit of the tolerable degree of, say, noise may be so chosen as to preclude ascertainable physical damage or bodily hurt—given our present knowledge of the effects of noise on people and property. Yet noise below that limit can be highly irritating to a lot of people. If a man were subjected at regular intervals to the gentlest tap on the back of his head, his subsequent exasperation would hardly surprise us. Neither the fact that he emerged from the treatment without bruises, nor the affirmation that this head-tapping

business was, in some mysterious way, an unavoidable by-product of the operation of modern industry and, indeed, could be counted on to promote exports, would assure us about its moral justification. And if the occasional, or frequent, bombarding of a man's ears with noise, as a consequence of other people's pursuit of pleasure or profit, can be said to differ from this imaginary case, it is only in our having over time become accustomed to it, and more obtuse as to the issues it raises. If the liberal economist rejects such social engineering norms as a 'tolerance level', it is not merely because the choice of such a level for society is necessarily arbitrary, but because the adoption of such tolerance norms on behalf of all members of society runs counter to the doctrine that each man is deemed to be the best judge of his own interest, particularly in matters that affect him intimately.

3.   It must be acknowledged however that economists have, as a rule, more eagerly defended this doctrine when man is regarded as a consumer of man-made goods than when he is regarded as a consumer of the goods provided by nature. The mere suggestion, say, that lace underwear should be withdrawn from production can be counted upon to provoke an outcry in the community, notwithstanding that lace underwear is not a requisite of the good life. Economists are usually well to the fore, though the issue be no more than that of offering the consumer a cheaper price for butter by removing import restrictions. Yet, when it comes to preventing avoidable suffering that accompanies the destruction of environmental amenity—something, it can be argued, that is a prerequisite of the good life—the response is all but perfunctory. The citizen can apparently be robbed of choice on those things—clean air, quiet, attractive surroundings—that critically affect his sense of well-being, without the public offering much resistance.[1] For far too long the public has been accepting the physical environment much as it has been accepting the weather; as a phenomenon to which it can perhaps adapt but which, in itself, is outside the control of men.

---

1   This was written in 1968. Since that time, much more prominence to environmental deterioration has been given by news media, and much more concern has been evinced by the public.

Such an attitude, however, is not justifiable. Some framework of law is necessary if markets are to function in an orderly fashion, and if trade and enterprise are to flourish. But not all laws are equally effective in harmonizing the search for commercial gain with the welfare of society. The economist's interest in social welfare or, more simply, in extending the citizen's area of choice, can do more than offer suggestions to promote a smoother functioning of the existing economic mechanisms. At a time of rapid deterioration of the environment, he can suggest alteration in the legal framework itself as something that can make significant contributions to social welfare.

Already we have pointed out that the more significant environmental spillovers do not lend themselves to any method of internalization, and that, therefore, they can be very costly to avoid. If, in spite of this difficulty, some improvement is possible working within the existing system of laws, more yet can be done—it will be argued—by changing laws from being tolerant of spillovers to being intolerant of them. Before broaching this more novel aspect of the problem, however, let us summarize the traditional consensus among economists on the subject of spillovers which prevailed until very recently.[2]

4. *A*. For any adverse spillover that varies with the output of a good x, the optimal output of x is uniquely determined. Given costless decision-making this optimal output can be reached as well by levying an excise tax on x as by offering an excise subsidy for reducing the output of x, as well by the manufacturer being compelled to compensate the public as by the public's bribing the manufacturer to reduce output. One is to conclude that the question of liability for the spillover—the question of who compensates whom—in such cases of manifest conflict of interest, has no bearing on the allocative problem of determining the optimal output.

B. Nor apparently can this question of who should compensate whom be settled by considerations of equity. If, for example, the smoke produced by a soap works can be said to damage the interests of the inhabitants living in the vicinity, so also can the curtailment of the smoke-producing output (or the compulsory installation of

---

2 Perhaps the most recent statement of such views can be found in Coase's 1960 paper.

anti-smoke devices) be said to damage the interests of the manu-facturer. The fact is simply that the interests of the two groups—the manufacturer (or the personnel of the soap works) on the one hand, the inhabitants on the other—are mutually opposed, and only a misuse of language can detract from the essential symmetry in respect of equity.[3]

C. In the event, whether an excise tax or an excise subsidy is to be employed in adjusting to optimal output, or whether the manu-facturer bribes the inhabitants or they bribe him, the optimal output (at least within a partial analysis). is uniquely determined The differ-ences in the devices by which this optimal output may be attained merely affect the *distribution* of welfare. They do not affect the optimal output.

D. Finally, whatever the institutional framework, the party suffering the damages has a clear interest in bribing the other party to modify the initial (uncorrected) output in the direction of the optimal output. But recognition of the opportunity for mutual gain in moving to an optimal position, leads to a consideration of the costs of negotiating such agreements between the two parties. For instance, in the absence of such negotiating costs, the potential gain in reducing the output of x by one or more units is the excess of the maximum amount the inhabitants will pay for the benefit of the accompanying reduction of smoke *less* the minimal amount the manufacturer will accept for having to reduce his output of x by one or more units. And if the output of x is reduced by one or more units, the distribution of this gain, say $100, will depend upon the respective bargaining power of the two parties.[4]

If, now, negotiating costs amount to $120, they will exceed the $100 of mutual gain; and the contemplated reduction in x's output is no longer mutually advantageous. The observed absence of negoti-ation over particular spillover effects is then explained on the argu-ment that the potential mutual gain, in a movement toward the

---

3 This proposition seems to have arisen from too exclusive an attention to spillovers as between firms where it appears to be more plausible. The examples produced by Coase (1960) are predominantly of this sort.

4 The loss to the manufacturer of x is the profit forgone by producing one or more units less of x. If, however, we are thinking in terms of a long-period supply curve of a competitive industry, the loss of profits is zero (though there may be losses of rent).

optimal output, is more than offset by the potential costs of negotiation. Since these negotiating costs are real enough, involving as they do the use of scarce resources, they may swamp the (costless) mutual gain of a movement toward an optimum. If so, such 'improvements' should obviously not be undertaken.

By such reasoning, some economists found themselves perilously close to the ultra-conservative conclusion that, in respect of spillovers at least, what is, is best. For the rest, one could do no more than to await the advent of innovations, technical or institutional, which could reduce the costs of preventive devices or the costs of negotiating and administration.[5]

5. This fairly widespread doctrine must now be subjected to critical examination. True, cost-benefit analysis addresses itself primarily to the question of the economic justification of a single project, or of the choice among a numberof technically feasible projects, and only in a secondary way to estimating the optimal outputs of such projects once they are established. But the arguments summarized above, dealing as they do with negotiating costs and compensatory payments involved in movements to an optimal output, can just as well be extended to cover the principles used in determining the outcome of specific cost-benefit studies.

What the critical examination is intended to reveal are two things: first, a simple though important point, that the question of who is to compensate whom, though it may be Pareto-symmetric, is not symmetric with respect to equity; second, a less simple though no less important proposition, that, in general, changes in the law of liability do indeed alter the relevant optimal outputs, even in the assumed absence of negotiating costs. However, the magnitude

---

5 Several minor propositions appeared since 1960, all of them rather obvious.

(1) If, in response to an adverse spillover an optimal excise tax is imposed on the manufacturer's output, any subsequent mutual agreement reached between the spillover victims and the manufacturer, will reduce output below optimal. See Turvey (1963).

(2) If the spillovers are 'overheads' (that is, unrelated to output) the firm responsible either closes down or continues to produce the same competitive output. See Davis & Whinston (1962), and Mishan (1965).

(3) Owing to the difficulties of calculating ideal excise taxes or subsidies for two firms inflicting spillovers on one another, especially in conditions of changing demand and supply, the merger solution is recommended. See Davis & Whinston (1967).

both of compensatory payments and negotiating costs can alter significantly as a result of a change of the law from being permissive of environmental spillovers to being prohibitive of them. Since environmental spillover effects, though hard to measure, may be critical to a cost-benefit evaluation, the reader should be quite clear about the difference made by such legal changes, and also about the relevance of this difference in appraising the economic feasibility of projects having such spillover effects. The process of clarification requires that the reader acquaint himself further with the economic concept of *exact* compensation—the subject matter of the following chapter.

Chapter 18
THE ECONOMIC CONCEPT OF EXACT COMPENSATION

1. In discussing the alleged uniqueness of an optimal output in the presence of spillovers, economists have recently made explicit the assumption that, in estimating the potential mutual gain in costlessly moving to an optimal output, the so-called income effects—or 'welfare effects' as it is more accurate to call them[1]—are to be ignored. The impression conveyed is that any impact these welfare effects have on the magnitude of compensatory payments, or on the resulting measure of the potential gain in moving to an optimal output, is best ignored: taking them into account would, apparently, clutter up the analysis without adding to it anything of practical value.[2]

2. Before going into this question, however, let us turn aside in order to demonstrate briefly that, even if we ignore completely any impact on the magnitude of the Pareto gain arising from changes in the welfare effects of the two opposing groups, and even if we suppose all negotiating costs to be zero, optimal outputs are not uniquely determined.[3]

We can illustrate this point with an example used by Coase (1960) of cattle-raising in ranches that are adjacent to corn-growing farms. Since in the absence of adequate fencing the cattle stray into the farms and spoil some of the crop, the farmers are obliged to put up with the losses, bribe the ranchers, or erect fences, whichever is the cheapest. If perfect competition prevails in both occupations, the resulting outputs of corn and cattle are optimal.

---

1   For reasons given in my 1959 paper (p. 387).
2   For two recent instances see Buchanan and Stubblebine's 1962 paper, also Turvey's 1963 paper. In contrast, my 1961 paper regarded these welfare effects as central to a formulation of partial welfare criteria in the presence of adverse spillovers. The effect of the law itself on compensatory payments was not explicitly introduced, however, until my 1967a paper.
3   The argument follows that outlined by Donald   Regan (1970) in an unpublished paper.

If legal liability were now to shift to the ranchers, they would in future have to bear the costs formerly borne by the farmers. Such costs, we are allowing, are the same whichever side bears them. Indeed, in the short period, this redistribution effect as between farmers and ranchers will cause no alteration in the amounts produced of either corn or cattle. In the long period, however, the equilibrium, and optimal, outputs of the two industries will alter.

Since, prior to the change in the law, long-period profits were zero in each industry, the shift in liability to the ranchers results, initially, in negative profits being made in the cattle-raising industry, and positive profits being made in the corn-growing industry.[4] There will then be an expansion of the number of corn-growing farms, and a contraction of the number of cattle-raising ranches until, in the new long-period equilibrium, the supply of corn is greater than it was before the legal change, and its price is lower, while the supply of cattle is smaller than it was before the legal change, and its price is higher. We may conclude that, contrary to the traditional doctrine, and even under the most abstract assumptions—zero welfare effects and zero negotiating costs—an alteration of legal liability for damages does alter the optimal outputs of the two industries concerned, that inflicting and that receiving the spillover in question.

3.   We now remove the assumption of zero welfare effects in order to consider those spillovers in which substantial changes in people's welfare are involved—important enough, at any rate, to make the question of whether a Pareto improvement is possible or not dependent directly upon the law's favouring one party's interest as against that of the other. In evaluating those projects having significant environmental spillovers, these welfare effects cannot be neglected.

There can be any number of ways of measuring exact compensation, but in all familiar circumstances only two of them need concern us. Their treatment is simplified by assuming that all welfare

---

4   Some concerns may carry on both corn-growing and cattle-raising, in which case—if the damage suffered by such concerns is created only by their own cattle—they are no better or worse off than before. But provided there are firms that carry on either business separately (and there is no economic reason, on the assumptions made, why the two activities should be merged) the results in the text are valid.

effects are positive, or 'normal',[5] which is to say, that a rise in a person's welfare raises the amount demanded of a good. This proposition in turn implies that the maximum sum he will pay for a given amount of it—or alternatively the minimum sum he will accept to forgo some amount of it—rises with an increase in his welfare.

In Chapter 16, on the valuation of spillovers, we used the term V_i to indicate the ith individual's compensatory payment, positive or negative—respectively a payment *from* the individual and a payment to him—and then d*efined* it to coincide with the compensating variation (CV), a concept that has to be distinguished from the other exact measure, the equivalent variation (EV).[6] The CV will now be defined, more generally as a measure of the money transfer necessary, following some economic change, to maintain the individual's welfare at its *original* level. If the price of one or more of the goods he buys rises, or of the service he sells falls, or if the air he breathes becomes more contaminated, his welfare falls, and some minimum payment to him is necessary to restore his welfare to its original level. *Per contra*, if one or several of the goods that he buys falls in price, or the price of his labour rises, or a by-pass is constructed that reduces the flow of traffic past his private residence, his welfare is increased. It is then restored to its original level by exacting from him some maximum sum of money.

The EV, on the other hand, is defined more generally as a measure of the money tranfer which, *in the absence of* the contemplated change, affords the individual an exactly equivalent change in his welfare. If, therefore, the price of a good he buys rises, or the price of his labour falls, or his environment becomes noisier, his welfare declines. But in the absence of any of these adverse circumstances, his welfare could be made to decline to an equivalent extent by exacting from him a sum of money. *Per contra*, if one or more of the goods he buys falls in price, or the price of his labour rises, or the airport near his home is abandoned, his welfare, we assume, rises. But in the absence

---

5 Although 'normal' welfare effects are plausible for the major spillovers suffered by the public, the significance of the analysis or, indeed, of the general conclusions reached in the following chapters, do not in the least depend upon this particular assumption.

6 These terms were first defined by Hicks (1944), following a seminal paper by Henderson (1941). (See references to Note B Part VI).

of any one of these favourable events, his welfare can be raised to the equivalent level by paying him a certain sum of money.

4. Let us work through a homely example involving a change of law, and then generalize from it. A confirmed smoker, S, and a total abstainer, N, are compelled to share a compartment on a train. The law is permissive with respect to smoking, and S prepares to indulge himself freely when N attempts to bribe him to desist. A pledge from S to cease smoking in exchange for a sum that N can afford clearly improves the *status quo*, since both would then be better off than if, instead, S smoked and N suffered in silence. The maximum sum N would pay for S's total abstention from cigarettes during the journey is, say, $20. This is N's CV, since this maximum sum he is prepared to pay for this improvement to his welfare is such as to offset it completely. As for N's EV, if on learning of N's sensitivity to smoke S decided not to smoke at all during the journey, N's welfare would rise compared with what it would otherwise have been. We can then ask the question: what is the minimum payment to N which, in the absence of S's pledge not to smoke, would provide N with the equivalent rise in welfare? If this minimum sum he would accept instead of the pledge is, say, $25, this sum is equal to N's EV.[7]

Now suppose there is a no-smoking regulation, though one which may be waived in the event of mutual consent. The smoker S has then to approach N for permission. What is the minimum sum that N will accept to forgo the advantages of smokeless air? We already know the answer, $25, from the last sentence of the preceding paragraph. But under the prohibitive regulation, the initial situation is that of no smoking. If, therefore, N puts up with the smoking of his companion for a sum of $25, he simply maintains his welfare at its initial level. This minimum sum he will accept to put up with a bad, which minimum sum restores his level of welfare to the initial no-smoking situation, is—according to our definition—a CV for person N. What about the EV under the prohibitive regulation? Applying our definition, we can say that in the absence of the adverse change that is being contemplated by N (smoking by S), the

---

7 The statement that the minimum sum N would accept to forgo a particular good (smokeless air) is greater than the maximum sum he would pay to acquire it, is an implication of a 'normal' (or positive) 'income effect' or, rather (as suggested), welfare effect.

EV is the maximum sum which, if paid by N, would reduce his welfare by as much as if the change in question did, instead, take place. The EV is therefore equal to $20. For we already know, from the preceding paragraph, that $20 is the maximum sum N will pay to prevent S from smoking.

On a first reading, the above analysis may seem a bit elusive, and the reader may want to read it over more than once—bearing in mind, always, that the CV is the sum which *maintains* welfare at the original level when the economic event takes place, while the EV is the sum which provides a change in welfare that is *equivalent to*, and in lieu of, the economic event in question. Having got the gist of it, the reader might like to go through the exercise again on behalf of the smoker, S. With a little care he will find it symmetrical in every respect with the treatment of individual N.

4. What we can infer from the above example is that, for each person whose welfare is affected by the two alternative states of the law—L and L̄, where L is permissive with respect to an activity and L̄ prohibitive[8]—four measures of exact compensation can be deduced; namely, a CV and an EV for each person for the L law, and a CV and an EV for the L̄ law. But as the example above makes clear, the CV and EV for any person under the L law corresponds, respectively, with the EV and the CV under the L̄ law. Thus, only two different measures are involved for each person. For example, if the CV involves a maximum payment of $20 for person N under the L law, under the L̄ law this same maximum payment of $20 is, as we have seen, the EV. The reverse is true for the minimum sum of $25 acceptable to N for bearing with the smoke: it is the EV under the L law and the CV under the L̄ law.

What is also *a propos* in this connection, is that if the CV involves a *maximum* payment of $20 for person N under the L law, the CV of the other person S, whose interest conflicts with that of N, is a *minimum* acceptable sum, say $35. If instead of comparing the CVs

---

8 Whether L law or L̄ law, we shall assume that rights are negotiable as between the offending and the offended party. Under the existing law negotiation is feasible. A feature of L̄ law would also be that rights are negotiable and enforceable.

Deficiencies of the present law, even where the damaged party is awarded an injunction by the courts, is discussed by Burrows (1970).

of the opposing parties, we compared their EVs, under the same L law, we should compare a minimum sum, \$25, acceptable to N with a maximum sum, say \$28, payable by S. The same reversal of maximum and minimum for CV and EV occurs under the L̄ law. Thus, the CV measure alone, used first under the L law and then under the L̄, provides the two measures—a maximum payable and a minimum acceptable—for each person affected. So, also, does the EV measure alone used under each kind of law. This duplication of results is, by itself, enough to absolve us from having to use both the CV and the EV measures in comparing the effects under each law, L and L̄.

5. In fact, we do not have much choice in the matter. Since we are committed to the concept of a potential Pareto improvement, we must allow ourselves to be guided by its implications. The notion of an economic event, or reorganization, that can make everyone better off requires that we use the CV concept only.

To be more explicit, all those affected by the economic event can be divided into gainers and losers. Irrespective of which law is operative, the CV of each of the gainers is the maximum sum he is willing to pay for the event. The CV of each of the losers, on the other hand, is the minimum sum he can be made to accept to put up with the event in question. If, then, with respect to some specific economic event, the maximum sums the gainers are prepared to pay (treated as a *positive* magnitude) exceed the minimum sums acceptable to the losers (treated as a *negative* magnitude), the algebraic sum of the CVs will be positive, and, by definition, a potential Pareto improvement will have been realized by the event.[9]

---

9 If, instead, we opted for using the EV measure under either law, the EV of each of the gainers from an economic event would be a minimum sum he accepts (as equivalent to forgoing the event), and the EV of each of the losers is a maximum sum he will pay (again, as equivalent to forgoing the event). Maintaining the above convention about signs, if the algebraic sum of all the EVs is *negative* we can infer only that the minimum sums required by gainers if they are to forgo the event exceeds the maximum sums that the losers will be glad to pay to forgo the event. But a resultant negative sign does not of itself imply a potential Pareto improvement—that is, the fact that losses from *not* introducing the event exceeding the gains from *not* having it does not, of itself, imply that gains from having it exceed losses from having it. All we can conclude from the negative sign is that there is a Pareto loss in not having the event; which is not the same thing as saying there is a Pareto gain in having it.

On the other hand, if the algebraic sum of the EVs is positive with respect to an event, there is a Pareto improvement in *not* having it.

The use of the EV, instead of the CV measure, is somewhat awkward both in respect of sign and interpretation.

Having decided to use the algebraic sum of the CVs in order to determine whether a particular economic change is a potential Pareto improvement under the existing state of the law, say L, we then reverse the state of the law to L̄ and ask the same question. It should not surprise us too much to discover that apparently contradictory results arise from asking the same question, first under the one law and then under its opposite. If a movement from an existing situation I to a new situation II appears as a potential Pareto improvement under the L law, it is simultaneously possible that, under the L̄ law, the reverse movement, from II to I, will also appear as a Pareto improvement. These paradoxical possibilities depend on the difference between the minimum sum a person will pay to go without a good and the maximum sum he will pay to have it—a difference which can be significant when the welfare effect is substantial, as it is likely to be in the presence of environmental spillovers.[10] These possibilities, and their relevance to cost-benefit analysis, will be demonstrated in the following chapter.

---

10 This apparent paradox which arises in a *partial* context—that is, one in which market prices are taken to be constant—is different in nature from that associated with the so-called Kaldor-Hicks or Scitovsky criteria. In the latter, the potential Pareto criterion, that is met in a movement from I to II and also from II to I, arises from movements in relative product prices being associated with the distributional changes in moving from I to II, or back from II to I. The interested reader should consult my 1961 paper.

Chapter 19

THE EFFECT OF LEGAL LIABILITY ON THE EVALUATION OF SPILLOVERS

1. The law concerning the liability for adverse spillovers, far from being neutral, affects the outcome of the Pareto criterion in two ways: one, through its effect on the magnitude of the compensatory payments which, in the last resort, is the value of the spillover effect; and two through its effect on the magnitude of the negotiating costs between the opposing parties. In this chapter, we shall deal only with the first of these.

2. Let us return first to our example in the preceding chapter of Messrs S and N sharing a compartment. As indicated there, if the law were permissive (L law), N would pay up to $20 to prevent S from smoking during the journey—or, for that matter, for having the law changed from L law to L̄ law. Person S, we now assume, will not accept less than $22 to abstain from smoking—or to allow the L law to be changed to L̄ law. If, on the other hand, the law initially prohibited smoking in the compartment, the minimum sum N would accept to put up with his companion's smoking—or for agreeing to have the existing L̄ changed to L law—is $25. Person S, we now assume, will pay as much as $18 for permission to indulge his craving—or to have the L̄ changed to L law.

The reader is reminded, in passing, that in accordance with our decision, all the above sums are CVs—exact measures of the compensation necessary to maintain the welfare of each person at his initial level—so that a positive algebraic sum for the CVs of persons N and S represents a potential Pareto improvement, whereas a negative algebraic sum represents a potential Pareto reduction of welfare.

These figures are set out in Table I below. The first row is interpreted as follows: under the permissive L law, the + 20 (under the N column) is the maximum sum N will pay to change the law in order to stop S smoking. The next figure, −22 (under the S column),

132

is the minimum sum S will accept to tolerate a change to $\bar{L}$ law. The excess benefit from changing the law from L to $\bar{L}$ is the algebraic sum of these two figures, $+ 20$ and $- 22$, or $- 2$, which is the figure given in the final column. It is plain that the change from L to $\bar{L}$ law does not entail a potential Pareto improvement, but the contrary, a potential decline in welfare—N's gain of 20 from the change falling short of S's loss of 22.

Let us elaborate this conclusion. If we regard S's smoking as a spillover effect on N, which it is on our definition, then, under the L law, a prohibition of the spillover appears to involve an excess benefit of *minus* \$2, in other words, a net loss of \$2. Put otherwise, a change of the existing L law to $\bar{L}$ law involves society in a net loss— all members (here only persons N and S) could be made worse off by the movement to the $\bar{L}$ law.[1] From this consideration alone, we should be compelled to regard the *status quo*, in which S is allowed to smoke freely, as Pareto optimal: for there is no way of making either person better off without making the other worse off. If N cannot compensate S to stop smoking, a change to the $\bar{L}$ law, which would prevent S from smoking, would make him worse off (by \$22) by more than N would be made better off (by \$20).[2]

Table I

State of law	CV of person N	CV of person S	Sum of CVs (equals Excess Benefit)
L	$+20$	-22	-2
$\bar{L}$	-25	$+18$	-7

1   Thus N could be made to pay \$21 to *S* for changing the law to $\bar{L}$, in which case N would be worse off (since the most he is willing to pay for the change in law is \$20), and S will be worse off also (since the minimum he is prepared to accept for the change in law is \$22.)
2   We are excluding, for the present, the possibilities open to N and S of making arrangements other than this all-or-nothing sort. It is perfectly possible for N to bribe S to smoke a little less, or not to smoke at certain times, or not after (or before) a certain hour. But this would complicate the argument without elucidating the principle, which is valid irrespective of the arrangements made. We do however touch on 'divisibility' shortly.

Now, we read along the second row of the Table, and interpret as follows: the existing law is $\bar{L}$, which prohibits smoking (in the absence of mutual agreement). In this situation, person N has a higher welfare than he had under the L law, and he will not agree to a reversal of the *status quo* (from the existing $\bar{L}$ law to L law, under which S can smoke freely) for less than $25. Person S, whose welfare is lower under the $\bar{L}$ law, will not pay more than $18 for the privilege of smoking and, therefore, for having the $\bar{L}$ changed to the L law.

The algebraic sum of the two CVs, -27 and $+18$, is -7, which again is the excess benefit to society arising from the change from the existing $\bar{L}$ law to L law. Again, therefore, the contemplated alteration in the *status quo* involves society in a net loss. Consequently, the existing situation under the $\bar{L}$ law is, by definition, also a Pareto optimal: there is no way of making either of them better off without making the other worse off.[3]

So, we may conclude in a light-hearted vein, 'you pays your money and you takes your choice'. Under the L law, the existing smoke-permissive law is Pareto optimal. Under the $\bar{L}$ law the existing no-smoking law is Pareto optimal.

3. The example we have used to illustrate this apparent paradox may be thought trivial—too trivial perhaps in its effects on the welfare of the two persons, N and S, to warrant the supposed difference between the maximum and minimum sum for each person. But one can think of more significant examples. The reader could, for instance, imagine that the figures given in Table I refer to $ millions, with N standing for the members of the public that suffer from aircraft noise and S standing for an airport authority representing, as it does, the interests of the airlines using the airport. If the existing law were L, permissive of aircraft noise, then $20 million along the first row is an exact measure of the public's collective CV. But this maximum sum the public is prepared to pay falls below the $22 million, which is the minimum sum the airport authority will re-

---

3 The reader who would like to follow up this idea is referred to my 1967 paper in which an $n \times n$ matrix is used in the Appendix to represent the n-person problem in which the interest of each person is deeemed to be opposed to that of every other.

quire for supressing all aircraft noise, or closing down the airport. The net loss of doing either, amounts to $2 million, and the *status quo* would then appear as the optimal outcome. The unsophisticated economist would then prove that supressing the noise 'does not pay', or recommend, on purely allocative grounds, that the airport remain in operation.

If, instead, we now suppose the $\bar{L}$ law to be in force, in which case all noise is forbidden (unless, of course, all parties willingly agree to accept the current noise level), we reach the opposite conclusion. The public's collective CV, $25 million, is now the minimal sum it will accept in compensation for changing the existing $\bar{L}$ law to L law. The maximum sum the airport authorities would pay to promote the change to L law is, as before, $22 million—*not* the $18 million in the Table, if we assume the airport authority to be a profit maximizer, with the sum, $22 million, being the full amount of the excess revenue. Beginning with the $\bar{L}$ law there will be a net loss in changing to the L law equal to $3 million. Once again, therefore, the *status quo* is a Pareto optimum, and there is no economic case for maintaining the airport.

4. We were able to talk about a Pareto optimal outcome in the above example because we took the noise spillover to be the only effect relevant to the decision, and because we supposed the airlines to have been in operation for long enough to enable a calculation to be made of their excess revenue. If, however, the question facing the economist is whether an airport should be constructed in the area, he has to evaluate the noise spillover as a negative good, or a bad, along with all other spillover effects, positive or negative. He then adds the algebraic total for all spillovers taken together to a separate estimate of the excess benefits in the absence of spillovers. Under an L law, the value of the noise spillover, and those of other adverse environmental spillovers, will in general be lower than they would be under an $\bar{L}$ law. In our example, in which noise is the only spillover, it will be valued as a loss of $20 million under the L law, and as a loss of $25 million under the $\bar{L}$ law. Now it may be the case that with either estimate, $20 million or $25 million, the cost-benefit calculation will still show a net excess of benefit over cost. Conversely, there may be a net negative excess benefit whichever of the

two estimates of the noise spillover is adopted. But it is also possible that the adoption of an estimate of the spillovers based on the L law, $20 million, would result in the scheme's showing a net excess benefit, so vindicating the scheme by a cost-benefit study, while if the other estimate of noise spillover, based on the $\bar{L}$ law, were adopted the cost-benefit calculation would show a net loss for the scheme.

5. Once a wide range of such projects is under consideration, each differing only in respect of size, the question arises of determining the optimal plant size. Or, once the size of the project has been decided, and the project built, the question arises of choosing the optimal output. Recourse to $\bar{L}$ law rather than to L law will, in all cases where negative spillovers predominate,[4] reveal a smaller optimal output, as is illustrated in Figure III.1 below.

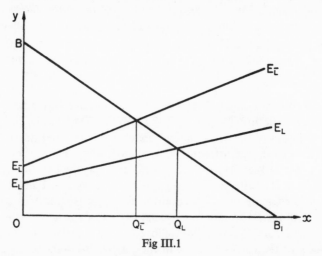

Fig III.1

Along the x axis we measure output, and along the y axis we measure marginal benefit or loss. Ignoring spillovers, the BB_1 curve measures excess benefit over cost. In the absence of spillover effects optimal output is, therefore, equal to OB_1. If output x is associated with, say, noise, we draw the $E_L E_L$-curve indicating, vertically, the collective CV compensation for successive units of

---

4 Always assuming that welfare effects are 'normal'.

noise-cum-output. Under the L law this CV is the maximum sums the noise victims will pay to prevent noise. If the law were changed to $\bar{L}$, and noise banned in the absence of mutual consent, the CV compensations for successive units would be above those under the L law, the relevant spillover curve being $E_{\bar{L}}E_{\bar{L}}$, above $E_L E_L$ at all points. Under the L law the optimal output would be OQ_L. Under the $\bar{L}$ law, the optimal output would be smaller at $Q_{\bar{L}}$.

Chapter 20
OPTIMAL METHODS OF CORRECTING SPILLOVERS

1. Prior to a discussion of the impact of the law on the costs of implementing potential Pareto improvements, let us look at several of the ways in which an existing competitive equilibrium output can be corrected for spillover effects. The exposition will be simplified by assuming, provisionally, that the welfare effects, or 'income' effects, on the public's spill-over-valuation are zero. In terms of Figure III.2 below, this means that the cost of spillover curve, EE_1, is uniquely determined. In all other respects, however, Figure III.2 is the same diagram as Figure III.1 of the preceding chapter. Thus, in the absence of spillovers, the excess benefit curve BB_1 would determine the optimal output of x as that equal to OB_1, excess marginal benefit (or price *less* marginal cost) at B_1 being equal to zero.

There can be a number of ways, or combinations of ways, of dealing with the spillover. We illustrate three alternative methods.

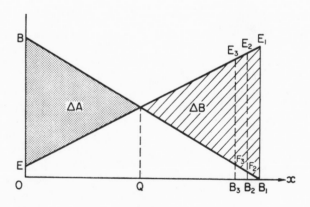

Fig III.2

2. *Method I.* If the only way of dealing with the spillover was to reduce the output of good x, we should want to reduce it to OQ, the optimal output. If the output were at OB_1, where it would be initially under the L law, the sum of the CVs (offered for eliminating the last, B_1th, unit of noise) would be equal to B_1E_1, while the excess commercial[1] benefit over cost would, as mentioned, be zero. A social loss is, therefore, incurred in producing this final unit, since there is no commercial gain in its production while the noise-affected public is willing to spend up to B_1E_1 for its withdrawal. If the final unit is withdrawn, the measure of the improvement is the elimination of this loss, equal to the whole of B_1E_1. Further Pareto improvements are made by the elininating of successive units up to the output OQ. Since further reductions of output would issue in potential losses— the collective CV gain of eliminating any additional unit of noise being exceeded by the loss of the excess commercial benefit, resulting from eliminating also the unit of $x - OQ$ is the optimal output. The measure of the Pareto improvement in reducing output from OB_1 to OQ is equal to the shaded triangular area, $\triangle B$. If, instead, we had begun at zero output, the measure of the maximum Pareto improvement in moving to output OQ is equal to the area of the dotted triangle $\triangle A$. We shall find it useful to identify a triangular area such as $\triangle A$ with the *excess social benefit* (ESB) of producing the optimal amount of x as compared with an initial non-optimal output—in this instance with not producing any of it. This brief analysis follows the traditional approach which abstracts, implicitly or explicitly,[2] from the impact of welfare effects on the spillover-valuation curve EE_1.

3. *Method II.* Rather than reduce output, one could concentrate wholly on preventive devices, such as anti-noise or anti-smoke devices. We shall suppose the effectiveness of these devices can be varied. For example, by spending an extra $1,000, say, we can raise the effectiveness of noise-muffling on aircraft by the smallest discernible difference. The expenditure of this first $1,000 does not reduce output or, to continue with the aircraft example, the number

---

1 The word *commercial* will be used as an adjective to describe calculations in which spillover effects are ignored.

2 An example of the latter appears in the paper by Buchanan and Stubblebine (1962) who use total curves rather than the marginal curves in Figure III. 2 above.

of flights per week. It reduces the suffering of the victims directly. With a lower volume of noise created by each aircraft, the maximum sums that would be offered to eliminate each aircraft flight would, therefore, be somewhat smaller than the original amounts. We should therefore construct a new spillover-value curve, $E'E'_1$ in Figure III.2, that is below the original EE_1 curve. This is shown in Figure III.3, which is the same diagram as Figure III.2 except for having spillover-valuation curves below EE_1.

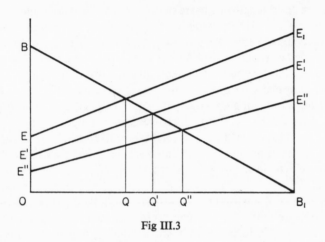

Fig III.3

The exact shape of the $E'E'_1$ curve is not at issue. If the $1,000 were spent instead on wholly supressing the noise from a single plane, the nth plane, the new $E'E'_1$ curve would coincide with the old EE_1 curve except near B_1, where it would fall far below EE_1. If, as first assumed, the $1,000 were spent on reducing the noise of all aircraft by a little, the $E'E'_1$ curve would, as drawn, lie everywhere below the EE_1 curve. The strip enclosed between these two curves, $EE_1E'_1E'$, would then represent the total value of the benefit experienced by the public from the spending of this $1,000. Obviously this benefit must be worth more than $1,000 if the introduction of this $1,000 expenditure on noise-preventive devices is to be regarded as a Pareto improvement.

We can, of course, repeat this $1,000 expenditure in order to secure the benefits of additional quiet, and draw the resulting curve

140

$E''E''_1$ below the $E'E'_1$ curve. The additional benefits are represented by the area of the strip $E'E'_1E''_1E''$, and, again, can be justified only if they exceed \$1,000. Clearly, we can continue doing this until the value of the additional quiet is no greater than the additional \$1,000 expenditure. In this way we maximize the Pareto improvement possible by means of this method alone while maintaining output at OB_1.

It should be clear, however, that if having gone as far as society can profitably[3] go in reducing noise directly by this second method, the resulting optimal output will have increased from OQ to some output greater than OQ, possibly greater than OQ''—the optimal output that corresponds to the expenditure of the second \$1,000 on anti-noise devices. The more effective is this second method, the more can the original EE_1 curve be profitably lowered, and the closer to B_1 is the resulting optimal output.

4. *Method III* involves bribing the victims to move from an existing spillover locality. Under our provisional assumption of zero welfare effect, it makes no difference whether, under the L law, the victim discovers that it pays him to incur the costs of moving away from the airport zone or whether, under the L̄ law, the airport authorities discover that it pays them to bribe him to move. Since the EE_1 curve is the vertical sum of the marginal loss curves for all noise-victims, the departure of any one of them reduces the width of the area OEE_1B_1 by a strip comparable with the $EE_1E'_1E'$ strip of Figure III.3. The resulting optimal output is then OQ'. As one after another depart, strip after strip is 'peeled off' the width of the original area OEE_1B_1, and the optimal output moves from OQ' to OQ'', and so on to OB_1. If all leave the vicinity, the spillover-valuation curve vanishes, and the resulting optimal output becomes OB_1.

Once more it should be apparent that unless the benefit from moving (the area of one of the strips) exceeds the cost of moving, there is no Pareto improvement in moving people from the locality. And, on the assumption that this is the only method of dealing with the spillover, the optimal number of emigrants from the area occurs when there is no person left in the vicinity whose migration would

---

3 The word *profitable* in this context has reference to social gain, and is therefore a shorthand for Pareto profitable.

produce an excess benefit over the cost of moving etc.[4]

5. Now it need hardly be said that these three methods, among others that are possible, are all available at the same time—and not only singly, but in combination. We have therefore to choose as between them or, rather, to pick out some optimal combination of them. With a little patience, plus the assumption of perfect divisibility, it should be possible to evolve pleasing diagrams and elegant mathematical solutions. But since the problems of an optimal combination of methods of dealing with spillover effects have, at present, limited application, we shall settle here for a rough and ready construct claiming only heuristic value.

Let us confine our ambition, for the moment, to comparing methods I and II only, asking ourselves whether the first $1,000 should be used up in pursuit of method I or II. In order to forgo $1,000 by method I, we must reduce the output of x in Figure III.2 by, say, B_1B_2, since the elimination of that much output of x entails a sacrifice of $1,000 of excess commercial benefit, as measured by the area of the triangle $B_1B_2F_2$. A further reduction of output by B_2B_3 corresponds to a further sacrifice of $1,000 excess commercial benefit, as measured by the area $B_3F_3F_2B_2$, and so on. The public gains from the accompanying reductions of spillover, the sum of the CVs, are measured by the relevant areas between the BB_1 and EE_1 curves, being $B_1F_2E_2E_1$ for the first $1,000 forgone, and $F_3F_2E_2E_3$ for the second $1,000. For successive expenditures of $1,000 on the II method of removing spillovers, on the other hand, the correspond-

---

4 The reverse of this process, migration into the noisy vicinity, obviously reduces the optimal amount of activity. It may indeed occur to the reader that, if legal liability for spillovers were placed on the shoulders of the entrepreneur, there would be an incentive for people to migrate into the area.

But, like the case of introducing an optimal excise tax on output and *also* permitting subsequent mutual agreement between the opposing parties (which then reduces output *below* optimal), introducing legal liability for entrepreneurs, and *also* after establishing a 'separate areas' situation—one in which there is a noisy area for industry and a quiet area for residential purposes—permitting people freely to migrate to the noisy area reduces welfare below the optimum.

Given the establishment of separate areas—which, as has been shown in my 1967 paper, increases social welfare beyond that attainable by the optimal outcome within a single area—the maintenance of the right of any family to move into the industrial area and claim adequate compensation reduces social welfare. It makes the family no better off while raising the costs and reducing the outputs of goods in the industrial area.

ing gains are given, as previoulsy indicated, by the area of the strips, in descending order, in Figure III.3.

The difference between the $1,000 forgone in eliminating spillover and the consequent gain (the sum of the CVs) it generates is the measure of the resulting potential Pareto improvement. The magnitude of the potential Pareto improvement of the first $1,000 forgone by method I is plotted as the area of a solid rectangle of unit width, equal to $1,000, in Figure III.4. The first $1,000 forgone by method II produces a like magnitude whose area is the dotted-line rectangle which, here, is taken represent $5,000 and is, therefore, greater than the $4,000 represented by the area of the solid-line rectangle of method I. If there is only $1,000 to be spent on reducing spillover, method II brings better results. (The reader will notice, in passing, that the use of method II by itself does not reduce the output of x below its initial amount OB_1. If, however, we now turned to method I, we should recognize that the optimal output is no longer OQ, in Figure III.3, but the larger output OQ'.)

We next consider a further 'expenditure' of $1,000 by either method. If method II's rectangle has an area equal to $4,000, and method I's rectangle an area equal to $3,500, we again choose to spend $1,000 by method II. Method II could be dominant throughout, with total expenditure on reducing the spillover expanding unit by unit until the final rectangle was of zero height, or close to it. In Figure III.4 we have shown method II to be superior to method I for the first two increments of $1,000, and inferior to it for the third increment. Although not shown in Figure III.4, we should want to continue the $1,000 units of expenditure in reducing spillover by whichever of the two methods, at any point, is the better until the final rectangle, of (close to) zero height, is reached. The outer-envelope of these successive rectangles cover an area equal to the maximum potential Pareto improvement arising from an optimal combination of the two methods.

If we now allow sufficient divisibility of anti-spillover expenditure, measured along the horizontal axis, we can trace a continuous downward-sloping solid curve for method I, and a continuous downward-sloping dotted curve for method II. In general these two curves intersect, as illustrated in Figure III.5. The outer envelope of the two intersecting curves encloses an area between the two axes that is equal to the largest potential Pareto improvement that is

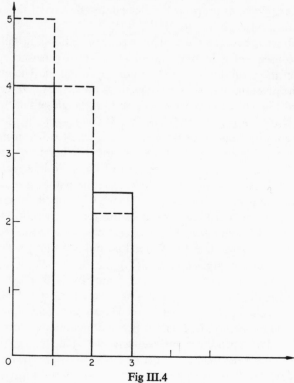

Fig III.4

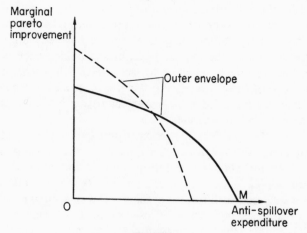

Fig III.5

possible through a combination of the two methods, by a total expenditure of OM.

There is no difficulty in extending this construct to cover the case of three, or more, different methods of spillover-reduction.

Chapter 21

THE COSTS OF IMPLEMENTING PARETO IMPROVEMENTS

1. Let us now turn to the costs of implementing potential Pareto improvements, in particular those improvements that can be effected by method I, involving, as it does, a movement in the level of output toward optimal output. Several ways of bringing about such movements are familiar. If, on political grounds, they are all equally desirable, the choice of which to adopt can be decided upon by reference to cost alone.

(a) The tax-subsidy scheme[1] is perhaps, owing to the great work of Pigou (1932), the best-known method of inducing a firm or an industry to produce an optimal output. The difficulties of calculating the optimal excise tax, or subsidy, under conditions of changing tastes and techniques has been stressed recently.[2] Although the costs of calculating and administering the taxes are not likely to vary closely with the size of the expected revenues, they are likely to vary with the degree of accuracy aimed at. However, if the economist is not over-fastidious about realizing the exact optimal conditions, he will settle for a substantial improvement. It may not be troublesome to calculate an excise tax that reduces output to within 10 per cent or 20 per cent of the optimum, and it is certainly worth while since such a tax is likely to capture well over 90 per cent of the potential Pareto improvement. Indeed, if we assume the costs of calculating the required excise tax can be anticipated for each proposition of the potential Pareto improvement it makes possible, one can go on to formalize the conditions for an optimal degree of accuracy.

---

1 Excise taxes are usually associated with adverse spillovers, and excise subsidies with favourable ones. But an excise subsidy could be used to curb outputs having adverse spillovers. Such a subsidy has, however, to be paid to the manufacturer for *reducing* his output below the profit maximizing output.

2 For instance by Davis & Whinston (1968). Their model is confined to *reciprocal* spillovers as between two concerns and so appears to exaggerate the difficulties.

(b) Government regulation of the volume of production—in so far as it is guided by optimality considerations—would seem to require more direct intervention than collection of taxes. Since the same calculations have to be made of cost schedules, demand schedules, and spillover damage, government regulation is likely to cost more, and possibly to be more resented also, then the tax solution.

(c) Direct prohibition of certain spillover effects can be justified in certain circumstances which we shall indicate shortly. Enforcement of such prohibitions are cheaper to implement than output-regulations or the levying of excises, but they are frowned upon as leading, generally, to non-optimal solutions.

2.   (d) Finally, potential Pareto improvements can be negotiated by mutual bargaining between the producers and receivers of spillovers. This scheme deserves particular attention, since the case for non-intervention is sometimes defended on the argument that, if the costs of negotiating agreement between the parties are smaller than the maximum potential Pareto improvement, such negotiations will indeed take place. Thus, the fact that no such negotiations are initiated, it is held, can be accepted as *prima facie* evidence that the potential Pareto improvement is exceeded by the costs of negotiation and administration. In other words, if the total cost of the real resources involved in the necessary negotiations and administration is denoted by G, and the maximum potential Pareto improvement is denoted by ESB (Excess Social Benefit in the absence of all such negotiating and administration costs), the condition for negotiation to take place required that RSB, the *Residual* Social Benefit— defined as equal to (ESB$-G$)—be positive. Clearly, ESB can be positive while RSB is negative. But it is the RSB that measures the Pareto improvement (positive, or negative) in the wider sense that includes all the costs needed to implement the ESB. If it happens that, in moving to a new position, the RSB is negative then the existing *apparently* optimal situation (where ESB, alone, is positive) is in fact truly non-optimal; for it will not really be possible to make everyone better off by moving to this seeming optimal output once we include the G costs necessary to reach it.

These G costs—sometimes referred to as 'transaction costs'— can be broken down into sub-categories. Let G_1 stand for the costs of negotiating agreement between the parties having conflicting interests over adverse spillover effects. Let G_2 stand for the costs of administration and supervision that are necessary to *maintain* the mutually agreed solution. And let G_3 stand for the capital outlays. if any, required to implement the agreement in question.

The G_1 costs would appear to be the more significant of the three, and those more likely to vary with the law on legal liability—at least for the case of environmental spillovers suffered by the public at large. Under the existing L law these costs would include, for the public, (a) the costs associated with taking the initiative, plus the costs (b) of identifying the victims of the spillover effects in question, (c) of communicating with each of them, (d) of persuading enough of them to agree to the idea of making a joint offer to the spillover-generating industry, (e) of reaching agreement among themselves on the sums to be offered to that industry, and also on the contribution toward these sums to be made by each of them, and (f) the costs of negotiation with the industry.

Once the representatives of the public approach the industry, a favourable response will involve it in a parallel breakdown of expenses. Thus, there will be the costs (b′) of identifying the firms responsible, (c′) of communicating with each of them, (d′) of persuading the firms to consider accepting an offer from the public, (e′) of reaching agreement between the firms concerned about the sums acceptable for their cooperation, and also about the formula on which any agreed sum is to be shared among them, and (f′) of negotiation with the representatives of the public.

It would seem that such costs are much higher for the public than they are for the industry. For instance, the costs (b), (c), (d), and (e) for the public will increase rapidly with the numbers of spillover victims and with their dispersion over the affected area, whereas, for the industry, the costs (b′), (c′), (d′), and (e′) will not increase so rapidly with numbers. For the numbers are small (it may be only a single firm) in any case, and they tend to be concentrated within an area rather than dispersed over it. Moreover, reaching decisions on behalf of their stockholders is a routine matter for business executives

3.   This difference in the G_1 costs as between the public, on the one hand, and the spillover-generating industry on the other is, however, of incidental interest. The relevant question is whether, taken to-

gether, they are likely to be any less under the $\bar{L}$ law than they are under the existing L law.

Under the $\bar{L}$ law, the initiative has to be taken by the spillover-generating industry, and the sequence is reversed. The breakdown of the costs incurred by the industry in preparation for an approach to the public is in the order (b'), (c'), (d'), and (e'), and they now have reference to the industry's making an offer, rather than to its accepting one. Once it is approached by the industry, the public has to incur costs (b), (c), (d), and (e), before being ready to negotiate, this breakdown of costs now having reference to the acceptance of offers made to them.

If we ignore (a) the costs of initiative, for the moment, it is hard to give convincing reasons for expecting that any of these items should, in general, be markedly different under one form of law as compared with the other—exception being made for item (d). The cost of persuading a large enough number of spillover victims to accept the idea of *making* a joint offer to the industry, under the L law, is sure to be much heavier than that of persuading them, under the $\bar{L}$ law to accept the idea of *receiving* a joint offer from the industry. In contrast, for (d'), the cost of persuading each firm under the $\bar{L}$ law to accept the idea of making a joint offer to the public is virtually nil, and it is likely to be the same for persuading them, under L law, to accept the idea of receiving a joint offer from the spillover victims. For the firms' financial interests are to the fore in the minds of their business executives, and virtually no persuasion is required to ensure receptivity to a scheme, under either law, which may add to their profits. If this argument is valid, the G_1 costs will be heavier to some extent under the existing L law than they would be under an $\bar{L}$ law.

4.   The question of initiative in (a) has been left to the last because of its crucial importance in determining the resultant allocation in the economy. If initiative were a productive service having a supply price, or at least a determinable cost, there could be no argument for intervention in the allocation thrown up by a competitive economy— so long as the existing law were accepted as a political datum. The mere fact that an economic rearrangement promising a potential Pareto improvement or, to use our notation, having a positive ESB,

149

had not been negotiated could be regarded as *prima facie* evidence that the G costs were too high and, therefore, that the RSB would be negative. This notion of a supply price for initiative is, however, untenable, and the inference that, in the circumstance envisaged, the RSB must be negative is unwarranted.

In the first place, from the observation that an economic re-arrangement having a positive ESB is not adopted, one cannot infer that the RSB is negative. For to infer, from the fact that mutual agreement has not been negotiated, that the RSB must be negative and in particular that the costs of initiative must be prohibitive, is invalid. Moreover it is an inference that is not to be refuted by empirical evidence. Such inference precludes, that is, any independent evaluation of G costs, and in particular any independent enquiry into the costs of initiative. If such tautological statements are accepted, one is bound to support the *status quo*, and to argue that the absence of mutual agreement in the presence of schemes having a positive ESB indicates simply that the RSB must be negative. It is such reasoning that reinforces the reluctance of some economists to intervention in the competitive market solution.

The import of this way of thinking, which rationalizes the *status quo*, is to encourage complacency rather than to draw attention to methods whereby initiative might be made available at low cost by institutional changes. If, for example, a government agency were set up, empowered to investigate instances of public disamenity arising out of the activities of modern industry and its products, it could, under the existing L law, lower all the other G_1 costs, from (b) to (f) to such an extent that, after allowance has been made for the costs of such an agency, optimal arrangements would be entered into which hitherto—in the absence of such an agency—would be quite impracticable.[3]

---

3 Allowing that the idea of making an approach to the industry in question occurs to a private individual, or to a number of them, the risk of failure at any of the stages (b) to (f) grows with the numbers of the victims and their dispersion. Apart from the sense of civic satisfaction, and the chance of gain from publicity, the benefit to the initiating party is no more than the difference between the maximum he (or they) will pay to reduce some of the spillover effects and the amount that he (or they) will actually pay, including a share of all the costs incurred in the hope of eventual agreement. This limited benefit, if positive, has to be set against the risk of irrecoverable loss of expenses plus the certain loss of time and effort until such time, if ever, as he, or they, succeed in setting up a representative organization which takes over subsequent risks and expenses.

Under an $\bar{L}$ law, in contrast, the necessary initiative would devolve upon the management of a firm or the executive body of an industry. Even if there were costs of initiative that could be identified, they would not be likely to add much to routine costs of decision-making by these bodies. The risks of failure, which in any case fall on the shareholders and not the executives taking the initiative, are smaller since, under an $\bar{L}$ law, firms can be assumed not to venture into a market without first having reasonably reliable information about the extent of their legal liability for the spillovers they generate. Indeed, a firm under $\bar{L}$ law is hardly likely to invest in plant and machinery for the manufacture of a range of goods unless it has good reason to expect that, after all economic preventive devices have been installed, it can afford to meet the costs of any residual damages from its net revenues.

All the above arguments apply also to method II—the installing of preventive devices—in which public initiative is required under the L law to bribe the manufacturers to instal preventive devices.[4]

5. In evaluating a project that is expected to produce one or more pollutants it should be clear that, irrespective of the prevailing attitude of the law with respect to pollution, the economist must cost them as if the law prevailed. In the first instance, that is, the prospective damage and inconvenience has to be estimated as a minimum sum acceptable to the potential victims of the expected pollution—and not as a maximum sum that the victims would be willing to pay to be rid of them. For what is relevant here, as in the evaluation of all items in a cost-benefit analysis, is the sum of compensating variations. And to value the pollution by reference to the maximum sum the potential victims are prepared to pay is to substitute a lower figure, that of the sum of their equivalent variations.

It need hardly be remarked that an estimate of these compensatory payments represents an upper limit of such costs, for it may be possible to reduce them by the use of preventive technology and/or by relocating the project in a more remote area.

---

4 We have confined ourselves to the G costs incurred in implementing voluntary mutual agreements under L and $\bar{L}$ law, simply because other schemes for potential Pareto improvements call for government intervention.

Given the state of the law actual compensation may not be required, and if not, transactions costs incurred in making arrangements for their payment do not arise. After all, in a cost-benefit calculation it is required only that pollution costs, along with all other costs, be compared with total benefits. There is no call for transfer payments to be made.

Finally, any inputs from a pollutant-producing industry A have to be valued at their social cost; that is to say, the cost of A's inputs used in the project has to include an estimate of the compensatory payments needed to restore the loss of welfare associated with the expansion of A's outputs (that are inputs to the project in question). If the A industry itself does not give rise to adverse spillover effects but uses inputs from some other polluting industry B, the additional social damage from the expansion of the B industry, needed to meet the expansion of A's inputs that are demanded by the project under evaluation, has to enter into the cost-benefit analysis, and so on. To the extent that spillovers generated by the project itself, by industry A, and/or by industry B, are benign, however, they will obviously have to be entered on the benefit side of the ledger.

Chapter 22
LOSS OF LIFE AND LIMB

1. As cost-benefit studies grow in popularity, it is increasingly important to make proper allowance for losses, or gains, arising from changes in the incidence of death, disablement, or disease caused by the operation of new projects or developments.

Since the analysis of saving life is symmetrical with that of losing it, it will simplify the exposition if, initially, we confine ourselves to the analysis of *loss* of life and limb—or, more briefly, to loss of life alone—indicating the necessary extensions later on.

2. (a) Despite repeated expressions of dissatisfaction with the method, the most common way of calculating the economic worth of a person's life and, therefore, the loss to the economy consequent upon his decease, is that of discounting to the present the person's expected future earnings.

A precise expression for the loss to the economy calculated on this method would be L_1, where

$$L_1 = \sum_{t=\tau}^{\infty} Y_t P_\tau^t (1 + r)^{-(t-\tau)}$$

Y_t is the expected gross earnings of (or, alternatively, value added by) the person during the tth year, exclusive of any yields from his ownership of non-human capital.[1] P_τ^t is the probability in the current, or τth, year of the person being alive during the tth year, and r is the social rate of discount expected to rule during the tth year. This sort of calculation is occasionally supplemented by a suggestion that auxiliary calculations be made in order to take account of the suffering of the victim, his loss of utility from ceasing to be alive, and/or of the bereavement of his family.[2] More recently, and as an

---

1 For the returns on his (non-human) assets continue after his death, or during his disablement.
2 For examples, see Kneese (1966, p. 77) and Ridker (1967), p. 34. The suggestions, needless to remark, have not been taken up. Presumably they are made in response to an uneasy conscience about the methods actually being employed.

153

example perhaps of the economist's finesse, it has been proposed that such calculations be supplemented also by the costs of 'premature burial'[3]—the idea being that the present discounted value of the funeral expenses is higher if they are incurred the sooner owing to an untimely death.

A related calculation, no less plausible than the above, would restrict itself to the individual's loss of expenditure on himself alone. The above formula will serve once Y_t is displaced by C_t, where C_t stands for the personal expenditure of the individual expected during the tth period. Alternatively one could attempt to calculate the individual's loss of consumer's surplus or rent.[4] Neither of these measures have been explicitly proposed however, possibly because a consideration of a man's personal expenditure leads inevitably to a consideration of the utility he also obtains from transferring part of his income to his family and, by extension, to the gains and losses of other members of society.

---

3   The expression occurs in Ridker's book (1967) on the costs of pollution. For those prone to morbid curiosity, the formula used is on page 39, and takes the form

$$C_a = C_o \left[1 - \sum_{n=a}^{\infty} \frac{P^n}{(1 +r)^{(n-a)}} \right]$$

where C_a is the present value of the net expected gain from delaying burial at age a. C_o is the cost of burial. P_a^n is the probability that an individual age a will die at age n, and r is the discount rate. It is not impossible that these calculations were made with tongue in cheek, and, if so, it is perhaps an oversight on his part that he omitted a countervailing consideration, viz. that, if the unfortunate person died at a very early age, some useful savings might be effected from the lower cost of a smaller coffin.

4   Although the concept of rent or economic surplus is conventionally employed within a partial context, it is quite valid in a more general setting (Mishan, 1959, p. 394). However generalized the concept, it still involves comparisons between alternative situations. Any idea of evaluating this surplus by subtracting from a man's total income, or total expenditure, some estimate of a subsistence level of expenditure, can be successful only if this level can be so chosen that the man is indifferent as between surviving at this subsistence level and expiring. But there is no warrant for believing that such a level exists. What casual evidence there is supports the popular impression that, no matter how precarious or hopeless a man's condition, he continues to hang on grimly to his life.

3. (b) At all events, a second method, which might be thought of as more refined than the first, is that of calculating the present discounted value of the losses over time accruing to *others only* as a result of the death of this person at age τ. A precise expression for the loss to the economy based on this method would be L_2, where

$$L_2 = \sum_{t=\tau}^{\infty} P_\tau^t \cdot (Y_t - C_t)(1 + \Omega_t)^{-(t-\tau)}$$

where C_t is the personal expenditure of the individual during the tth period that is expected at time τ. This sort of measure, sometimes referred to as being based on the 'net output' approach, in order to distinguish it from the 'gross output' approach associated with the L_1 measure, though occasionally mentioned in the literature,[5] has not been employed apparently because of the assumed policy implications.

(c) A third possible method would repudiate any direct calculation of the loss of potential earnings or spending. Instead, it would approach the problem from a 'social' point of view. Since society, through its political processes, does in fact take decisions on investment expenditures that occasionally increase or reduce the number of deaths, an implicit value of human life can be calculated. This approach receives occasional mention[6] and, indeed, the appeal to the political, or democratic, process is sometimes invoked to provide guidance on broader issues.[7]

(d) The insurance principle is a departure from any of the aforementioned methods. By making use of the premium a man is willing to pay, and the probability of his being killed as a result of engaging in some specific activity, it is thought possible to be able to calculate the value a man sets on his life.[8]

---

5   For instance, by Devons (1961, p. 107) and Ridker (1967, p. 36).

6   For instance, by Fromm (1965, p. 193) and by Schelling (1968, p. 147).

7   Indeed, Rothenberg (1961, pp. 309–36) ends his examination of social welfare criteria by proposing that the democratic process itself be regarded as such a criterion. More recently, Nath (1969, pp. 216–17) proposes that the task of the economist be limited to that of revealing the locus of 'efficient' economic production possibilities available to society, leaving it to democracy to select the collection of goods it wishes.

8   An example is given by Fromm (1965, p. 194).

4. Each of these four possible methods of measuring the loss of life is now briefly appraised.

Method (a), turning on the loss of potential future earnings, can be rationalized only if the criterion adopted in any economic reorganization turns on the value of its contribution to GNP, or, more accurately, to net national product, But although financial journalists manage to convey the contrary impression, maximizing GNP is not an acceptable goal of economic policy. If it were, the simplest way of promoting it would be to adopt a policy of virtually unlimited immigration—accepting immigrants up to the point at which the value of their marginal product is zero. Recourse to this method by the practicing economist does not, therefore, rest on the clear recognition of the desirability of maximizing GNP but rather, obviously on the fact that it lends itself easily to quantification. Notwithstanding its usage, most writers have mental reservations about its validity, and tend to regard it as only part of the total measurement. For instance, Schelling (1968) makes a distinction between the value of livelihood, which is the L_1 measure, and the value of life, which poses a perplexing and possibly unsolvable problem.

The so-called net output method (b) might seem, at first glance, more acceptable than the gross output method: taking a cold-blooded attitude, what matters to the rest of society is simply the resulting loss, or gain, to it following the death of one or more of its members. This *ex post* approach, however, appears to strike some writers as either absurd or dangerous.[9] If accepted, it certainly follows that the death of any person whose L_2 measure is negative confers a net benefit on society. And this category of persons would certainly include all retired people irrespective of their ownership of property. Yet from this undeniable inference, no dread policy implications follow. If the method were satisfactory on economic grounds, the inference would not, of itself, provide any reason for rejecting it. But the method is not satisfactory for the simple reason that it has no regard to the feelings of the potential victims. It restricts itself to the interests only of the surviving members of society: it ignores society *ex ante*, and concentrates wholly on society *ex post*.

---

9 For example, Devons (1961, p. 108) concludes ironically: 'Indeed if we could only kill off enough old people we could show a net gain on accidents as a whole!' As for Ridker (1967, p. 36), the net output method 'suggests that society should not intefere with the death of a person where net value is negative'.

As for method (c), which would build on implicit values placed on human life by the political process, the justification appears somewhat circular even when we ignore the political realities of Western democracies: in particular (i) the fact that decisions to invest in certain projects are not determined by popular vote; instead, governments avail themselves of a general mandate, conferred on them by an election, to delegate powers of decision at various levels of the political hierarchy; (ii) the fact that investment decisions are not motivated primarily by the desire to advance the *general* welfare, on any plausible criterion, but are rather the outcome of political conflicts; and (iii) the fact that an implicit value attributable to loss of life by a particular public programme will differ widely from an implicit value derived from another public programme. Ignoring these political realities, and assuming that democratic voting alone determines whether or not a particular investment project, or part of a project, is to be adopted, the idea of deriving quantitative values from the political process is clearly contrary to the idea of deriving them from an independent economic criterion. And where the outcome of the political debate is that of calling upon the economist to provide a quantitative evaluation of the project under consideration, the economist fails to meet his brief in so far as he abandons the attempt to calculate any aspect of the project by reference to an economic criterion and instead attempts to extricate figures from previous political decisions.[10] By recourse to a method that refers a question, or part of a question, received from the political process back again to the political process, the economist appears to be concealing some deficiency in the relevant data or some weakness in the logic of his criteria. Moreover, even if it were agreed that the loss of human life should not be estimated by 'ordinary' economic criteria used in evaluated other gains and losses, the requirements of consistency cannot be met by such implicit—and also arbitrary and erratic—valuations of political outcomes, though they might be met by particular criteria that make the valuation of loss of life explicit

---

10 Which is not to deny that the economist's criterion or criteria—though independent of the outcome of any particular political process that is sanctioned by the constitution—must themselves be vindicated ultimately by reference to value judgments widely held within the community. The reader interested in this aspect is referred to my monograph (1969a, pp. 13–23).

and systematic. As we shall see, however, there is no call for evaluating loss of life on a criterion different from that which is basic to the economist's calculation of all the other effects comprehended in a cost-benefit analysis.

Finally, there is method (d) based on the insurance principle. This has about it a superficial plausibility, enough at any rate to attract some attention.[11] But the insurance policy makes provision, in the event of a man's death, only for compensation to *others*. Thus, the amount of insurance a man takes out may be interpreted as a reflection, *inter alia*, of his concern for his family and dependents, but hardly as an index of the value he sets on his own life.[12] A bachelor with no dependents could have no reason to take out flight insurance, notwithstanding which he could be as reluctant as the next man to depart this fugacious life at short notice.

---

11 An early attempt, for instance, was made by Fromm (1965, pp. 193–6) to attribute a value for loss of life raised on the implied assumption of a straight-line relationship between the probability of a person being killed and the sum that he would pay to cover the risk. If, therefore, the premium y corresponding to the additional risk p is known, the value he places on his life is to be reckoned as y/p. Thus, if a man would pay $100 to reduce his chance of being killed by one per cent—say from an existing chance of $1/10$ to $2/50$—the value he places on his life is to be estimated as $10,000 (or to use Fromm's own calculation, if the probability of being killed in air travel were to be reduced from the existing figure of 0.0000017 per trip of 500 miles to zero, a person who values his life at $400,000 should be willing to pay 68 cents to reduce the existing risk to zero).

The implied assumption of linearity, which has it that a man who accepts $100,000 for an assignment offering him a four to one chance of survival will agree to go to certain death for $500,000, is implausible to say the least. And, indeed, this linearity assumption was later criticized by Fromm himself (1968, p. 174) when it was incidentally posited by Schelling (1968). But even if it were both plausible and proved, the insurance principle does not yield us the required valuation.

12 An ingenious paper by Eisner and Strotz (1961), after some theorizing on the basis of the Neumann-Morgenstern axioms about the optimal amount of insurance a person should buy, addresses itself to the question of why people continue to buy air-accident insurance when ordinary life insurance is cheaper. They suggest, among other things, that flight insurance could be a gamble (related formally to the increasing marginal-utility segment of the income-utility curve), and they point also to the existence of imperfect knowledge, imperfect markets, and inertia.

However, the paper does not, and is presumably not intended to, throw any light on this question of the valuation of human life. The observation that a man does not insure his life against some specific contingency cannot be taken as evidence that he is indifferent as between being alive and being dead.

5. The crucial objection to each of these four methods, however, is that not one of them is consistent with the basic rationale of the economic calculus used in cost-benefit analysis. If we are concerned, as we are in all allocative problems, with increasing society's satisfaction in some sense, and if in addition we eschew interpersonal comparisons of satisfactions, we can always be guided in the ranking of alternative economic arrangements by the notion of a Pareto improvement—an improvement such that at least one person is made better off and nobody is made worse off. A *potential* Pareto improvement,[13] one in which the net gains *can* so be distributed that at least one person is made better off with none being made worse off, provides an alternative criterion, or definition, of social gain—one which, as it happens, provides the rationale of all familiar allocative propositions in economics, and therefore the rationale of all cost-benefit calculations.

When the full range of its economic effects is brought into the calculus, the introduction of a specific investment project will make some of the community of n members better off on balance, some worse off on balance, the remainder being indifferent to it. If the j th person is made better off, a compensating variation (CV) measures the full extent of his improvement, this CV being a maximum sum V_j he will pay rather than go without the project, the sum being prefixed by a positive sign. Per contra, if the j th person is made worse off by the introduction of the project, his CV measures the full decline of his welfare as a minimal sum V_j he will accept to put up with the project, this sum being prefixed by a negative sign.[14]

---

13 A 'potential Pareto improvement' is an alternative and simpler nomenclature than a 'hypothetical compensation test'. The problems associated with the concept are important, but need not concern us here if we accept the fact that cost-benefit analyses take place within a partial context, one in which changes in the prices of all the non-project goods can be ignored. If this much is granted, the relevant individuals' compensating variations which is what we are after will be uniquely determined.

14 These sums may be calculated as annual transfers or as capital sums according to the method being used in the cost-benefit study. Since the flow of costs and benefits are to be valued at a point of time, consistency would require that the CVs also be reckoned as a capital sum at that point of time. If there are no external effects of saving for future generations, as posited by Marglin (1963), the existence of imperfect capital markets will result in different rates of time preference among the persons concerned. In that case, capitalizing their CVs reckoned as annual sums at some single rate of discount will result in corresponding capitalized CVs which would differ from those chosen directly by these same persons, which latter sums should, of course, prevail.

If, then, in response to the introduction of this specific project, the aggregate sum $\overset{n}{\underset{j}{\Sigma}} V_j > 0$ (where j runs from 1 to n)—if, that is, the algebraic sum of all n individual CVs is positive—there is a potential Pareto improvement, its positive value being interpreted as the excess of benefits over costs arising from the introduction of the project.[15]

Consistency with the criterion of a potential Pareto improvement and, therefore, consistency with the principle of evaluation in cost-benefit analyses, would require that the loss of a person's life be valued by reference to his CV; by reference, that is, to the minimum sum he is prepared to accept in exchange for its surrender. For unless a project that is held to be responsible for, say, an additional one thousand deaths annually can show an excess of benefits over costs *after* meeting the compensatory sums necessary to restore the welfare of these one thousand victims, it is not possible to make all members of the community better off by a redistribution of the net gains. A potential Pareto improvement cannot then be achieved, and the project in question ought not to be admitted.

If the argument is accepted, however, the requirements of consistency might seem to be highly restrictive. Since an increase in the annual number of deaths can be confidently predicted in connection with a number of particular developments—those, for example, which contribute to an increase in ground and air traffic—such developments would no longer appear as economically feasible. For it would not surprise us to discover that, in ordinary circumstances,[16] no sum of money is large enough to compensate a man for the loss of his life.

---

15 Within the same broad context, and allowing for sufficient divisibility in the construction of such projects, the corresponding rule necessary to determine the optimal output of such projects—or, in short periods, the optimal output of the goods of the existing projects—takes the simple form that $\overset{n}{\underset{j}{\Sigma}} v_j = 0$, where v_j is the CV of the jth person in response to a marginal increment in the size of the industry, or (in the short period) the size of its output.

16 If a man and his family were so destitute, and their prospects so hopeless, that one or more members were likely to die of starvation, or at least to suffer from acute deprivation, then the man might well be persuaded to sacrifice himself for the sake of his family. But without dependents, or close and needy friends, the inducement to sacrifice himself for others is not strong.

6. In conditions of certainty, the logic of the above proposition is unassailable. If in ordinary circumstances we face a person with the choice of continuing his life in the usual way, or of ending it at noon on the morrow, a finite sum large enough to persuade him to choose the latter course of action may not exist. And indeed if the development in question unavoidably entailed the death of this specific person or, more generally, a number of specific persons, it is highly unlikely that any conceivable excess benefit over cost, *calculated in the absence of these fatalities*, would warrant its undertaking on the potential Pareto criterion.

It is never the case, however, that a specific person, or a number of specific persons, can be designated in advance as being those who are certain to be killed if a particular project is undertaken.[17] All that can be predicted, though with a high degree of confidence, is that out of a total of n members in the community, an additional x members per annum will be killed (and, say, an additional $10x$ members will be seriously injured). In the absence, therefore, of any breakdown of the circumstances surrounding the additional number of accidents to be expected, the increment of risk of being killed imposed each year on any one member of the community can be taken as x/n (and $10x/n$ for the risk of being seriously injured). And it is this fact of complete ignorance of the identity of each of the potential victims that transforms the calculation. Assuming universal risk aversion,[18] the relevant sums to be subtracted from the benefit side are no longer those which compensate a specific number of persons for their certain death, but are those which compensate

---

17 Cf. Schelling's remarks (1968, pp. 142–6).

18 Risk-aversion is assumed throughout (unless otherwise stated) solely in the interests of brevity. If some people enjoy the additional risk, their CVs will be positive. In general if the aggregate of the CVs for the additional risk is negative, which is the case for universal risk aversion, there is a subtraction from the benefit side. If, on the other hand, it were positive, there would be an addition to the benefit side.

each person in the community for the additional risk to which he is to be exposed.[19]

In general, of course, every activity will have attached to it some discernible degree of risk (even staying at home in bed bears some risk of mishap—the bed might collapse; the wind might blow the roof in; a marauder might enter). Any change, from one environment to another, from one style of living to another, can be said to alter the balance of risk, sometimes imperceptibily, sometimes substantially. Only the dead opt out of all risk. Yet the actual statistical risk attaching to some activity may be so small that only the hypersensitive would take account of it. In common with all other changes in economic arrangements, there is some *minimum sensible* beyond which an increment, or decrement, of risk will go unnoticed. More important, however, what is strictly relevant to the analysis is not the change in the statistical risk *per se*, but the person's response, if any, to such a change. For the change in risk may go unperceived and, if perceived, it may be improperly evaluated. Indeed, people do have difficulty in grasping the objective significance of large numbers and, where chance or risk is at issue, they are prone to underestimate it. One chance in 50,000 of winning a lottery, or of having one's house burned down, seems a better chance, or a greater risk, than it actually is. And if so, the existence of gambling and insurance by the same person is explicable without recourse to the ingenious Friedman-Savage hypothesis (1948).

---

19   In a most engaging, and highly perceptive paper, Schelling (1968) divides the problem into three parts: (a) society's interest, (b) an economic interest (in which category, a man's contribution to GNP is placed), and (c) a 'consumer's interest,' Discussing this third interest, in connection with a life-saving programme, Schelling correctly poses the relevant question: what will people pay for a government programme that reduces risk? (p. 142). But being uneasy about the actual measurement of such a sum, and absorbed with other fascinating, though in the context irrelevant, considerations, he does not develop the analysis systematically. Indeed, he goes on later to discuss the value of certain loss of life, and comes up with the suggestion that college professors would be prepared to pay an amount equal to something between ten and a hundred times their annual income in order to save the life of one of their family.

If one is interested solely in the conceptual measure, as I am here, one can make use of the notion of external effects to develop the analysis. Fromm's hypercritical comments (1968), on the other hand, make use of external effects, along with the difficulties of measuring, largely to cast doubt upon this valid part of Schelling's paper.

The analysis which follows does not, however, depend upon the veracity of such conjectures. All the reader has to accept is the proposition that people's subjective preferences of the worth of a thing is to count. In the market place, the price of a good, or a 'bad' (such as labour-input or other disutility), is fixed by the producer, and the buyer or seller determines the amount by reference to his subjective preferences. Where, however, the amount of a (collective) good, or 'bad', is fixed for each person—as may be the case with a change in risk—a person's subjective preference can only determine the price he will accept or offer for it: in short, his CV. People's imperfect knowledge of economic opportunities, their imprudence and unworldliness, has never prevented economists from accepting as basic data the amounts people freely choose at given prices. Such imperfections cannot therefore consistently be invoked to qualify people's choices when, instead, their preferences are excercised in placing a price on some increment of a good or 'bad'. True, attempts to observe the change of magnitude when people adjust the price to the change in quantity—rather than the more common assumption that they adjust the quantity to the change in price—does pose problems of measurement. But the problems of measurement must not be allowed to obscure the validity of the concept.

Placed within the broadest possible context then, any additional risk of death, associated with the provision of some new facility, takes its place as one of a number of economic consequences (including employment gains and losses, new purchase and sale opportunities, and the withdrawal of existing ones) all of which affect the welfare of each of the n members of the community.

Chapter 23
LOSS OF LIFE AND LIMB (Continued)

1. We shall now consider four types of risk, two of them direct, or physical, risks, the remaining two being indirect, or derivative, risks.

(1) First, there are the direct, or physical, risks that people *voluntarily* assume whenever they choose to buy a product or avail themselves of a service or facility. Inasmuch as such risks are evaluated by each jth person as a CV, equal say to r_{jj}^1, his benefit from the service or facility is estimated net of such risk; that is, after r_{jj}^1 has been subtracted from it. If smoking tobacco causes 20,000 deaths a year, no subtracting from the benefits, on account of this risk, need be entered in a cost-benefit analysis of the tobacco industry inasmuch as smokers are already aware that the tobacco habit is unhealthy. And if, notwithstanding their awareness, they continue to smoke, the economist has no choice but to assume that they consider themselves better off despite the risks. Indeed, the benefits to smokers, net of risk—that is, after subtracting the aggregate $\sum\limits_{j}^{n} r_{jj}^1$—are reflected in the demand schedule for tobacco. Once the area under the demand curve has been estimated, and used as an approximation of the benefit smokers derive from the use of tobacco, any further subtraction for such risks would entail double counting.

Another example will help to clarify the principle and will extend the argument. If, in an initially riskless situation, we observe that the jth person buys a car, we may infer that C_j is positive; that, in his own estimation, he is better off with the car than without it.

---

1 The nice distinction made by Schelling (1968, pp. 132–5) between loss of life and loss of livelihood is possibly meaningful, but difficult to capture. Given the 'conjuncture' of circumstances in which a man finds himself, there is, in principle, some amount of money that will just induce him to assume a particular risk of being killed. But it is hardly likely that he will be able to apportion that sum as between 'life' and 'livelihood', and it is not necessary, in this analysis, that he should be able to do so.

The introduction, now, of some personal risk associated with driving the car does not alter this inference.[1] Once he is aware of the additional element of risk in driving the car, the consequent reduction in the j th person's welfare is valued at the risk compensation r^1_{jj}. If, in spite of the additional risk, the j th person still offers to buy the car, we are compelled to infer that $(C_j. - r^1_{jj}) > 0$, i.e. his original consumer's surplus exceeds the risk compensation or, but otherwise, his consumer's surplus *net of risk* is positive. The evaluation of a new automobile plant will, therefore, disregard this type of risk, since the benefits are roughly equal to the aggregate of consumers' surplus net of risk. Similarly, a cost-benefit study of a highway project which is expected to increase the number of casualties need make no allowance for the expected loss of life, provided, again, that this is the only type of risk. For in this case also, the benefits to be measured are ultimately the maximum sums motorists are willing to pay for the new highway system in full cognizance of the additional risks they choose to assume.

Occasionally, as in the automobile example, the risk assumed by each person will depend also upon the numbers availing themselves of the service or facility. Since the additional degree of risk generated by all the others are imposed on each one, in addition to the risk he would assume in the absence of all others, the analysis must extend itself to include 'external diseconomies internal to the industry'.[2] If we let r^1_{ij} stand for the risk compensation sum required by the j th person for the risk imposed on him by the i th individual, the compensatory sums for the extra risks contributed by all other individuals is given by $\sum_i^n r^1_{ij}$ ($i \neq j$). Now, although these additional risks are imposed on the j th person, they can always be avoided by his refusal to avail himself of the new service or facility. If, however, he decides to avail himself of it, the economist cannot but assume that he believes he is better off with it than without it. Again, therefore, we must assume that $(C_j - \sum_i^n r^1_{ij}) > 0$, where i now includes j so as to make provision also for the risk that person j

---

2 The distinction between external effects *internal* to the industry, and those *external* to the industry, was proposed in my 1965 paper.

would run if he alone enjoyed the new service or facility.[3] Aggregating over all n members, the net consumers' surplus is $\sum_{i}^{n} (C_j - \sum_{i}^{n} r_{ij}^1)$, which can be abbreviated to $C - R^1$.

In so far, then, as additional risks associated with the service or facility are all voluntarily assumed, no subtraction for loss of life need be placed on the benefit side, since the benefits to be measured are already net of risk. However, once we turn from risks that can be voluntarily assumed to those which cannot be avoided (or, rather, cannot be avoided without incurring expenses) we are in the realm of 'external diseconomies that are *external* to the industry', and cost-benefit analyses have to make provision for them.

2. The additional risks that are imposed on the community as a whole as a by-product of some specific economic activity, and are therefore to be regarded as external diseconomies external to the industry, can be separated into three types. Although all three can be inflicted on the same person, who could propose a single sum in compensation, it is useful to separate them, there being circum-

---

3 The external diseconomies of traffic risk are therefore treated exactly as the external diseconomies of traffic congestion. But, as distinct from the problem of estimating the excess benefit of a *given* project, the determination of an *optimal* traffic flow does require intervention by the economist in consequence of these mutual diseconomies. For the question raised in determining an optimal traffic flow is no longer that of showing that, for a given volume of traffic, total benefits (*net* of risk and congestion) exceed total costs. The question, now, is to *choose* a volume of traffic so as to *maximise* excess benefit over cost, this being realized by equating marginal social benefit to marginal cost. The standard argument is then invoked: although the effects on all others of risk and congestion grow with each additional car, the jth, or marginal vehicle-owner, in deciding whether to use the highway, considers only the term $\sum_{i}^{n} r_{ij}^1$. (ignoring the similar congestion term), as indeed does each of the other members, i.e. he takes account only of the costs to him of each of the n vehicles on the road, including his own. What he does *not* take into account is the effect he himself produces on each of the others by his decision to add his vehicle to theirs; which is to say, he ignores the cost $\sum_{i} r_{ji}^1$. ($i \neq j$), the costs imposed on each of the intra-marginal vehicles by introducing his own jth vehicle. This term therefore represents the cost of those external diseconomies generated by the marginal vehicle, diseconomies that are internal to and absorbed by all intra-marginal vehicles, and which are properly attributable to the marginal vehicle in determining the optimal flow of traffic.

stances where only one or two types of risk are of any importance.

(2) The direct *involuntary* risk of death that is inflicted on the j th person by some specific project can be compensated by the sum r_{jj}^2. For example, the establishment of a nuclear power station and the resulting disposal of radioactive waste materials is held to be responsible for an increase in the annual number of deaths. Again, if supersonic flights over inhabited areas are introduced as a regular service, we can anticipate an increase in the annual number of deaths, at least among the frail, the elderly, and among those suffering from heart ailments.

In addition to this primary risk, there is a secondary risk to which the j th person is exposed, which will arise in other instances. For example, in the absence of legal prohibition, a works pours 'sewage' into the air and increases the incidence of death from a number of lung and heart diseases. Apart from those who are the direct victims of this activity, there will be a number of fatalities arising from infection through others. And this possibility of infection obviously increases the risk since, within a given area, every person becomes a source of risk to every other. In addition, therefore to the sum r_{jj}^2 to compensate the j th person for the risk imposed on him even if he were the sole inhabitant, he requires also a sum $\sum_{i}^{n} r_{ij}^2 \, (i \neq j)$ to compensate for the risk that each of the other $(n-1)$ persons impose on him.

There does not seem to be any advantage, however, in upholding this distinction between primary and secondary physical risk. Where the risk of infection through others is acknowledged, it is difficult, if not impossible, to separate primary from secondary risk. In such cases the risk compensation required by each person covers both. We shall therefore employ the general term $\sum_{i}^{n} r_{ij}^2$ for the j th person (which includes the term r_{jj}^2 for the risk he runs in the absence of others). Aggregating over the n members of the community, this total risk compensation is to be valued at $\sum_{j}^{n} \sum_{i}^{n} r_{ij}^2$, which can be denoted by R^2.

(3) There is, finally, the indirect, or derivative, risk arising from the general concern of each of the n persons with the physical risks,

voluntary and involuntary, to which any of the others is exposed. This additional concern, to which, in general, each member is prone (as a result of the additional physical risks run by others), has, first, a purely financial aspect. If, on balance, the death of the i th person improves the financial position of the j th person, the additional chance of i's death is a benefit to j, and the risk-compensatory sum r_{ij}^3 is therefore positive. This means that the j th person is willing to pay up to a given sum for the improved chance of his losing some dependent or inheriting some asset—or of inheriting it the sooner.[4] If, on the other hand, the death of the i th person would reduce j's real income, the sum r_{ij}^3 is negative; that is, the j th person would have to receive a sum of money to compensate him for the increased risk of suffering a reduction in his real income. Although the j th person's financial condition is likely to be affected by the death of only a few members of the community, his risk compensation, on this account, can be written in general as $\sum_i^n r_{ij}^3 (i \neq j)$. Bearing in mind that most of the terms in the sum will be zero, the total expression will be positive or negative according as the increased risk of death run by others makes him, on balance, better off or worse off.

For this financial risk to which the community as a whole is exposed, the total risk compensation is given by aggregating the above expression over the n members to give $\sum_j^n \sum_i^n r_{ij}^3 (i \neq j)$, which can be represented by R^3. This sum can, as suggested, be positive or negative according as the community as a whole expects

---

4 It might at first appear that an asset which is transferred from the deceased to his beneficiaries cancels out, as it does in the L_1 or L_2 measure. But although a transfer of wealth is clearly a distribution effect, it may be entered into the calculation of a potential Pareto improvement. And if transfers are generally omitted from such calculations it is simply because they take place between living persons: a transfer of $10,000 from person A to person B implies that the sum of their CVs is zero. On our criterion there is neither gain nor loss.

Where the issue is no longer a voluntary transfer of wealth, but the risk of an involuntary transfer through death, the case is different. If there is an increased risk of person B losing his life, the CV for that risk is negative; that is, there is some minimum amount of money which will restore his welfare. To person A, however, who cares nothing for B's person but who expects to inherit B's vast estate, the increased risk to which B is now exposed is a benefit for which he is willing to pay up to some maximum sum.

to be made financially better off, or worse of, by the death of others.[5]

(4) The other aspect of the concern to which, in general, each member is prone, in consequence of the additional physical risks to which others are exposed, is of a psychic nature. It is convenient, as well as charitable, to suppose that this concern entails a reduction in people's welfare. Thus the compensatory sum $\sum_{i}^{n} r_{ij}^4 \ (i \neq j)$ for the jth person's increased risk of bereavement carries a negative sign, being the sum of money necessary to reconcile him to bearing the additional risk of death to which his friends and members of his family are exposed. The increased risk of bereavement to which the community as a whole is exposed is to be valued at a sum equal to the aggregate $\sum_{j}^{n} \sum_{i}^{n} r_{ij} \ (i \neq j)$, which sum is abbreviated to R^4.

3. Simplicity of exposition has restricted the analysis to an increase only in the risk of death. The qualifications necessary for the treatment of an increase also in the risk of injury and death are too obvious to justify elaboration. Application of the above analysis to reduced risk of death, and to reduced risk of injury and disease, is perhaps slightly less obvious, and it may reassure the reader if its symmetrical nature is briefly illustrated by an example. Just as an increase in the number of accidents and fatalities can be a by-product of some growth in economic activity, so also can a reduction in the number of accidents and fatalities. More familiar, however, is public investment designed primarily to reduce the incidence of disease, suffering and death. And although such activity is to be regarded as a collective good, the relationship between collective

---

5 Only in an economy in which income was wholly from human capital would the R^3 component be comparable with the L_2 measure. A figure for the latter could be got by subtracting the net *losses* to the surviving members, arising from the death of breadwinners, from the net *gains* to the surviving members, arising from the death of dependents. As for R^3, the better the information, and the more constant the relation between income and utility along the relevant range, the closer the figure would be to the aggregate of the actuarial values of the net expected gain or loss to each person. It is the existence of non-human assets, and the possibility of their transfer from deceased to survivors, that adds to the positive value of R^3, and raises it above the L_2 measure.

goods and external effects (which can be thought of as incidental, 'nonoptional', collective goods and 'bads'), is close enough to permit us to make use of our conceptual apparatus without significant modification.

Suppose, then, that the government has a scheme for purifying the air over a vast region, one which is expected to save 20,000 lives annually.[6] The costs of enforcing a clean-air act, and of installing preventive devices wherever needed, has to be set against the above social benefits. In accordance with our scheme, they are to be evaluated as follows.

(1) Since, in this example, the reduced risk of death is a collective good, and not an external economy that is internal to some specific economic activity (as there could be, say, in a development that promoted horticulture, regarded as a healthy occupation), there is no R^1 term. There is here no question, that is, of how much a person will pay for some market good after making allowance for the *incidental* reduction of risk. The only good in question here is the collective reduction of risk itself.

(2) If the population of the area is 100 million, and the chance of dying from causes connected with air pollution is independent of age, location, occupation, physical condition, etc., the risk of death to each person in the region is reduced by 2/10,000. More generally, there is for the j th person a reduction of the risk of death from factors connected with air pollution (including infection by others suffering from air-pollution diseases) for which he is prepared to pay up to $\sum_{i}^{n} r_{ij}^2$, which, on our assumption of universal risk-aversion, is

---

6 Again, for simplicity of exposition we omit reference, in this example, to the reduction of suffering or enjoyment of better health.

positive. Aggregating over the n members, the total sum R^2 is, therefore, also positive.[7]

(3) A reduction in the risk of death for everyone implies, for the jth person, a reduction in the chance of his being financially worse off or better off in the future. The risk compensation $\sum\limits_i^n r_{ij}^3 \, (i \neq j)$ can therefore be positive or negative. The greater the proportion of aggregate income arising from non-human capital, the more likely is the total sum R^3 to be negative for the reduced risk.

(4) Finally, there is the reduced risk of the jth person's suffering bereavement over the future, the corresponding risk compensation $\sum\limits_i^n r_{ij}^4 \, (i \neq j)$ being positive. The total sum R^4 will, therefore, also be positive.

Evaluation of the benefits of the government scheme is, then, to be based, ultimately, on the aggregate of maximal sums that all persons in the region affected are willing to pay for the estimated

---

7 It is frequently alleged that at low levels, risk can have a positive utility. (In the absence of 'income effects' one can, for example, hypothesize a curve relating the person's CV to increasing risk of death. Such a curve would be above the horizontal,—probability—axis for low risk, and below it for all risk exceeding a critical level. As the probability of death falls towards unity, we should expect the curve to increase its rate of decline, and become asymptotic to a vertical axis passing through the unity point.)

But whether this is so, and the extent to which it is so, would seem to depend upon the activity associated with the risk. Driving at 100 miles per hour increases the risk of a fatal accident. And if some people choose gratuitously to drive at this speed, it is not simply in response to the additional risk *per se*. It is partly because a test of skill, physical courage, or manhood, is involved. Even where skill is absent, as in playing Russian roulette, there is a certain bravado in openly flirting with death. On the other hand it is hard to imagine a man deriving positive utility from the information that henceforth he is to be exposed—though anonymously, along with millions of others—to an increased risk of death, one over which he has no semblance of choice or control. The risk of increased infection by some new disease, or by increased radioactive fall-out, would be examples.

Nevertheless, the question of whether risk, at some levels, has a positive utility or a negative utility, in any particular case, is an empirical one, and does not affect the formal analysis.

171

reduction of the risks of death,[8] an aggregate which can usefully be split into three components, R^2, R^3, and R^4.

4. A word on the deficiencies in the information available to each person concerning the degree of risk involved. These deficiencies of information necessarily contribute to the discrepancies experienced by people between anticipated and realized satisfactions. For all that, in determining whether a potential Pareto improvement has been met, economists are generally agreed—either as a canon of faith, as a political tenet, or as an act of expediency—to accept the dictum that each person knows his own interest best. If, therefore, the economist is told that a person A is indifferent as between not assuming a particular risk and assuming it along with a sum of money, V, then, on the Pareto principle, the sum V has to be accepted as the relevant cost of his being exposed to that risk. It may well be the case that, owing either to deficient information, or congenital optimism, person A consistently overestimates his chances of survival. But once the dictum is accepted, as indeed it is in economists' appraisals of allocative efficiency, cost-benefit analysis has to accept V as the only relevant magnitude—this being the sum chosen by A in awareness of his relative ignorance.[9] Certainly all the rest of the economic data used in a cost-benefit analysis, or any other allocative study, whether derived from market prices and quantities, or by other methods of enquiry, is based on this principle of accepting as final only the individual's estimate of what a thing is worth to him at the time the decision is to be made. The thing in question may, of course, also have a direct worth, positive or negative, for persons other than the buyer or seller of it, a possibility which requires a

---

8 It has been put to me by a colleague that 'the benefits of increased safety from a project can be worth no more than the cost of preserving human life (or of a reduction in accidents) by alternative means'. This statement, however, confuses the measure of the benefits themselves with the measure of the expenditures necessary to produce such benefits. The economist must obviously consider 'alternative means' in order to produce any good at its lowest cost. But he cannot know whether incurring the lowest possible cost is justified until he has independently calculated a figure for the benefits in question, so enabling him to estimate the excess social benefit, or social loss, of preserving human life, etc.

9 Person A, for example, may find himself disabled for life and rue his decision to take the risk. But this example is only a more painful one of the fact that people come to regret a great many of the choices they make, notwithstanding which they would resent any interference with their future choices.

consideration of external effects. Yet, again, on the above dictum, it is the values placed on this thing by these other persons that are to count. Thus, while it is scarcely necessary to urge that more economical ways of refining and disseminating information be explored, the economist engaged in allocative studies traditionally follows the practice of evaluating all social gains and losses solely on the basis of individuals' own evaluations of the relevant effects on their welfare, given the information they have at the time the decision is taken.

5.   In sum, any expected loss of life, or saving of life, any expected increase or reduction in suffering, in consequence of economic activity, is to be evaluated for the economy by reference to the Pareto principle; in particular, by reference to what each member of the community is willing to pay, or to receive, for the estimated change of risk. The resulting aggregate of CVs for the community can be usefully regarded as being made up of four components, and, of these, R^1—where it exists—can be ignored on the grounds that the benefit to each individual of the direct activity in question (often estimated as equal to the area under the demand curve) is already net of this risk.

The other components, R^2, R^3, R^4, cannot, in general, be ignored, though one can surmise that with growing material prosperity their magnitude will grow. With the growth in the welfare state, and in particular with an increasingly egalitarian structure of real disposable incomes, the financial risk-compensation, R^3, will tend to decline. The gradual loosening of family ties and the decline of emotional interdependence should cause the magnitude of the bereavement risk-compensation R^4 to decline also. In a wholly impersonal society, in which, for any j^{th} person, the loss of any member of the community is easily replaceable in j's estimation by many others, R^4 will tend to vanish. R^2, however, is wholly selfish in the sense that it depends on people's preference for staying alive. Until such time as a genetical revolution turns men into pure altruists, or pure automatons, ready, like some species of ants, to sacrifice themselves at a moment's notice for the greater convenience of the whole, it can be expected that R^2 will grow over time.

Before concluding, however, it should be emphasized that the basic concept developed in this chapter is not simply an alternative or an auxiliary to, any existing methods[10] that have been proposed for measuring the loss, or saving, of life. It is the only economically justifiable concept. And this assertion does not rest on any novel ethical premise. It follows as a matter of consistency in the application of the Pareto principle in cost-benefit calculations.

In so far as an immediate application of the concepts to the measurement of loss or saving of life is in issue, one's claims must be more muted. In the attempts to measure social benefits and losses, price-quantity statistics lend themselves better to the more familiar examples in which people choose quantities at given market prices then they do to examples in which people have to choose prices for the given quantities. For one can observe the quantities they choose, at least collectively, whereas one cannot generally observe their subjective valuations. In the circumstances, economists seriously concerned to come to grips with the magnitudes may have to consider the possibility that data yielded by surveys based on the questionnaire method are better than doing nothing, or better than persisting with some of the current measures such as L_1 or L_2.

In view of the existing quantomania one may be forgiven for asserting that there is more to be said for rough estimates of the precise concept than precise estimates of economically irrelevant concepts. The caveat is more to be heeded in this case, bearing in mind that currently used, and currently mooted, measures of saving or loss of life, such as L_1, L_2, L_3 and L_4, have no conceptual affinity with the Pareto basis of cost-benefit analysis.

---

10 It is far from impossible that society may choose to refer decisions in matters involving life and death to a representative body or committee, and that a decision may be reached that differs from the one which would arise from the consistent application of cost-benefit techniques. Nevertheless, the economist is free to criticize the decision, to point up inconsistencies, and to discover what features, if any, warrant a departure from the Pareto criterion.

Consistency in this instance requires that the expected change in risk, associated with any contemplated scheme, be evaluated by reference to the same principle as all other relevant economic gains and losses. To evaluate the welfare effect of risk on some other principle, say by a voting procedure, entails the adding together of incommensurables: an implicit figure for the effect of risk on welfare attributable to a decision taken by a smaller group (or even by the whole group), by the method of counting heads, is added to a figure for the other economic effects which, using the Pareto principle, aggregates the valuation of each member determined on a CV basis.

Chapter 24

HORSE AND RABBIT STEW

1. As several conscientious economists have pointed out, the outcome of all too many cost-benefit studies follows that of the classic recipe for making horse and rabbit stew on a strictly fifty-fifty basis, one horse to one rabbit. No matter how carefully the scientific rabbit is chosen, the flavour of the resulting stew is sure to be swamped by the horseflesh. The horse, needless to say, represents those other considerations among which environmental spillover effects loom large. For all that, mention of environmental spillovers seldom takes up more space than a sentence or two in a footnote, or in the preamble to the expert's study which is, of course, the scientific rabbit, one having all the earmarks of professional competence.[1]

In our growth-fevered atmosphere there is always a strong temptation for the economist, as for other specialists, to come up with firm quantitative results. In order to be able to do so, however, he finds that he must ignore the less easily measured spillovers. In so far as the ignored spillover effects are adverse, this common response to the temptation imparts a bias toward favouring commercially viable projects, irrespective of their ability to withstand more searching criteria. As a matter of professional pride, and of obligation to the community he elects to serve, the economist should resist this temptation.

2. Yet, it may well be asked, until such time as more reliable methods are evolved to bring these spillovers into the calculus, what can the economist do? The least he can do is to reveal clearly the area of ignorance. After measuring all that can be measured with honesty, he can provide a physical description of the spillovers and some idea of their significance. Secondly, he may offer a guess, or a range of guesses, of the value of damage to be expected. He will

---

1 This was written in 1968, at a time when economists were becoming more concerned to capture these spillovers. Volume VII of the *Commission for the Third London Airport* (the cost-benefit analysis put out by the Roskill Commission) was appreciative of the environmental damage a third airport would cause. But their quantitive methods fell short of the principles they adopted.

certainly avoid spurious quantification—spurious because based on invalid concepts.[2] Thirdly, and as a development of the preceding suggestion, he can have recourse to what I have called elsewhere (1969a) *contingency calculations*, these being the estimates of a critical magnitude for the spillovers which will just offset the excess benefits of a project that is calculated in disregard of the spillovers.

2   Worse, perhaps, than the attempt to measure the social cost of loss of life and limb by the present value of forgone earnings (the L_1 measure criticized in the preceding chapter) is the attempt to measure noise or pollution costs by differences in property values.

The simple idea behind this method is that if the increase of spillovers over time is enough to cause people to want to move away from the areas worst hit, and if they cannot sell their properties in a competitive market without suffering a loss, such losses can be regarded as the present discounted value of losses of future income, or welfare, and regarded, therefore, as the costs of the spillover. If the spillover were aircraft noise, we should expect to find that the market value of houses nearer the airport, *ceteris paribus*, lower than houses farther away. All that is needed, apparently, is a multivariate analysis of residential property values within the region as a whole, from which to extract a positive relation between 'value of freehold property' and 'distance from source of aircraft noise'. From this relationship the economist, it is believed, can calculate the social cost of aircraft noise of varying volume.

It may be noted in passing that even if the method were valid, we not only ignore the costs of movement (which, like negotiation or transaction costs, can be a formidable barrier to revealing choices on the market), but we provide a CV measure under the existing law, whereas equity would prescribe the larger EV measure (which would be equal to a CV measure if legal liability were placed on the creators of spillover).

But these are not fundamental objections. What is fundamental is the argument that, for such a relationship to be useful in costing the aircraft noise, the noise-level of the quietest area in the region covered must remain unchanged. For it is quite possible, and under modern developments highly probable, that the level of noise will tend to rise in all areas. What is more, as the level of aircraft noise is everywhere increased the *differences* as between areas within the region may become—indeed, under modern developments, are likely to become—smaller than they originally were. The differences may even disappear completely, in which case the social cost of aircraft noise, calculated on this method, will be zero. And this, at a time when the whole region will be submerged beneath an intolerable volume of aircraft noise.

Nor, incidentally, can the economist regard with any satisfaction statistics purporting to show that over time, and in response to continued and increasing environmental disamenities, people become accustomed to them, and resent them the less. The resignation of populations to such disamenities may be accompanied by a deterioration in their health and good nature. The least the economist should do in the face of such evidence, is to say nothing at all, simply because 'tastes' have changed over the period. But, if the economist happens to be a civilized being, he will observe also that they have changed for the worse. A yet stronger objection to such spillovers than the fact that they cause innocent people to suffer is, surely, that they cause the victim population eventually to lose its sensitivity to environmental deterioration.

To illustrate, if the cost-benefit calculation of a new airport produces an excess benefit over cost of some $10 millions per annum for the next t years, but only by ignoring the aircraft noise it generates, the increased traffic congestion it causes, and the increased loss of life that is expected to follow, the economist can impress the authorities, and the public with the importance of these consequences by making hypothetical estimates of a critical *average* loss per person, or per family, based on rough calculations of the numbers of people likely to be affected. Thus (a), if it were reckoned that about half a million additional families would suffer in varying degrees as a result of the newly located airport, an annual compensatory sum averaging as little as $20 per family would wholly offset the excess benefit. Again (b), if the new airport becomes responsible for adding to the road congestion within the region of the airport, so as to cause an average delay of one hour a week to about one million motorists, this delay alone if valued at 20 cents an hour, would wholly offset the $10 million of excess benefits of the project. Similarly for loss of life, and any other remaining side effects.

Even though the estimate of the number of people affected is speculative, provided it is not altogether implausible, the resulting contingency calculations may well cast doubt as to the economic feasibility of the scheme—enough doubt, at least, to delay a decision until estimates of these less tangible, but socially important, features of the scheme can be made with greater assurance. On the other hand, there may be instances in which the per person, or per family, valuation of the spillover deriving from the contingency calculation will be so large as to place the economic feasibility of the scheme beyond doubt.

3. Finally, there is nothing to prevent the economist from using the questionnaire method to secure information that is not thrown up, directly or indirectly, by the pricing system. True, economists have tended to scorn this source of data, and their scorn may be forgiven wherever more dependable information is to be had by observing what a man does rather than hearkening to what he says of himself. In particular, where behavioural relations are at issue, as they are in 'positive economics', there is everything to be said for this conservative practice: if the evidence does not suffice, we can always

wait. But when it comes to evaluating spillover effects in a cost-benefit analysis, one cannot wait for more 'objective' information. Without some market mechanism by which people can express their attitudes to spillover effects, there can be no 'objective' way of measuring their costs. Indeed, the description of the nature of adverse environmental spillover effects, as unavoidable *collective* bads, itself suggests that the likelihood of a market mechanism being established for such effects is remote. Surveys based on the questionnaire method may be suspect for a number of reasons, but they are sometimes better than guesswork, and assuredly better than no information at all, The economist in earnest about making cost-benefit analysis a more discriminating technique will be giving plenty of thought to the measurement of environmental spillovers and, in consequence, plenty of thought also to the possibilities of evolving questionnaire techniques for eliciting critical information.[3]

---

3 No matter how fastidious the recommendation of the economist it cannot be depended upon to secure majority approval. The economic policies adopted by majorities will generally be less than ideal. Such losses arising from existing political mechanisms have not been treated in these chapters. The reader interested in such problems should find stimulating reading in Buchanan and Tullock's *Calculus of Consent*.

REFERENCES AND BIBLIOGRAPHY FOR PART III

Baumol, W. J. "External Economies and Second-Order Conditions," *American Economic Reveiw*, 1964.

Bohm, Peter. *External Economies in Production*. Stockholm: Almquist & Wiksells, 1964.

Buchanan, J. M. 'An Economic Theory of Clubs', *Economica*, 1965.

— and Stubblebine, W. C. 'Externality', *Economica*, 1962.

— and Tullock, G. *The Calculus of Consent*. Michigan: University of Michigan Press, 1962.

Burrows, P. 'Nuisance: The Law and Economics', *Lloyd's Bank Review*, 1970.

Coase, H. 'The Problems of Social Cost', *Journal of Law and Economics*, 1960.

Davis, O. A. and Whinston, A. B. 'Externality, Welfare and the Theory of Games', *Journal of Political Economy*, 1962.

—and Whinston, A. B. 'On the Distinction between Public and Private Goods', *American Economic Review*, 1967.

Devons, E. *Essays in Economics*. London: Allen & Unwin, 1961.

Dobb, M. *Welfare Economics and The Economics of Socialism*. Cambridge: Cambridge University Press, 1969.

Duesenberry, J. *Income, Saving and the Theory of Consumer Behaviour*. Cambridge, Mass.: Harvard University Press, 1949.

Eisner, R. and Strotz, R. H. 'Flight Insurance and the Theory of Choice', *Journal of Political Economy*, 1961.

Friedman, M. and Savage, L. J. 'Utility Analysis of Choices Involving Risks'. *Journal of Political Economy*, 1948.

Fromm, G. 'Civil Aviation Expenditures', in R. Dorfman (ed.), *Measuring Benefits of Government Investment*. Washington D.C.: Brookings Institution, 1965.

—. Comment on T. C. Schelling's paper, 'The Life You Save May Be Your Own', in S. B. Chase, Jr. (ed.), *Problems in Public Expenditure*. Washington D.C.: Brookings Institution, 1968.

Graaff, J. de V. *Theoretical Welfare Economics*, Cambridge: Cambridge University Press, 1957.

Kneese, A. V. 'Research Goals and Progress Toward Them', in H. Jarrett (ed.), *Environmental Quality in a Growing Economy*. Washington, D.C.: John Hopkins Press, 1966.

Marglin, S. 'The Social Rate of Discount and the Optimal Rate of Investment', *Quarterly Journal of Economics*, 1963.

Margolis, J. 'A Comment on the Pure Theory of Public Expenditure', *Review of Economics and Statistics*, 1955.

Marshall, A. *Principles of Economics* (8th *edn*.). London: Macmillan, 1924.

McKean, R. *Efficiency in Government Through Systems Analysis with Emphasis on Water Resource Development*. New York: John Wiley & Sons, 1958.

Meade, J. E. 'External Economies and Diseconomies in a Competitive Situation' *Economic Journal*, 1962.

Mishan, E. J. 'A Reappraisal of the Principles of Resource Allocation', *Economica*, 1957.

— 'Rent as a Measure of Welfare Change', *American Economic Review*, 1959.

— 'Reflections on Recent Developments in the Concept of External Effects', *Canadian Journal of Economics and Political Science*, 1965.

— 'Pareto Optimality and the Law', *Oxford Economic Papers*, 1967.

— *Welfare Economics: An Assessment*. Amsterdam: North Holland Publishing Company, 1969 (a).

— 'The Relationship between Joint Products, Collective Goods, and External Effects', *Journal of Political Economy*, 1969 (b).

Nath, S. K. *A Reappraisal of Welfare Economics*. London: Routledge & Kegan Paul, 1969.

Oort, C. J. *Decreasing Costs as a Problem of Welfare Economics*. Amsterdam, 1958.

Pigou, A. C. *Economics of Welfare* (4th edition). London: Macmillan, 1946.

Regan, D. Unpublished MS. 1970.

Reynolds, D. J. 'The Cost of Road Accidents', *Journal of the Royal Statistical Society*.

Ridker, R. G. *The Economic Costs of Air Pollution*. New York: F. A. Praeger, 1967.

Rothenberg, J. *The Measurement of Social Welfare*. New Jersey: Prentice Hall, 1961.

Samuelson, P. A. 'The Pure Theory of Public Expenditure', *Review of Economics and Statistics*, 1954.

— 'Aspects of Public Expenditure Theories', *Review of Economics and Statistics*, 1958.

179

Schelling, T. C. 'The Life You Save May Be Your Own', in S.B. Chase, Jr. (ed.) *Problems in Public Expenditure*. Washington, D.C.,: Brookings Institution, 1968.

Scitovsky, T. 'Two Concepts of External Economies', *Journal of Political Economy*, 1954.

Turvey, R. 'On Divergencies between Social Cost and Private Cost', *Economica*, 1963.

PART IV. INVESTMENT CRITERIA

Chapter 25
INTRODUCTION

1. The benefits flowing from any project, as also the costs incurred, have a time profile which poses a problem of evaluation. Given an expected time profile of costs and benefits, we can ask a first question: should we recommend that the investment in question be undertaken? This question could be thought of as a special case of the second and more general question: given a number of investment projects which one, or which several, should we recommend, if any, always supposing that the funds at our disposal are limited? We shall begin by considering the problems that arise in the attempt to answer the first question, after which we shall have little difficulty in coping with the problems posed by the second question.

2. Let us be clear about the nature of these costs and benefits. Investment in, say a railroad requires an initial outlay of capital spread over the first one or two years. These expenditures are clearly costs. So also are the anticipated outlays at future periods of time, whether for repairs, maintenance, or for adding equipment, though their magnitudes are usually smaller than the initial outlays. Benefits are understood in the most comprehensive sense to include all additions to social welfare that can, in Pigou's words, 'be brought into relation with the measuring rod of money'.

Benefits should therefore include not only expected receipts over time since the services produced may not in fact be sold to the public but provided free, or sold at a price below its cost (rail travel could, for instance, be made free). Even if the good produced is sold at a price that covers its cost the revenue collected is almost always less than the full amounts people would be willing to pay rather than go without. As indicated earlier, an estimate of the full benefit to the buyers of the good is roughly equal to the area under the market demand curve. Again there are positive and negative spillover effects to be evaluated and added, algebraically, to the benefits of the direct recipients of the goods purposely produced by the project. The very existence of the railroad is a form of insurance even to those who use other means of transport, a form of insurance for which they would presumably be willing to pay something. Such sums, the estimated value of indirect benefits, are to be added to the direct benefits. Thus, any compensatory sums called for by those people whose assets or whose welfare decline as a result of the noise or pollution, or any other disamenity associated with the railroad service, are to be subtracted from the benefits.

We remind ourselves in passing that if we correct the benefit calculation for all spillover effects in order to come up with a net figure for social *benefits*, we *cannot* also invoke the concept of social *costs*—else we should be entering some spillover effects *twice*, i.e. on the cost side as well as on the benefit side. Outlays therefore remain as the actual money disbursements; the sums spent on the project at any time during its life. All incidental effects on society that arise either in the building or in the operation of the project are to be added to, or subtracted from, the social benefits at the time they appear.

3. A distinction is sometimes made between 'capital costs' and 'operating costs', the former being the sums needed to build the project, the plant, machinery, and the like, the latter being the sums disbursed at regular intervals so as to maintain the flow of products or services. These operating costs can be met from a 'revolving fund', which can take the form of a line of credit from the bank to be drawn on in order to meet the weekly wage bill, repairs, salaries and payments for materials. The indebtedness to the bank is limited by continual repayments either from the sale of goods or from government revenues. It is possible then to ignore all these operating costs and include in the benefit-cost stream outlays only for capital expenditures and interest-payments to the banks. In that case one has to be careful to subtract from gross receipts all expenditures on wages, salaries, materials, etc., leaving only a stream of net benefits or, more narrowly, net revenues.

In principle, however, it is simpler to disregard the distinction between capital costs and operating costs and enter *all* payments as costs, in which case *all* receipts (or 'gross receipts'), taken together with a net figure for the algebraic sum of all other indirect gains and losses, are entered as benefits. By subtracting, in each period, all the costs from all the benefits, we end up with a succession of net benefits (some negative, some positive or zero) to which we can conveniently apply any adopted investment criterion.

The advantages of setting out, initially, the gross figures in full may be illustrated by a simple example. Suppose a capital outlay of 100 in year one is expected to be followed by an outlay on labour and materials of 130 in year two, and by sales of the resultant output, valued at 150, in the third year. The series generated would then begin −100, −130, 150, If, however, one were to use the revolving fund concept, and omit setting down payments for labour and materials, the series might look like—100, 0, 14, the last figure being reached by subtracting from the sales of 150 both the value of labour and material inputs of 130 and also the interest payments of 6 on borrowing 130 for about a year. This figure of 14 clearly depends on the rate of interest at which the bank lends. For private businesses that seek to maximize profit the rate at which they expect to be able to borrow will indeed feature as no more than an unavoidable expense. But for public investment, the criterion to be used calls either for a special rate of discount, which in general differs from the actual borrowing rate, or else for a calculation of the internal rate of return, which is a product of the stream of net benefits *in the absence of* any discounting or compounding.[1]

For this reason it is advisable to set out in the first instance the gross figures as they appear period by period. Having decided the length of the period, we can subtract all outlays from all benefits only for the period within which they both occur. If, for example, we have the following stream of benefits and outlays:

Benefits	0	0	150	160	.	.
Outlays	100	130	135	0	.	.

1   It might be thought that if we are given the rate of discount to be adopted, we could charge interest on money borrowed (for labour and material payments) at that rate throughout the lifetime of the project. But this procedure would be valid only if all the opportunities for reinvesting future returns were those yielding a rate equal to that rate of discount, which in general is too restrictive an assumption.

it can be written as (0–100), (0–130), (150–135), (160–0), . ., or, taking the algebraic sum in each of the brackets as equal to the net benefits, −100, −130, 15, 160, . .

In general, that is, we can summarize the stream of expected data as $(b_1 - c_1)$, $(b_2 - c_2)$, . . ., $(b_n - c_n)$, where b_1 is the gross benefit in the first period and c_1 the gross outlay, and so on, the subscript referring always to the period.[2] If we define net benefit in any tth period, B_t, as $(b_t - c_t)$, we can write the above as a stream of net benefits, B_1, B_2, . . ., B_n, where the Bs can, of course, be either negative, zero, or positive.

4. The choice of the size of the discrete periods into which a given length of time is to be divided is arbitrary. The year is customarily chosen for obvious reasons and, unless otherwise stated, we shall abide by the custom in the following chapters. For a comparison of very short investment streams, the breakdown into six-monthly, quarterly, or even monthly periods may be desirable.[3] There may not appear to be much to choose from as between two investment streams each running to three years. Broken into quarterly periods— and using quarterly rates of return and discount—one may be easily superior to the other.

It is perhaps unnecessary to remark that, since we are concerned with *social* benefits and not business profits net of tax,[4] our task is simplified somewhat. Neither corporation tax, income tax, nor excise tax for that matter is to be subtracted in the estimate of social benefits. Whether or not the government collects such taxes from the public enterprise in question, the value of such taxes is part of the social benefit.

---

2 Sometimes it is more convenient to begin with period 0 rather than period 1, as we shall see later.

3 Indeed, for theoretical purposes at least, there is a mathematical convenience in postulating a *continuous* time-profile of net benefits.

4 Given an annual progressive income tax, a business concern does not equate, or prefer, a stream 30, −10, 10 to a stream 10, 10, 10. The former will pay more tax over the three-year period. After tax, for example, the former stream might be 20, −10, 8, and the latter 8, 8, 8. Unless the discount rate was very high, the latter would be preferred.

Chapter 26
CRUDE INVESTMENT CRITERIA

1. Suppose we are faced with a choice of four investment options having the net benefits shown in Table IV·1 below. Which do we choose, if our budget is limited to 100?

TABLE IV.1

	1	2	3	4	5
A_1	−100	115	0	0	0
A_2	−100	20	30	50	170
A_3	−100	100	110	−50	0
A_4	−100	80	110	−50	−10

If we had to choose *only one* from the four, we could be sure that it would never be A_4, irrespective of the criterion used. For A_3 is as good as, or better than, A_4 period for period. In the jargon, investment option A_3 'dominates' A_4. Thus, if we subtract A_4's net benefit stream from that of A_3 the difference is a series, 0, 20, 10, 0, 10, these figures showing the amounts by which A_3's net benefits exceed those of A_4 in successive periods. In no period is A_3's net benefit less than that of A_4.[1]

Let us now consider three rather crude investment criteria, which however are commonly employed in the business sector, especially where the venture contemplated is risky.

2. *Cut-off period.* This is perhaps the crudest possible criterion that is used in business in order to decide whether or not to invest in a project. A period is chosen over which the money invested must be fully recouped. The period could be ten years, though usually a shorter period such as five years, or even less, is chosen. Such a criterion

---

1   If, on the other hand, we had funds enabling us to choose two or more of these investment options, we might choose both A_3 and A_4. But we should never include A_4 while rejecting A_3.

may be justified in cases of innovation in products, or methods, that cannot be protected by patent, and which innovations are likely to be copied by competing firms within two or three years. A cut-off period of three years, for instance, may be chosen in the belief that after three years further profits are uncertain, and increasingly unlikely. Glancing down the Table, it is clear that a cut-off period of three years *after* the initial outlay would admit the A_1 investment option. Indeed, more than the initial 100 is recouped in the first year after the outlay. The A_2 option only just scrapes home. A_3 would be able to recoup as much as 160 in the three years, while A_4 would recoup 130 (which, however, would be 120 if the outlay of 10 in the 4th year were certain).

The shortcomings of this criterion are easy to perceive. If the returns were not expected to accrue mainly in the first few years but mainly after the first few years, worthwhile projects would be rejected. A stream $-100, 0, 0, 20, 40, 60, 80, 120, . .$ would be rejected. So also would a stream $-100, 20, 20, 20, 20, 20, 20, . .$

3. *Pay-off period.* Instead of choosing an arbitrary cut-off period, we may rank the investment options according to the number of years necessary to recoup the initial outlay. Clearly the A_1 project would be ranked first, since its pay-off period is less than a year. For the A_2 project it is exactly three years. For the last two investment projects it is two years—even after subtracting the later outlays.

The so-called *pay-off period rate of return* is but another way of expressing the same results. It is obtained simply by dividing 100 by the number of years in the pay-off period. If the A_1 investment option requires only a year to pay off the initial outlay, it is equal to 100 per cent (actually it is a bit more than 100 per cent as the outlay of 100 is paid off in less than a year). For the A_2 project, the pay-off-period rate of return is equal to 100 divided by 3, or $33\frac{1}{3}$ per cent. For the other two investment options it is about 50 per cent.

The justification for either form of this ranking device is similar to that for the cut-off period. When imitation by competitiors, or rapid obsolescence is anticipated, or in circumstances of political uncertainty, one of the over-riding considerations is safety. One looks for quick returns and prepares for a hasty exit. A project such as A_1, which pays 115 within a year of 100 being invested is likely, in such circumstances, to be looked on with greater favour than option A_2 which would not show any profit until the fourth year.

In the complete absence of uncertainty, however, it would be impossible to justify either of the above rules-of-thumb. If interest rates happened to be low A_2 would be far more profitable than A_1, and more profitable than A_3 for that matter.

4. *The average rate of return* is the simplest way of taking account of all the figures in the investment stream. Just because all the figures are taken at face value in calculating the average rate of return, there is an implied assumption that all the figures have been corrected for uncertainty.

For all investment options having only the initial outlay of 100, such as A_1 and A_2 in Table IV.1, there is no ambiguity in the method. One simply adds together all the subsequent positive net benefits, divides this sum by the number of years, and expresses the resulting figure as a percentage of the initial investment outlay. For the A_1 option, the sum of positive benefits is 115. This sum divided by one gives an average sum of 115 per annum, and expressed as percentage of the outlay of 100, is 115 per cent. For A_2 the sum over four years of the positive benefits is 270. This sum divided by 4 gives an annual average return of $67\frac{1}{2}$ and, expressed as a percentage of the original outlay of 100, is $67\frac{1}{2}$ per cent.

The weakness of this method is apparent at once. For it is by no means evident to any one thinking of investing 100 that A_1, with an average rate of return of 115 per cent, is superior to A_2. It might be added in passing, however, that the weakness is not particular to this method, but arises also in the more sophisticated internal-rate-of-return method which will be treated later.

For investment options A_3 and A_4, having outlays in later years, the method has not been specified. On the one hand, we could add together all the figures, both positive and negative, after the initial outlay and proceed as before. For A_3 the algebraic sum of 100, 110, and -50, is 160. This sum divided by 3 yields an average of $53\frac{1}{3}$ per cent per annum. Similarly for A_4 which yields an average return of $32\frac{1}{2}$ per cent. Alternatively, we could total the outlays first, work out the average amount of the remaining positive figures (210 for A_3, 190 for A_4), and divide by the number of years yielding a positive investment. This sum is then taken as a percentage of the sum of the outlays (150 for A_3, 160 for A_4). Using this method the average yield for A_3 is 70 per cent, and for A_2 is 56 per cent.

5. *Net average rate of return.* The above results can be regarded as 'gross' average yields since they are derived from adding together only the positive net benefit figures. One obvious modification is to calculate a 'net' average yield in the same way except that the outlays are subtracted from the sum of the benefits before dividing by the number of years. In A_1, for example, we should first subtract the outlay of 100 from the 115, to give 15, this being 15 per cent of the 100 outlay. In A_2 we subtract the outlay of 100 from the positive sum of benefits, 270, before dividing by 4. Hence a net average rate of return of $42\frac{1}{2}$ per cent. The comparison between A_1 and A_2 looks a lot more plausible on this 'net' average method than on the 'gross' average method above. Again, we can treat A_3 and A_4 in the two alternative ways indicated above. The first way gives 20 per cent for A_3 and 15 per cent for A_4. The second gives 20 per cent for A_3 and 9 per cent for A_4.

Under conditions of certainty at least, the net average rate of return, though clearly superior to the other investment rules, is unsatisfactory for two reasons.

(1) It depends upon the number of years chosen. To choose the length of the investment stream by reference to the number of consecutive years showing a positive net benefit is arbitrary. For example if project A_1 in Table IV.1 yielded the slightest positive net benefit in year two—say, a return of 0·1—the average rate of return would result from dividing the total benefits, $115 + 0·1$, *less* the initial outlay of 100, by 2 instead of one, giving 7·51, which on this method has to be accepted as the net average rate of return per annum on the 100 investment. This slight addition to the net benefit of the A_1 investment option makes it look, on this calculation, a very much less attractive proposition, a paradoxical result which could obviously cause a lot of trouble.

(2) A less apparent but no less serious defect is that the method takes no cognizance of the *pattern* or *profile* of the net benefits over time. Given the total amount of the net benefits, say 300, arising over a number of consecutive years, whether the net benefits are bunched together over the first years, spread evenly over the years, or bunched toward the end of the period, makes not the slightest difference to the net average rate of return. An investment stream of $-100, 5, 20, 25,$

250 is to be valued as highly as one of −100, 250, 25, 20, 5; or, for that matter, we should on this calculation be indifferent as between an investment option having the stream −100, 1, 1, 1, 297, and one having the stream −100, 297, 1, 1, 1. But which person would not prefer the latter to the former? For people do take notice of the timing of benefits. They are not, that is, perfectly indifferent as between receiving $10,000 in ten years time and receiving $10,000 today. Once we take into account the time dimension, we are impelled to move away from these rather primitive investment criteria to those more familiar to economists.

6.   These more sophisticated investment criteria are all based on the common procedure of reducing a stream of net benefits (some negative, some positive) to a single value at a point of time. This is done by using some rate of interest as a weighting device through time. The more familiar fall into two categories: (1) those which determine the *value* of an investment stream at an arbitrary point of time by reference to a given rate of interest—the more popular procedure being that of determining a *present* value of the investment stream; (2) those which determine an average *rate of return* by reference to the condition that the value be reduced to zero at the initial point of time. The more popular criterion in this connection is that known as the internal rate of return.

These two popular investment criteria, the present discounted value criterion and the internal rate of return criterion, will be compared in the following two chapters.

Chapter 27

THE PRESENT DISCOUNTED VALUE CRITERION

1. If we have an investment stream such as −100, 50, 150, and we are given a rate of interest (or discount rate) of 10 per cent per annum, the present discounted value of the stream of benefits alone —50 after the first year, 150 after the second year—is given by the calculation

$$\frac{50}{(1 + 0 \cdot 1)} + \frac{150}{(1 + 0 \cdot 1)^2} = 166 \cdot 5.$$

The present value of the outlay of 100 is also 100, since the 100 is, in these examples, supposed to be incurred right at the beginning, at year zero; that is, at the *beginning* of the first year or, for the sake of conformity, at the end of the zero[th] year. It is incurred just at the point of time to which we are reducing all subsequent net benefits or net outlays, and therefore does not require discounting to that point of time.

The *Net* Present Discounted Value of the investment stream above, being the present value of the benefits less the present value of the costs, is 166·5 − 100, or 66·5. If we wish to regard outlays as negative net benefits, the net present discounted value of an investment stream is simply the sum of all the net benefits when discounted to their present value.

In more general terms, given a stream of net benefits, $B_0, B_1, B_2, \ldots, B_n$, where the Bs are positive, zero, or negative, the net present discounted value is given by

$$B_0 + \frac{B_1}{(1 + r)} + \frac{B_2}{(1 + r)^2} + \ldots + \frac{B_n}{(1 + r)^n},$$

or, more briefly,

$$\sum_{t=0}^{t=n} \frac{B_t}{(1 + r)^t},$$

where r is the rate of discount.

The necessary instrument in this criterion is the appropriate rate of interest or rate of discount by which the net benefit at any point of time is weighted. It is commonly assumed that the correct rate of interest is that which reflects society's rate of time preference. (If, for example, society is taken to be indifferent between having $100 million today and $106 million next year, the *social* rate of time preference is 6 per cent per annum.) We shall, for the present, go along with this assumption though later on it will be argued that it is correct only under special conditions. In a Crusoe economy, if 120 bushels of corn next year are deemed by Crusoe to be equivalent in satisfaction to 100 bushels of corn today—by which is meant that he is perfectly indifferent to having an extra 100 bushels of corn today and 120 bushels of corn in a year's time—Crusoe's rate of discount is 20 per cent per annum. Until Man Friday arrives, and has some say in the decision, Crusoe's individual rate of discount can also be thought of as the social rate of discount.

2. To be more accurate, however, Crusoe's reaction to the choice presented to him gives us no more than the social rate of discount for the one year and, for that matter, is strictly valid only for 100 bushels of corn this year, not for more or for less. If, indeed, the same rate of discount did hold for successive years, then Crusoe would be indifferent as between 100 today, 120 next year, 144 in the year following that, and so on. It is however, quite possible that his discount rate rises with the passage of time. Instead of being indifferent as between 100 today and 144 in two years time, he might specify 150 in two years time. This would mean that for the first year his rate of discount is 20 per cent, but for the second year he uses a discount rate of roughly 25 per cent per annum.

Again, even if we confine ourselves to the one year, it is not true that the same rate of discount holds for *any* amount of corn. If Crusoe agrees, though only just, to postpone consumption of 100 bushels of corn this year in order to have an additional 120 bushels next year, it does not follow that he will be prepared to forgo another 100 bushels of corn this year in exchange for another additional 120 bushels next year. It is more plausible to suppose that he should want more than an additional 120 bushels next year to persuade him to forgo this year the consumption of yet another 100 bushels; say an additional 140 bushels next year. We could say that Crusoe's marginal willingness to sacrifice 100 today for 120 next year reflects a discount rate of 20 per cent per annum, while his marginal willingness to sacrifice 200 today for 260 tomorrow reflects a discount rate of 30 per cent over-all. Put otherwise, we could say that for the first 100 bushels the marginal discount rate was 20 per cent, and that the marginal discount rate for another 100 bushels was 40 per cent.

These possibilities are to be noted before passing on. For it is also the case in society at large that, however the social rate of discount is determined, it is invariant neither with respect to the magnitude of the intertemporal exchange of goods nor to the length of time involved. If we have information about the variation of the rate of discount with respect either to magnitude or time, however, there is no difficulty, in principle, in adapting our chosen investment criterion accordingly. In the meantime, our task will be simplified by assuming but a single social rate of discount. Moreover, since we are to examine this concept in Chapter 29, we shall also assume that this social rate of discount is known to us. If the reader prefers, he can suppose, provisionally, that it has arisen from the interplay of market forces plus, perhaps, some form of government intervention that has the object of ensuring that the resulting rate of interest in the economy correctly reveals society's preference as between present and future goods, If, for instance, the social rate of discount is 10 per cent per annum, we shall take it that society as a whole is indifferent as between 100 today, 110 in a year's time, 121 in two years' time, and so on. And that, therefore, the present value of 110 in one year's time, or 121 in two years' time, is exactly 100.

3.   Having made these provisional simplifications, let us go on to consider the following three propositions, all of them commonplace in the literature on the subject.

1.   The Net Present Value[1]—or Excess of Present Value over Cost—of a particular investment stream depends upon the rate of discount used. If, for instance, the stream of net benefits is —100, 0, 150, the net present value of the stream would be a little less than 48 if the discount rate were one per cent. If, instead, the discount rate were 50 per cent, the net present value would be —33⅓.

---

1   The term 'Net Present Value' will be used occasionally as an abbreviation of 'Net Present *Discounted* Value'.

2. Which of a number of investment streams yields the largest net discounted present value depends, in general, on the rate of discount used. If the two investment streams are, respectively, −50, 20, 80, and −60, 20 70, then the first, being dominant, will have a larger net present value irrespective of the rate of discount employed. If, instead, the two streams are, respectively, −100, 0, 180 and −100, 165, 0, a discount rate of one per cent ranks the first, with a net present value of about 76, above the second, which has a net present value of about 63. If, however, the rate of discount is 50 per cent, the net present value of the first stream is −20 and is, therefore, ranked *below* the second stream, which has a net present value of 10. From these two examples it should be manifest that there is a particular social rate of discount—between 1 per cent and 50 per cent—for which the two streams have exactly the same present value. Let us call this social rate of discount r^*. Then r^* is easily determined by equating the net present value formulae for the two streams, i.e. we set

$$- 100 + \frac{180}{(1 + r)^2} = - 100 + \frac{165}{(1 + r)} \cdot$$

and solve for r^*, which turns out to be about 9 per cent.

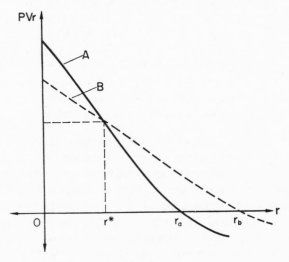

Figure IV.1

In general we can determine a net present value of a particular investment stream, say A, for each conceivable rate of discount. The resulting relationship can be plotted in Figure, IV.1 where the vertical axis measures PV_r, or net present value of the investment stream in question, and the horizontal axis measures r, the social rate of discount. The net present value of the A stream becomes smaller the larger is the rate of discount r; hence the negative slope of the A curve. It will be noted that the negative slope crosses the horizontal axis and continues below it into the south-east quadrant. This indicates that at discount rates above some critical rate of discount the net present value of the stream becomes negative (for example, at a 50 per cent discount rate, the stream $-100, 0, 180$, has a net present value of -20). A similar relationship can be plotted for a different investment stream B.

If one of these two investment streams were dominant, it would lie above the other at all rates of discount. In the absence of dominance the A and B curves will intersect, either in the positive quadrant, as in the Figure, or else in the negative quadrant (not shown). For all conceivable (positive) discount rates—save one, r^*—the present value of the two streams differ. At discount rates below r^* the A stream has a higher net present value than the B stream, the reverse being true for discount rates above r^*. Only at r^* do both streams have the same net present value. It is obvious that if the rate of discount, from being a little above r^*, fell to a figure below r^*, the net present value of the A stream would change from being less than that of the B stream to being greater than it.

It may be observed finally, that there is a discount rate corresponding to each investment stream, r_a and r_b respectively, for which the net present value of the A and B streams are both zero.

4. 3. As a corollary of the preceding proposition, it is simple to show that given the growth-path of an asset, the optimal 'gestation period'—that period giving the maximum net present value—is also determined by the rate of discount. Such a growth path is represented in Figure IV.2, time, in years, being measured along the horizontal axis. Total real value at any point of time is measured vertically and, therefore, at time zero total present value is measured. Common examples of growth curves are those of the growth in value of timber and wine. If a tree is planted, the value of the tree increases

proportionally with the growth of the tree (assuming the price of timber constant). As for a bottle or barrel of wine, its value increases with time because of the improvement in its flavour. Let us consider the timber example.

A continuous growth path is given by G_0 G in Figure IV.2. Initially, that is, at time zero, the value of the timber is OG, a negative magnitude, this being the cost of the sapling and the labour required to plant it. The net value of the timber at any point of time is given by the vertical distance from the horizontal axis, at the point of time in question, to the G_0 G curve. Thus at the point the growth curve cuts the horizontal axis—which in our Figure happens to be the end of the second year—the net value of the timber is zero, the initial cost OG_0 being offset by the increase in the volume of timber when valued at the end of the first two years.

In order to appreciate better the connection between this growth curve and the preceding Figure IV.1, along with its examples, we could split the time axis into discrete units of a year, and measure vertically the total volume, and value, of timber at the end of each year. Instead of a continuous growth path we should then have a succession of vertical lines increasing in height up to point M. The heights of these vertical lines should then be regarded as the value of *alternative* investment streams. For instance, the vertical line above 4 on the horizontal axis could measure exactly 100. If OG_0 measured an initial cost of 50, the investment option corresponding to $t = 4$ would be 50, 0, 0, 0, 100. The investment option corresponding to $t = 5$ could be 50, 0, 0, 0, 0, 112. The investment option corresponding to $t = 6$ could be 50, 0, 0, 0, 0, 0, 120, and so on for $t = 7, 8, 9, \ldots, n$. Which of all the investment options would we choose? Bearing in mind the preceding proposition, we need have no hesitation in affirming that, in general, it will depend upon the social rate of discount.

If, then, we are given the social discount rate r, we can construct any number of *discount curves*, each different from the other by an increment of present value. Suppose the social discount rate is 5 per cent, one such discount curve V_1 V_1 would measure, say, 80 along the vertical axis. At a point above $t = 1$ the height would be 84, at $t = 2$ the height would be 88·2, and so on, the height at the end of each successive year being 5 per cent more than that of the preceding year. Society is deemed indifferent to being anywhere along such a curve, any increase in time being exactly compensated by an increase in value. V_2V_2 can be drawn measuring, say, 90, along the vertical axis; V_3V_3 measuring, say, 100, and so on. Conceptually, these VV curves are infinitely dense, and we should select the highest among them that touches the growth curve. In the Figure, V_2V_2 is represented as the highest VV curve, touching the growth curve at Q, a point that corresponds to $t = 6\cdot2$. We should conclude that the maximum *present* value of the net benefits at a 5 per cent discount rate is given by the height OV_2. The gestation period is $6\cdot2$ years, and *net* present value is OV_2 minus OG_0. It will be correctly surmized by the reader that the point Q is one of tangency between the discount curve and the growth curve. If there is any doubt about it, this property can be inferred by approaching the gestation period by a slightly different route.

The growth path G_0G, when looked at as a succession of vertical lines, or alternative investment options, is so shaped as to place these

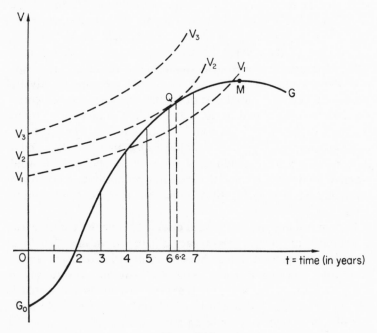

Figure IV.2

alternative investment options, eventually,[2] in order of increasing value. We need then only consider the increment by which the value of each investment option exceeds the one preceding it by a year, and compare the resulting increment in value with the given discount rate. There is always a social gain to be obtained provided the increment of value by waiting a year exceeds the social rate of interest. Postponing the cutting down of the tree from the fourth year to the fifth year will result in an increase in value from 100 to 112. Since society is indifferent as between 100 in the fourth year and 105 in the fifth year, there is a social gain of 7 (in the fifth year) from postponing the cutting down of the tree by a year. If we postpone the cutting for another year, the value of the timber rises by a further 8, to 120 altogether. But society is indifferent as between 112 in the fifth year and 105 per cent of 112, or about 118, in the sixth year, so there is a further social gain of 2 (in the sixth year) by postponing the cutting to the sixth year. Postponing the cutting to the seventh year would increase the value of the wood to 125. Society, however, would require a minimum of 126 in year seven to induce it to give up 120 in year six. If therefore it did postpone the cutting until the seventh year, a social *loss* of one (in the seventh year) would be incurred. We conclude that the tree should be cut down some time between the sixth and the seventh year.

Once we return to the assumption of a *continuous* growth curve, however, the successive periods of time can be made as small as we like. In the limit, the increment of growth and the necessary time premium are equalized at a point of time. Visually, there is a mutual tangency at this point of time between the growth curve and one of the 5 per cent discount curves.

---

2   Initially, the annual rate of growth increases, but while it does this there is no sense in stopping the process. Only when the rate of growth begins to decline does the time arrive for comparing the increment of value with premium required to induce society to wait for this increment of value.

197

Chapter 28

THE INTERNAL RATE OF RETURN

1. The internal rate of return is a more respectable form of the average rate of return mentioned in Chapter 26 in that, like the present discounted value method, it takes account of time.

A simple example will illustrate how the internal rate of return is calculated. If we have a stream of net benefits, $-100, 50, 86\cdot4$, we can discount each of these net benefits to the present, $t = 0$, using a discount rate of 20 per cent. The present value of the net benefit of 50 in year one, when discounted at 20 per cent, is $50/(1 + 0\cdot2)$. or 40, while the present value of $86\cdot4$ in year 2, when discounted at 20 per cent, is $86\cdot4/(1 + 0\cdot2)^2$, or 60. The present value of both 50 in year one and $86\cdot4$ in year two is, therefore, $40 + 60$, or 100; which is exactly equal to the initial *negative* net benefit, or net outlay, of 100. This 20 per cent discount, just because it equates the present value of the positive net benefits to the present value of the net outlay, is taken to be the internal rate of return of the above stream of net benefits.

We can, for the present, simplify the terminology a little by referring to *positive* net benefits simply as *benefits*, and by referring to *negative* net benefits simply as *costs* or *outlays*. The internal rate of return is, then, the rate of discount which makes the present value of the benefits exactly equal to the present value of the costs. Put otherwise, the internal rate of return is that rate of discount which makes the present value of the entire stream—benefits and costs—exactly equal to zero. Thus, if we have an investment stream,

$$B_0, B_1, B_2, \ldots, B_n, (B_i \geqslant 0, \text{ for } i = 0, 1, 2, \ldots, n),$$

then the internal rate of return λ, is that for which the sum

$$\frac{B_0}{(1 + \lambda)^0} + \frac{B_1}{(1 + \lambda)^1} + \frac{B_2}{(1 + \lambda)^2} + \cdots + \frac{B_n}{(1 + \lambda)^n} = 0,$$

or, more briefly , that for which

198

$$\sum_{t=0}^{n} \frac{B_t}{(1 + \lambda)^t} = 0.$$

The sense in which the internal rate of return, so defined, is an average over time is conveyed by the example of a man investing, say, 100 for five years. If the internal rate of return were 25 per cent per annum, the man would have in mind an equivalent, though simpler, investment in which his 100 in the present grows by 25 per cent each year. He sees his 100 in the present becoming 125 by the end of the first year, $156\frac{1}{4}$ by the end of the second year, and so on, to reach $100(1 + 0.25)^5$ by the end of the fifth year. More generally, if the investment stream in question were -100, B_1, B_2, B_3, B_4, B_5, where the Bs are any pattern of benefits, and the internal rate of return were known to be 25 per cent, then an *equivalent* investment stream would be -100, 0, 0, 0, 0, 100 $[(1 + 0.25)^5]$. For this given investment stream, when discounted to its present value at 25 per cent, is, by assumption, equal to zero, and so also is the equivalent stream. Consequently, if a man is told that the internal rate of an investment stream over n years is equal to λ, he is justified in thinking of the investment as equivalent to one in which his initial outlay is compounded forward at the rate of λ per annum for n years.

Thinking of the internal rate of return in this way, the man will want to compare any such investment with the opportunities for putting his money into other securities, either equities or government bonds. If the only alternative open to him, or the only alternative he will consider, is long-term government bonds, perpetuities say, yielding 6 per cent per annum,[1] then an investment yielding a rate of return of more than 6 per cent (always assuming certainty or, at least, equal certainty) will be preferred to the purchase of these 6 per cent government bonds.

2.   Let us now return briefly to the growth curve of the preceding chapter, depicted here in Figure IV.3 The reader will recall that

---

1   In the modern economy there is, of course, a wide diversity of government bonds even if we restrict outselves to long-term issues. We simplify the treatment, for the time being, by assuming there is only one type of long term government bond, say 'perpetuities'—that is, interest-bearing bonds having no redemption date, such as British Consols.

using the tangency condition between the growth curve, G_0G, and the highest 5 per cent discount curve at Q determined the optimal gestation, or investment, period. We have here followed the convention of drawing the discount curve as straight lines by measuring the *logarithms* of the values along the vertical axis—thus successive x per cent differences appear along it as equal distances.

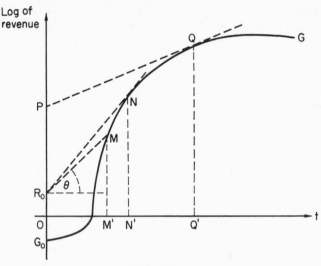

Figure IV.3

If the highest present value, OP, at the given social rate of discount (which we continue to suppose is 5 per cent), determines the optimal investment period OQ', do we obtain the same result using, instead, the internal rate of return criterion? But first, how do we represent the internal rate of return on this diagram? If we choose OR_0 to be equal—in *absolute* value—to OG_0, then the slope of a straight line from R_0 to any point of the growth curve, say M may be taken to represent the internal rate of return. For the slope is determined by $\tan.\Theta$, which is equal to the total compounded benefit $M'M$ less OR_0 $(= OG_0)$, divided by OM'. The discount rate given by $\tan.\Theta$ must be the internal rate of return simply because, as required, it reduces the future benefit $M'M$ to a present value of OR_0 which is equal to the initial cost OG_0. The highest internal rate of return possible is determined by the slope of the straight line from R_0 that just touches the growth curve at N, there being no straight line from R_0 steeper than R_0N that touches the growth curve.

If the optimal investment period is defined as that yielding the highest internal rate of return, it will be ON', which is clearly shorter than OQ', the optimal period on the present value criterion. So which is it to be? Do we let the tree grow for a period OQ' or do we cut it down after ON' years? This is not the only sort of problem in which the results obtained by using these two investment criteria differ. We shall defer the resolution of this apparent discrepancy, then, until we have illustrated similar discrepancies in other investment problems.[2]

---

2 A hint may be allowed the impatient reader, however. If, after time ON', the proceeds NN' could be reinvested in an identical tree-growing project, there would be a loss by letting the tree continue to grow to $Q'Q$. What is at issue, then, are the reinvestment possibilities whenever the tree is cut down. This reinvestment aspect of the problem is treated in some detail in Chapters 34–36.

Chapter 29

INVESTMENT CRITERIA IN AN IDEAL
MARKET ECONOMY

1. Investment criteria, whether based on present discounted value
or internal rate of return, are devised so as to enable us to choose
between alternative uses of investible funds. If there are two or more
alternative investment options each has to be compared with the
others.[1] If there is only one investment project under consideration,
the alternative would be either to use the funds for private expenditures, or for buying government securities. The latter course of action
may be thought of as a financial transaction that does not of itself
result in any new investment. Initially it is but a purchase of government bonds on the open market: a transfer of funds from the indi-
dual to the government. For society as a whole, however, and certainly for public investment, we must transcend all financial transactions and, in the last resort, consider at least two alternatives:
either consumption or else investment in this particular project.
If there is only one rate of interest on the market, which we are
assuming to be the case for the present, it will be generally used as
the relevant rate of discount in the present value criterion, provided
that this market rate reflects society's rate of time preference. A rate
of interest of 5 per cent that reflects society's time preference implies
that society is indifferent as between $1 today and $1.05 in a year's
time. If therefore one removes $1 worth of consumption today and
returns $1.06 worth of goods next year, society is deemed to gain
by the transaction. If, instead, one returns $1·04 in a year's time,

---

1 It is just possible that the reader may be wondering why we have continuously
ignored mention of depreciation in the treatment of investment criteria. The
short answer is that the principles which guide the rate of *amortization* are unrelated to those that arise in *selecting investments*. There is nothing mysterious
about this. All investment criteria, whether based on present discounted value or
internal rate of return, implicitly make allowance for the maintenance of capital
through the requirement that the outlays on the investment project be (more
than) covered by the present discounted value of its expected future benefits.

society is deemed to be worse off from having postponed consumption. Consequently if a particular investment yields more than 5 per cent in a year's time, society is deemed better off from switching resources from the production of consumption goods to this particular investment good, and vice versa.

In circumstances where the only two alternatives open to the use of present resources are either investment to day in a specific project or else consumption today, the investment project will be chosen if its internal rate of return exceeds the 5 per cent social rate of time preference. As for the net present discounted value of this investment project, it is sure to be positive (since, by definition of the internal rate of return, the net present value of this investment stream is zero when discounted by a rate *higher* than 5 per cent), and is therefore admissible also on the present value criterion. A positive net present value, given the rate of discount equal to the social rate of time preference, indicates that the present value equivalence of the future benefit stream—as valued by society at its own rate of time preference—exceeds the present value produced by the same resources if, instead, they are used to produce consumption goods. Society is therefore better off by investing these resources and consuming the future products than by consuming their product today. In sum, undertaking *any* investment project that has a higher internal rate of return than the 5 per cent social discount rate, and therefore yields a net present discounted value greater than zero, makes society better off than it would be using the resources instead for present consumption.

2. In an ideal market economy, in which the existing rate of interest reflects the social rate of time preference, the economy is in equilibrium. If this rate of interest is 5 per cent, the marginal product of the existing capital stock is also equal to 5 per cent and, indeed, the internal rate of return on the current volume of investment—the so-called marginal efficiency of investment—is also equal to 5 per cent. In such an ideal economy, at the moment of equilibrium, any new investment opportunity having an internal rate of return above 5 per cent—or a net present value above zero when discounted at 5 per cent—will add to social welfare, as indicated above, and will be undertaken. Such investments will also appear immediately profitable to private persons and corporations. For, in a perfect

capital market, they can sell the prospect of the future stream of returns (expected with certainty) for a present value that is larger than the initial outlay. The difference between the initial outlay and the present value so calculated is an immediate profit. If the investment stream is −100, 63, 66, the value of the benefits, 63 in year one and 66 in year two, when discounted to the present at 5 per cent discount, is 120. Once these subsequent benefits are assured by spending an initial outlay of 100, he can sell them on the market for a present sum of 120, the difference, 20, being pure profit.

In this long run equilibrium, with social rate of time preference equal to the existing (riskless) rate of return on investment, a straightforward application of the present discounted value formula, or the internal rate of return formula, as already outlined, will suffice for an investment criterion. If, however, the rate of return on investment is well above the social rate of time preference either (a) because of short period disequilibrium, or (b) because the interest rate thrown up by the competitive capital market does not reflect the social rate of time preference, investment criteria become less simple, and indeed there are controversies about the 'correct' criterion we shall have to examine. The former discrepancy depends obviously on how far the economy diverges from long-period equilibrium. The latter discrepancy, however, does not disappear in long-run equilibrium. It may be attributed to some deficiency in people's character which disenables them from having proper regard to the future— Pigou's lack of telescopic faculties—or to some deficiency in the market mechanism. What seems to complicate the issue further is that even in the absence of such deficiencies, the long-run equilibrium rate of interest that would emerge, is not uniquely determined by the interaction of individuals' preferences and investment opportunities, but may be varied through monetary and fiscal management. We shall face these several difficulties in the following chapters.

Chapter 30

THE RATE OF DISCOUNT AND THE
SOCIAL RATE OF TIME PREFERENCE

1. Assumptions we have been working with—a perfectly competitive economy and, therefore, a perfectly competitive capital market dealing in a single government long-term bond—may appear pretty stringent. A perfectly competitive capital market, for instance, would imply that every person could brorrw, for a particular purpose and length of time, on exactly the same terms as could any other person. We could, instead, have introduced a large number of markets that specialize according to the length of time of the loan and according to the type of investment for which the money is raised. All such markets could be conceived to be working perfectly if all men were equally eligible to trade, in any amounts they wished, in any of the markets. There are however one or two implications of such a construct that are so far from being satisfactory as to make it appear unworldly and impractical. If a man were permitted to borrow any sum from one of such markets at the going rate, he could borrow a large sum for any period, say ten years, and could repay the loan on maturity simply by borrowing a larger sum, repeating the operation, if necessary, to the end of his life so that in fact the loan would not be repaid. For such a perfect capital market to promote optimal economic arrangements then, it would be necessary to have a population of perfectly honest men. But even this requirement would not suffice, for although all men were perfectly honest, they are yet likely to make errors of judgment or become the victims of untoward events. The wealthier a person is, however, the better placed he is to weather any adversity arising from misjudgment or misfortune. Given that differences in wealth are substantial, it would be irrational for lenders to be willing to lend as much to the impecunious as to the richer members of society, or to lend the same amounts on the same terms to each. In order to make perfect capital markets a plausible assumption, we should have to require not only that men are perfectly honest but also that they are equally

wealthy and wise or, alternatively, that there is perfect foresight in respect of the outcome of all investment projects and repayments.

One might conclude that the model of a single perfectly competitive capital market is so exacting in its requirements as to seriously mislead us in any further discussion based on *the* rate of interest. And it has to be confessed that the conditions under which a single perfect capital market could operate are far removed from circumstances that ever existed or are ever likely to exist. Nevertheless, this consideration alone need not inhibit us from adopting the perfect capital market construct; for the problems that we are to examine closely would arise no less if there were a large number of capital markets, if differences in risk were of the greatest importance, and if therefore, in consequence, such capital markets were highly imperfect. Nothing of economic significance is lost, in fact, but unnecessary complication by proceeding for some time with the fiction of a single perfect capital market, one trading in a single long-term government bond and perfectly riskless private securities all having the same yield. The yield on government bonds we shall call the market rate of interest, r.

2.   Under what conditions could such a market rate of interest be regarded also as the social rate of time preference?

In the modern economy, the market for the existing stock of securities is so large relative to new issues that the prices at which securities as a whole are bought and sold are not much influenced by the volume of new issues. This state of affairs accords with the common 'Keynesian' assumption that the price of long term bonds is highly stabilized. Starting from any underemployment equilibrium for the economy, an exogenous increase of investment, entailing an excess current supply of bonds over the current demand for them (the current demand for bonds being equal to current saving) cannot then restore equilibrium in the bond market by raising the interest rate (lowering bond prices). If the rate of interest is perfectly stabilized, the excess of current investment over saving causes a rise in income and employment until, in a new employment equilibrium, saving again equals investment and therefore the bond market is in equilibrium at the perfectly stabilized rate of interest. The converse operation is assumed to take place if there is an exogenous decline in investment. More generally, the rate of interest is taken to be *im-*

perfectly stabilized, as reflected in the elasticity of the so-called liquidity preference function. In that case, an exogenous increase in investment results in a new equilibrium level of employment having a somewhat higher rate of interest, and vice versa. We should therefore have to conclude that, in general, the rate of interest varies positively with the equilibrium level of output and employment.

We might get around this problem, however, by arguing that what is wanted is a rate of interest that is consistent with full employment and price stability. Such a rate of interest could be taken to reflect the interaction between a fully employed society's current saving schedule and its current investment opportunities. No matter what a person's time preference pattern is like, he is able to borrow and lend all he wishes at the resultant market rate of interest. Each person's rate of time preference is therefore equated at the margin to the market rate of interest; which means that, in equilibrium, everyone has the same rate of time preference. For this reason it may be called the social rate of time preference, and adopted as the social rate of discount in any investment criterion.

But a problem can arise if aggregate current saving, and possibly aggregate current investment also, depend not only on the rate of interest and income, as it can in a simple 'classical' or 'Keynesian' economy, but also on the community's accumulated wealth. If, for instance, people save less as their real wealth grows then the apparently unique full-employment rate of interest, which we hoped to adopt as the social rate of discount, no longer obtains. Imagine the government, beginning from a position of full employment with stable prices and a stable interest rate, deliberately lowering the interest rate by continued open-market purchases of bonds. At a lower interest rate, the resulting excess investment over saving and, therefore, excess aggregate demand, causes a rise in the general level of prices. The price level will, we know, continue to rise until real saving is increased to the extent necessary to restore equilibrium. However, the increase in real saving cannot come through changes in real income, or output, for the economy is already at full employment. We must have recourse to some other mechanism. Now the rise in the level of prices causes both the stock of fiat money and the stock of government bonds held by the public to decline in real value. This apparent decline in wealth has no effect on government expenditure, but it does cause people to save more. Prices therefore

207

continue to rise until the saving-investment equilibrium is restored through this 'Asset–Expenditure Relation' (Metzler, 1951). The outcome of the government's open-market policy in lowering the interest rates turns out to be a new equilibrium at a lower rate of interest, but at a higher level of prices. If this mechanism is accepted, it follows that by use of open market operations, the government can ultimately establish any full employment equilibrium rate of interest over a wide range, leaving prices to find their own level. There is, therefore, no longer a unique rate of interest corresponding to the full-employment economy.

How important is this possibility if we intend to use the equilibrium rate of interest in a full-employment economy as the social rate of discount? It is generally conceded that if real income, or real wealth, increases autonomously, or if other exogenous changes take place, such as a change in tastes or in technological opportunities, the equilibrium rate of interest would also alter. We should not think of repudiating the use of the market rate of interest on that account. Why then should we feel uneasy if it is supposed that an alteration of the market rate of interest can result also from a believed change in the value of money and bonds held by the public? Whatever people's beliefs are about the current value of their assets, and however the government's actions have influenced this belief, it is not misleading to state that the resulting rate of interest provides the terms on which everyone is ready to forgo consumption today for consumption tomorrow. Thus, although the determination of the rate of interest may now be said to depend upon an additional factor, wealth (indirectly manipulated by the government in setting this rate of interest), it is nonetheless as valid an expression of the social rate of time preference in any new equilibrium as in the old.

3. It should be mentioned in passing, however, that if the real value of the public debt varies with the price-level, via the above mechanism, it is simply because the public debt is what is sometimes called 'deadweight' debt—indicating that, at some time in the past, the government sold bonds to the public and used the revenues, not for investment in real assets, but simply to meet current expenditures. Interest payments on such deadweight debt are, therefore, not met from the yields of real assets, since these do not exist, but from additional taxes raised for this purpose. To the public it may be a

matter of indifference whether the government securities are backed by real assets or not. But when the price level changes it does make a difference. For if the government does hold real assets, they rise or fall in price along with the general level of prices, and the public's holding of real wealth does not alter.[1] It is, then, only when the government securities have no 'real' backing; when the 'wealth' they represent is in effect illusory, that a rise in the price level creates the illusion of a fall in real wealth, and vice versa. If somehow the community recognized that it was no better or worse off in consequence of its internal ownership of the public debt and therefore valued it correctly at zero, the relationship between the rate of interest and the price level described above would not exist.[2] Once more the full-employment rate of interest would be uniquely determined.

---

1 Nevertheless, inasmuch as the government, like any private firm, has issued fixed-interest bonds, a doubling, say, of all prices would enable it to pay double the nominal interest payments; for its nominal return from the real assets it has acquired will also have doubled. Since debtors are not, however, required to pay out any more than the fixed nominal interest payments, the government gains to exactly the extent that its bondholders lose. Though it may be said that the community as a whole is no worse or better off as a result of this redistribution of income in favour of debtors and against creditors, it is far from impossible that it will not affect aggregate expenditure. But we follow tradition here in mentioning the possibility, while disregarding the distribution effects on aggregate expenditure. We are left, then, only with the wealth illusion expenditure effects of movements in the price level.

2 If people were all perfectly informed and rational, they would indeed perceive the connection between the interest on such bonds and the additional taxes required to meet the interest payments. In that case the community as a whole could not regard itself as having increased its wealth by buying such bonds. If then the price-level rose, their *tax payments* to meet interest on the deadweight debt would fall in real terms, and by exactly the same amount in real terms as their *interest-receipts* from these deadweight bonds. They would be neither better off nor worse off. Apart from possible distribution effects—operative when there is any price-change in the economy—their real saving would not alter. In such a situation the full-employment interest rate is indeed uniquely determined.

Chapter 31

THE RATE OF DISCOUNT AND THE SOCIAL RATE OF TIME PREFERENCE
(Continued)

1. Even if we suppose the full-employment rate of interest to be uniquely determined, there may be other reasons for rejecting the market rate of interest as an expression of the social rate of time preference. If they are valid, we cannot use the market rate of interest as the social rate of discount in investment criteria. It may be the case, as argued by Pigou (1946), that people suffer from an absence of 'telescopic faculties' which causes them to discount their future wants too heavily. They would then tend to save less than they would if they were not afflicted with this defective vision. Put otherwise, their rate of time preference would be 'too high', and they would save and invest less than they would if they were, in some sense, perfectly rational beings. The case for government intervention might be strengthened by regarding the state as custodian of the future, responsible for the welfare of future generations. In order to correct the imperfection of vision and/or of institutions, and to give more weight to the future, investment decisions should be guided by a 'true' social rate of time preference, one that is below the rate of interest thrown up by the market.

But this argument, as indicated by Marglin (1963b) presents difficulties. In a liberal democracy some of the decisions are made through the voting mechanism, other decisions being made through the price mechanism. Since both sorts of decisions are made by the same people it is distinctly unsatisfactory that the rate of interest emerging from the political process should differ from that emerging from the market. Whether we call this schizophrenia or not, however, it is not hard to conceive of a rate of interest, determined in a perfect capital market, that is different from that adopted by the political process. The distribution of wealth would in general, affect the equilibrium market rate of interest, as indeed it would affect any price in the economy, though it would not necessarily affect the

210

rate of interest as determined by the voting mechanism. A politically-determined rate of interest is more likely to be influenced by the existing proportion of borrowers to that of lenders; numbers would count more than the distribution of financial power. Be that as it may, if democracy agreed to be guided in the formation of the rate of interest, as indeed in the formation of any other price, by the Pareto principle, no political opposition to the equilibrium rate of interest, produced in a perfectly competitive economy, could be justified—*provided there were no external effects*. And this indeed is how Marglin proposes to justify the notion of adopting a social rate of discount below the equilibrium rate of interest thrown up by a competitive economy. The explanation draws on a particular type of external effect, one arising from the experience of welfare at the thought of additional consumption of future generations. It is possible that, quite apart from being concerned with the real income of his heirs, and the heirs of his friends and relations, a man is not completely indifferent to the prospective real income of future generations. If he is not indifferent, then the prospect of an additional one dollar of income to be enjoyed, say, by the next generation adds to or subtracts something from his present satisfaction.

2. Suppose it is known that a contribution today of $1 to an investment fund for future generations will realize $2, in real terms, in thirty years' time, which additional $2 will then be at the disposal of the future generation, how will a man react? He may be prepared to pay, at most, 20 cents today to be certin that the future generation enjoys an additional $2. But 20 cents falls short of the $1 necessary to bring this about. However, there may be a number of other people who also have a soft spot for the generation yet to be born, and derive some satisfaction from the thought that they will inherit more than the provision being made for them by the economic system. The maximum sum each of such persons will be willing to pay now, in order that the future generation has an additional $2, is his compensating variation (CV). Clearly, if the sum of the CVs, taken over all of such people exceeds the dollar of investment that is necessary to produce $2 in 30 years' time, there is a net gain to society from investing the extra $1. If, say, there are 15 people altogether, each willing to give, at most, 20 cents today to the 'Posterity Fund' for the satisfaction of knowing that posterity will receive $2, then, by

contributing 20 cents each, all 15 of them are made better off. Altogether they contribute $3 today which, when invested, produces $6 for posterity, which obviously afford these 15 people more satisfaction than if only $2 were made available to posterity.

In general every person in the community can have different feelings about posterity, and the welfare of a number of persons may fall if an additional $2 is made available to future generations by the Posterity Fund. For such persons the CV is negative. However, so long as the *algebraic* sum of the CVs of all people today is positive and exceeds the sum of $1, there is a case for the state investing an additional $1. Clearly, additional dollars today should be invested beyond the market volume of investment so long as there continues to be a potential Pareto gain. The volume of extra-market investment, that is, should continue to the point where the algebraic sum of all CVs of the future $2 is exactly equal to the $1 of investment necessary to produce it.

There can be, then, a case for assuming that, accepting people's preference as ultimate data, the equilibrium rate of interest is too high, and that a careful calculation of people's CVs would reveal that the volume of current investment should be increased to a given optimal amount. This optimal amount of investment would be realized by the market if the rate of interest were set below the equilibrium at some predetermined figure. This lower rate of interest should be regarded as the true rate of society's time preference and, for investment criteria, should be adopted as the social rate of discount.

3.   The formal logic of the argument is sound enough, but the particular notion that on balance people today would like to see consumption reduced in order to provide more consumption for posterity has to be verified in order to rationalize the common assumption that the social rate of time preference is generally below the market rate of interest. This notion, however, appears to be at variance with the familiar distributional judgment which favours transferring income from rich to poor both within, and as between, communities. If society survives the hazards that science and technology have made possible, then, in the wealthier countries at least, one can be almost certain that our grandchildren will be far

better off materially than we are today, even if the rate of net saving were to fall to zero. To suggest that real income has to be transferred from the poorer generation of today to the richer generation of tomorrow in order to attain an optimal volume of investment is to suggest that, when properly questioned, people would on balance reveal notions of distributional justice that are the opposite of those traditionally adopted by most poeople, including economists, and indeed adopted today by all governments. Such a finding cannot be ruled out *a priori*, but no reliable evidence has been adduced to support it.

Nevertheless, in order to put our investment criteria through their paces, we shall follow the convention of supposing a market rate of return on current investment, ρ, that is expected to remain above society's rate of time preference, r, in conditions of certainty. This assumption obviously implies long-period disequilibrium in the capital market. In equilibrium the two rates would, of course, coincide, and there would be no difficulty in formulating investment criteria.

So long as current investment is below the optimal level—that necessary to equate ρ to r—social welfae will be increased for every $1 taken out of current consumption and invested in the private sector, there to yield an annual return equal to ρ: for $1 consumed today is, according to society's time preference, equal to $1(1 + r)$ tomorrow, whereas $1 invested today becomes a larger sum to-mortow $1(1 + \rho)$. Clearly, if there are no limits on the amounts the government can raise from the public for investment purposes, it should continue, in the interest of maximizing social welfare, to reduce consumption in favour of investment—even if there are no opportunities other than those available in the private investment sector—until the difference between ρ and r have vanished. In a short period, however, there are political restraints on the amounts the government can budget for. And though whatever investment is undertaken in the short period will act to lower the market rate of return, ρ, for simplicity of exposition we shall choose a period so short as to make the decline in ρ negligible.

Maintaining the fiction of a perfect capital market, each person in this economy must have a time preference equal to ρ, the certain market yield on private investment, this private time preference

213

being in contrast with, and below, the 'true', or social, time preference, r. Under these conditions how is the present discounted value formula to be used in choosing between investment options?

Chapter 32

PRESENT DISCOUNTED VALUE AS AN INVESTMENT CRITERION

1. Let us briefly restate the problem before discussing the solutions proposed. In a competitive full-employment economy—one in which public expenditure of any kind can be increased only by displacing private expenditure—the market rate of return on private investment, ρ, expected with certainty, is above the social rate of time preference, r. If ρ were equal to r, we should have no hesitation in using the straightforward discounting procedure introduced in Chapter 27. If the net present value of the entire stream (including initial outlay) of some public investment project were positive, society always gains by introducing the particular investment project. For example, if the initial outlay of this project were $1 million, and the discounted value of all benefits generated by it amounted to $1,090,000, we must regard the latter figure as the present value equivalent for society arising from using the $1 million for investment rather than for consumption. Consequently, by accepting this public investment option rather than the consumption option, society increases its present value by $90,000. Moreover, there are no other opportunities to consider, for the $1 million can fetch no more if placed in the private investment sector than if used for consumption: $1 million $(1 + \rho)$ is exactly equal to $1 million $(1 + r)$. However, once r is taken to be below ρ, as we shall assume henceforth, the $1 million public investment project may be said to have an 'opportunity cost' of more than $1 million, for there is now the opportunity of investing the money instead in the private investment sector at a yield of ρ.[1]

---

1 Where ρ is above r, there is a case for government intervention to accelerate the expansion of investment so as to eliminate the difference between the two rates.

We are considering, therefore, a period so short that additions to capital equipment have negligible effects on r and ρ.

215

Proposed investment criteria, which have become familiar in recent years,[2] turn on the notion of calculating what is called a *social opportunity cost* (SOC) (which is greater than the actual capital cost, K, according as ρ is greater than r. It is then required that the present r-discounted value of the benefit stream, which we shall henceforth denote as $PVr(B)$—where B stands for the stream of benefits that succeed the initial outlay K, and r is the rate of discount used—shall not merely exceed K itself, but exceed the SOC of K. This SOC of K can be calculated as aK, with $a \geqslant 1$.

2.   What the SOC is, and therefore how a is to be calculated, is taken to depend upon the way the government raises the money to finance this public investment. In particular, the distinction is made between raising the funds directly by taxes and raising the funds by selling bonds in the open market. These criteria, and their supposed rationale, can be illustrated by supposing the social rate of time preference, r, to be equal to 5 per cent per annum and the market rate, or yield on private investment, ρ, to be equal to 10 per cent per annum, the cost of the investment project being $1 million, as above. Suppose this sum is raised by direct taxes, and that the aggregate marginal propensity to save is $\frac{1}{5}$ of disposable income. Then because taxation reduces aggregate disposable income by $1 million, aggregate saving is reduced by $\frac{1}{5}$ of $1 million. In a full employment economy, this reduced saving of $\frac{1}{5}$ of $1 million implies a reduction of private investment of $\frac{1}{5}$ of $1 million, the remaining $\frac{4}{5}$ of $1 million coming out of consumption. We now ask, what is the present value of this reduction of $1 million of private expenditure, of which $\frac{1}{5}$ becomes a reduction of private investment, and $\frac{4}{5}$ a reduction of consumption. Since private investment yields 10 per cent per annum in perpetuity, every $1 invested in the private sector yields an annual payment of $0.10 for ever. At a social rate of time preference of 5 per cent, a stream of $0.10 for ever has a present discounted value of $2, $(0.10/0.05 \times \$1)$. Thus the $\frac{1}{5}$ of $1 million of reduced private investment, the consequence of raising $1 million by taxes, has a present discounted value of $\frac{1}{5}$ of $1 million

---

2   The better known papers in connection with these proposed criteria are those of Eckstein (1957), Marglin (1963a), and Feldstein (1964). Since the basic ideas are the same, I have chosen to follow Marglin's procedure as being the most forceful and explicit.

times 2. To this reduction of present value we now add the reduction of $\frac{4}{5}$ of \$1 million of consumption. The total reduction in present value, when \$1 million is raised by direct taxes, is therefore $(2 \times \frac{1}{5})$\$1 million *plus* $\frac{4}{5}$ of \$1 million, or altogether \$1.2 million, which is taken as the SOC of public investment by this method of finance. The coefficient a, is 1.2 in this case. In more general terms,

$$\text{SOC} = K \left\{ \varTheta \left(\frac{\rho}{r} \right) + (1 - \varTheta) \right\} = aK,$$

where $\varTheta$ is the aggregate marginal propensity to save from disposable income.

In order that the \$1 million investment project yield a social gain, it is required that $PV_r(B)$ exceed its SOC, which is here equal to \$1·2 million. If, on the other hand, the \$1 million were raised instead entirely in the capital market, it would entail a subtraction of \$1 million of private investment—a potential loss, therefore, of 0·10 of \$1 million per annum in perpetuity, having a present value of \$2 million when discounted at 5 per cent. The SOC of the \$1 million project when the sum is raised entirely by loans, is therefore \$2 million.

3.   Before subjecting this sort of reasoning to scrutiny, let us follow a further development of this line of thought. Of each *primary* return accruing from the investment, one-fifth will be saved and invested in the private sector, there to earn 10 per cent per annum in perpetuity. And of these streams of private yields generated from each such reinvestment of primary returns, a subsidiary stream is generated equal to one-fifth of the return reinvested *times* 10 per cent, and so on. This perpetual reinvestment process obviously increases the present value of the public investment undertaking. The same logic,[3] however, has to be extended to the calculation of the SOC. Thus the one-fifth of \$1 million of displaced private investment entails a 10 per cent per annum loss of income, equal to

---

3   Though based on different premises, a related procedure is used by Galenson and Leibenstein (1955). Where the supreme objective in a poor country is to squeeze as much saving as possible from the economy, the present discounted value of an investment is not the decisive factor. The proportion of the return, or profit, that is likely to be saved also becomes a crucial consideration.

$\frac{1}{5} \times$ \$1 million $\times \frac{1}{10}$. Of this potential reduction in the stream of income, however, $\frac{1}{5}$ represents a further reduction of saving, and therefore of private investment. And of this consequent reduction of income, $\frac{1}{5}$ constitutes yet a further reduction of private saving and investment, and so on. SOC, in short, has to be 'blown up' in much the same way for valid comparison with present value of the stream of benefits.

It goes without saying that this perpetual reinvestment procedure can become quite complicated. The reader, however, need not trouble to familiarize himself with the formulae reached for the simple reason that, under the conditions posited, such procedures can be shown to be either invalid or unnecessary, and this for three reasons: the first two reasons bear on the formulation of the opportunity cost of public investment, the third reason has to do with the reinvestment assumption.

4. First, then, and disregarding for the moment the reinvestment opportunities open to the stream of benefits flowing from the initial \$1 million capital outlay, the present worth of the $\frac{4}{5}$ of \$1 million reduction in consumption (when the \$1 million is raised entirely by taxes) ought to be valued, *not* at its nominal value, $\frac{4}{5} \times$ \$1 million, as in the proposed procedure. For the $\frac{4}{5}$ of \$1 million taken from consumption, in order to invest it in the public project, can just as well have been invested instead in the private sector where it would have earned an annual yield of 10 per cent. There is no warrant, therefore, for spending the $\frac{4}{5}$ of \$1 million, withdrawn from consumption, on the public project (any more than there is for spending on it the $\frac{1}{5}$ of \$1 million withdrawn from private investment) unless each dollar so withdrawn can earn in the public project at least as much as the 10 per cent per annum yielded with certainty by private investment. At the social rate of time preference of 5 per cent per annum the opportunity cost of *any* dollar taken from the private sector is therefore two dollars—and this is so *irrespective* of whether the funds for the public investment project are to be raised wholly by taxes, wholly by loans (through the capital market[4]) or by a mixture of both methods.

---

4 It could be raised through the capital market only by offering the public an issue of government bonds yielding at least 10 per cent per annum.

In short, since $1 million raised from current expenditure can, in this model, always be used in the private investment sector, there to yield 10 per cent per annum in perpetuity, its potential yield of $100,000 is forgone if the $1 million is used instead in some public investment. So long, then, as the social rate of time preference remains at 5 per cent, this annual yield of $100,000 forgone has a present value of $2 million. And this $2 million is the true SOC of the $1 million invested in a public project, no matter how this $1 million is raised.

5.   Secondly, if we accept 10 per cent as the opportunity yield for all public investment funds, no matter how the funds are raised, it simplifies matters to choose 10 per cent as the appropriate discount rate. And since $1 invested in the private sector yields 10 cents per annum in perpetuity, the *opportunity* cost of investing $1 in the public sector becomes—at 10 per cent—exactly $1 (not $2, as it would at 5 per cent). The criterion now to be used is simply that the present value of future benefits, *when discounted at* 10 *per cent*, exceed the initial capital outlay.

Writing $PV\rho\ (B)$ for the present discounted value of the benefit stream of the B investment being contemplated, when this is discounted at yield ρ, and writing the initial capital outlay as K, the correct investment criterion is therefore written as $PV\rho\ (B) > K$, or $PV\rho\ (B) - K > 0.$[5]

The reader should take note, however, that the present sum $PV\rho\ (B)$ does *not* represent the present social welfare equivalence of the B stream of benefits. So long as r is the social rate of time preference, the present social welfare equivalence continues to be equal to $PV_r(B)$. What the correct investment criterion, $PV\rho(B) > K$, does,

---

5   If outlays appear at a later date, these 'negative benefits' are also discounted to the present at ρ. As indicated earlier, the initial outlay, K, can itself be taken as a negative benefit at time zero, and, if so, the criterion can be written, more generally, as

$$\sum_{t=0}^{n} \frac{B_t}{(1 + \rho)^t} > 0.$$

In the present chapter, however, we shall continue to use $PV\rho\ (B) > K$.

however, is to meet the requirement that the present social welfare equivalence of any public investment costing an initial sum K be *higher* than the present social welfare equivalence of the benefit stream that arises from investing this sum K in the private sector at yield ρ.

One more *caveat* is in order. The reader may think that if, notwithstanding the simplifications introduced by adopting ρ as the discount rate, one continued to use r as the discount rate then, provided he estimated the opportunity cost of capital outlay K at ρ/r (or, using the figures in the context, estimating the opportunity cost of the \$1 million capital outlay as equal to \$2 million), he could use $PV_r(B) > (\rho/r)K$, and regard this as equivalent to the correct criterion $PV\rho(B) > K$. But this is so *only* so long as the reinvestment potential of the benefits are ignored. Once we take into consideration the possibility of reinvesting the primary benefits in the private sector at yield ρ, as we do below, the two criteria are *not* equivalent. Put otherwise, once reinvestment at yield ρ is introduced the sum $PV_r(B)$ is not necessarily equal to $(\rho/r)PV\rho(B)$.

6. Thirdly, we must turn to the question of reinvestment. Suppose, first, that all benefits appear as collectible revenues and that there is no constraint on their use, what proportion is to be reinvested?

To assume that only that proportion of the income (received from the yield of the investment in any period) which is neither taxed or consumed is to be reinvested cannot be regarded as an allocative proposition. For if the primary benefits of the public investment project is, or can be made, encashable there is no case for consuming any portion of them so long as the social rate of time preference r (5 per cent) is below the yield ρ (10 per cent) in the private sector. Any \$1 consumed of a future benefit B_t, collected at time t, has a social worth of but \$1 at that time t. If, instead the \$1 is reinvested at time t in the private sector at 10 per cent, it generates a stream that has a value of \$2 at time t. In order to maximize the present value of any primary stream of benefits it is necessary then to reinvest in the private sector the *whole* of the revenues accruing in each future period and, for that matter, to reinvest the whole of the secondary stream of revenues, the whole of the tertiary stream of revenues, and so on. Provided there are no reinvestment opportunities open to these revenues generated by the public investment other than the opportunity to invest in the private sector at yield ρ, which is a common assumption, the one-hundred-per-cent reinvestment requirement gives no trouble. For the compounding forward of the whole of any primary return B_t at 10 per cent from period t onward adds nothing at all to the value of B_t in the tth period provided we use 10 per cent as the discount rate as we do in the correct criterion. If, for example, B_t were equal to 150, reinvesting the whole at 10 per cent would yield $150 (1 + 0\cdot1)$ in the $t + 1$ period, $150(1 + 0\cdot1)^2$ in the $t + 2$ period, and $\ldots 150 (1 + 0\cdot1)^n$ in the $t + n$ period. Discounting back to the tth period, this $150 (1 + 0\cdot1)^n$ in the $t + n^{\text{th}}$ period becomes 150 again in the tth period. In this way all reinvestments of primary returns can be discounted back initial to their primary returns.[6] The criterion $PV\rho(B) - K > 0$, then, needs no emendation wherever we adopt the standard assumption in this sort of model that the opportunities for reinvestment of revenues are restricted to the private investment sector.

7. The modification necessary for reinvestment opportunities other than those presented by the private investment sector is straightforward. If one can anticipate some more advantageous reinvestment opportunity than the ρ yielded by the private investment sector which is available specifically to any one of the primary revenues from the project, the whole of the primary revenue, if possible, is to be reinvested in this special opportunity for as long as possible. If the amount that can be channelled into this special investment opportunity is limited, as much as that primary benefit as possible must be invested there for as long as possible. For obviously, to the extent that some part of the primary revenue is not reinvested in this special greater-than-ρ-yielding opportunity, the present value of the benefit stream is smaller than it need be.

---

6 In general, any primary return B_t, when discounted to the present at ρ is equal to $B_t (1 + \rho)^t$. If B_t is now compounded forward for n more periods to equal $B_t (1 + \rho)^n$ in the $(t + n)^{th}$ period, its present value discounted at ρ is equal to

$$\frac{B_t(1 + \rho)\text{s}}{(1 + \rho)^{(t+n)}} = \frac{B_t}{(1 + \rho)^t}$$

or $PV\rho(B_t)$.

The further modification, necessary for those benefits that do not take the form of cash revenues, depends upon the attitude we take to political or administrative constraints. One might take up the position that since, in principle, the benefits of all public investment projects *could* always be made available as cash revenues—even where it happens that no revenues whatever are collected—simply by raising through taxes a sum equal to the calculated benefit, a correct criterion *should* make allowance for a one-hundred-per-cent reinvestment of all primary benefits (whether these encashed benefits are to be reinvested in the private sector at ρ or in some specific and more advantageous opportunities). But an investment criterion that followed this injunction could be said to yield only a hypothetical maximum present value of the benefit stream. For if, notwithstanding the transformability of non-cash benefits into cash through taxation, the constraints are known to be operative, the actual present value of the stream of benefits will be smaller than its potential present value.

One may, of course, calculate the maximum potential present value of a benefit stream, if only as part of an argument for persuading politicians or officials to remove constraints which prevent exploitation of further reinvestment opportunities. But in so far as the constraints are not in fact removed, they cannot be ignored. One cannot proceed as if the effective losses caused by the constraints do not in fact occur. If, for example, a benefit worth \$1,000 accrues at time t and is not to be made available for reinvestment, it has to be regarded as consumed at time t.[7] It cannot, therefore, be compounded forward at ρ, the private sector's yield. One year after t it is not worth \$1,000 $(1 + \rho)$, but only \$1,000 $(1 + r)$. For, the social rate of time preference being r, the community is indifferent as between \$1,000 at time t and \$1,000 $(1 + r)$ at time $t + 1$. At some terminal period for the benefit stream, say $t + n$, this t^{th} benefit will have a compounded value of \$1,000 $(1 + r)^n$, and its discounted present value at ρ will be

$$\frac{\$1,000\,(1 + r)^n}{(1 + \rho)^{\,t+n}}$$

---

7   It can be argued that the non cash benefits are not wholly consumed since they can be treated as an increment of real income, and some fraction of this increment of real income will be invested in the private sector. Whether people would in fact respond in this way is an empirical matter. If they do, the modifications are obvious, though they would complicate the calculations. It is of small importance, however, and is not taken up here.

which is smaller[8] than $\$1,000/(1 + \rho)^t$, the latter being the present value (discounted at ρ) of $\$1,000$ collected in year t where the $\$1,000$ could be wholly reinvested at ρ for any number of years.

8. In sum, the criterion is as follows: Where there are no advantageous opportunities peculiar to the benefit stream and all benefits are encashable, $PV\rho(B) - K > 0$ is applicable without modification. If any part of a primary benefit accruing at time t can be reinvested in a specific opportunity that yields more than ρ over any period, as much of that part of the primary benefit is to be reinvested there as the specific opportunity allows. This special reinvestment portion is to be compounded forward to the terminal period and discounted back to the present at ρ. Finally, the portion of any future benefit at time t that, for institutional or political reasons, is not available for reinvestment, and has therefore to be consumed at time t, must be compounded forward to the terminal period at r, the social rate of time preference, and, as above, discounted back to the present at ρ.

9. Before ending this chapter it is, perhaps, advisable to make quite explicit that the logic of the forgoing analysis depends upon an absence of political or administrative constraints on public projects.

Earlier in the chapter it has been asserted that there is no economic warrant for spending, say, the $\frac{4}{5}$ of $\$1$ million, withdrawn from current consumption expenditure, on the public project unless each dollar so withdrawn can earn in the public project at least the ρ which it can always earn in the private investment sector. If, however, economically unjustifiable conditions are attached to the use of funds raised from the public, the conclusion that the approrpiate discount rate is ρ has to be qualified.

---

8 Since $r < \rho$, $\$1,000 \, (1 + r)^n < \$1,000 \, (1 + \rho)^n$ and

$$\frac{\$1,000 \, (1 + r)^n}{(1 + \rho)^{t + n}} < \frac{\$1,000 \, (1 + \rho)^n}{(1 + \rho)^{t + n}},$$

where the latter expression is equal to $\$1,000/(1 + \rho)^t$.

The required qualification, and its explanation, are most easily grasped by an example in which r is taken to equal 5 per cent, ρ is taken to equal 10 per cent, and the perpetual yield on some public project C is 8 per cent. Clearly, if we use 10 per cent as the discount rate the C project will be rejected, whereas if we use the 5 per cent rate it will be accepted. Under what political conditions should we use r?

Assuming, first, that the funds, say 100, are raised wholly by reducing current consumption, it is surely better that the 100 of resources should yield 8 per cent in the C public project than the equivalent of 5 per cent when used in current consumption—though it is obviously better yet if the 100 is placed in the private investment sector, there to yield 10 per cent per annum. Assuming, secondly, that the 100 is raised wholly by reducing private investment, placing this amount in the public project C, which yields only 8 per cent, immediately involves the economy in a potential loss of 2 per cent per annum. This result being too apparent, it is only under circumstances corresponding to the first assumption that political constraints are occasionally introduced.

Granted then that the funds for public investment are made available by reducing current consumption, adopting 10 per cent as the discount rate is justified on condition that such funds may always be switched to the private investment sector in the event that the estimated yields of the mooted public projects are less than 10 per cent. But the assumption that such funds can always be switched to the private investment sector is implicit within the framework of the analysis we have adopted. Thus, in the absence of any explicit statement to the contrary, it has to be accepted.

If, now, we are apprized of political constraints that allow funds to be raised by reducing current consumption *only on condition that the funds so raised be wholly invested in some public project*, adopting 10 per cent as the discount rate is not justified. For the adoption of a 10 per cent discount rate would reject the C public project yielding 8 per cent in favour of current consumption deemed to yield but 5 per cent. It follows, therefore, that wherever such a constraint is operative, the 5 per cent social rate of time preference, r, is the appropriate rate of discount. For if, in any case, there is no opportunity of placing funds (raised by reducing current consumption) in the private investment sector, at least some improvement is effected by employing them in public projects such as C that yield more than 5 per cent.[9]

Finally, if private firms or investors also act in an apparently arbitrary fashion in regularly consuming some fixed proportion of their investment yields, the appropriate rate of discount for public projects is somewhat less than ρ. For a given investment in the private sector now grows at a rate somewhat below ρ per annum. We shall, however, be in a better position to deal with this minor amendment in the opportunity rate of growth, afforded by the private investment sector, after reading the three chapters on normalization procedures. The matter is then discussed briefly in the last footnote of chapter 36.

---

9 Explicit introduction, then, of such a policy constraint—*plus* the assumptions (i) that a public project, if acceptable, is to be financed through reducing private consumption and private investment in fixed proportions, and (ii) that (as in the final paragraph above) private investors regularly consume a given fraction of their investment yields—would warrant Marglin's procedure (1963a).

Chapter 33

THE ALLEGED SUPERIORITY OF THE PRESENT DISCOUNTED VALUE CRITERION

1.   Consider three alternative investment streams, A, B and C, listed in Table IV.2. The undiscounted net benefit ratio, $(B - K)/K$, where B represents the benefits in the first, and only, benefit period, and K represents the initial capital outlay, would rank C greater than A. Why the *undiscounted* net benefit ratio? Since any rate of discount affects each of the benefits at t_1 in exactly the same proportion, we may infer that whatever be the discount rate, the resulting discounted net benefit ratio would give the same ranking as the undiscounted ratio.

This conclusion is valid, however, only for a two-period investment in which the outlay appears in the first period, and the benefit in the second. Add but one more period, and the ranking will in general depend upon the discount rate. For instance a stream $- 100, 10, 100$ cannot be ranked with respect to the stream $- 100, 90, 10$ without knowing the discount rate. If this were 1 per cent the first would clearly yield a larger net benefit ratio than the second. If, however, the discount rate were 50 per cent, the second would yield a larger net benefit ratio than the first.

The two-period investment stream has also another property: the ranking of investment streams by their internal rates of return, as shown in the last column of Table IV.2, is equal to the undiscounted net benefit ratio, $(B - K)/K$, and therefore produces the same ranking. There is no mystery about this: the excess benefit, $B - K$, as a fraction of the capital cost, K, is equivalent to one year's growth of the initial capital, K. Thus the capital of 100 in A will have been perceived to grow by 5 per cent, and in C by 25 per cent. A discount rate of that same percent—5 per cent for A and 25 per cent for C—will therefore reduce the magnitude of the benefit so as to equal the original cost; which result follows the definition of the internal rate of return.

226

For such two-period investment streams, then, the ranking is unambiguous. Whatever the rate of discount, whether zero or any positive or negative figure, the ranking remains unchanged, and indeed gives exactly the same order as a ranking based on the internal rate of return.

TABLE IV.2

	t_0	t_1	$(B - K)/K$	Internal rate of return
A	−100	105	$\dfrac{5}{100}$	5%
B	−100	115	$\dfrac{15}{100}$	15%
C	−20	25	$\dfrac{25}{100}$	25%

2. This harmony between the present value criterion and the internal rate of return criterion will, however, as the reader surely suspects, break down if any of the investment streams being compared contains more than two periods. Indeed, this implication accords with the proposition exemplified above: that for investment streams in excess of two periods the ranking will vary with the rate of discount used. The internal-rate-of-return ranking does not, however, at all depend on the adopted rate of discount, but is independently determined. If it then so happens that at the ruling discount rate a number of investment streams show the same ranking by the two criteria, an alteration of the discount rate, which changes the present value ranking of the investment projects, will also produce a discrepancy between this new present-value ranking and the ranking by internal rates of return.

The two three-period investment streams, A and B in Table IV.3, illustrate this simple inference. Both investment streams are ranked equally by the internal rate of return criterion, each yielding 10 per cent. Not surprisingly, if the rate of discount were 10 per cent, discounted net benefit ratio would be zero in each case, and they would be ranked equally. If the rate of discount were 1 per cent,

TABLE IV.3

	t_0	t_1	t_2	Internal rate of return	$(B-K)/K$ at 1%	$(B-K)/K$ at 10%	$(B-K)/K$ at 20%
A	-100	110	0	10%	$\dfrac{9}{100}$	0	$\dfrac{-8}{100}$
B	-100	0	121	10%	$\dfrac{19}{100}$	0	$\dfrac{-16}{100}$

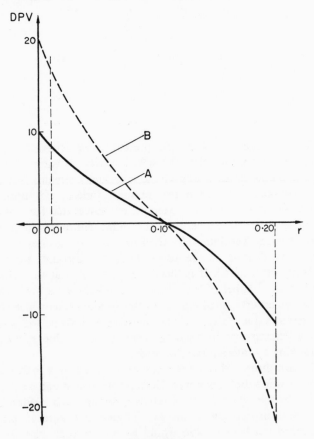

Figure IV.4

investment stream B would show a higher discounted net benefit ratio, 19/100, compared with that for A, 9/100. The reverse ranking is produced if the discount rate were changed to 20 per cent—B's net benefit ratio being—16/100 compared with $-$ 8/100 for A. A diagrammatic representation of these results appears in Figure IV.4 (page 228). The discounted present value of the investment streams, and therefore the discounted net benefit ratio of each investment stream A and B, varies inversely with the rate of discount measured horizontally. At a 10 per cent rate of discount the two investment streams have the same present value, which is zero. Since a 10 per cent rate of discount reduces each of these investment streams to zero, their internal rates of return are, by definition, equal to zero. For discount rates of less than 10 per cent, at which the net present value of both streams are equal,[1] B's present value exceeds that of A, the reverse being true for rates in excess of 10 per cent.

3.   In spite of this discrepancy between the two criteria, the internal rate of return has been recommended in some circumstances, particularly as a method of allocating a given capital budget among a number of potential investment projects. Thus, it has been proposed by McKean (1958) that one select a number of public investment streams, subject to a budget, provided that the internal rate of return on each investment stream that is chosen exceeds the adopted rate of discount. The scheme is illustrated in Table IV.4, which shows five investment streams in declining order of internal rate of return. The discounted present value of the net benefit ratio is also given for a discount rate equal to 3 per cent.

If the capital budget were 1,000 on this selection criterion, only 350 of it would be spent. We should admit A, B, C and D. But we should not admit E. Only the first four projects have an internal rate of return in excess of the 3 per cent discount rate. Project E has an internal rate of return of only 2 per cent, which is below

---

1   Irving Fisher has defined the term *rate of return over cost* as the discount rate at which the $(PV_r(B) - K)/K$ ratio of two alternative investment streams are equal. In general this rate of return over cost is *not* equal to zero, as in the example above, and as depicted in Figure IV.4. The significance of this rate of return over cost figure is simply that of revealing the discount rate at which ranking reversal takes place.

TABLE IV. 4

	t_0	t_i	t_2	Internal rate of return	$PV_r (B-K)/K$ (for $r = 0.03$)
A	−100	110	0	10%	$\dfrac{7}{100}$
B	−100	0	115	7%	$\dfrac{8}{100}$
C	−100	106	0	6%	$\dfrac{3}{100}$
D	−50	52	0	4%	$\dfrac{1}{100}$
E	−200	2	208	2%	$\dfrac{-2}{200}$

the 3 per cent discount rate. The reader will doubtless observe that the ranking by present discounted value (at 3 per cent) of the four selected investment options differs from the ranking produced by their internal rates of return. But this is no matter, since the same four investment options would be admitted also, and the E product excluded, on the present value criterion.

If the capital available were only 200, the internal-rate-of-return criterion would select A and B, a choice which would be confirmed by the present-value criterion. However, let the capital available be only 100, and we are, again, faced with a problem. The internal-rate-of-return criterion chooses the A investment option. The present-value criterion chooses instead the B investment option.[2] Again, the reader may be inclined to put his faith in the present value method If the rate of discount that is operative is 3 per cent, he will choose the B stream since he can exchange it for a net profit of 8 today, whereas the A stream can be exchanged for a net profit of only 7 today.

2 The problem would arise even with a capital budget of 300 or more if the A and B investment streams were *mutually exclusive*, i.e. if, in any list of investment projects, we could include either A or B, but not both.

4. A further consideration also seems to tell against the use of the internal-rate-of-return criterion: more than a single rate of return may correspond to a given investment stream. A necessary, though not sufficient, condition for more than one internal rate of return to correspond with an investment stream is that not all the costs be incurred in the initial period: there will have to be net disbursements at later periods.

A simple example of such an investment stream, H, would be — 100, 350, — 400, which yields two internal rates of return, λ_1 of 46 per cent, and λ_2 of 456 per cent, since using either of these rates as a discount rate would reduce the present value of this stream to zero, as required by the definition of the internal rate of return.[3]

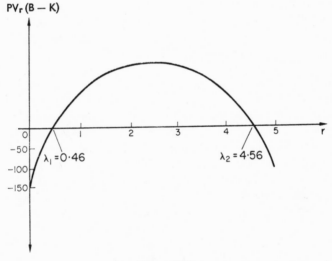

Figure IV.5

---

3 From the definition of the internal rate of return, say λ, we require a λ for which

$$- 100 + \frac{350}{(1 + \lambda)} - \frac{400}{(1 + \lambda)^2} = 0.$$

The reader will recognize the expression as a quadratic equation with two solutions for λ, 0·46 and 4·56.

Figure IV.5, (page 231) depicts the curve relating the net present value of the H stream to the rate of discount, r. The curve will be seen to cut the horizontal axis, not once (as does each of the investment streams in Figure IV.4), but twice; once at the point where r is 0·46, and once where r is 4·56. Since either of these two discount rates reduces the present value of the H stream to zero, they are identified as the two internal rates of return, λ_1 and λ_2.

Of course, the reader might think that of these two internal rates of return, λ_1 (46 per cent) is the more reasonable. If he were obliged to adopt an internal rate of return for such a stream, he would probably choose 46 per cent. But he would find it difficult to justify such a choice, if he were not allowed to draw on intuition. Moreover, even if the reader did feel confident about the 46 per cent internal rate of return for the H stream,[4] this example of two internal rates of return is only a special case. For one can devise investment streams to yield three, four, or indeed, any number of internal rates of return.[5] However open-minded the reader may wish to remain, he cannot deny that the case for preferring the present-value criterion above the internal-rate-of-return criterion looks very strong.

5. If, provisionally, we accept the present-value criterion, there is still the question of whether we are to rank investment streams by excess benefit over cost, by the ratio of benefit to cost, or by the ratio of excess benefit to cost (which we used in Table IV.4). These three alternative present-value criteria are worked out in Table IV.5 for two investment streams, A and C, where K' is the present value of the outlays, and B' is the present value of the benefits both discounted, say, at 10 per cent. In the $(B' - K')$ column, A having excess benefit over cost of 50 is ranked above C with an excess benefit over cost of only 30. In the next, B'/K' column, however, C having a ratio of benefit to cost of 2·5 is ranked above A having a ratio

---

4 In fact, as we shall see in Chapter 34, *neither* of these internal rates of return may correspond with the concept of an average rate of growth over time.

5 Determining the values of the internal rates of return corresponding to any investment stream implies solving for the roots of a polynomial. Any investment stream having n periods can be transformed into a polynomial having a maximum of $n - 1$ different roots, each being a possible internal rate of return. Only those that are positive will matter for investment criteria. Negative internal rates of return make sense, but are not usually of much importance. Complex roots do not appear to make sense in this context.

TABLE IV.5

	K'	B'	$B' - K'$	B'/K'	$(B' - K')/K'$
A	100	150	50	1·5	0·5
C	20	50	30	2·5	1·5

of benefit to cost of only 1·5. In the final column showing $(B'-K')/K'$, the ratio of *excess* benefit to cost continues to show C ranked above A. A glance at the last two columns will assure the reader that B'/K' and $(B' - K')/K'$ will give the same ranking, since the latter ratio is derived from the former simply by subtracting one from it. We can, then, ignore the B'/K' ratio and compare $B' - K'$ with $(B' - K')/K'$.

Now if there is a capital budget of exactly 100, it may seem reasonable to be guided by the $(B' - K')/K'$ ratio ranking, and therefore to choose C rather than A. This is rational enough if it is established that he can have either A alone or, instead, five of the C streams. The outlay for five of the C streams uses up exactly the budget of 100, and produces a discounted present value of five times 50, or 250—which is 100 more than can be got by choosing to invest the budget of 100 in A. But suppose, now, that there is an opportunity for only a single C investment, what then? We should have 80 left over after putting 20 of the capital into C. If we could use this 80 left over in A (the A investment stream being divisible) it would be better to invest 20 in C and the remaining 80 in A, than to put the whole 100 in A; for, in the former case, the present value of the benefits would be $\{(0·8 \times 150) + 50\}$, or 170, while in the latter case the present value of the benefits is only 150. But just as it may not be possible to increase the C investment, the A investment stream may not be divisible. In that case we have a choice; all the A stream, or all the C stream. If there were no other opportunities for the 80 left over from choosing the C stream, we should choose the A investment stream. Even if the funds left over from a choice of C did not have to be returned, but could be used to invest in the private investment sector of the economy at, say, 10 per cent, the A stream would still be chosen. For the adoption of 10 per cent as the discount rate ensures that the outlay of 80 invested in the private sector at 10 per cent per annum in perpetuity has a present value of

233

no more than 80. There is, then, no excess benefit from using the 80 left over in the private sector if C were chosen: the excess benefit resulting from this course of action would still be 30—just as little as it would be if, instead, the 80 were returned to the government.

It is apparent that, under these conditions, investment stream A should be chosen. And if such conditions did prevail we should use the $(B' - K')$, or excess benefit, method of ranking which would place A, having an excess benefit of 50 above C having an excess benefit of only 30. It is no less apparent that if any multiple of the C investment stream were technically feasible, we should be maximizing the excess benefit of the given capital funds of 100 by opting for C rather than A. Under those conditions, the $(B' - K')/K'$, or excess benefit over cost ratio, method is the correct one to employ. Put differently, if we adopted the $(B' - K')$ method of ranking, we tacitly suppose that the alternative investment streams are of exactly the size given: no increase is possible. If, however, we adopt the $(B' - K')/K'$ method of ranking, we tacitly suppose the opposite; that either stream can be increased in any proportion. Where neither of these suppositions are true, we should not repose confidence in either method of ranking. We should then want to compare the present value of the benefits from using the given 100 of funds in each of the feasible number of ways.

Chapter 34

A NORMALIZATION PROCEDURE FOR PUBLIC INVESTMENT

1. The reader is now aware that the ranking of a number of investment streams may differ according as the internal rate of return criterion is used or according as the present value criterion is used; or, with respect to the latter, according as excess benefit over cost is used, or excess benefit-cost *ratio*. Broad hints have been dropped in preceding chapters as to how such differences arise, though for the most part we were concerned chiefly to point them up. This task being accomplished, it is now necessary to understand just how these differences in ranking arise.

Table IV.6 below sets out three investment streams A, B and C, and their ranking in columns (3), (4) and (5), by reference to the conventional methods of using the three investment criteria shown.

TABLE IV.6

	t_0	t_1	t_2	t_3	(1) B	(2) K	(3) $(B-K)$	(4) $(B-K)/L$	(5) λ
A	-20	15	16	$\cdot$	27·5	20	7·5	0·375	0·34
B	-100	$\cdot$	$\cdot$	160	120·2	100	20·2	0·202	0·17
C	-45	351	402	$\cdot$	315·0	375	$-59·0$	$-0·13$	0·46
									4·56

In the right hand part of the Table, the B in column (1) stands for the usual present value of the benefits when discounted at the given rate of social time preferenc, r, here assumed 10 per cent. The K in column (2) stands for the present value of outlays when discounted to the present in the same way. The $(B-K)$ in column (3) is, therefore, the excess of benefits over costs, being positive for the investment streams A and B, and negative for C. Column (4) shows the excess benefit cost ratio $(B-K)/K$, which, again, is positive for A and for B, and negative for C. The final column (5) shows the

235

value of the internal rate of return of each investment stream, λ, with the C project yielding two internal rates of return.

The excess benefit criterion of column (3) would rank the projects in the order, B, A, C, with C being inadmissible inasmuch as its discounted costs exceed its discounted outlays. The excess benefit cost ratio criterion, $(B - K)/K$ of column (4) would, however, rank the investment streams in the order A, B, C, though again C being inadmissible would not be undertaken.. The ranking based on the internal rate of return, as defined in Chapter 28, however, would rank the investment streams in the order C, A, B, investment stream C being ranked first on either of its internal rates of return.

2. It is tempting to set out, at once, to uncover the features that give rise to these discrepancies. There are, however, pedagogical advantages in first stating the three conditions that are sufficient, though not necessary, to preclude discrepancies between the investment criteria used in Table IV.6. After doing so, we shall illustrate briefly the importance of each of these three conditions. We then lay down the general procedure that ensures consistency of project ranking in the application of all investment criteria. Following a general proof of this consistency theorem, we shall return to re-examine the examples given in Table IV.6.

The three conditions which, if met, are sufficient to ensure a unique ranking of the alternative investment streams in question irrespective of the investment criterion used, and can therefore be spoken of as a 'normalization' procedure, are: (1) that the reinvestment opportunities open to each of the benefits be made explicit and be fully utilized; (2) that a common outlay, and (3) a common investment period, be estabished for all the investment streams under comparison.

We shall now resort to three simple examples to convince the reader that if any two of these conditions are met, but not all three of them, discrepancies in the ranking of investment streams can still arise. In all three examples the calculations are facilitated by limiting the investment period to three years and by supposing ρ, the certain yield in the private sector, to be zero—an assumption which, on the arguments produced in Chapter 32, justifies our adoption of a discount rate, r, of zero.

3. The two investment streams, A and C, in Table IV.7a, have the same total outlay of 100, and run for the same three periods. Thus conditions (2) and (3) are met. We notice that in the first two columns of the right-hand side of the Table, the results given by the excess benefit criterion, $PV_r(B) - K$, and the excess benefit ratio criterion, $[PV_r(B) - K]/K$, both rank the A stream above the C stream in the proportion 42 to 26.

TABLE IV.7a

	t_0	t_1	t_2	(1) $PV_r(B) - K$	(2) $[PV_r(B) - K]/K$	(3) λ
A	-100	10	132	42	0·42	0·20
C	-100	121	5	26	0·26	0·25
						λ'
A'	-100	0	142	42	0·42	0·19
C'	-100	0	126	26	0·26	0·12

The internal rate of return, λ, in the last column, appears to be 20 per cent for A and 25 per cent for C. This ranking of C above A clearly conflicts with the ranking of the other two criteria.

It transpires however that the internal rate of return criterion is at fault, and it is at fault because the first condition is not met. It is true that the calculation of the internal rate of return follows the conventional definition as given in Chapter 28. But this conventional definition, alas, violates our first condition. For it produces an implicit rate of reinvestment that, in general, is not warranted by the objective situation. It is certainly unwarranted in this example in which the only reinvestment opportunity open to any of the benefits in t_1 is that of reinvestment in the private investment sector at an annual yield equal to zero. Notwithstanding this feature of the example, the implicit reinvestment rate produced by the conventional definition of the internal rate of return turns out to be that equal to the internal rate of return itself, In investment stream C, for instance, the reinvestment rate implied by using the conventional internal rate of return is 25 per cent. This inference is easily borne out by transforming the two benefits, 121 at t_1 and 5 at t_2, into a single benefit at t_2.

237

Adopting the implicit reinvestment rate of 25 per cent, the 121 at time t_1 becomes 121 (1 + 0·25), or 151, at time t_2. Add this to the existing 5 at t_2, and we obtain a total of 156 at t_2. Now this 156 can be discounted back to give 100 at t_0, by adopting a 26 per cent discount rate. If beginning with 100 one could produce no more than 156 at t_2, then the average rate of growth would indeed be 26 per cent. But clearly one cannot produce 156 at time t_2, and the implicit 26 per cent reinvestment rate is wrong. For the yield in the private investment sector is ρ. Therefore, when the 121 at t_1 is invested for a year in the private investment sector it emerges at t_2 as being worth 121 (1 + ρ), or, since ρ is equal to zero, as worth no more than 121. This sum when added to the 5 appearing at t_2 gives a total of 126.

In other words, the C stream *cannot* be transformed into the equivalent stream − 100, 0, 156, as would seem to be implied by the conventional internal rate of return. By reference to the opportunities open to it in the economy, the C stream can be transformed only into the stream, − 100, 0, 126, which is that given in the Table as C'. Of this C' stream, the average rate of growth over the two years is 12 per cent, and this average growth-rate is denoted in the Table by λ', to indicate the *reinvestment-corrected* internal rate of return; one that is appropriate to the concept of an average growth-rate, and one moreover that is consistent with the requirement of condition (1), that reinvestment rates be made explicit and utilized. It is now also necessary, of course, to correct the conventional internal rate of return for the A stream, calculated at 20 per cent, for the equally unwarranted implicit reinvestment rate, 20 per cent that is implicitly applied to the benefit of 10 appearing at t_1. When the growth of this investment is calculated by reference only to the market opportunities, the A stream is transformed into the A' stream, − 100, 0, 142, one having a corrected internal rate of return λ' of 19 per cent. The use of these corrected internal rates of return, as can be seen in Table IV.7a, will rank the original streams A above C, as also do the other two investment criteria.

We may conclude that the satisfying of conditions (2) and (3) alone does not suffice to ensure consistency in the ranking of investment criteria. Consistency in the above example is achieved only after condition (1) is met; that is, only after the reinvestment opportunities are explicitly recognized and utilized so as to correct the unwarranted reinvestment rates implicit in the conventional definition of the internal rate of return.

4.   Investment streams A and C in Table IV.7b illustrate the case where condition (2), that requiring equal outlays, is not met, while the other two conditions are met.

There is now a discrepancy in the ranking by the two discounted value criteria. On the excess benefit criterion, $PV_r(B) - K$, A is ranked above C, whereas on the excess benefit ratio criterion, $[PV_r(B) - K]/K$, the two streams are ranked as equal. As pointed out in the preceding chapter, however, the use of the excess benefit ratio criterion tacitly assumes that the stream having the smaller outlay, C here, can be multiplied so as to use up all the available funds, 100. But if this tacit assumption were true in this example, we should have been given the information that the 80 left over from choosing the C investment stream could have been used to invest in four more of these C investment streams. In that case, the five C streams together give exactly the same result as the A stream. If we are not given this information, however, we must assume that the 80 left over after putting 20 into the C stream, can be placed only in the private investment sector. Since the private investment sector is taken to yield a zero rate per annum, the 80 placed there at t_0, to emerge as $80(1 + 0)^2$ at t_2, is worth no more than 80 at t_2. The transformed investment stream C', and the transformed investment stream A'—in any case necessary to calculate the corrected internal rate of return—now have the same outlays, 100, run for the same three periods, and have the same reinvestment rate of zero up to t_2. The ranking of A and C is now clearly the same on each of the three criteria.

TABLE IV.7b

	t_0	t_1	t_2	$PV_r(B) - K$	$[PV_r(B) - K]/K$	λ'
A	−100	50	71	21	0·21	
C	−20	10	14·2	4·2	0·21	
A'	−100	0	121	21	0·21	0·10
C'	−100	0	104·2	4·2	0·042	0·022

239

5. Finally, investment streams A and C in Table IV.7c illustrate the case where the first two conditions are met, but not the condition requiring that the investment period be uniform. Since the outlays for A and C are equal to 100, both the present value criteria produce the same ranking, C's shorter period making no difference to these criteria. This ranking, however, conflicts with that given by the internal rate of return. Notice, however, that the reinvestment-corrected internal rate of return for A, 7 per cent, is the same as the conventional internal rate of return—λ' is here the same as λ. For A, the first benefit appears at t_2, and there is no opportunity for further reinvestment and none, therefore, for implicit reinvestment rates. The same remarks apply to C. There is only one benefit at t_1 of 110·25, and the investment stream ends there.

TABLE IV.7c

	t_0	t_1	t_2	$PV_r(B) - K$	$[PV_r(B) - K]/K$	$\lambda = \lambda'$
A	−100	0	114·5	14·5	0·145	0·07
C	−100	110·25	—	10·25	0·1025	0·1025
A'	−100	0	114·5	14·5	0·145	0·07
C'	−100	0	110·25	10·25	0·1025	0·05

However, let us meet condition (3) by extending C to t_2. This can be done by investing the sum 110·25 collected at t_1 for one year in the private sector at ρ. Since ρ is equal to zero, the sum at t_2 is no more than 110·25. This equivalent stream C' can now be compared with A, or A' (which is the same as A since, in this example, no transformation is required). This stream C', however, in virtue of advancing its benefit forward a period, so as to be uniform in this respect with stream A, produces an internal rate of return of only 5 per cent. The ranking of A above C is now consistent with that arising from the application of the other investment criteria.

We may conclude, therefore, that of the three sufficient conditions laid down to ensure consistency of ranking by these various investment criteria, none can be regarded as superflous. Let us now turn in the next chapter to a more general statement.

Chapter 35
A NORMALIZATION PROCEDURE FOR PUBLIC INVESTMENT (Continued)

1. The steps to be taken to ensure identical rankings of a number of alternative investment projects for all investment criteria are those necessary to meet the three sufficient conditions for 'normalization' discussed in the preceding chapter. (a) The first step—which is, incidentally, sufficient to bring into harmony the excess benefit criterion and the excess benefit cost ratio criterion—is that a capital outlay common to all the investment projects be established. (b) The second step requires that the maximum reinvestment potential for the benefits of each investment stream be calculated and utilized. (c) The third step is that all investment streams under comparison be extended to run for the same period of time.

Finally, in the further discussion that accompanies the implementation of these conditions, we shall find it convenient to depart from the discounting method (inherent in both present discounted value, and internal rate of return criteria). Instead, we shall adopt the method of compounding forward. All benefits, and all outlays, of each investment stream, that is, will be compounded forward to yield a terminal value. Let us now discuss some of the implications of this procedure.

(a) The uniform capital outlay need not be reckoned at the initial point of time, t_0. It may be reckoned at any time that is common to all investment streams. Since we are to compound benefits forward in the first instance, it will be convenient to compound all outlays forward to the terminal period also. Whether, however, the outlays are compounded forward, or discounted backward, to a common point of time, the rate of interest to use is ρ, the common opportunity yield, say 20 per cent, in the private investment sector (which is, by assumption, greater than r, the social rate of time preference, which we can take to be 10 per cent). The reason for using ρ as the relevant interest rate is that all outlays can earn ρ in the private investment sector if they are not otherwise employed—as in fact

241

they will be in all admissible public investment projects.[1]

In calculating the magnitude of the outlay that is to be made common to all the alternative investment projects, we cannot assume indivisibility. If none of the outlays are divisible, the largest is adopted as the common outlay. Any project having a smaller outlay than this common outlay must employ the difference as advantageously as it can; which generally means putting the difference in the private investment sector. If, for example, project A is the most costly, requiring an outlay of \$10 million at t_0, which sum the capital budget allows, then if some other project B requires an outlay of only \$8 million at t_0, the \$2 million left over can always be placed in the private investment sector, there to earn ρ per annum. If, on the other hand, one of the investment projects under consideration, C, involved an outlay of \$4 million at t_0, it may be possible to invest in two of such projects, again leaving \$2 million to be placed in the private investment sector. If this were not possible, we should have \$6 million left over all of which would be placed in the private investment sector.

2. (b) No reinvestment of any of the *primary* benefits—those benefits that would exist in the absence of all reinvestment opportunities—at a rate below ρ is to be undertaken, while all opportunities for yields greater than ρ that are particular to any one of the investment projects must be full exploited. Wherever there is a number of alternative reinvestment paths open to any one, or more, of the primary benefits of an investment project, the choice of such paths is made with the aim of maximizing the terminal value of the benefits of that particular project.

In those cases where the primary benefits do not accrue as cash revenues, or where there are political constraints on the reinvestment of any revenues, they are deemed consumed at the time they accrue. As indicated in Chapter 32, we are required in such cases to com-

---

1 There is nothing illogical about taking the benefits of some specific project, involving a capital outlay K, as the opportunity cost of some alternative K-costing project. But such pair-wise comparisons are cumbersome even where the alternative investment projects are few. If, therefore, we want to rank a number of public investment projects and, at the same time, exclude from admission any of them having a corrected internal rate of return of less than ρ (the private sector yield), the simplest way is to adopt ρ as the opportunity yield common to all of them.

pound these consumed benefits forward to the terminal date, n, at the social rate of time preference, r.[2]

3. (c) The shorter the common period of investment, the simpler it is to apply the normalized procedure. However, the shortest common period has to be chosen subject to the obvious proviso that any further extension of the common period does not alter the ranking of the investment projects. Wherever there is no political or other constraint on reinvestment, the common terminal date is to be chosen as the date after which no further *specific* reinvestment opportunity is available to any of the investment streams under comparison. If, on the other hand, there are consumption constraints, which entail compounding a consumed benefit forward at r, rather than at ρ, the rule just mentioned may not meet the situation. Owing to some portion of say A's stream being consumed at t, and therefore being compounded forward at a lower rate r, as compared with the benefits of another project B (which are compounded forward at ρ), further movement forward through time allows the compounded B benefit to grow faster than the compounded A benefit. If at period t, the terminal value of A were higher than that of B then, although there may be no more specific investment opportunities open to either project, there will come a time when the terminal value of the A project will fall below that of B, and thenceforth remain below. Clearly, in cases where benefits have to be consumed, we may need to go beyond the date at which specific investment opportunities are exhausted in order to ensure that there is no potential reversal of terminal benefit values.

4. Finally, once the terminal values of each of the benefit streams, normalized for common outlay and common period, have been calculated, the investment projects can be ranked directly. Alternatively these terminal values can be reduced to present values without in any way altering the ranking, irrespective of the discount rate

---

2   If the un-reinvestible benefit occurs at time t, its worth then, B_t, and its worth on the terminal date, n, after being compounded forward at r, $B_t(1 + r)^{(t-n)}$, are deemed equivalent on society's reckoning.

used.[3] It transpires, also, that the normalized internal rates of return to be derived from these terminal values reveal the same ranking—but we shall postpone further discussion of the normalized internal rates of return for a page or two.

5. An investment stream K_0, B_1, B_2, . . , B_m, in which the negative benefits may, for convenience, be referred to as outlays, is converted by the normalization procedure into a stream

$$0, 0, 0, \ldots, \{TV^n(B) - TV^n(K)\}.$$

The $TV^n(B)$ stands for the maximum normalized terminal value of the sum of all the positive benefits in the nth, or terminal, period, while $TV^n(K)$ stands for the normalized terminal value of the sum of all outlays incurred over time.

The reader is now to be reminded that the maximum normalized terminal value of the benefits is assured by the following rules. (1) Each primary benefit is compounded forward to the terminal date either (a), at r if it is to be consumed in the period it accrues, or (b), at ρ if it is not so consumed yet has no reinvestment opportunities other than that in the private investment sector. (2) If, however, there are specific greater-than-ρ reinvestment opportunities open to any portion of a primary or secondary benefit, they are assumed to be fully utilized. As for the normalized terminal value of the initial and any later outlays, they are to be compounded forward at ρ to the terminal date. Such a terminal sum is what these outlays would have amounted to by the terminal date if they had been invested wholly in the private investment sector. And it should be manifest that unless the terminal value of the benefit stream of some specific public investment exceeds the terminal sum of its outlays, the specific public investment project offers no advantage compared with the alternative of placing the outlays in the private investment sector. Thus $TV^n(B) - TV^n(K) > 0$ constitutes an acceptable investment criterion for any investment project. If it is met we can deduce at once that $PV_i^*(B) - K^* > 0$, where $PV_i^*(B)$

---

3 Although the ranking remains invariant to the discount rate used, the excess present value over cost of each project varies inversely with the size of the discount rate. Using ρ as the discount rate, as positive excess value over cost implies a 'social surplus' from using the funds in the public investment sector as compared with their use in the private investment sector.

is the normalized present value of the stream of benefits obtained by discounting the normalized terminal value by *any* rate of interest, i, while K^* is the normalized present value of the outlays also obtained by discounting the terminal value of costs by the same interest rate i. This result is obvious since it is derived by multiplying both $TV^n(B)$ and $TV^n(K)$ by the discount factor $1/(1+i)^n$.

The definition of the normalized internal rate of return, λ^*, is that λ^* for which

$$\frac{TV^n(B)}{(1+\lambda^*)^n} = K^*.$$

Clearly, this expression provides only a single value for λ^*, which value, in addition, accords with the concept of an average rate of growth of the investment over time, since K^*, the normalized present value of the outlays, does indeeed grow at λ^* per annum to become $TV^n(B)$ in the nth year.

6.   It remains only to show that the normalization procedure ensures all criteria produce the same ranking of alternative investment projects, after which we shall return to re-examine Table IV.6.

Since normalization requires that $TV^n(K)$ be the same for all investment projects under comparison, if the normalized terminal benefit of investment project A exceeds that of C, that is if:

$$TV^n(B_A) > TV^n(B_C) \tag{1}$$

then

$$\{TV^n(B_A) - TV^n(K)\} > \{TV^n(B_C) - TV^n(K)\} \tag{2}$$

and project A is ranked above project C on the normalized terminal value criterion.

If we multiply all the terms in inequation (2) by the same discount factor, $1/(1+i)^n$, where i is any rate of interest, we have the inequation:

$$\{PV^*(B_A) - K^*\} > \{PV^*(B_C) - K^*\} \tag{3}$$

and project A is ranked above C on the normalized excess present value criterion.

Dividing both sides of the inequation (3) by K^*, we have:

$$\frac{PV^*(B_A) - K^*}{K^*} > \frac{PV^*(B_C) - K^*}{K^*} \tag{4}$$

and project A is ranked above C on the normalized excess present value over cost ratio criterion.

Finally, since λ^* is defined so that $K^*(1 + \lambda^*)^n = TV^n(B)$, we substitute the $K^*(1 + \lambda^*)^n$ expression for each side of the inequation (1) above, and obtain:

$$K^*(1 + \lambda_A)^n > K^*(1 + \lambda_B)^n$$

(where λ_A^* and λ_B^* are normalized internal rates of return for projects A and C respectively).

Therefore

$$\lambda_A^* > \lambda_B^* \tag{5}$$

and project A is ranked above C on the normalized internal rate of return criterion.

Chapter 36

A NORMALIZATION PROCEDURE FOR PUBLIC INVESTMENT (Concluded)

1.   Let us now apply these normalization rules to the data given in Table IV.6 in Chapter 34, for the present restricting our attention to the A and B projects. Under this normalization prodedure the data of Table IV.6 is transformed into those of Table IV.8. Allowing that the capital sum available for investment is not less than 100, we can multiply the A stream by 5 only if it is known to be possible to increase its scale by a factor of 5, or to be possible to undertake 5 of such investment projects. If this is not possible; if, say, no more than a scale factor of 3 is possible, we shall have a capital surplus of 40 which we shall have to compound forward at the existing ρ of 20 per cent to the terminal date. For expository purposes, however, we shall suppose that the A stream can be increased five-fold, the figures now reading −100, 75, 80, as shown in Table IV.8.

Turning to the B project, we assume that there is open to it a specific reinvestment opportunity; which is that the return of 160 in period t_3 can be invested in some specific project of one year's duration to emerge as 210 in t_4. If there are no specific opportunities open to the A stream, and no consumption of the benefits of either projects, we should choose t_4 as the terminal period.[1]

---

1   If, instead, we had supposed, for example, that the A benefit of 75 at t_1 was to be wholly *consumed* in t_1, and therefore, according to our procedure, this 75 was to be compounded forward to the terminal date at r, or 10 per cent per annum, we could *not* be sure that t_4 was to be the terminal date for reasons given in the preceding chapter. By doing the calculations with t_4 as the terminal date, and then with t_5 as the terminal date, it can in fact be shown that the ranking of A and B would be reversed. Since further periods would cause no further reversal, t_5 would then be adopted as the terminal date. Thus, at t_5, the normalized terminal benefit of the B project would exceed that of the A project. From t_5 onward B's terminal benefit would compound at 20 per cent per annum, while A's terminal benefit would compound at *less* than 20 per cent per annum (since a part of A's terminal benefit, traceable to the consumed benefit of 75 at t_1 would be compounded forward at only 10 per cent).

The normalized terminal value of the B stream is, therefore, its value at t_4 which, as stated, is 210, this figure being entered opposite the B project of Table IV.8 in column 1, under B'—where B' here stands for normalized terminal value of the benefits. The terminal value of the A stream, on the other hand, requires that the 75 in t_1 be compounded at 20 per cent to t_4 and added to the terminal value of the 80 in t_2 after this 80 also has been compounded to t_4 at 20 per cent. The normalized terminal value of the benefits of the A stream is therefore, $75(1 + 0\cdot2)^3 + 80(1 + 0\cdot2)^2$, or $244\cdot8$, which sum is entered under B' in column (1). The normalized terminal value of both streams, equal to $100 (1 + 0\cdot2)^4$, or $207\cdot4$, is indicated by K' and shown in column (2). The figures in columns (3) and (4), containing the criteria $(B' - K')$ and $(B' - K')/K'$ respectively, are easily calculated from the figures shown in the first two columns of the Table.

TABLE IV.8

	t_0	t_1	t_2	t_3	t_4	(1) B'	(2) K'	(3) $B'-K'$	(4) $(B' - K')/K'$	(5) λ^*
A	-100	75	80	·	·	$244\cdot8$	$207\cdot4$	$37\cdot4$	$\dfrac{37\cdot4}{207\cdot4}$	$25\cdot1\%$
B	-100	·	·	160	·	210	$207\cdot4$	$2\cdot6$	$\dfrac{2\cdot6}{207\cdot4}$	$20\cdot4\%$
C	-14	109	$-124\cdot5$	·	·	$188\cdot4$	$207\cdot4$	$-19\cdot0$	$\dfrac{-19\cdot0}{207\cdot4}$	$17\cdot2\%$

Normalized internal rates of return are entered in the last column and, according to our definition, are to be calculated by reference to B' and K^*, which, for the normalized outlays of projects A and B, is equal to K_0, the single initial outlay of 100. Thus for A, λ^* is equal to $25\cdot1$ per cent, since $100(1 + 0\cdot251)^4 = 244\cdot8$. Similarly, for B, λ^* is equal to $20\cdot4$ per cent since $100(1 + 0\cdot204)^4 = 210$.

Given that $\rho = 20$ per cent, both the A and B projects qualify for admission: each gives better results than the using of the 100 of initial capital in the private investment sector where it would emerge as $100(1 + 0\cdot2)^4$, or $207\cdot4$, at t_4. For the normalized terminal value of the A project at t_4 is $244\cdot8$, which provides an excess over the private sector alternative of 37·4. This 37·4 is entered into column (3) under $(B' - K')$. Similarly, the normalized terminal value of the B project at t_4 is 210, so providing an excess over the private sector alternative of 2·6, which 2·6 is also entered into column (3). Clearly, if we express the excess benefit of either project as a fraction of a common denominator, K', as in column (4), it makes no difference to the ranking of A and B. Thus A is ranked above B on the normalized excess terminal benefit criterion and also on the normalized excess terminal benefit over cost criterion. As shown in the final column, A is again ranked above B on the normalized internal rate of return criterion. Both these normalized rates also give an average rate of return over the period higher than the 20 per cent obtainable in the private investment sector.

2. Let us now turn to project C which, in Table IV.6, has a single collectible benefit of 351 at t_1. Since normalization requires a common magnitude for capital outlays, project C can be included in the comparison only if it is scaled down to the finance that is available, this being equivalent to 100 at t_0. Assuming, for argument's sake, that this is possible the C stream in Table IV.6 has to be multiplied throughout by 0·31. The resulting normalized C stream appears in Table IV.8 as -14, 109, $-124·5$.[2] This normalized C stream has a K' of 207·4 or, discounted at 20 per cent, a K' of 100 at t_0, as do both the A and B streams.

The C stream's benefit of 109 at t_1 is compounded forward at 20 per cent to t_4, to become 188·4, which is entered in the B' column. With a K' of 207·4, $(B' - K')$ is $-19·0$, and the normalized C stream would not be admitted on this normalized excess terminal benefit criterion. Neither would it be admitted on the normalized excess terminal benefit over cost criterion of column (4). As for the C stream's normalized internal rate of return λ^*, it is 17·2 per cent inasmuch as $100(1 + 0·172)^4$ is equal to the 188·4 in the B' column. Since the normalized internal rate of return at 17·2 per cent is below the 20 per cent rate of return that can be earned in the private

2 The terminal value, of the C outlays in Table IV.6, of 45 at t_0 and 402 at t_2, when comppunded at 20 per cent to t_4, is equal to 672·2 compared with a K' for A and B of 207·4. The terminal outlay of the C stream of Table IV.6 is, therefore, 672·2/207·4 too large. To normalize the C stream for outlay requires that we multiply it by the reciprocal of this fraction, or 0·31

investment sector, the C stream would not be admitted on the norma-lized internal rate of return criterion either.

The reader will observe, finally, that the ranking A, B, C, is common to each of the three criteria of columns (3), (4) and (5). He will also recognize that the present-value criteria equivalents to (3) and (4), obtained by multiplying each of the K' and B' terms by a common discount factor $1/(1 + \rho)^4$—or, for that matter, by $1/(1 + i)^4$, where i is any rate of interest—maintains the ranking, and admissibility, of the three projects.

3. This is as far as we need go in illustrating the normalization procedure. Though it ensures that all investment criteria produce identical results, it is plain that the simplest criterion to use is the normalized excess terminal benefit criterion, $(B' - K')$ of column (3). Dividing this expression by K' to obtain the $(B' - K')/K'$ criterion of column (4), or discounting either (3) or (4) to *present value* equivalent criteria, by multiplying them by the common dis-count factor $1/(1 + \rho)^n$, is gratuitous work which adds nothing to the results. The normalized internal rate of return criterion also involves additional calculation. Thus if K' has to be calculated in order to normalize the outlays, as was the case for project C in Table IV.8 (for the purpose of scaling down the C stream of Table IV.6 by a factor 0·31), as well as B', then we already have informa-tion enough to meet the $(B' - K')$ criterion without engaging in further calculation to determine the normalized internal rate of return. Even if the outlays of all the projects are initially equal, and occur only at t_0, it is simpler to use $(B' - K')$. For we have, in any case, to calculate B'. But whereas for the $(B' - K')$ criterion we have (in addition) to calculate K', or $K_0(1 + \rho)^n$, for the λ^* criterion we have (in addition) to calculate $n\sqrt{(B'/K_0)} - 1$, which equals λ^*. And clearly the former calculation is simpler than the latter.

4. There may, however, be two features of this procedure which are puzzling to the reader. First of all there is the fact that discounting back to the present of $(B' - K')$ at *any* rate of interest i does not alter the ranking of the projects and does not affect the conclusions regarding their admissibility. If the $(B' - K')$ criterion were positive for four projects A, B, C and D, and its value for each were in the proportion 7:6:5:3, then the present value equivalent criteria (either

in excess benefit form or in excess benefit over cost form) will all be positive also irrespective of the discount rate i used, and will all maintain the proportion 7:6:5:3. Very satisfying, thinks the reader; but what has happened to the social rate of time preference r, about which everything is supposed to hinge?

The social rate of time preference r does, however, continue to play an essential role, even in an economy having a private sector yield ρ above r. For only when r is used to discount the normalized terminal value of the benefit stream does the resulting figure represent the equivalent present value to society—the present value, that is, as between which and the normalized terminal value society is deemed to be indifferent.

The social rate of time preference r has another normative function: it provides a lower limit to the opportunity rate at which benefit streams may be compounded forward. Primary and secondary benefits are on no account to be reinvested at a rate below r. For example, the reinvesting of 100 of benefit today at a rate i, below r, would yield but $100(1 + i)^t$ in t years' time, whereas 100 today should not be surrendered for less than the larger sum, $100(1 + r)^t$, this being the exact sum that would compensate society t years hence for surrendering 100 today. In our model, however, the private investment sector yield is ρ, assumed greater than r, so that no reinvestment of any revenues at yields below ρ need be contemplated. As for benefits that are not reinvestible, but are consumed when they appear, they are, as explained, to be compounded forward to the terminal date at r.

5. The second feature that may puzzle some readers is the contrast between the results of the conventional method of calculating the internal rate of return used in Table IV.6 and normalized method used in Table IV.8. The conventional definition can be depended upon to produce a single internal rate of return only in the case of a single capital outlay.[3] In order for the conventional rate of return to be the same as the normalized version it is sufficient, in addition,

---

3 A single capital outlay is a *sufficient* condition for a single internal rate of return, on the conventional definition, though *not* a necessary condition. There may, that is, be a unique internal rate of return corresponding to particular investment streams that have more than one outlay. An obvious example would be -120, 120, -1, having an internal rate of return of a little less than 20 per cent.

that there be a *single benefit occuring at the terminal date*. For instance, the *B* stream in Table IV.6 has a conventional internal rate of return of 17 per cent. If the normalized period *were* three years (instead of the four periods adopted in Table IV.8—in consequence of the specific opportunity open to the *B* stream at t_3) the normalized internal rate of return would also be 17 per cent.

In general, however, and apart from these special conditions, the conventional definition of the internal rate of return not only yields a different figure from the normalized definition, but also departs from the underlying concept of this sort of criterion, that of an average rate of return, or average rate of growth of the (equivalent) initial outlay over time. Thus, if there is more than a single benefit, as there is in the *A* stream of Table IV.8 (where a benefit of 75 at t_1 is followed by a benefit of 80 at t_2), the normalized internal rate of return, even if calculated over this two-year period, is 30·2 per cent,[4] in contrast to the conventional internal rate of return of 34 per cent (as given in Table IV.6). In the normalized internal rate of return, the 75 at t_1 is compounded forward—as it should be—at the private sector rate of 20 per cent for one year, to be added to the 80 at t_2, the supposed terminal date. In the conventional internal rate of return, on the other hand, the 75 at t_1 is implicitly compounded forward— as it manifestly ought *not* to be—at the conventional internal rate of 34 per cent.[5]

Since the normalized period in Table IV.8 happens to cover four years rather than two, the normalized internal rate of return will

---

4 If

$$\frac{75(1 + 0·2) + 80}{(1 + \lambda^*)^2} = 100$$

then the normalized internal rate of return, λ^*, equals 0·302.

5 If

$$\frac{75}{(1 + \lambda)} + \frac{80}{(1 + \lambda)^2} = 100$$

then λ, by definition, is the conventional internal rate of return. If, how, we multiply this equation through by $(1 + \lambda)^2$, we have:

$$75(1 + \lambda) + 80 = 100 (1 + \lambda)^2,$$

where λ is equal to 0·34, or $75(1 + 0·34) + 80 = 180$. But at t_2, the benefits are worth only $75(1 + 0·2) + 80 = 170$.

compound the benefit-sum at t_2 for a further two periods at 20 per cent, thereby reducing the above two-period normalized internal rate of return of 30·2 per cent to 25·1 per cent. In contrast, the conventional internal rate of return takes no account of the additional periods and, as in Table IV.6, remains at 34 per cent.

6. Turning to cases in which there is more than a single outlay, there may be more than one conventional internal rate, as there would be for the C stream of Table IV.8. And in the conventional calculation, any later outlays, like benefits, are operated on by implicit discount rates that are equal to the conventional internal rates of return themselves. Thus, in discounting the outlay of 124·5 at t_2 to a value at t_0, the implicit rate of 46 per cent or 456 per cent would be employed, whereas the outlay of 124·5 at t_2 ought to be discounted to t_0 at the private sector rate of 20 per cent. It follows that either of the conventional internal rates of return, used as implicit discount factors, will understate the correct present value of the outlays.

Let us illustrate this crucial point further. In order to calculate the growth potential of the C stream we must first transform the outlay of 124·5 at t_2 into an equivalent sum at t_0. This is done by recourse to the market rate of 20 per cent. Society is indifferent as between paying 124·5 at t_2 and paying $124·5/(1 + 0·2)^2$, or 86, at t_0, since payment of 86 today can be transformed, through the private investment sector, into payment of 124·5 in two years time. The correct equivalent initial outlay for C is therefore $86 + 14$, or 100, which puts it on par with those of the other two projects, A and B, as required by the normalization procedure.

What we must *not* do is to discount this outlay commitment at t_2 back to t_0 at either of the conventional internal rates of return, 46 per cent or 456 per cent. Using the first conventional rate would offer us a present equivalent outlay of $124·5/(1 + 0·46)^2$ or 56; the second conventional rate would offer a present equivalent outlay of $124·5/(1 + 4·56)^2$, or 6. But it is not possible to discharge an obligation of 124·5 at t^2 by payment today of 56, or 6 (if it were possible, the average growth rates of the t_0 equivalent outlays in reaching 109 at t_1, would indeed be 46 per cent, or 456 per cent, respectively). The sum required today to produce 124·5 at t_2 is, as indicated above, 86.

The correct market equivalent outlay of the C stream being 100, the benefit of 109 in the following year produces an annual growth of only 9 per cent. This consideration alone would suffice to disqualify the C project since the 109 is the only benefit. For if the 100 at t_0 were instead invested in the private sector it would emerge in a year's time as 120, 11 more than is offered by the C project.

The common terminal date, however, is t_4, and this has the effect of raising C's internal rate of return above the 9 per cent for the one year. For although there are no further benefits beyond this 109 at t_1, the normalized requirement that this 109 be reinvested at the market rate of 20 per cent raises the average growth rate. In fact, the greater the number of subsequent periods the closer will the average rate of growth approach to 20 per cent. The terminal period being t_4, as stated, the average growth rate over that period (made up of 9 per cent for one year and 20 per cent for three subsequent years) works out at 17·2 per cent, our normalized internal rate of return over cost.

7. A caveat should be entered before ending this extended treatment. The express purpose of the normalization procedure, as elaborated in these three chapters, has been to sort out a number of critical issues within a familiar analytic framework. The chief conclusions emerging from the exercise spring from the formulation of sufficient conditions to ensure consistent ranking of investment projects irrespective of criteria used, in particular the rejection of r as a discount rate in calculating present value of future benefits, and after making explicit the implicit reinvestment rate of return on primary benefits, the determination of a unique internal rate of return.

There are, however, implications of this analysis which are incidental and not significant in themselves. One of them is the rule for determining the shortest common investment period. Within the analytic framework adopted, with $\rho > r$, and both ρ and r constant, the only consideration that impels us to limit the length of the common period is that of economy in calculation: why compound further into the future if the ranking and admissibility of the set of investment projects will remain unaffected?

Now, if among the set of investment projects there is one (or more) having only non-collectible benefits—benefits that are consumed at the time they occur and are, therefore, compounded forward at the social rate of time preference, r—then, in order to reach a common terminal date beyond which no ranking-reversal takes place, we should have to go forward in time until the terminal value of such a project falls below those of all those other projects whose benefits are taken as being reinvestible. Since the benefits of this former project, when compounded forward, grow at the lower rate r, as compared with the growth of the benefits of the latter at the rate ρ, the time must come when the terminal value of the former falls below those of the latter. What is more, however, the terminal value of the benefits of this former project, being compounded at r, will also fall below the terminal value of its outlays, since they are being compounded forward at ρ. Thus investment projects whose benefits, no matter how large, are destined partly to be consumed cannot meet any of the investment criteria: they will always be rejected.

This implication, which is obviously unsatisfactory, has not been brought out until now simply because, although it is perfectly valid, and economically intelligible, *within the framework of assumptions used*,[6] it has no significance in any actual application of investment criteria. In contrast, the other features of the normalization procedure we have emphasized—the use of ρ as the compound or discount rate, the corrected calculation of the internal rate of return, and the conditions sufficient for ranking consistency—remain significant in any actual application of investment criteria.

Whether this distinction, between significant and non-significant implications of a model, is methodologically acceptable is still an open question. In the meantime, however, economists do continue to write as if such distinctions are allowable. The perfectly competitive model, for example, has, as one of its implications, that firms never alter product or factor prices. And since neither the government nor any outside body alters them either, one must infer that

---

6 This means, however, that the problem cannot be circumvented simply by resorting to present discounted value methods. If we are, say, to rank two investment streams, we cannot ignore differences in their length, or the possibility of extending them through reinvestment of benefits, without first establishing the validity of doing so. We can establish this, however, only by demonstrating that it makes no difference if we extend either or both streams by reinvesting benefits, which requires that wholly consumed benefits be reinvested at r. This is tantamount to determining a minimum common terminal date.

product and factor prices never change. Again, if the U-shaped cost curve is held to determine plant size, the number of plants a firm can acquire is unlimited. For that matter, the popular assumption of production functions homogenous of degree one implies that the plant size is completely indeterminate, while the assumptions of a perfectly competitive capital market would imply that any person can live a prosperous life by the simple expedient of borrowing all he wishes to meet his future wants, repaying past debts by borrowing anew until the day he expires.

Notwithstanding such 'unrealistic' implications, these artificial models continue to do yeoman service in economic analysis. The 'unrealistic' implications are, perhaps, noted, but the purpose of the models are found in other implications. If, indeed, the economist is interested in the size of the firm or of the plant, or in the limitations on borrowing, it is not to these perfectly competitive models that he turns to for answers. Nor then does the economist turn to the familiar analytic framework used in this and the preceding chapters in order to determine the exact length of the (shortest) common terminal period. Once we look at the question in a more practical light, other factors assume importance in limiting the common period. And such factors will tend to make it shorter (never longer) than that determined by reference strictly to this analytic framework.

The chief of these factors is, of course, the increasing uncertainty of benefits (and outlays) that occur over the future. Although the treatment of uncertainty is left for the following section, what is relevant here is that allowance for it is sometimes made by raising the estimates for r over the future and, perhaps also, for lowering those for ρ. A more acceptable way, it can be argued, is to reduce the value of future expected benefits on the one hand and, on the other, to increase the value of future expected outlays. Either method ensures that after some future date the additions made to the equivalent present values of each of the projects under comparison are negligible and that, therefore, it is pointless to extend the common period beyond that date. In addition, the government may impose a time limit on the returns to a project, say twenty five years, beyond which no further return is to be counted. Whether justified or not in the particular circumstances, it has to be accepted as a political constraint. Without such outside constraints, however, no economist —in view of the uncertainties of the future—is likely to consider a common period greater than a half century or so, and seldom will he go beyond thirty years.

What exactly must be done in practice about a common period will become known only when we have solved the problems arising from uncertainty. But whatever the method turns out to be, the more significant implications of the normalization procedure that we have emphasized in these three chapters will remain a valid part of the apparatus of cost-benefit analysis.[7]

---

7 We have disregarded in this chapter the 'arbitrariness' (at least within the framework of assumptions posited) of private investors who forgo the maximum terminal value of their investments by consuming some part of their investment receipts—which consumption is, as indicated, equivalent to a private yield of ρ per annum—instead of wholly reinvesting them at ρ. Whether, within our framework of analysis, such behaviour is admissible at all is a moot point. But assuming that it were, for the sake of argument, it would have to be accepted as a datum in estimating the opportunity rate of growth in the private investment sector. In that event, the ranking, and the admissibility, of public projects have to be reconsidered.

With respect only to the question of *ranking* of public investment projects, no alteration in our procedure is necessary. We should, that is, continue to use ρ as the minimal reinvestment rate wherever the returns are collectible, on the principle of aiming for the highest terminal value of each project. Whatever private investors do with their returns has no bearing on the method of ranking, *per se*, of the public projects.

With respect to *admissibility*, however, the public investment whose terminal value is discounted at ρ is somewhat over-discounted if the $PV\rho(B)$ investment criterion is to be used for rejecting or accepting public projects, since the opportunity rate of growth of an investment outlay in the private sector is now somewhat less than ρ. It is simple, however, to make allowance for this 'arbitrary' private investors' behaviour by including along with the alternative public projects a private investment stream, call it Z, having the same common outlay and the same common terminal period—which period, as indicated, can be determined in any real situation only by taking into account future uncertainty (and also the negligible contribution made by returns occuring in, say, fifty years' time or so, to the present value of the project). The outlay of Z is, then, compounded forward to the terminal date, but not at ρ: for the consumed portions in any period will be compounded forward only at r. Consequently a public project having an annual yield just equal to ρ (or, for that matter, a little less than ρ) will have a terminal value higher than that of Z, and will qualify for admission on any of our investment criteria.

Discounting these normalized terminal values, including that of the Z project, does not, of course, make any difference to the result irrespective of the rate of discount used.

Finally, if there is also an 'irrational' policy constraint permitting public funds—raised, say, wholly by reducing private consumption—to be used only for public investment, we compare the resulting TV of the benefits of the public project with the TV, of the outlays when compounded at or to the terminal date. Alternatively we could discount the TV of the public investment at r, and approve of it only if its present value, so discounted, exceeds the present value of the outlays so discounted.

Chapter 37

SELECTING A SET OF INVESTMENT PROJECTS

1. We now take the final step in exploring the uses of investment criteria: that of selecting, from a large number, a set of investment projects subject to a budget constraint. The methods proposed here build on the normalization technique elucidated in the preceding chapters. In other respects, however, they will depart only in limited ways from the more familiar methods put forward in the last decade or so.[1]

The general features of this problem are, first, that there are several objectives or purposes, single or multiple to be served, such as pest-control, flood-control, irrigation, electricity provision, or flood-control plus irrigation, or flood-control plus irrigation plus electricity, in one or in several regions. Second, that for each of these single or multple objectives in a given region there is a number of alternative investment projects, all of which are technically feasible. Given the same competitive full-employment economy, with ρ greater than r, the problem is that of choosing, from among all the technically feasible investment projects, one project for each of some number of specific purposes—within the limits of the finance available. The set of investment projects chosen must be an optimum in the sense that society would prefer the capital budget to be used for this set of projects rather than for any other set.

2. Since we have argued, in precious chapters, that the use of r as a discount rate in calculating the present value of an investment stream is defective, and since we have also argued in the the preceding chapter that normalized terminal values of both benefits and outlays are the components of a correct investment criterion, and that no advantage derives from transforming them either into

---

1 I have in mind the particular contributions of McKean (1957) and Steiner (1959), among others.

normalized internal rates of return or discounted present value criteria, we shall describe a method of investment selection based on the method of terminal values. The terminology will be simplified by omitting from now on the adjective 'normalized', notwithstanding that terminal figures will be normalized in all the respects mentioned in the preceding two chapters, save that which requires uniformity of capital outlays. For, in general, the technically feasible investment projects, from which the selection must be made, will not all have the same (equivalent) initial outlay.

As for the question of how the purposes, or required services, and the alternative investment options that can be used to provide them, are to be counted, occasions may well arise when the treatment has to be arbitrary. The following rules, however, provide some guidance. (a) The same type of service required in a different locality, or region, is conceived as a different service. (b) If, within a single locality, two or more services can be produced in combination by a single investment project, each different combination of services so producible qualifies as a distinct service. Thus if it is possible to provide flood control alone, possible also to provide electricity alone, and possible also to provide both, though in three different proportions, there will be five different services in that locality. (c) *Per contra*, if two or more investment projects need to combine in order to provide a single service, or a complex of services, each of such combination of investment projects is to be treated as a single investment option. (d) If there are scale effects in any investment project, each scale of the project is to be distinguished (in the light of the expected demand for the service or services in question) and is to be treated as a separate investment option.

Turning to the question of finance, the more general approach will suppose that the finance for the resulting investment programme is raised in part from the capital budget and in part from the displacing, or at least the not renewing, of existing public enterprises. There may also be arrangements to encourage private investment to compete with public investment, both sorts of investment being judged solely by the criterion we evolve.

3. Having listed the number of services to be met and the number of alternative investment projects for each service, the first step, after deciding the length of the common period, is to divide the

calculated excess terminal benefit (terminal benefit *less* terminal cost) of each of the investment projects by its terminal cost. This gives us a *per dollar* excess terminal benefit (ETB) for each investment option. We can then place in a single row the ETBs of all investment options that are technically able to provide a particular service. There will then be as many such rows as there are services, single and complex, under consideration. The array of such ETBs provides the data we have to work with.

The method of selection will be illustrated, however, under the assumption that there are but three possible services under consideration: A, a passenger and traffic bridge across the Flo River at point X; B, a dam across the Flo River in order to generate electricity for an area marked Y; and C, another dam which can provide irrigation and electricity for the same area.

The simplest context in which to solve the problem is that in which (I) there is no possibility of private enterprise undertaking to meet any of these services, and in which (II), the initial capital available, say $5 million, is met wholly by the government, say by raising additional taxes.[2] The hypothetical ETB data are set out in Table IV.9 where the bracketted figures represent the terminal value of the costs of each of the investment options in $ millions.

TABLE IV.9

A	0·05	(1·8)	0·20	(1·5)	0·30	(2·0)			·	
B	0·10	(4·5)	0·20	(4·0)	0·40	(4·0)	0·45	(3·0)	0·50	(3·5)
C	0·22	(5·0)	0·25	(4·0)	0·30	(2·5)	0·35	(3·0)	·	

The ETB figures in the Table are all positive, as they have to be to qualify for admission, since a positive sum indicates that there is an excess of terminal benefit over costs (costs, as stated, being compounded forward to the terminal date at a ρ of 20 per cent). In other words, all the investment options included in the Table produce a greater terminal value than if, instead, their outlays were invested in the private sector at 20 per cent.

---

2 The (II) assumption will be removed later on, but the (I) assumption will be maintained throughout. For a more general treatment in which both assumptions are removed the reader is referred to my 1967 paper.

As there is only $5 million in the investment budget there is no point in including among the set of investment options any one requiring an initial outlay of more than $5 million. However, since we are dealing in terminal values, the initial capital outlays have to be compounded to the common terminal date, t_n, at 20 per cent. We can suppose then that the $5 million budget today becomes $7 million at this terminal date t_n.

4. The problem now reduces itself to the mathematical one of using the data in Table IV.9 so as to choose no more than one of the alternative options in each of a number of rows (since no more than one investment option can be adopted for each of the services to be provided), but choosing them so as to obtain the highest total of terminal benefits for the given terminal cost of $7 million.

If, for instance, we pick the investment option in the C row having an ETB of 0·22, and the investment option in the A row having an ETB of 0·20, we shall be picking two investment options which between them have a terminal cost of $7 million, so exhausting the budget. The total excess benefit for this choice will be (0·22 × $5 million) *plus* (0·30 × $2 million) or $1·7 millions. If, instead, we pick the 0·50 ETB option in the B row and the 0·35 ETB option in the C row, these two investment options between them use up $6·5 million of terminal capital. Unless we assume that investment options can be increased in any proportion, an unlikely contingency, we shall have left over $0·5 million of capital which, of course, produces no excess terminal benefit. The total excess benefit from this latter choice, however, is (0·50 × $3·5 million) *plus* (0·35 × $3·0 million), or $2·8 million. Clearly, the latter choice is better than the former. And so we could continue, picking out other combinations of investment projects, the total terminal costs of which do not exceed $7 million, in order to discover the combination yielding the highest total excess benefit.

Where there are many rows, and many investment options in each row, the selection process can be a lengthy business. A computer programme so as to pick the optimal combination of projects from all those allowed by the given budget constraint would require that the problem be formalized, as it is in the footnote below.[3]

But if it so happens that along any one row the terminal costs of all the options are equal (though the amount differs from row to row) we can dispense with the computer's service. We should, in that case, choose the highest ETB in each row, and list them in descending order starting from the highest. We work down this list, summing the terminal capital requirements (given in brackets) until the total sum is as close as possible to the available (terminal) capital without exceeding it. This condition that the terminal capital costs (the bracketed figures) in each row be uniform may seem stringent, but the method will probably work even where the condition is only approximately met. Indeed, if we tried the method out on the data in Table IV.9 where the condition is far from being met, we should form the list:

---

3 The problem is to maximize

$$\sum_{i=1,j=1}^{q} \sum^{m} \tau_{ij} \, w_{ij} \, K_{ij} \tag{1a}$$

$$\left. \begin{array}{l} w_{ij} = 0, 1 \\ \tau_{ij} > 0 \end{array} \right\} \tag{2a}$$

$$\sum_{i=1,j=1}^{q} \sum^{m} w_{ij} \, K_{ij} < K \tag{3a}$$

$$\sum_{j=1}^{m} w_{ij} < 1 \; 1 \; (\text{for all } i) \tag{4a}$$

There are q possible services, and for each service there are never more than m alternative investment options.

τ_{ij} is the ETB of the jth investment option that caters to the ith service, and K_{ij} is the terminal capital cost corresponding to the ij^{th} investment option.

The first part of the condition (2a), that $w_{ij} = 0, 1$, indicates that the weight w_{ij} is equal to unity if that investment option is selected as part of the programme, and is equal to zero if it is excluded from the programme. The second part of condition (2a) $\tau_{ij} > 0$, indicates that no investment option is to be included in the programme unless it can do better with its capital outlay than can be done with it in the private sector.

Condition (3a) states that the sum of the terminal capital costs of the investment options in the programme should not exceed the terminal value of the capital available ($7 million in the example above).

Since no more than one option from each row can be chosen we require condition (4a), that the sum of the weights in any row does not exceed unity. This condition means in effect that either one option can be chosen from the ith row, or none.

B	0·50	(3·5)
C	0·35	(3·0)
A	0·30	(2·0)

The highest ETB options for rows B and C respectively will use up $6·5 million of terminal capital. Obviously the highest ETB option (0·30) in the A row cannot also be included without infringing the budget constraint of $7 million of terminal capital. The total excess benefit from the highest ETB options of rows B and C is equal to (0·50 × 3·5 million) + 0·35 × 3·0 million), or $2·8 million. And this investment programme happens to be the one yielding the maximum excess terminal value possible under these conditions.

5.   We now remove the (II) assumption, and consider the case where the capital sum is to be raised in part by discontinuing existing public enterprises. Let there be three such public enterprises, x, y and z, that are due to expire this year, but, having recouped their capital through amortization,[4] these enterprises could either be renewed, or their funds used for the new investment programme. If they are renewed their ETBs are calculated respectively as, say, 0·05 (2), 0·15 (1), and 0·35 (3), where, again, the figure in the brackets refers to the terminal worth, in $ million, of the capital required. Let us suppose that the terminal value of the total capital available is $7 million, as before, but that now only $4 million of it is to come from additional taxes, the remainder coming from the amortization funds of the three public enterprises mentioned above. How do we now proceed to select a programme giving the maximum excess terminal benefits for the available funds?

The opportunity cost of obtaining capital *in excess* of the $4 million (in terminal value) being raised by taxation is not simply ρ— as it will be for this $4 million of new investment. On the assumption that the existing enterprises yield at least ρ (for if they yield less than ρ they should not, in any case, be renewed), the opportunity cost of using an additional $3 million by displacing existing public enterprises must be the expected yields of these enterprises. The procedure, then, is to discontinue first that enterprise having the

---

4   The amortization funds are assumed to be invested in the private sector at ρ, where they are left until particular projects offering more than ρ are available within the existing political constraints.

lowest ETB, provided that the funds so released are used to introduce a new investment option having a higher ETB. The second existing public enterprise to discontinue is, clearly, that having the next lowest ETB, again provided that it is replaced by a new investment having a higher ETB (although one that is as low or lower than the ETB of the new investment(s) replacing the first public enterprise). If this plan is followed, a number of new public investment projects will be financed, up to $3 million, by the funds made available from discontinuing a number of existing public enterprises. Moreover, on this procedure, the ETB of the last public enterprise to be discontinued, though the highest among the discontinued enterprises, will be lower than the ETB of the new investments that replace it (this being the lowest ETB of all the newly introduced investments).[5] It should be manifest that if this latter condition were not met, if the ETB of the last incoming new investment(s) were below that of the last outgoing public enterprise, then we could improve matters by forgoing these new investment(s) in favour of the otherwise to-be-discontinued public enterprise.

Assuming that the new investment options A, B, and C, are as before, we should continue to rank them in order of ETB as B, C, A. The B option will certainly qualify, and the $3.5 million outlay will be financed from the $4 million available from the budget. If no more funds were available, the $\frac{1}{2}$ million left over would be invested in the private sector. However, by discontinuing existing enterprises x and y, having ETBs respectively of 0·05 and 0·15, another $3 million can be made available to finance the new investment C which offers an ETB of 0·35. Since we should require an additional $2 million to introduce A as well, this is as far as we can go within the budget constraints. But the reader will notice that if the budget restraint were extended, say, to $9 million, we could not introduce A by displacing existing enterprise z without violating our rules. For the ETB of enterprise z is 0·35, while that of new investment A is only 0·30.

As in the previous case, that in which the whole of the capital budget is raised by taxes, the solving of the problem appears to be difficult once we have a large number of services to be met, each

5   The procedure is analogous with that of increasing output so long as diminishing marginal revenue is above rising marginal cost. In this case, however, the ETB of the incoming new investments takes the place of marginal revenue, and the ETB of the outgoing public enterprises take the place of marginal cost.

attainable by any one of a number of alternative investment projects, and also a large number of public enterprises that can be discontinued and their funds made available for the investment programme. Nevertheless, the problem can be formalized, as in the footnote below,[6] and a systematic procedure devised to enable the

---

6 Let aK be the terminal value of the capital to be made available from the budget, where a is positive and less than one (in the text, a is 4/7, and aK, therefore is $4 million). We have then to maximize

$$\sum_{i=1}^{q} \sum_{j=1}^{m} \tau_{ij} \, w_{ij} \, K_{ij} \tag{1a}$$

subject to:
$$\begin{cases} w_{ij} = 0, 1 \\ \tau_{ij} > 0 \end{cases} \tag{2a}$$

subject also to:
$$\sum_{i=1}^{q} \sum_{j=1}^{m} w_{ij} \, K_{ij} \leqslant K - M$$
$$\text{(where } M \geqslant 0) \tag{3a'}$$

$$\sum_{j=1}^{m} w_{ij} \leqslant 1 \text{ (for all } i) \tag{4a}$$

In addition, we are to minimize:
$$\sum_{h=1}^{H} \tau_h \, w_h \, k_h \tag{5a}$$

subject to
$$w_h = 0, 1 \tag{6a}$$

$$\sum_{h=1}^{H} w_h \, K_h \geqslant (1 - a) \, K - M \tag{7a}$$

$$\tau_i{}^* > \tau_h{}^* \text{ (for all } i) \tag{8a}$$

M is the amount by which the capital to be raised from discontinuing public enterprises will fall short of the maximum allowable (the maximum allowable being $3 million in our example) with M happening to be zero, since the discontinuing of existing enterprises x and y make the whole of this $3 million available. If, instead, they had only made $2\frac{1}{2}$ million available, M would be $\frac{1}{2}$ million). To the extent given by the magnitude of M, less capital than K is available for the total of new investments to be introduced, as in equation (3a'), and less capital is to be released from the discontinuation of the existing enterprises, as indicated by equation (7a).

Minimizing the (5a) equation expresses the requirement that we discontinue those among the existing public enterprises that together show the least possible loss of excess benefit.

The last condition (8a) determines the sum M. The symbol $\tau_i{}^*$ are the ETB's of each of the new investment options that are finally selected, while $\tau_h{}^*$ is the highest ETB of the outgoing public enterprise. The condition (8a) requires that all the adopted investment options have an ETB that is higher than the highest ETB of the outgoing public enterprises.

All the other equations carry the same interpretation as that given for the previous case.

computer to select the optimum investment programme.

6. In conclusion, one must concede the possibility that, owing to past habits of thought, economists might continue to find it easier to think of the problem in terms of the present value of costs and benefits rather than in terms of their terminal values. There is nothing wrong in conceiving and solving the problem in these terms. The method of selecting the investment programme outlined in this chapter can just as well be used if the present value of excess benefits is substituted for their terminal value, and if the present value of outlays is substituted for their terminal values, provided, always, that the normalization technique continues to be employed.

REFERENCES AND BIBLIOGRAPHY FOR PART IV

Alchian, A. 'The Rate of Interest, Fisher's Rate of Return over Costs, and Keynes Internal Rate of Return', *American Economic Review*, 1955.

Bailey, M. J. 'Formal Criteria for Investment Decisions', *Journal of Political Economy*, 1959.

Eckstein, O. 'Investment Criteria for Economic Development', *Quarterly Journal of Economics*, 1957.

— *Public Finances, Needs, Sources and Utilization*. London: National Bureau of Economic Research, 1961.

— *Water Resource Development—the Economics of Project Evaluation*. Cambridge, Mass: Harvard University Press, 1958.

Feldstein, M. 'Net Social Benefit Calculation and the Public Investment Decision', *Oxford Economic Papers*, 1964.

Galenson, W. and Liebenstein, H. 'Investment Criteria, Productivity and Economic Development', *Quarterly Journal of Economics*, 1955.

Hirschliefer, J. 'Theory of Optimal Investment Decision', *Journal of Political Economy*, 1958.

Lind, R. C. 'The Social Rate of Discount and the Optimal Rate of Investment: Further Comment', *Quarterly Journal of Economics*, 1964.

Lorie, J. and Savage, L. J. 'Three Problems in Rationing Capital', *Journal of Business*, 1955.

Mabro, R. 'Normalisation Procedure for Public Investment: A Comment', *Economic Journal*, 1969.

Marglin, S. 'The Opportunity Costs of Public Investment', *Quarterly Journal of Economics*, 1963 (a).

— 'The Social Rate of Discount and the Optimal Rate of Investment', *Quarterly Journal of Economics*, 1963 (b).

Margolis, J. 'The Economic Evaluation of Federal Water Resource Development', *American Economic Review*, 1959.

Massé, P. *Optimal Investment Decisions: Rules for Action and Criteria for Choice*. New Jersey: Prentice-Hall, 1962.

McKean, R. N. *Efficiency of Government through Systems Analysis*. New York: Wiley, 1958.

Mishan, E. J. 'A Normalisation Procedure for Public Investment Criteria', *Economic Journal*, 1967.

Nichols, A. 'Normalisation Procedure for Public Investment Criteria: A further Comment', *Economic Journal*, 1970.

— 'The Opportunity Costs of Public Investment: Comment', *Quarterly Journal of Economics*, 1964.

Robinson, R. 'The Rate of Interest, Fisher's Rate of Return over Costs, and Keynes' Internal Rate of Return: Comment', *American Economic Review*, 1956.

Sen, A. K. 'Capital-intensity in Development Planning', *Quarterly Journal of Economics*, 1957.

Solomon, E. 'The Arithmetic of Capital-budgeting Decisions', *Journal of Business*, 1956.

Steiner, P. O. 'Choosing among Alternative Public Investments in the Water Resource Field', *American Economic Review*, 1959.

Subcommittee on Benefits and Costs (Federal Inter-Agency River Basin Committee) *Proposed Practices for Economic Analysis of River Basin Projects*. Washington, 1950.

Usher, Dan. 'The Social Rate of Discount and the Optimal Rate of Investment: Comment', *Quarterly Journal of Economics*, 1964.

PART V. UNCERTAINTY

Chapter 38
CERTAINTY EQUIVALENCE

1. The treatment in this section of the methods for dealing with uncertainty in project evaluation is, inevitably perhaps, the least satisfactory feature of this introductory volume. In the evaluation of any project there is sure to be some guesswork about the magnitudes of future costs and benefits, arising in the main from technological innovations and shifts in demand which may affect the prices of the inputs and outputs. In consequence, economists making use of the methods discussed in this section cannot be sure of arriving at a common figure or set of figures for a specific project. The problem of how to make decisions in any situation where the past affords little if any guidance is not one that can be satisfactorily resolved either by logic or empiricism, and what rules have been formulated are either of limited application or of no practical value. We shall, however, consider briefly and in a simple-minded way the various methods that have been proposed to deal with this problem of uncertainty, beginning with the device of reducing an uncertain prospect to an equivalent certainty.

2. Suppose that I am uncertain of the price my house will fetch on the market when I come to sell it in five years' time. Though uncertain of the exact price, I will surely entertain some ideas of what the price is likely to be. With luck, I think it could be $60,000, possibly even more. Allowing for this, that and the other, it is, however, more likely to be $50,000. Yet it could well be as low as $40,000, and one cannot altogether exclude the possibility of its fetching a sum lower even than this.

I should be glad to be free of the anxiety caused by this uncertainty about the sales price of my house for a guaranteed price of $50,000 five years hence. Indeed, I could be induced to agree to a smaller sum than $50,000. The question naturally arises: what is the lowest guaranteed sum I would be prepared to accept in five years' time to be rid of uncertainty? If it were $45,000, then $45,000 is said to represent the certainty equivalent that corresponds to the range of uncertain prospects.

If, on the other hand, I contemplated buying a particular house in five years' time for a sum which could be as low as $72,000 but might be as high as $100,000, I might be induced to agree to pay, in five years' time, as much as (but no more than) $86,000. If so, $86,000 becomes the certainty equivalent corresponding to the uncertain purchase price.[1]

In general, it is asserted that to any uncertain future sum of money—to be paid or to be received—there corresponds a guaranteed sum as between which and the uncertain sum in question the individual is indifferent.

On the more common assumption of risk-aversion for transactions of some importance, a person is prepared to pay some premium for safety. If, therefore, the expected figure for the sale of his house appears to be $50,000, by accepting a guaranteed price of $45,000 he can be said to be paying a risk premium of $5,000. If, on the other hand, he is concerned with the problem of buying a particular house in five years' time, and the most likely price is $80,000, by accepting a guaranteed future price of $86,000, he can be said to be paying a risk premium of $6,000. It goes without saying that the higher the degree of uncertainty about the future price,[2] the greater the risk premium a person will be willing to pay.

---

1 If there were only two possible outcomes, $100,000, expected with a probability of $\frac{1}{4}$, and $72,000 expected with a probability of $\frac{3}{4}$, the certainty equivalent might be thought equal to ($\frac{1}{4} \times$ $100,000) + ($\frac{3}{4} \times$ $72,000), or $79,000. In 'normal' cases, it would be less than $79,000, as explained in Chapter 43. In the present chapter we cannot, however, assume that probabilities can be attached to each of a range of possible outcomes.

2 The higher degree of uncertainty might be measured by a higher degree of variance if it were possible to talk of likelihood in a probabilistic sense, one arising from repeated experiment in an unchanged universe—which is not, however, the case for uncertainty.

3. This notion of uncertainty equivalence is, perhaps, a useful ploy in working through abstract economic constructs where the troublesome fact of uncertainty can be formally accommodated, without any amendment to the theory, simply by attributing a certainty equivalent to every uncertain magnitude. But it provides no guidance to the economist engaged in evaluating a project. If he cannot be sure of a figure at any time in the future he will have to guess at it, and if he is at all sensible he will choose to err on the conservative side. There is no way of insuring himself. The knowledge that some rational being, when faced with the problem of placing a value on some future magnitude, might well choose a value very different from that chosen by another equally rational individual, may be of some consolation to him in his perplexity. But it cannot provide him with any guidance.[3]

---

3 By measuring expected value (or arithmetic mean) along the horizontal axis and variance on the vertical axis, a 'Gambler's indifference map' can be constructed. The indifference curves slope upward from left to right indicating that increased uncertainty (as measured by variance) has to be compensated by an increase in expected value. If we now have a number of alternative future benefits to choose from (all incurring the same cost), each identified by a particular expected value and variance, that touching the highest indifference curve is to be chosen.

This construction enables one to rank a number of alternative uncertain benefits without first reducing each to a certainty equivalent. Though, formally, a more direct method than that indicated in the text, exception can be taken to measures of mean and variance in situations of genuine uncertainty. Moreover, in the absence of a community indifference map, and in the absence of agreement on the characteristics of the data, the method provides no more guidance in the face of uncertainty than does the method of certainty equivalents; which is to say it provides no guidance at all.

Chapter 39
GAME THEORY

1. Since game theory may be regarded as a technique invented to deal with cases of complete ignorance in respect of initial probabilities of the possible outcomes, the reader might be inclined to pitch his hopes for useful guidance a little higher. Again I think he will be disappointed, but before pronouncing judgement we shall illustrate the relevant technique known as the 'two-person zero-sum game'[1] with one or two simple examples.

2. Consider first a reservoir which is full at the beginning of the season and can be used both for irrigation and flood-control. Without any prior knowledge of whether or not a flood will occur, a decision is required on how much water is to be released. If a little water is released it will be good for the harvest, but it will be ineffectual in preventing flood damage. If a lot of water is released it will make flood damage virtually impossible, but it will damage the harvest to some extent.

Now the amount of water which can be released from the reservoir can range in general from nothing at all to the whole lot. As for the flood, if it occurs, it can be either negligible or destructive. In order to illustrate the principle, however, we can restrict ourselves to two possible outcomes, (b_1) full flood and (b_2) no flood, The options open to the decision-maker are also to be restricted to a_1, release one-third of the reservoir, a_2 release two-third of the reservoir, a_3 release the lot.[2] In addition to the possible 'states of nature' (b_1 and b_2), and the options open to us (a_1, a_2 and a_3), we are also assum-

---

1 So-called for the rather obvious reason (1) that the game is played between two persons, or groups, one of which may be 'nature', and (2) that there are no mutual gains to be made—the gains to one party being equal to the loss for the other party. An introduction to such games is given in Williams (1954).
2 The example is borrowed from R. Dorfman in Maass (1962), pp. 130 ff.

ed to have a clear notion of the result of any occurance given the particular option adopted. If, for example, a decision is taken to release two-thirds of the reservoir (option a_2), and a full flood (b_1) occurs, the net benefit—that is, the value of the harvest *less* the value of the damage done—is equal, say, to $140,000. Again, if we choose the a_3 option instead, the value of the net benefit becomes $80,000. Since there are three options for each of the two possible states of nature, b_1 and b_2, there will be altogether six possible outcomes each with a net revenue figure. The scheme is depicted in Table V.1 below:

TABLE V.1

	(b_1) Flood	(b_2) No flood
a_1	130,000	400,000
a_2	140,000	260,000
a_3	80,000	90,000

A glance at the Table will convince the reader that, provided the six figures above are accepted as correct estimates of net benefits, option a_3—requiring the release of all the water in the reservoir— will not be adopted. Whether b_1 or b_2 occurs the net benefits of adopting the a_3 option will be lower than those of either a_1 or a_2. In the jargon, option a_3 is dominated by the other options, a fact that is revealed by the figures in the a_1 row (130,000 and 400,000) and those in the a_2 row (140,000 and 260,000) both sets of figures being larger than the a_3 row figures (80,000 and 90,000). We could then save some unnecessary calculation by eliminating the dominated option a_3, since there are no circumstances in which it would pay to adopt it. Nevertheless we shall retain it in this simplified example as the additional exercise will be useful while the additional calculation will be slight.

Given no information other than that in Table V.1 we could employ either of two standard methods to produce a decision:

3. *A. Maximin procedure.* If he looks along the first row of Table V.1, showing the net revenues, 130,000 and 400,000 corresponding to each of the two possible alternative states of nature, b_1 and b_2, the decision-maker will realize that if he chooses option a_1 the worst that can happen is that b_1 takes place, yielding a revenue of only 130,000. Assuming that he is a conservative person, he will want to

272

compare this worst result, or minimal net revenue, he can obtain from choosing a_1 with those minima he might obtain if instead he adopts the a_2 or a_3 option. Now the choice of a_2 can realize a net yield of either 140,000 or 260,000 according as b_1 or b_2 occurs respectively. He can then be sure of at least 140,000. Similarly if he chooses option a_3 he can be sure of obtaining at least 80,000. These three row minima, 130,000 for a_1, 140,000 for a_2, and 80,000 for a_3 are all shown in the third column of Table V.2—which is the same as Table V.1 except for the addition of two columns.

TABLE V.2

	b_1	b_2	Row minima	Maximin (maximum of row minima)
a_1	130,000	400,000	130,000	
a_2	140,000	260,000	140,000	140,000
a_3	80,000	90,000	80,000	

Down this third column he reads off the worst possible outcome corresponding to each option. If he chooses a_1, he can be sure of not getting less than 130,000. If he chooses a_2, he can be sure of not getting less than 140,000. If he chooses a_3, he can be sure of not getting less than 80,000. It will then occur to him that if he chooses any option *other than* a_2 he might get less than 140,000; for example, if having chosen a_1, b_1 occurs, he will receive only 130,000, whereas if he chooses a_3 he will receive only 80,000 or 90,000 according as event b_1 or event b_2 occurs. The largest net revenue he can be *sure* of obtaining is, then, $140,000. The maximin principle therefore requires that he choose option a_2 (releasing two-thirds of the reservoir), and assure himself of no less than $140,000.

The guiding idea has been to pick out the maximum figure from column three, which column contains the minimum possible net revenues corresponding to each option. Hence the figure chosen—140,000 in column four of Table V.2—is spoken of as the *maximin*.

4. One feature of the above example is that capital costs are taken to be constant for each of the alternative options. This enables us to compare directly the net revenues—annual revenues *less* annual loss

—in each of the first two columns. If we assume instead that revenues are fixed and that costs alone vary according to the decision made and the event which takes place, we can go through the same sort of exercise.

An example would be the installation of a boiler in a works.[3] Again we can suppose three options: a_1, installing a coal-fired boiler, a_2, installing an oil-fired boiler, or a_3, installing a dual boiler, one that could be switched from using coal to using oil, and vice versa, at negligible cost. Three possible occurrences are to be considered: b_1, coal prices rise relative to oil prices over the next twenty years by an average of 25 per cent; b_2, the reverse of this; and b_3, the relative prices of the two fuels remain on the average unchanged.

The outcomes of the relevant calculations are summarized in Table V.3, the figures being the present discounted values (in thousands of dollars) of the streams of future costs associated with each option for each of the three possible outcomes.

TABLE V.3

	b_1	b_2	b_3	Row Minimum	Maximin
a_1	−13·0	−12·0	−12·0	−13·0	
a_2	−11·3	−12·5	−11·3	−12·5	−12·5
a_3	−12·8	−12·8	−12·8	−12·8	

By convention costs are to be regarded as negative revenues, so the figures in Table V.3 are all negative. Looking along the a_1 row the worst outcome is −13·0. If a_1 is chosen and b_1 should occur, the cost would be 13. (13 is the highest absolute figure in the row, but seen as a nagative revenue and considered algebraically − 13 is less than −12. Thus −13 is the lowest figure in the row.) The largest costs, or the smallest gains, corresponding to options a_2 and a_3 are, respectively, −12·5 and −12·8, which figures are entered in the fourth column. Of these row minima, the maximum (or least cost) is −12·5 corresponding to option a_2 which, on the maximum principle, would be the one to be chosen. Having chosen a_2, we can

3   This example has been adapted from that given in Moore (1968).

be sure that the cost to which the firm can be subjected cannot exceed 12·5. This cost would be incurred if event b_2 took place. If, however, event b_1 or b_3 occurred the cost would be only 11·3.

Chapter 40
GAME THEORY (Continued)

1.   There is one implication of this maximin principle that is obviously unsatisfactory. It seeks security above all, and is therefore highly conservative. In Table V.1, for instance, we are led by it to choose a_2 rather than a_1 simply because in choosing a_2 we can be sure of obtaining at least $140,000 whereas if we choose a_1 we can be sure of obtaining at least $130,000. If we feel pretty certain of getting the least in all cases, we should indeed be wise to choose that least which is largest. And the least for a_2 is $10,000 larger than that for a_1. But if it so happens that the event b_2 does take place, our choice of a_2 yields us only $260,000, whereas we instead choose if option a_1 event b_2 yields as much as $400,000. In other words, if b_2 takes place after all, we shall forgo an extra gain of $140,000 ($400,000 *minus* $260,000). The cost of playing safe—of ensuring $10,000 more if the worst should happen—is that of losing the opportunity of gaining $140,000 more if the best should happen.

2.   We can 'cook up' another set of figures for this example, those in Table V.4 below, in order to bring out this defect even more sharply.

TABLE V.4

	b_1	b_2	Row Minimum	Maximin
a_1	13	5,000	13	
a_2	14	15	14	14

The row minima for options a_1 and a_2 are shown, in the third column, to be 13 and 14 respectively. On the maximin principle, the a_2 option is to be chosen as that which guarantees a net receipt of no less than 14—but, also, no more than 15. By comparing this choice with the rejected option a_1, we cannot but realize that we are sacrificing the chance of gaining 5,000, in order to increase our guaranteed minimum receipt from 13 to 14. With outcomes such as those in the columns of Table V.4, it is hard to think of any one employing the maximin method and choosing a_2. For he cannot but be aware that if event b_2 turns up, he receives 15 whereas if he had chosen a_1 he would receive 5,000: he is aware then that by choosing a_2 he lays himself open to a potential loss of 4,985 (5,000 *minus* 15).

A less conservative person would not want to direct his choice on the maximin principle even if the figures were less enticing than those in Table V.4. Indeed, if he were at all enterprising, and had an eye open for the larger gains that are possible, he would adopt something like the reverse of the maximin principle. What he would want to avoid is the possibility of an outcome which will make him regret his choice. Since his regret will increase with the size of the loss of possible gain—4,985, in the above example, if he chooses a_2—he will adopt the principle of minimizing his regret. Hence, the alternative *minimax-regret* procedure suggested by economists.

3. *B. Minimax procedure.* We can illustrate this procedure by constructing Table V.5 below using the primary data given in Table V.1. Suppose a flood occurs, which is to say that the b_1 event takes place, the initial choice of option a_2 would have secured a net revenue of 140,000. If, on the other hand, a_1 instead had been chosen, the net revenue would have been 130,000; or 10,000 less than could have been got had we chosen a_2. We therefore put a 10,000 in the cell opposite a_1 and below b_1 in Table V.5. This 10,000 entry is to be interpreted as follows: if b_1 occurs, the prior choice of option a_2 yields the largest receipt, 140,000. By choosing some other option, say a_1, we receive only 130,000, a potential loss of 10,000. Below b_1 and opposite a_3, however, we place the figure 60,000 since, if b_1 occurs, our prior choice of a_3 would yield 80,000—a potential loss of 60,000 (140,000 *minus* 80,000) compared with the largest yield of 140,000 that would come from having chosen a_2. Opposite a_2 itself we obviously put a zero, as there is no potential loss from having chosen a_2 if event b_1 occurs.

We now fill the cells down the second column. The highest net revenue if event b_2 occurs is 400,000 corresponding to the choice of option a_1: hence a zero opposite a_1 and below b_2. If a_2 instead is chosen only 260,000 can be collected—a potential loss of 140,000

(400,000 minus 260,000) is involved. Opposite a_2, therefore, we place the figure 140,000. If, finally, a_3 is chosen, only 90,000 can be collected, a potential loss of 310,000 (400,000 *minus* 90,000). Opposite a_3 we therefore place the figure 310,000.

TABLE V.5

	b_1	b_2	Row Maxima (of potential losses)	Minimax (minimum of row maxima)
a_1	10,000	0	10,000	10,000
a_2	0	140,000	140,000	
a_3	60,000	310,000	310,000	

Since the figures in the first two columns are to be regarded as potential losses, row a_3 is again dominated by the other rows. Its potential losses for either event, b_1 or b_2, are larger than those of any other row. The standard computational procedure would be to eliminate a_3 before calculating the figures for the Row Maxima column. But, again, in so simple an example, it adds to the interest while causing no difficulty.

Since it is regret at potential losses we now seek to minimize we glance along the rows and pick out the largest potential loss that could arise from each option in turn. The largest figure along the a_1 row is 10,000. It is therefore placed opposite a_1 under the third column containing the row maxima. For the a_2 row the largest potential loss figure is 140,000, and it is entered accordingly opposite a_2 and in the third column. For the a_3 row the largest potential loss figure is 310,000 and this is shown opposite a_3 in the third column.

Of these largest potential losses from choosing a_1, a_2 or a_3, the decision-maker chooses the smallest, which is 10,000 corresponding to option a_1. Accordingly the figure of 10,000 is entered in the fourth column of Table V.5. By choosing option a_1 he can be sure of one thing; that whichever event occurs his potential loss—that is, the additional gain he might, in that event, have obtained had he instead selected one of the other options—can be no greater than 10,000. For clearly, if he chooses instead a_2, the potential loss he may suffer s 140,000. While if he chooses a_3 the potential loss he may suffer is 310,000.[1]

As a further illustration of the minimax regret method, Table V.6 below is constructed from the primary data given in Table V.3. For the first column, below b_1 the best choice is a_2, since it would entail the least cost 11·3. If option a_1 were chosen instead, the cost would be 13, and therefore the loss of potential saving would be 1·7 (13 *minus* 11·3). Similarly, if a_3 were chosen the cost would be 12·8, and the loss of potential saving 1·5 (12·8 *minus* 11·3). The figures in the next two columns are obtained in the same way. In the fourth column we put the row maxima. From these the smallest potential loss, 0·5 corresponding to option a_2, is chosen and entered in the fifth column.

TABLE V.6

	b_1	b_2	b_3	Row Maxima	Minimax
a_1	1·7	0	0·7	1·7	
a_2	0	0·5	0	0.5	0·5
a_3	1·5	0·8	1·5	1·5	

4. Not surprisingly perhaps, the more obvious defect of this minimax method is the opposite of that found in the maximin. The conservatism of the maximin, it will be recalled, is such that cases can

1 This 'minimax-regret', or 'minimax-risk' (of loss), principle, as it is sometimes called, is really a misnomer. The figures for losses in Table V.5 are given without sign. But if we follow the convention of treating losses as negative signs we should write all the figures in Table V.5 with a minus sign. For instance, if a_3 is chosen and b_1 occurs, the potential *gain* is 80,000 *minus* 140,000 or −60,000.

The largest potential loss in each row of Table V.5 should then really be expressed as a *negative* figure: −10,000 for a_1, −140,000 for a_2, −310,000 for a_3. These negative figures can then be regarded as the lowest or minimal row gains. Of these (algebraic) row minima we choose the (algebraic) maximum; namely −10,000 corresponding to option a_1.

The formal procedure is in fact no different from that used in connection with Table V.3, where the negative items happen to refer to costs.

In effect then the same *maximin* procedure as before is employed, with the important difference that the row minima figures we are now maximizing refer to (negative) *potential* gains (as compared with other options) instead of, as in Chapter 39, *actual* gains.

However, we shall here follow the convention of using positive figures to refer to potential losses, and of describing the procedure as 'minimaxing-regret'.

arise in which large potential gains are sacrificed for very little extra security. In order to skirt this contingency, the so-called minimax-regret method courts the opposite danger. For cases can arise in which the application of this more enterprising minimax method will effectively jettison the chance of a good gain for the hope of getting a bit more.

The net revenue figures in Table V.7 below are chosen to bring out this defect of the minimax regret procedure.

TABLE V.7

	b_1	b_2	b_3	b_4
a_1	300	300	300	300
a_2	120	500	120	120

Application of the maximin principle, as discussed in Chapter 39, would select option a_1 so assuring a receipt of 300. Table V.8 below, however, uses the data in Table V.7 to derive corresponding figures in each cell for potential losses.

TABLE V.8

	b_1	b_2	b_3	b_4	Row Maxima	Minimax
a_1	0	200	0	0	200	
a_2	180	0	180	180	180	180

In the concern (should event b_2 occur) *not* to regret the loss of 200, the person employing the minimax-regret principle incurs instead the risk of the somewhat smaller potential loss of 180 should any of the other three events, b_1, b_3, b_4, occur. Put more directly, his choice of a_2 ensures that if event b_2 occurs he will obtain 500 rather than the 300 he would obtain by choosing a_1. If, however, either b_1, b_3 or b_4 occurs, he will collect only 120 rather than the 300 he would obtain by choosing a_1.

5. It would appear then that the choice of maximin or minimax-regret would not be adopted in advance, and independently of the primary data, by any person unless he were cautious to a fault (in

which case he would always apply the maximin principle) or reck-lessly opportunistic, or, more precisely, fearful of losing potential gain (in which case he would always apply the minimax regret principle). One must conclude that even where conditions are such that these methods can be applied, the fact alone that the choice of whether to use maximin or minimax regret will depend both upon the person and upon the data makes the application of game theory techniques somewhat unsatisfactory. Since subjective judgment enters into the choice of whether to use maximin or minimax-regret, competent economists inspecting the same data can come up with different decisions.

Chapter 41

THE USE OF PROBABILITY IN DECISION-MAKING

1. The techniques, illustrated in the preceding two chapters, are based on the assumption that there is no knowledge at all available that could throw any light on the likelihood of each of the alternative events, b_1, b_2, b_3, occurring over the period in question. In the complete absence of such knowledge we can no more suppose that b_1 is as likely to occur as b_2 than we can suppose that b_1 is more (or less) likely to occur. We can say no more of the events in question than that each is *possible*. Once a suspicion about the greater likelihood of one, or more, of the possible events occuring begins to form, the simple game-theory method may require modification. In general, the more information about likelihoods we can obtain the more agreement about the best decision we can hope to secure. If, from years of keeping records about floods, we could attach probabilities to each of the possible outcomes in our first example, our procedure would be to include those probabilities as weights in working out a solution.

2. Suppose that event b_1 (flood) can be expected with a probability of p_1, say 3/5, and event b_2 (no flood) therefore with a probability p_2 of $(1 - p_1)$, or 2/5, we make our calculations in a way to be illustrated by reference to Table V.9 below.

TABLE V.9

	$b_1 (p_1 = 3/5)$	$b_2 (p_2 = 2/5)$	Weighted average	Largest weighted average
a_1	$130,000 \times 3/5$	$400,000 \times 2/5$	238,000	238,000
a_2	$140,000 \times 3/5$	$260,000 \times 2/5$	188,000	
a_3	$80,000 \times 3/5$	$90,000 \times 2/5$	84,000	

282

If option a_1 is chosen each of the outcomes—130,000 and 400,000 —corresponding to the possible events, b_1 and b_2 respectively, is multiplied by the probability of the occurrence of the event, 3/5 and 2/5. The weighted average, or mathematical expectation, of the gains from choosing a_1 is entered in the third column, as also is the weighted average of gains from choosing a_2 and a_3. The largest weighted average is obviously 238,000 arising from the choice of option a_1, which can be regarded in the circumstances as the proper decision.

Now if this figure of 238,000 could be regarded as the anticipated value of net revenue from choosing a_1, in the sense that there is a stronger likelihood of a net revenue 238,000 occuring than of any other single value, we might have less hesitation in opting for a_1 rather than a_2 or a_3. But this figure of 238,000 can be regarded as the expected value only in the conventional statistical sense; that is to say, if it were possible to repeat this experiment year after year for, say, the next hundred years or so then—provided that the relevant climatic conditions remain unaltered—the *average* net revenue taken over the hundred years would be close to 238,000. For roughly ⅗ of the century, or for roughly sixty out of the hundred years, event b_1 would occur, and for the remaining years event b_2 would occur.

It is clear, then, that if we are thinking in terms of many years ahead, we can (if relevant conditions are not expected to change very much) expect to come close to the (undiscounted) average of 238,000 by repeatedly opting for a_1. If, on the other hand, we are interested in the outcome next year alone we cannot expect a net revenue of 238,000 from choosing a_1. In one year only one event will occur. If b_1 occurs the net revenue will be 130,000. If, instead, b_2 occurs the net revenue will be 400,000. All we can say is that, on the basis of past evidence, there is more chance of b_1 occuring than b_2. And the higher the probability of b_1's occuring the more we are disposed to expect it and to have our decision governed by the thought of its occurrence.

If, to take more extreme probabilities, we discovered from the records that floods occur, on the average, in nine years out of ten, we should be justified in expecting a flood next year, and in being surprised if it did not occur. The net revenue we can most reasonably expect if we choose a_1 is therefore 130,000. By the same logic, the net revenue we should be inclined to expect by choosing option a_2

is 140,000. This being so, we might conclude that the rational thing is to choose a_2. But once we have probabilities attached to the various events it would not be very sensible to focus our expectations on the event with the highest probability and ignore the possibility of the other events occurring. Whether the probability of event b_1 occurring is 3/5 or 9/10. the decision-maker is not completely indifferent to the outcome arising from event b_2—unless that outcome is the same, say 200,000, whatever option is chosen. The greater the gain (given that b_2 occurs) in choosing a_1 compared with that in choosing a_2, the more weight he will give to the a_1 option. To illustrate with extreme figures; if choice of a_1 would entail an outcome of 1,000,000 if event b_2 occurred whereas the choice of a_2 entailed an outcome of zero for the same event, the nine chances out of ten that b_1 would occur—conferring an additional 10,000 if a_2 were chosen rather than a_1—would hardly be likely to prevail against the thought that if, despite its slim chance, b_2 did occur a net gain of 1,000,000 would be collected.

3.   We may conclude tentatively that dependable probabilities will be taken into account by the decision-maker in such cases; moreover, that the use of these probabilities as weights in the method indicated above, by reference to Table V.9, would be acceptable to many as a rough general rule. By choosing an option on the basis of a weighted average of events, rather than on the basis of a single most likely event, we are in effect refusing to neglect the possible impact of the less likely event(s) on our decision, and doing so in a systematic and conventional manner.

Chapter 42

CONDITIONAL PROBABILITY IN DECISION-MAKING

1. Records covering many years can provide information additional to the probability of each of a number of alternative events such as b_1 and b_2. For instance, in addition to discovering that over, say, a hundred years event b_1 (flood) occurred in sixty out of a hundred years, that is with a frequency of $3/5$, and event b_2 (no flood) therefore with a frequency of $2/5$, the records may reveal the following information: (1) prior to event b_1, a period of several weeks of cloudy weather—a condition we refer to as z_1—was observed in half the number of b_1 events; (2) prior to event b_1, a period of several weeks of mixed weather—referred to as z_2—was observed in one-third of the number of b_1 events; (3) prior to event b_1, a period of several weeks of clear weather—say z_3—was observed in one-sixth of the number of b_1 events.

The same sort of information will be available for event b_2 which, it is assumed, is completely independent of b_1. Let us suppose, therefore, that z_1 was observed prior to one-sixth of the number of b_2 (no flood) events; that z_2 was observed prior to one-third of the number of b_2 events; and that z_3 was observed prior to one-half of the number of b_2 events. If we can assume that basic climatic and other relevant conditions will remain much the same, we can treat these frequencies as probabilities. And if so, we can get better results than those reached by adopting what are called 'pure' strategies; that is, by adopting *either a_1 or a_2 or a_3*. These better results are attained by recourse to 'mixed' strategies, which are no more than a *combination* of pure options—adopting a_1 a fraction of the time, a_2 another fraction of the time, and a_3 the remainder of the time.

2. Thus, instead of the choice between the three simple options, a_1, a_2 and a_3, let the reader think of a larger number of quite arbitrary mixed strategies; call them s_1, s_2, s_3, .., s_n. For example, strategy s_1 might require that *if z_1 is observed then a_1 is to be chosen*;

285

if z_2 occurs a_2 is to be chosen; if z_3 occurs a_3 is to be chosen. Strategy s_2 might be as follows: if z_1 occurs choose a_1; if z_2 occurs choose a_2, while if z_3 occurs choose a_2 again. Strategy s_3 might be, if either z_1 or z_2 or z_3 occurs choose a_2, and so on.

Now suppose event b_1 were to take place, we should, as indicated above, expect to observe weather condition z_1 with a probability of $\frac{1}{2}$, z_2 with a probability of $\frac{1}{3}$, and z_3 with a probability of $\frac{1}{6}$. The expected outcome from adopting, say, strategy s_1 (in the event that b_1 occurs) is got by weighting each of the net revenues attaching to the options designated by strategy s_1 by the probabilities of the z's. Thus, strategy s_1 prescribes that we select option a_1 (with outcome 130 in case of event b_1) should z_1 occur, which it does with a probability of $\frac{1}{2}$. The first component of strategy s_1, in that event, is $\frac{1}{2} \times 130$. The second component of strategy s_1 requires we select a_2 (with outcome 140 for event b_1) should z_2 occur, which it does with a probability of $\frac{1}{3}$. Consequently the second component of strategy s_1 is equal to $\frac{1}{3} \times 140$. Similarly, the third component of strategy s_1 prescribes option a_3 (with outcome of 80 for b_1) should z_3 occur, which it does with a probability of $\frac{1}{6}$. Hence it is equal to $\frac{1}{6} \times 80$.

Given event b_1 then, the expected value of revenue from employing strategy s_1 is equal to

$$(\tfrac{1}{2} \times 130) + (\tfrac{1}{3} \times 140) + (\tfrac{1}{6} \times 80) = 125.$$

Given the same b_1 event, we could work out the expected value of the revenue from employing strategy s_2. The same steps in the calculation give it as

$$(\tfrac{1}{2} \times 130) + (\tfrac{1}{3} \times 140) + (\tfrac{1}{6} \times 140) = 136.$$

Given the same b_1 event again, the employment of strategy s_3 will realize an expected value equal to

$$(\tfrac{1}{2} \times 140) + (\tfrac{1}{3} \times 140) + (\tfrac{1}{6} \times 140) = 140.$$

And so we could go on calculating expected revenues, in the event b_1 takes place, for all the other strategies.

If, instead, event b_2 occurred then the relevant probabilities of z_1, z_2 and z_3, would be $\frac{1}{6}$, $\frac{1}{3}$ and $\frac{1}{2}$ respectively. And employing the original s_1 strategy would, therefore, yield an expected value of revenue equal to

$$(\tfrac{1}{6} \times 400) + (\tfrac{1}{3} \times 200) + (\tfrac{1}{2} \times 90) = 199.$$

Employing strategy s_2, however, would yield an expected value of net revenue equal to

$$(\tfrac{1}{6} \times 400) + (\tfrac{1}{3} \times 260) + (\tfrac{1}{2} \times 260) = 284.$$

While recourse to strategy s_3 would yield an expected value of revenue equal to ,

$$(\tfrac{1}{6} \times 260) + (\tfrac{1}{3} \times 260) + (\tfrac{1}{2} \times 260) = 260.$$

TABLE V.10
(in thousand dollars per annum)

	b_1	b_2
s_1	125	199
s_2	136	284
s_3	140	260
.	.	.
.	.	.
s_n	140	260

These results can be displayed in Table V.10, for all n possible strategies, though in fact only the first three strategies and the last strategy is represented there. Some strategies are likely to be dominated by others and would not stay in the Table. After eliminating all the dominated strategies, we are left with a choice of mixed strategies which we could renumber $S_1, S_3, \ldots, S_m$.

3.   What is the advantage of all this? On the surface of things it would appear to offer a larger range of choices.[1] Granted that the use of these strategies offer us more choice, how do we go about selecting the best strategy?

In fact we are 'back to square one'—*except* that there are apparently many more choices of strategy than the initial three options. With the data given by Table V.10, that is, we could employ the

---

1   We can, of course, include the pure strategies (the choice of option a_1 alone, a_2 alone, or a_3 alone) among these mixed strategies. The choice of a_1 alone might be numbered strategy S_8, with a_1 being chosen irrespective of the occurrence of z_1, z_2 and z_3, so yielding 130 for b_1, and 400 for b_2 as in Table V.9. The choice of a_2 alone would enter, say, as strategy S_9 with a_2 being chosen regardless of the occurrence of z_1, z_2 and z_3, so yielding 140 for b_1 and 260 for b_2 as in Table V.9.

maximin method, or the minimax-regret method, or some other method in order to select one of these new strategies. Indeed, since we can also attach probabilities to events b_1 and b_2, we can employ the method outlined in the preceding chapter: we can, that is, calculate the weighted average net revenue for each of the listed strategies, and choose that yielding the highest revenue.

Again, however, if we are concerned with the outcome over the next one or two years only, the method outlined is of much less use than if, instead, we can adopt the strategy for a largish number of years. Consider, for instance, the calculated net revenue of 125 that arises from employing strategy s_1 in the event that b_1 takes place. True, if b_1 is to occur, we shall observe z_1 with a probability of $\frac{1}{2}$, z_2 with a probability of $\frac{1}{3}$, and z_3 with a probability of $\frac{1}{6}$. But in responding to the z's according to the adopted stretagy, here s_1, we cannot hope to realize this same year a revenue of 125. For in the one year *either* z_1 *or* z_2 *or* z_3 is observed and, therefore, according to the strategy chosen, *either* a_1 *or* a_2 *or* a_3 is adopted. The net revenue in that event is *either* 130 *or* 140 *or* 80—*not* 125, however, which is but an average figure to which the revenues will converge only if, whenever b_1 occurs (which is about 3/5 of the total number of years), we continue to use strategy s_1. Similar remarks apply to the figure of 199. It follows that if, say, over the next hundred years event b_1 could be expected to occur 3/5 of the time and event b_2 the remaining $\frac{2}{5}$ of the time, the repeated of strategy s_1 could be expected to give a series of (undiscounted) revenues that would average about $(3/5 + 125) + (2/5 \times 199)$, or 155. If, over the same period s_2 instead were repeatedly employed, the average (undiscounted) revenue to expect would be $(3/5 \times 136) + (2/5 \times 284)$, or 196. We could work out the (undiscounted) average revenues for all the mixed strategies listed and expect in general that at least one such strategy would produce a weighted average figure above the highest (238) for the pure strategy (option a_1 in Table V.9 of the preceding chapter) which makes no use of the zs.[2]

4. We may conclude that the information about such indicators as the zs can be of use in improving the decision process through mixed

---

2 Given an appropriate rate of discount, we could, of course, calculate the present discounted value of any future net revenue, and produce a strategy that would yield a highest weighted average discounted net revenue.

strategies only when events over a large number of years or over a large number of projects are anticipated. If, for example, a reservoir is to be used under the same environmental conditions for many years to come, or if a large number of similar reservoirs are to be constructed, there can be advantages in using information provided by the z's in order to produce a variety of mixed strategies. Having chosen the maximum-yielding strategy, it has to be employed repeatedly over the future in the first case, or applied to each of the many reservoirs in the second case. If, however, what matters is the revenue for only one or two years and/or for only one or two reservoirs; or if, alternatively, environmental conditions cannot be expected to remain unchanged (so that one cannot reasonably attach probabilities to the events b_1, b_2, or to the indicators z_1, z_2, z_3), the method of contingent probabilities outlined above is of little practical use.

Chapter 43
THE UTILITY APPROACH

1.   Up to the present, net revenues or costs have been expressed in money terms, though they could just as well have been expressed in 'real' terms by using a price-index as deflator. Whether in money or in 'real' terms, however, the absolute or proportional differences between the figures may not be a good index of the sense of gain or loss to the decision-maker.

2.   A coin is tossed and if it comes down heads $10 is paid to me, while if it comes down tails I have to pay $10. This sort of gamble would be called an actuarially fair gamble if it were believed that an unbiased coin would have an equal chance of coming down heads as of coming down tails. In fact if the coin were tossed many hundreds of times, heads would appear about half the number of times, and at the end of the game I would be no better or worse off—or nearly so.

It might be thought then that, if I am indifferent to the joys of gambling, I could have no objection to taking part in an actuarially fair gamble. But if the coin is to be tossed only a few times—in the limiting case, say, once only—I may demur. To be more accurate, my willingness to gamble in this way may be observed to diminish the larger is the bet. If it is no more than $10, I may have no objection. If the bet is $10,000 I will not agree to a fair gamble.

Maintaining the fiction that I derive no pleasure from the act of gambling, the reluctance to participate in a fair gamble for large stakes is not irrational. For I would not feel the gain of $10,000 as keenly as I would feel the loss of $10,000. Put more formally, the utility added by $10,000 is for me smaller than the amount of utility lost when I lose $10,000. This inference would follow from the assumption that my income is subject to diminishing marginal utility.

Indeed, for any consistent person an ideal experiment can be planned. The truthful answers to the questions asked would enable us to draw a curve relating total number of utils to 'real' income. If we are interested, as we are here, only in differences in utility corresponding to differences in income, it is the shape of this utility curve that matters, not the particular scale we adopt.

3. To illustrate, let us suppose the experiment just mentioned has been performed and we have emerged with the utility curve, *UU*, shown in Figure V.1. On the vertical axis the utility index marked (a)

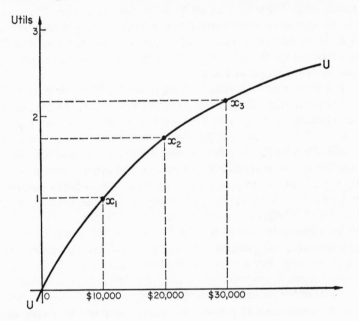

FIGURE V.1

1 util, 2 utils, 3 utils, and so on, could be changed to (b) 10 utils, 20 utils, 30 utils, respectively, or for that matter to (c) 200 utils, 400 utils, 600 utils respectively, without in any way altering the shape of the utility curve, *UU*. Again, if the origin were changed from zero, as shown in Figure V.1, to some other number, say 50, then instead of (a) we should read off 51 utils, 52 utils, 53 utils; instead of (b) we should read off 60 utils, 70 utils, 80 utils; or instead of (c) we should read off 250 utils, 450 utils, 650 utils. Thus, neither of these alterations—neither those of scale nor those of origin—will change

the shape of the *UU* curve in Figure V.1. In the jargon, the utility function is determined up to a linear transformation.

More specifically, suppose we moved from point x_2 on the *UU* curve, which point corresponds to an income of $20,000 to the point x_1 which corresponds to an income of $10,000, then using the (a)-scale (and irrespective of the value of the origin) the experienced loss of real income is measured as 0·8 utils. Using the (b) scale, the loss would be measured as 80 utils. Using the (c)-scale it would be measured as 160 utils. Now let us move from x_2 on the *UU* curve to x_3, an increase in utility corresponding to an increase in income from $20,000 to $30,000. Again, irrespective of origin, the gain in utility is measured on the (a)-scale as 0·5 utils, on the (b)-scale as 5 utils, and on the (c)-scale as 100 utils.

It follows that beginning with an income of $20,000 the ratio of utility lost by the *subtraction* of $10,000 to that gained by the *addition* of $10,000—that is, $U(-\$10,000)/U(+\$10,000)$—is for the (a)-scale $-0\cdot8/0\cdot5$, for the (b)-scale $-8/5$, and for the (c)-scale $-160/200$. Clearly the *ratio* of these differences in cardinal utilities remains the same regardless of the scale and origin.[1] And this ratio is, indeed, all we require to explain why our perfectly consistent individual will not accept an actuarially fair gamble. On the assumption that his behaviour is determined only by reference to the shape of his utility curve, it can be shown that he would accept such a fair gamble only if the marginal utility of his 'real' income were constant (or increasing). For in that case the total utility curve *UU* would be a straight line sloping upwards to the right. The utility lost would then be equal to (or less than) the utility to be gained. If, however, diminishing marginal utility prevails, the utility curve will be shaped as in the figure. In that case the utility of the loss of $10,000 exceeds the utility of the gain of $10,000 by 8 to 5, the actuarial value of the gamble in terms of utility being $5 - 8/2$, or $-1\cdot5$, which is negative.[2] From the utility-point of view it is obviously not a fair gamble, but one having a negative value.

---

[1]   Though we have recourse here only to the ratio of the first differences, it is easy to show that this constancy attaches to the ratio of the second, the third, fourth, ... and n^{th} differences also.

[2]   The actuarial value of the gamble as a *proportion* of the difference in utility as between an income of $10,000 and $30,000 remains constant at $-15/130$ for any scale and origin.

4. Now in order to be able to plot such a utility curve from the consistent and perceptive answers given by such a person, it should be clear that we could begin by attributing to some initial income, say $10,000, some arbitrary number of utils, say 100 utils, and also to some smaller income, say $1,000, a smaller but still quite arbitrary number of utils, say 95 utils—or it could be 10 utils, or zero utils, or even −55 utils. For as we have said, the origin is arbitrary: it can be zero or positive or negative. However, once we have chosen 100 utils for $10,000 and, say, 95 utils for $1,000, we can show how the answers given by our individual enable us to plot enough points to draw a total utility curve over the range $1,000 to $10,000, and indeed beyond that range.

The key assumption we have to make throughout, in order to be able to plot the points of his utility curve, is that which would equate (1) the utility of a $\frac{2}{3}$ chance of winning $100 with (2) $\frac{2}{3}$ of the utility of $100. Put generally, the assumption is that (1) the utility of the *probability* of winning a sum x, is equal to (2) that probability *times* the utility of the sum x. This assumption may or may not be plausible, but for the purpose in hand we have to accept it. As indicated above, we start the construct by choosing two levels of income and arbitrarily attribute a higher utility to the larger. Since within this limitation the choices are arbitrary, we may as well choose the figures with an eye to maximum convenience. We shall, therefore, choose zero income and $10,000 and attribute zero utils to zero income and 100 utils to the income of $10,000.

Now in order to discover the appropriate utility of some intermediate income, say $5,000, we have only to put the following question to our rational individual: which option would you choose: (1) $5,000 with certainty, or (2) a gamble in which the result is either zero or $10,000? The reply will always be that it depends upon the sort of gamble.[3] If there were 9/10 of a chance of winning $10,000 and therefore only $\frac{1}{10}$ of winning nothing, he would be very likely to choose the gambling option, If the odds were the other way round, he would almost surely choose the certain option (1). We may legitimately surmise, however, that there will be some gambling

---

3 We may suppose the individual begins with zero income, or else that the above sums are *additional to* his existing income.

odds which would make our individual indifferent as between the two options.

Suppose the gambling odds which make him indifferent as between options (1) and (2) are 7 chances of winning $10,000 to 3 chances of winning nothing. In other words, when the probability of winning $10,000 is set at 7/10 and that of winning nothing at (1–7/10), or 3/10, the utility to our individual of each of these two options is exactly equal. We, therefore, have the equation:

(1) Utility of $5,000 = (2) Utility of probability (7/10) of $10,000
+Utility of probability (3/10) of zero

More briefly, U (5000) = U of a 7/10 probability of 10,000 + U of a 3/10 probability of 0.

Our key assumption enables us to re-write the right hand side of the equation as $(0.7 \times U (10,000)) + (0.3 \times U(0))$.

However, we have already chosen 100 utils for $10,000 and zero utils for zero income. Substituting these utils into the right hand side we have:

U (5,000) = (0.7 × 100 utils) + 0.3 × 0 utils) = 70 utils.

In Figure V.2, we already have two points, zero utils corresponding to zero income, and a point where 100 utils corresponds to an income of $10,000. Since we have just discovered that $5,000 is valued at 70 utils, we mark off a third point 70 utils on the vertical scale above $5,000. We know the utility curve for this person must pass through this point.

To find another point, we could take some other certain sum, say $7,500, and once more put the question before our imaginary person who, we shall suppose, is now indifferent between the options only if there are 9 chances out of 10 of winning $10,000. Once again therefore we have an equation:

U (7,500) = U of a 9/10 probability of 10,000 + U of a 1/10 probability of 0

Which we can re-write, using our key assumption, as:

U(7,500) = (0.9 × 100 utils) + (0.1 × 0 utils) = 90 utils.

We mark off a fourth point 90 utils, on the vertical scale, above $7,500. Any number of additional points can be plotted by this means

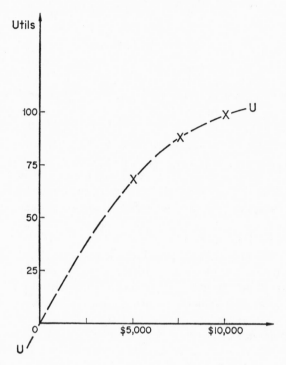

Figure V.2

and we may continue generating such points until we can draw the utility curve with confidence between zero and $10,000.[4]

5. Having mapped out the utilities corresponding to the $ values we can replace net revenues in each of the Tables V.1 to V.10 by utilities. The same decision rules discussed in the preceding chapters may now

---

4 Indeed, we can extend the utility curve beyond $10,000. Consider the point corresponding to $20,000. We let option (1) be the certainty of $10,000 and option (2) a gamble between $20,000 and $0. If the individual is indifferent between these options if there is a 0·6 probability of winning $20,000, we can write:

$$U(10,000) = (0·6 \times U(20,000)) + (0·4 \times U(0)).$$

Therefore, 100 utils $= 0·6 \times U(20.000)$, so that $U(20,000) = 166·2/3$ utils.

be applied to these new figures, the result being that, in some cases, a different option or decision strategy will emerge.

This method of deriving a utility curve from such experiments was originally put forward as a hypothesis to explain—by reference to both diminishing and increasing marginal-utility segments of the curve—why the same person both insures and gambles.[5] An extension of this procedure, whereby money, or 'real' revenues are translated into utilities, to the problems of practical decision-taking does not appear to have been a resounding success. For a one-man enterprise, or even a partnership, the experiment could conceivably be carried out and, if successful, the resulting utility curve might be used to replace money sums by utilities in the hope of approaching closer to an optimal decision. But, on the face of things, it would seem quite impracticable to derive such a curve uniquely for a large number of people; and for society in general quite impossible.[6] Even if the method were practicable it runs into the objection that its employment would be unnecessary and, indeed, would go beyond the Pareto basis of cost-benefit analysis. For the Pareto criterion requires only that the sum of the money gains in any project exceed the money sum of the losses: no weighting of these gains and losses by reference to a utility scale, nor their arbitrary addition, is called for.

---

5 The interested reader might wish to consult Friedman & Savage (1948) and Markowitz (1952).

6 The single figure for revenue that is used as a possible outcome is not a possible gain to a single person. In a cost-benefit analysis such a figure is the resultant of the possible gains and losses of a large number of different people. If we wanted to replace such a gain by a figure for total utility, the utilities of all the persons affected have to be added together by some arbitrary weighting system.

Chapter 44

HOW PRACTICABLE ARE THESE DECISION TECHNIQUES?

1. The final stage of a typical cost-benefit study requires that we evaluate a stream of net benefits,

$$(B_1 - K_1), (B_2 - K_2), \ldots, (B_n - K_n),$$

in which the Bs, or benefits, and the Ks, or costs, are uncertain, and, indeed, increase in uncertainty the further they are from the present.

The difficulties we encounter in the attempt to apply game theory principles may be illustrated by recourse to a simple example in which the net benefits of a project are spread over four years as follows: -100, 30, 80, 50. The -100 figure indicates a net capital outlay of 100 in the first year, and the remaining figures are net benefits in successive years. The penumbra of uncertainty surrounding each of these figures might suggest, for example, that for the -100 figure we substitute a *range* -95 to -105; for the figure of 30, a range 25 to 35, and so on. For practical purposes, however, we would not use a continuous range, only discrete figures. The range -95 to -105 could, for instance, be split into three possible outcomes, -95, -100, and -105. The range 25 to 35 could also be split into three outcomes, or perhaps five, say, 25, 38, 30, 32, and 35. Similarly for the other two figures. If we take these arbitrarily chosen figures from the range of net benefits in any period to be independent of the arbitrarily chosen figures from the range of any other period's net benefits, then a combination that included one of the possible net-benefit outcomes from each of the four periods—say -95 from the first period, 32 from the second, 75 from the third, and 50 from the fourth—would add up to the outcome of a single event. There are obviously as many events as there are combinations of such possible outcomes for the four-year period.[1]

---

1 It is hardly necessary to say that in adding these four figures, those for the second, third, and fourth periods have to be discounted at the relevant rate.

2. The uncertainty about the net-benefit figures in each period can, however, be attributed to the uncertainty about future price-movements of both the inputs and outputs associated with the project. It is true that the price-movements themselves depend upon a number of future possible events, such as technical innovations, changes in domestic and foreign policies, and alterations in the conditions of demand and supply. But for each combination of possible events there will correspond a range of possible prices for both the inputs and outputs in question. We may therefore express the uncertainty about all future events in each period by reference to some price-range of each of the inputs and outputs.

Suppose that in the A_1 investment project, giving rise to a four-year stream of net benefits (including the initial year's capital outlay), there are the prices of only four items to be anticipated; that of homogeneous labour, that of homogeneous material, that of homogeneous machinery, and that of homogeneous output. Since prices do become more uncertain as we move into the future, the range of possible prices becomes wider and, as it becomes wider, it may be split into a larger number of possible prices. In token of this consideration we shall divide the price-range of each item into three alternative prices for the first period, but into five alternative prices for the second, third, and fourth periods. In each of the four periods there will be a large number of possible net benefits, every one of them corresponding to a different combination of the prices of each of the four items. Thus, for the first period, the three alternative prices for each of the four items will generate 3^4, or 81, possible outcomes, each of such outcomes being an alternative net benefit. For the second period, the five different prices for each of the four items will generate 5^4, or 625, possible outcomes, each being an alternative net benefit. Similarly, there will be 625 possible net benefits for each of the two remaining periods.

Matching any one of the net benefits in the first period with any one from each of the other three periods so as to produce a particular permutation of four successive benefits, provides us with (in the terminology of game theory) an event, b_1. Since there are 81 different net-benefit outcomes in the first period, and 625 different net-benefit outcomes in each of the three remaining periods, the total number of different events which are possible is given by 81×625^3, or close to 20 billion different events.

3. If we now introduce another investment option A_2, which also yields a stream of possible net benefits over four years and uses the same inputs and outputs, we have to calculate figures for roughly another 20 billion events. If, on the other hand, the A_2 stream covers more periods than the A_1 stream, or if there are additional inputs or outputs to contend with, we shall have to increase the number of events. Each of these additional events will carry a net-benefit figure for A_2, positive, zero or negative. Corresponding to them there will be zeros for A_1. There may, however, be inputs or outputs in the A_2 investment option that replace those in the A_1 option; for example, steel may be the only material used in the A_1 investment option, and aluminium the only material used in the A_2 option. In that case there will be a number of b's that are strictly relevant only to A_1 and a number that are strictly relevant only to A_2. Corresponding to those events that are strictly relevant to A_1 there will be net revenues (positive, zero, or negative) for the A_1 option, and zeros for the A_2 option, and vice versa.

One has but to reflect (a) that the price-range of any important item can be split into more than three or five possible prices, (b) that the number of important items to be bought or sold over the lifetime of a project can exceed four, (c) that the number of periods of any of the investment streams under comparison can exceed four and, indeed, is often likely to exceed ten, (d) that there is frequently more than two investment options to compare, to realize that attempts to deal with the uncertainty aspects of cost-benefit studies in this game-theory fashion is hardly a practical proposition.

When it is further recalled that, as distinct from simple game-theory techniques, not only is the number of distinct events *not* given to us exogenously (as indicated above, it is generated from alternative prices chosen arbitrarily from guesses about the likely range), but also that not all events are equally likely, inasmuch as not all the alternative prices are equally likely, it is not surprising that in any practical evaluation of investment projects no recourse is had to the formal apparata of game theory. The practice, rather, is to estimate the *most likely* figure for net revenue in each period and, in addition, an upper and lower estimate derived, respectively, from more optimistic and more pessimistic evaluations. If all three estimates meet the required investment criterion, or all three estimates fail to meet it, there is no problem. If the optimistic estimate alone meets the criterion there is a case for rejecting the project. If the pessimistic estimate alone fails to meet the criterion there is a case for accepting the project.

The factors that will influence the judgment of the economist are, rather obviously, (i) the margin by which a pessimistic estimate falls below the figure required by the criterion, (ii) the degree of plausibility that can be attached to the pessimistic estimate, (iii) the size, duration, and flexibility of the project in question. It need hardly be remarked that what is deemed likely, optimistic or pessimistic, will be based more on subjective estimates than on past records. And though some people would object to invoking the term statistical probability unless there are records of a fair number of closely similar cases, the persisting view that experience has something to offer in forming 'plausible' estimates, that something useful can be gleaned from the past warrants the convenience of a term such as 'subjective probability'. Only if no notion at all of the outcome can be distilled from a knowledge of the past can we talk of uncertainty in an absolute sense.

4. Two simple devices have been proposed for dealing with the fact that later returns and costs are less certain than earlier ones. The cruder of the two is the adoption of a 'cut-off period': if the stream of benefits is expected to run, say, for twenty years or more, it can be laid down that the adopted criterion be met within the first ten, eight, or five years, according to the degree of increasing uncertainty about the future. The length of the cut-off period is clearly an arbitrary matter, and is often quite short—three to eight years—in some of the riskier private ventures. For public enterprise where, for the most part, the future is less uncertain, this device is likely to be superfluous. The farther into the future are the expected returns the smaller the weights attached to them. At a discount rate of, say, 10 per cent, a net benefit of $5 in fifteen years time is worth only about $1 today.

The other device is that of adding something to a riskless rate. There are, however, objections to its use in long-term investments. Not only is the method too indirect, evasive almost, it is based on the implied assumption that the uncertainty compounds itself at a given rate over the future. If, for example, we add 2 per cent for uncertainty then we are deducting more than 6 per cent in the third period, or more than three times as much for the third as for the first period and so on. Greater uncertainty of one project can be allowed for but not by means of a systematic and mounting rate of reduction of later returns.

It is quantitatively more justifiable to express the uncertainty of a particular net revenue by widening the upper and lower limits of the later period compared with those of an earlier period. If in the first and second period the upper and lower figures are set respectively at 90 per cent and 110 per cent of the most likely figure, the corresponding percentages for the fifth and sixth periods could be set at 80 per cent and 120 per cent, or at 70 per cent and 125 per cent. A certain arbitrariness enters into the subjective judgment required by either method, but the latter is more direct and more flexible than that of raising the discount rate.

5. So far we have not distinguished between public investment and private investment. We need to do so only in so far as the greater resources at the disposal of the government enable it to bear losses that could prove fatal to the private firm. These greater resources should take no account of the tax-raising powers of the government that would enable it to conceal a loss, but should take account only of its existing real assets and current investment expenditure. There is no warrant for ignoring any risk inhering in government investment projects simply because of the nature of its financial power. If risks were consistently ignored in government projects unnecessary waste would result over time.

The only valid distinction to be made between public and private is one that rests on the magnitude and variety of the investments undertaken. In virtue of its being a very large spender of investible funds decisions on government investments should tend to be rational in an *actuarial* sense, whereas, in virtue of its limited resources, private concerns can be expected to take rational decisions only in the *utility* sense described in the preceding chapter. The extreme example of an insurance company that underwrites a large number of risks compared to the risk borne by a single person, or firm, is suggestive in this connection—bearing in mind, however, that the risks undertaken by government investment are less homogeneous and much less calculable. Thus, if decisions on public investment can be guided by subjective likelihood and subjective variance, private investment decisions will tend (on the common assumption of diminishing marginal utility of money) to be more wary and to attach greater weight to the chances of loss than to the chances of gain.

6. Allowing that rationality in the actuarial sense is applicable to public investment, we can, however, make use of subjective estimates of likelihood to generate something less crude than a simple triple-valued outcome consisting of a most likely figure for the present value of excess benefits plus an upper (most optimistic) and a lower (most pessimistic) figure.[2] We can, as it happens, generate a probability distribution covering the full range of excess-benefit possibilities simply by making use of subjective probabilities attaching to several possible values of each variable in each period.

To appreciate the advantages of this latter procedure, we first illustrate the deficiency of the simple triple-value method. Consider a project in which there are only four uncertain variables, these being the buying prices of a specific input in periods 1 and 2, and the selling prices of some output in the same periods 1 and 2. To simplify further, we can suppose that the most likely price in all four cases is expected to have a 60 per cent chance of occurring. The corresponding most likely estimate of the excess benefit will then have only a $(0 \cdot 6)^4$, or 13 per cent, chance of occurring. Clearly, we should like to know more about the chances of other possible outcomes occurring before reaching a decision. We should, in fact, prefer to have as complete a distribution as possible of the range of alternative cost-benefit outcomes.

This subjective probabilistic approach can be illustrated by reference to the four uncertain prices mentioned above; call them p_1, p_2, p_3, and p_4. The first step is to obtain from the experts estimates of the most likely magnitude of each price over the future. In the case, say, of p_1, we should want from them not only their estimate of the chances of the most likely value of p_1, but also the chances of some lower and higher values. For example, after some discussion with

2 This still common practice is not inconsistent with the description given by Shackle (1949) of the behaviour of businessmen (based on 'potential surprise') in the face of uncertainty.

the experts, we might decide that there is a 60 per cent chance of p_1 being \$1.20, a 30 per cent of its being \$1.00 and a 10 per cent chance of its being \$1·40. Having obtained three such estimates for each of the four prices, the next step—given that the movements of p_1, p_2, p_3, and p_4 are independent of one another[3]—is to calculate an excess benefit figure with each possible combination of the four prices. Since each price has three alternative values, there will be $(3·0)^4$, or 81, possible excess-benefit outcomes, each with its own probability. For example, one of these 81 combinations of the four prices could be \$1·40 for p_1 with a 10 per cent probability, \$3·50 for p_2 with a 60 per cent probability, \$2·0 for p_3 with a 20 per cent probability, and \$1·80 for p_4 with a 30 per cent probability. This possible combination would have an excess-benefit figure of, say, \$125,000, and the probability of its occurring would be equal to the product of these four probabilities, 0·36 per cent (equal to $0·1 \times 0·6 \times 0·2 \times 0·3$) $\times$ 100 per cent. All together, these 81 possible outcomes, along with their corresponding probabilities, provide a fairly detailed probability distribution, one which, in general, will have the normal shape.

Such a distribution cannot, of course, be any more accurate than the initial estimates made by the experts. The information contained by such a distribution is the result only of bringing out the full implications of these initial estimates. But accepting the basis of such

---

3 If the values of different variables are *not* independent, then clearly they cannot enter the calculation as independent variables. The relationship between them has to be spelled out and attention given to the distribution of the 'independent' variable. For example, the amount of an output sold and the price of that output may both be uncertain, but if the quantity to be sold will depend upon the price, we need only an estimate of the distribution of the price. Suppose the relationship adopted was $S = 100 + 25p + e$, where S is the amount sold, p the price, and e an error term. If the most likely estimate for p is, say, 10, then the most likely estimate for S is 350. If the likelihood of a price of 10 occurring is 60 per cent then the likelihood of S being 350 is 60 per cent also (with a total sales value of 3,500) *provided* the error term e is zero. If, however, the error term is not zero, but instead is such that when p is equal to 10 the chance of S being 350 is 80 per cent, with a 10 per cent chance of its being either 400 or 300, a distribution of three possible sales values is generated. For the 60 per cent probability of p being 10, that is, we shall have a $(0·6 \times 0·8)$ or 48 per cent chance of a sales revenue of 3,500, *plus* a $(0·6 - 0·1)$ or 6 per cent chance of a sales revenue of 4,000, *plus* a $(0·6 \times 0·1)$ or 6 per cent chance of a sales revenue of 3,000. Once we take into account the two other possible prices, having between them a probability of 40 per cent, we generate nine independent values for the sales revenue.

information we can now say a good deal more than before. Having gotten the mean and standard deviation of the distribution we can say, for example, that there is a 90 per cent chance of the excess-benefit outcome falling between, say, $110,000 and $175,000; that there is only a 3 per cent chance of the excess benefit being zero or negative; and so on. When there are a number of investment projects to be ranked, this method of dealing with uncertainty implies that their corresponding excess-benefit distributions are to be compared. And unless some of these distributions are dominant, they can be ranked only by comparing some gains with smaller ones having a greater chance of occurring. Subjective judgement in project selection enters again at this final stage, for there is no economic expertise that can say just how much additional risk an additional one per cent is worth.

In the above simple example, involving four variables with a three-level estimate for each, the eighty-one possible outcomes could be worked out with pencil and paper. In general, however, there will be far more than four uncertain variables and sometimes—especially where there is information arising from variations in price or quantity over the past—more than three probability estimates for each variable. All possible cost-benefit outcomes of a single project might then run into millions or thousands of millions. Nevertheless, a sample distribution can be simulated with the aid of a computer that is set to select at random from the distributions of each variable (according to the probability of its occurring) one particular value, and from this combination of values to compute the corresponding excess-benefit figure. After a run of, say, 200 or 300 'observations' the resulting sample will usually be reliable enough a distribution to work with.[4]

7. Finally, in this consideration of more practical ways of adjusting cost-benefit calculations for uncertainty, we may return to the rate of discount. Earlier in the chapter, brief and slighting mention was made of the device of adding, arbitrarily, one or two percentage points to a riskless long-term rate of interest, a proxy for the social rate of time

---

4 If there is any doubt about the adequacy of the sample, the computer can be run for another 200 or 300 'observations.' If there is then no discernible difference in the resulting distribution, the sample is deemed to be large enough.

preference. More promising, however, is the notion of using a commercial rate of return as a discount rate. Already in Chapter 32, the adoption of the yield on private investment as an appropriate discount rate has been discussed within a context that abstracts from uncertainty. The argument is easily extended to cover the existence of uncertainty in the real world.

Owing to general risk-aversion and also, perhaps, to progressive income taxes, a higher actuarial return, it is alleged, is necessary to attract funds into the riskier types of private investment. Whatever the reason for the higher, or the highest, actuarial yield on any particular types of commercial venture, it is clear that public funds can always be placed there (in the absence of political or administrative constraints) as an alternative to using such funds for public investment. Since the option is always open to it, the government's use of this commercial yield as a discount rate will ensure that only those public projects having expected returns greater than those of the highest-yielding private investments are accepted.

Adopting the highest commercial rate of return as the discount rate for public projects[5] is allocatively correct provided only that those projects are numerous enough to realize an average rate of return over time that is not far from their expected average rate of return and will, in fact, exceed somewhat the commercial rate of return. Clearly, if only a few, possibly very large, public projects are undertaken, there may only be a small chance of the expected yield actually occurring. In such cases, although the actuarial return on commercial investment ought still to be used as a discount rate (or as the rate to be compared with the normalized internal rate of return on the public project), ordinary prudence would suggest the advisability of supplementing the data with the sort of subjective probability distribution described above. Indeed, since the costs of contriving such a probability distribution is not high, it may be usefully employed in connection with each public project even where

---

5 Under inflationary conditions, the *nominal* actuarial yield tends to exceed the real actuarial yield of any particular type of commercial investment by roughly the annual average rise in the price level. If this were, say, 6 per cent per annum, a nominal yield of 20 per cent implies a real yield of about 14 per cent. Inasmuch as the calculations of future costs and benefits are generally in terms of a base-year price level, it is the real actuarial yield that is to be used as discount rate in public projects.

large numbers of such projects are involved. It adds another dimension to the investment criterion and, according to the skill and consistency, with which it is used, it should serve to raise somewhat the average rate of return on some given amount of public investment.

REFERENCES AND BIBLIOGRAPHY FOR PART V

Carter, C. F. and others (eds.). *Uncertainty and Business Decisions.* Liverpool: University Press, 1957.

Churchman, C. W. *Introduction to Operations Research.* New York: Wiley, 1957.

Dorfman, R. 'Basic Economic and Technologic Concepts', in A. Maass and others. *Design of Water Resource Systems.* London: Macmillan, 1962.

Friedman, M. and Savage, L. J. 'The Utility Analysis of Choices Involving Risk, *Journal of Political Economy*, 1948.

Hertz, D. B. 'Risk Analysis in Capital Investment', *Harvard Business Review.* Jan./Feb. 1964.

Hillier, F. S. 'The Derivation of Probabilistic Information for the Evaluation of Risky Investments', *Managerial Science*, April 1963.

King, W. R. *Probability for Management Decisions.* New York: Wiley, 1968.

Luce, R. D. and Raiffa, H. *Games and Decisions: introduction to Critical Survey.* New York: Wiley, 1967.

Moore, P. G. *Basic Operation Research.* London: Pitman & Son, 1968.

Markowitz, H. 'The Utility of Wealth', *Journal of Political Economy*, 1952.

Reutlinger, S. *Techniques for Project Appraisal Under Uncertainty* (World Bank Staff Paper No. 10). John Hopkins Press, Baltimore, 1970.

Schlaiffer, R. *Probability and Statistics for Business Decisions.* New York: McGraw-Hill, 1969.

—— *Introduction to Statistics for Business Decisions.* New York: McGraw-Hill, 1961.

Shackle, G. L. S. *Expectations Economics.* Cambridge: University Press, 1949.

Williams, J. D. *The Compleat Strategyst.* New York: McGraw-Hill, 1954

PART VI. FURTHER NOTES RELATING TO COST-BENEFIT ANALYSIS

NOTE A: THE WELFARE BASIS OF COST-BENEFIT ANALYSIS

Chapter 45
THE SOCIAL BASIS OF WELFARE ECONOMICS

1. Since cost-benefit is an application of the theory of resource allocation, itself a subject at the core of welfare economics, the rationale of such analysis, along with that of allocation theory, can be understood and vindicated only by reference to propositions at the centre of welfare economics. It is frequently alleged[1] that allocative recommendations that flow from welfare theorems are misleading, for without being explicit about them the economist makes recommendations that depend ultimately on his political predilections. It is argued, moreover, that even if his political predilections were shared by society, such recommendations would be unnecessary: the decisions on economic policy can, and should, be left to the political decision-making machinery. In particular, in a liberal democracy, in which the goals of economic policy are chosen by the people's elected representatives, the role of the economist is that of consultant only. His is the task of disclosing the implications of the policies being mooted and, perhaps, that also of suggesting alternative policies. By discharging these tasks, the economist en-

---

1 Among others, by Graaff (1957), Nath (1969), Rothenburg (1961), and Tinbergen (1966).

ables the elected representatives to select policies having consequences that are consistent with one another, and that accord with the wishes of the majority of the electorate.

One might add, in passing, that if this more restrictive role of the economist were accepted by the profession, and acted upon, the consequences would be more inhibitive than is generally recognized. For one thing, not only would cost-benefit analysis have to be rejected; other popular techniques, such as those used in traffic control and pricing, would also have to go. For another, economists would be hard put to justify their general approval of a competitive pricing solution. Thus, if economists reject welfare economics, they may well have to reject also the economist's conventional presumption in favour of a competitive market.[2]

There can, moreover, be practical difficulties in the attempt to confine the economist to this more modest role of consultant, one whose task is only to reveal to decision-makers the implications of alternative economic policies. Allowing that the economist is both competent and honest, and produces a detailed list of all the 'economic' implications of each of the several policies under consideration, it is sure to baffle the ordinary politician. The economist can confidently anticipate a request that he, the economist, somehow 'organize' the raw data; that he provide some method by which the large variety of consequences expected from each policy be weighted in some way so as to enable the politician to compare the over-all merits of the alternative policies. Such a request itself, however, places arbitrary powers in the hands of the so-called economic consultant—unless (which is more likely than not) he has recourse to the familiar propositions of resource allocation. We might well surmise that, in the absence of any other incentive, the need for politicians to assimilate an otherwise unmanageable mass of price-quantity data in order to reach decisions on economic policy would impel economists to formulate allocative propostions.

---

2 The economist could, of course, approve of the market for other than allocative reasons: for instance, on the grounds that it is a cheap and relatively non-political administrative institution for coordinating economic activity (where coordination implies no more than an absence of shortages or surpluses of goods at given prices). Such coordination is possible with a wide variety of patterns of price-cost relationships.

2. The uncomfortable consequences, or the practical difficulties, that would follow the repudiation of welfare economics do not of themselves, however, constitute a sufficient argument for its acceptance. It must be able to offer more positive merits. These emerge from a brief examination of the arrangement alternative to a market economy—that of making economic decisions entirely through the political process.

Decision-making through the political process, especially in a liberal democracy, is time-consuming. Even if the democratic process, alone and unaided, were somehow able to offer to each person the same opportunities and the same combination of goods that he already receives through the market, economists would have no difficulty in convincing people that the substitution of voting mechanisms for the pricing mechanism would take up an unconscionable amount of time and effort. And yet, prodigal though it would be in the use of time and effort, it is hardly conceivable that the political process will bring about an allocation of goods and resources as satisfactory as that brought about through the market. Whatever the outcome of the political process, it is highly unlikely then that such an outcome could not be materially improved by introducing pricing mechanisms. And, if some improvements can be effected by the introduction of such pricing mechanisms, they can also be effected by simple allocation rules which 'simulate' the workings of the price mechanisms.

Nevertheless, allocation theory does not derive its justification from its being able to simulate the competitive market solutions—though this, no doubt, would suffice to commend it to many people. The reverse is rather the case: competitive markets are to be justified by reference to the propositions of welfare economics. And if so, it becomes necessary to understand the social basis of welfare economics, in particular the nature of an allocative improvement. The attempt to do this begins with a consideration of value judgments.

Economists are not alone in being unimpressed by the workaday wisdom of majority rule in modern societies. Notwithstanding conventional safeguards, a majority in power is capable of irresponsible and, even, tyrannical behaviour towards individuals and minorities. There can be no reasonable expectation, in particular where legislation is influenced by party doctrine, that majority decisions will always respect minority interests, or even views that are widely held in society.

The consequences of these deficiencies in the working of democracy can be limited by decentralized institutions, and by constitutional restrictions that rest upon a broad consensus. The existence of either, that is, depends on near-unanimous acceptance of a number of ethical premises. Ideally such ethical premises could be formulated by the members of society only if none of them had any idea beforehand of the circumstances into which he was to be born. Though this is impossible, a sufficient degree of detachment might be realized in existing societies to ensure near unanimous agreement on a number of provisions to be writ into a constitution.

In addition there may be a number of ethical propostitions which, though they appear to command widespread assent, are not written into a constitution. Either the society has no written constitution or, if there is one, such ethical propositions appear to be too obvious to warrant mention. They can then be said to form part of a virtual constitution. And if, among these ethical propositions that comprise a virtual constitution, there are several on which a welfare economics can be raised then—provided always that the logical structure was flawless—its guiding rules can truthfully claim to rest on a widely accepted ethical base. Such rules, on any ethical ranking, would therefore transcend economic decisions reached by poltical processes, democratic or otherwise, even when they are neither ephemeral, opportunitistic or foolish. For decisions reached by the political process will almost always rest on a narrower basis of consent.

One might add, in passing, that even without the explicit concept of a virtual constitution, a theory of welfare economics might be developed from the democratic process. If the latter operates not as a majority-rule decision mechanism—justified on the cynical view that, in the last resort, it is better to count heads than to break them —but rather as a method of reaching agreement through informed debate, then indeed the principles by which broad categories of decisions are reached becomes relevant. For if consensus is reached through informed debate on certain sorts of issues, the existence of

310

a common context of aspirations must be presumed. There is then likely to emerge a search for consistency in decision-taking on such issues, one that will tend to promote a common set of criteria. One such range of issues would comprehend certain kinds of economic problems, and the criteria sought for would be of an allocative nature. The incentive for discovering such criteria is, of course, economic. Once formulated, the implications of certain kinds of economic measures need not be debated at great length: they can be judged directly by reference to these allocative or 'welfare' criteria which, over time, will acquire a sort of constitutional status. In such an idealized democracy one might hope that time and intelligence would throw up those welfare propositions by which economists today seek to justify their prescriptive statements.

3. Now this notion of the welfare economist's ultimate appeal to a virtual constitution throws a clear light on the scope of welfare economics. For there appears, at first, to be only two propositions that would qualify for inclusion in such a constitution: (a) a Pareto improvement, and (b) a distributional improvement. A Pareto improvement takes place if some economic rearrangement makes one or more people better off without making any one worse off. A distributional improvement takes place if there is near-unanimity that the distribution resulting from the economic rearrangement is an improvement.

This may seem modest enough in all conscience, but a little thought on the matter will reveal that neither proposition can be regarded as unambiguous until the economist has made a choice between the alternatives of grounding his welfare economics in utility or in ethics. If he chooses the former, the utility base, then every effect on the individual's utility is to count. If he chooses the latter, the ethical base, only those effects sanctioned by the constitution as valid are to be admitted into the economic calculus.

Adoption of the utility base may be defended on the ground that if, for any reason, we ignore one or more individuals' reactions to an economic change, an apparent 'Pareto improvement' which may result may not, in fact, be a true Pareto improvement when such reactions are taken into account, or vice versa. In favour of the ethical base it can be argued that, if the concept of a Pareto improvement rests on an ethical consensus, this same ethical consensus may reject its validity unless it is restricted so as not to contravene other ethical judgments. Thus, notwithstanding that all members of society agree that an individual is the best judge of his own welfare, society may not wish to admit a Pareto improvement by reference to utility alone which otherwise affronts in any particular the moral sense of society.

The conflict between the utility and the ethical base of welfare economics can be observed most clearly in the generation of external, or spillover, effects, broadly defined. Outside the pricing mechanism, a person's welfare can be affected in an almost unlimited number of ways[3] by the actions of others. The ethical approach would admit as agenda only certain sorts of spillover effects. Among those to be excluded would be those external diseconomies sometimes referred to as interdependent utilities which, in more ordinary language, amount to the envy of any favourable change in the fortunes of others.[4] External diseconomies which take the form of a loss of an individual's welfare from the mere knowledge of events that have no palpable impact on his circumstances might also be excluded. Such individual reactions are understandable, but they do not evoke social approval or encouragement. Unlike, say, environmental spillovers, they are not of a tangible nature, and need have no bearing on a person's style of living. If, for example, a person dislikes Welshmen, his resentment of the fact that a Welshman dwells within the vicinity of his home is not likely to be accepted in such a constitution as grounds for compensation—much less any displeasure he suffers from the mere knowledge that Welshmen dwell somewhere within the same region, or county, with small likelihood of his ever

---

3 Although a great number of such spillover effects are 'trivial' in the sense that the minimal costs of attending to them exceed any potential mutual benefit.

4 If the 'interdependence' was positive, so that the person rejoices in the good fortune of others, society can approve, though without specifying that such responses enter the economic calculus.

meeting any.[5] Nor for that matter would such a constitution acknowledge the claims of a regular drinker that his enjoyment of life was being reduced by the abstention of his companions, or the claims of a smoker who insisted the presence of non-smokers was offensive to him.

A virtual constitution, then, has also to determine the broad nature of the spillover effects that are to count as a matter of course in any economic calculus: expressed in more pedestrian discourse, what is to count and what is not, has to be decided by reference to what men of good will regard as reasonable.

There are, of course, borderline difficulties to be invoked on this as on every other issue under the sun. But in existing Western societies I do not imagine there will be much difficulty in deciding what sort of spillovers are to be included in the economic calculus and what sort are not to be included. Certainly environmental spillover effects would qualify for inclusion, and equally certainly 'physic' spillover effects, such as envy, would be excluded. The reader may be able to amuse himself by thinking up some uncertain instances, but whether he manages to think of a few or many, the

5 Such constitutional provisions do *not*, however, appear to argue against political activity motivated by considerations of race, colour, culture, religion, or nationality. The principle of nationalism, or of self-determination, or of racial homogeneity, derives its strength from the deep satisfaction of peoples in having a homeland among their own 'kith and kin', from pride in long traditions, from an abiding affection for their own institutions, customs, characteristics, attitudes, and ways of life; and, therefore, also from a not irrational reluctance to suffer a risk of destruction, or possibly of dilution, of this social heritage, by having to share a common territory with a large number of people of altogether different origins and traditions.

Only fanatical addiction to a contrary ideal would unhesitatingly condemn those among a group, or race, or nation, who desire ardently to maintain their sense of continuity with the past, and who have no wish to alter their present ethnic mixture. Such aspirations, it can be argued, have no more to do with 'xenophobia', or 'chauvinism' than a strong preference for one's own home and family. They presuppose neither inhospitality to aliens, nor discrespect for the achievement of others. At the worst such aspirations are rooted in man's inner loneliness, insecurity perhaps, which translates itself into a desire for 'identification', and a need to belong.

Moreover, in a world where differences in national character, differences in race, class, dialect, culture, are being ironed out by rapid technological developments in transportation and in communication media, there is surely a particular case for viewing any counteracting movements to maintain differences, and to preserve some remnants of social variety in an increasingly anonymous universe, with more sympathy than is currently popular.

fact remains that if, instead, we base our welfare economics purely on utility, it will run into ethical objections and lose credibility.

4.   Having opted for the ethical base, let us return to this question of the scope of welfare economics. It should be manifest at once that not all economic issues can resolve themselves into a Pareto and a distributional change. Some economic issues will raise other questions, such as that of striking a balance between a high level of employment and a high level of price stability, or that of choosing from a variety of time paths by which the economy can reach some predetermined level of output, or that posed by Adam Smith between defence and opulence. Each of these problems presents a variety of alternative choices, none of which stands out on any widely accepted body of principles as superior to the others. For instance, price-stability alone, or high employment alone, is each accepted as a good thing. Near unanimity might be secured for the proposition that the more of each the better for society. Yet is is unlikely that any provision of the constitution, actual or virtual, will afford guidance where the chosen combination of these two social goods involves quantitative adjustments as between opposing incommensurables—where the more of one social good, that is, can be enjoyed only at some sacrifice of a different sort of social good. It follows that there will be many issues in the formulation of economic policy which cannot call for guidance on a welfare economics that raises itself only on those ethical premises sanctioned by the virtual constitution.

To conclude, inasmuch as current allocation economics derives its rationale from welfare economics, the socially relevant part of that subject can have no affinity with the species of sophisticated games which economists can play with any ranking device that catches their fancy. As the term suggests, welfare economics is to be regarded as a study of the contribution economics can make to advancing the social welfare. As such it seeks general, and conditional theorems, from which cost-benefit analysis and familiar optimizing techniques can be derived, all of them purporting to be independent of the current state of politics inasmuch as they take their sanction, ultimately, from the virtual constitution of the society for which they are intended.

However, since the relevant ethical premises are few—indeed, apart from those invoked to determine which effects are to count, only two would seem to qualify—it should be clear that while some issues of economic policy are fit subjects for welfare economics, it has little to contribute to other issues.

Chapter 46

COST-BENEFIT ANALYSIS AND THE PARETO PRINCIPLE

1. The welfare economics that is to be raised on the ethical provisions of a virtual constitution ensure only a *partial* ordering of conceivable economic arrangements. In other words, if each conceivable economic arrangement is identified by a distinct collection of goods and a distinct distribution of it among the members of society, only some can be ranked as unambiguously better than others by a consistent dual welfare criterion, one comprising the Pareto and the distribution improvement. Since these two provisions, each based on a social value judgment, are incommensurable, the welfare criterion is met only if neither provision is negated, and at least one is met. Such a criterion poses a number of problems which we need not stop to consider here,[1] for the simple reason that pure allocation theory and, therefore, cost-benefit analysis which is an application of this theory, is linked with but a single provision of the virtual constitution, a Pareto improvement. I say linked with, and not raised upon, simply because allocation theory is not raised on the Pareto-improvement provision, but rather on a 'diluted' version of it; what may be called a *potential* Pareto improvement. This can be defined as an economic rearrangement in which the gains *can* be so distributed as to make everyone in the community better off. So defined, the potential Pareto improvement will be recognized by some as a restatement of the familiar welfare test—that gainers be able to more than compensate losers—associated with the names of Hotelling (1938), Kaldor (1939), Scitovsky (1941), and others, though in fact going back to Pigou (1932).

2. Let us indicate briefly what is implied by a potential Pareto improvement. Following Hicks (1944), let us define the compensat-

---

1 The reader who would like to pursue the elusive issues connected with welfare criteria is referred to my 1965 paper.

ing variation, CV, as the sum of money which, if received or paid after the economic change in question, would make the individual no better or worse off than before the change. If, for example, the price of a loaf of bread falls by 10 cents, the CV is the maximum sum a man would pay in order to be allowed to buy bread at this lower price. *Per contra*, if the loaf rises by 10 cents the CV is the minimum sum the man must receive if he is to continue to feel as well off as he was before the rise in price. Since, in general, some people lose and some people gain following any economic change— which may involve a fall or a rise in several product and/or factor prices (or involve the introduction of a new good or the withdrawal of an old one)—the CVs of the gainers (the largest sums they are able to pay), which is a positive sum, may be added algebraically to the CVs of the losers (the smallest sum they will accept), which is a negative sum. If the resulting algebraic sum is positive, gainers can more than compensate losers, and the change will realize a potential Pareto improvement. If, on the other hand, this algebraic sum is zero or negative, the economic change contemplated does not realize a potential Pareto improvement. Moreover the magnitude of a positive algebraic sum measures the extent of the potential Pareto improvement, while the magnitude of a negative algebraic sum measures the extent of the potential reduction welfare.

Although it is seldom made explicit, the reader will do well to bear in mind that all calculations that enter into a cost-benefit analysis, when reduced to a single point of time by acceptable methods, are to be interpreted as contributions, positive or negative, to the magnitude of some resulting potential Pareto improvement. What is to be concluded, then, from a cost-benefit analysis showing, say, an excess gain of $100,000 is *not* that everyone concerned *is* made better off in varying degrees; only that it is conceptually possible, by *costless* redistributions, to make everyone better off, in total by an amount equal to $100,000. And since economists have, from time to time, vented their dissatisfaction with the notion of a potential Pareto improvement as a criterion and measure of social gain, we can hardly employ cost-benefit techniques with a clear conscience without examining some of the criticisms to which the concept has been subjected.

3. First, the potential Pareto improvement test clearly ignores the

resulting change in the distribution of incomes. Not only is it true that not everyone is made better off, it is also possible that those in the community who are made worse off are to be found largely among the lower-income groups. A change which makes the rich better off by $250,000 at the expense of the poor, who are made worse off by $150,000, still produces an excess gain of $100,000 for the community as a whole. As such, however, it is not likely to be accepted by all as an unexeptionable economic change—at least, not unless it was to be accompanied by redistributive measures which would make the poor no worse off than before, and possibly better off. A cost-benefit calculation may, indeed, be accompanied by observations on the resulting distribution, and even by recommendations in this respect. But the quantitative outcome of a cost-benefit calculation itself carries no distributional weight;[2] it shows that the total of gains exceeds the total of losses, no more.

Moreover, the appeal of such a test is diminished by its hypothetical nature. A Pareto improvement which positively requires that when some are made better off, no one is made worse off, is assured of fairly wide acceptance. It does some good to some, and apparently does no harm to others. A *potential* Pareto improvement, which is consistent with a great many people actually being made worse off, has much less appeal. One factor, however, does make it easier to countenance. The spread over the last century of increasing wealth, and increasing electoral power, has made for egalitarian tendencies. The more progressive is the tax structure, and the more intensive is competition, the greater is the likelihood that a potential Pareto improvement will result in an actual Pareto improvement, or something close to it. In the limiting case of a system of taxes and subsidies designed to maintain complete equality of incomes, every potential Pareto improvement (allowing for sufficient divisibilities) as transformed into an actual Pareto improvement. By redistributive transfers, that is, everybody in fact becomes better off.

In the existing world, however, where projects can have distributionally regressive effects, the economist can, as indicated above,

---

2 It is obviously possible to attach different weights to the dollars lost or gained by different income groups, but the weights—determined by the political process? are arbitrary. Revisions of the *differences* in weights used can admit projects hitherto rejected, and vice versa.

say something about the distribution resulting from the introduction of an otherwise feasible project. If the economist has reason to beleive that it will be unambiguously regressive, his duty is to mention it. It may, in some cases, be practicable to combine the project with a distributional scheme. More often than not, the distributional effects on society as a whole are not large. Provided no spillover effects are involved, the *direct* local effects of a number of familiar sorts of project are apt to be progressive. One thinks in this connection of flood-control, electricity generation, irrigation, and the like. Once spillover effects are entered, however, the net impact on the local inhabitants can be distinctly regressive. The spillover effects of through-traffic highways, and of fly-overs, constructed through working class neighbourhoods, provide a familiar example.

4. Secondly, as a result of the connection between relative prices and the distribution of the collection of goods, it is possible that a movement from one collection of goods, Q_1 to another Q_2, which realizes a potential Pareto improvement, is compatible with the reverse movement, one from Q_2 to Q_1, *also* realizing a potential Pareto improvement.[3]

To illustrate, let I_1 in Figure VI.1 be the community indifference curve passing through the initial collection of goods Q_1 comprising Y_1 of good Y and X_1 of good X. This collection of goods can be thought of as being divided between two persons (or two groups of persons), A and B, in a manner indicated by point d_1 on the contract curve from O to Q_1 of the box diagram, $O Y_1 Q_1 X_1$. The tangency of d_1 between A's indifference curve I_A and B's indifference curve I_B is, by construction, parallel to the tangency of the community curve I_1 at Q_1.[4] Since the alternative collection Q_2 is above the I_1 community indifference curve, it is possible to improve the welfare of everyone by moving to the Q_2 position (allowing, always, for sufficient divisibility). It is possible, that is, to make both A and B better off in the Q_2 than in the Q_1 position.

---

3 This was first demonstrated, using the box diagram technique (involving two goods and two persons) by Scitovsky (1941), though the possibility of this 'paradox' was mentioned earlier, by Pigou (1932).
4 A simple geometric technique for the construction of community indifference curves (that meet the optimum exchange condition) has been explained in my 1957 paper.

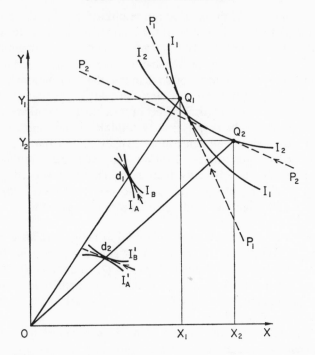

FIGURE VI.1

However, *having moved* to Q_2 on this recommendation [5], the resulting distribution of this Q_2 collection might be one such as is represented by point d_2 on the OQ_2 contract curve of the box diagram $OY_2Q_2X_2$, A's welfare (greater than it was in the Q_1 position) being represented by A's I_A' indifference curve, and B's welfare (less than it was in the Q_1 position) being represented by B's I_B' indifference curve. Again, the slope of the mutual tangency of I_A' and I_B' is, by construction, parallel with the tangent of the community indifference curve I_2 passing through Q_2. With this distribution resulting from the movement from Q_1 to Q_2, the slope at Q_2 is such that the I_2 curve passes below Q_1. And from this we infer that a movement from Q_2 to Q_1 realizes a potential Pareto improvement: beginning with the

---

5 Though *without* intervening in the resulting distribution so as, by transfer payments, actually to make both A and B better off.

d_2 distribution of Q_2, that is, a movement to Q_1 can make both A and B better off.[6]

The same apparent paradox results if, instead of community indifference curves, we make use of the relative prices arising from the respective distributions of the two collections of goods. The relative prices for Q_1 is represented by the slope of the line P_1P_1 tangent to the I_1 curve at Q_1, and at these relative prices it is clear that Q_2, being to the right of this price-line, is valued more highly than the Q_1 collection of goods. Once the community has moved to Q_2, however, the resulting relative prices are represented by the line P_2P_2 tangent to the I_2 curve at Q_2. At these relative prices it is equally clear that Q_1 being above the P_2P_2 line passing through Q_2, is valued more highly than the Q_2 collection of goods.

This apparent paradox is obviously a disconcerting theoretical possibility. It has to be taken seriously in attempts to prove some general propositions. for instance that some international trade is better for a country than no international trade.[7] The possibility of such a reversal actually occuring in the real world, where there are a large number of goods and people, is much smaller, however, than the impression conveyed by a two-good two-person diagram. Moreover, no matter how likely we rate the possibility, it diminishes as the focus of our analysis narrows, and the effects both of distributional changes on relative product prices and compositional changes on relative factor prices, become smaller. Nearly all cost-benefit calculations can be regarded as exercises in very partial analysis. Thus, all prices, outside those pertaining to the project, may be reasonably assumed constant.

---

6 If, instead, we constructed Figure VI.1 so that I_1 passed *above* Q_2 and I_2 passed *above* Q_1, the reverse paradox is illustrated: that Q_2 is potentially Pareto inferior to Q_1, and also that Q_1 is potentially Pareto inferior to Q_2.

7 In the attempt to prove that some international trade is better for a country than no international trade, Kemp (1963) ignored this theoretical possibility.

Chapter 47

CONSISTENCY IN PROJECT EVALUATION

1. Granted that a cost-benefit analysis seeks to establish the presumption of a potential Pareto improvement, measured in principle as the algebraic sum of all CVs, one must pass from the general concept to specific ways of estimating benefits and costs. The transition can be made by following the convention of the market economy, which regards people both as producers and consumers of goods. If *qua* producers, men are no worse off in consequence of some contemplated economic change, but are better off *qua* consumers then, on the whole, they are better off and a Pareto improvement is achieved. If they are all no worse off *qua* consumers, but better off *qua* producers, a Pareto improvement is also achieved. Similarly, if men are better off *qua* consumers and producers, there is a Pareto improvement.[1] Moreover, the value of goods and 'bads' to men, either as consumers or producers (factor-owners) are not worked out from scratch. Market prices can be deemed to provide these values in the first instance, following which they can be corrected for 'market failure'.

Except for marginal changes, in which case cost-benefit analysis is of little value, the notion of a surplus, or economic rent, is applicable. For measurement purposes this is customarily divided into consumers' surplus for changes in product opportunities and rents for changes in factor opportunities. A common practice, however, is to accept factor costs as given but to substitute some measure of consumers' surplus rather than use product prices, or changes in product prices, alone. This asymmetrical treatment is not wholly unwarranted in an economy in which factor groupings are few, but in which

---

1 A person is no worse off *qua* consumers if product prices do not rise against him, and better off if, on the whole, they fall. A person is no worse off, or better off, *qua* producer, if, respectively, factor prices do not fall or, on the whole, rise in his favour.

product groupings are many. A project that increases the output of a product or service may result in a large change in its price without appreciable effects on the relevant factor prices. The larger the change in that price, the more important it is to measure the gain, or loss, by consumers' surplus. Nonetheless, while there is some justification for paying more attention to consumer gains and losses than to the gains and losses of factor-owners, we have occasionally emphasized the importance of valuing factors at their opportunity costs in situations where they may differ markedly from their market prices.

2. There may be occasions, however, when the absence of data prevents the economists from putting a value on certain effects resulting from the project. Very often such effects are spillovers, which do not register on the market mechanism. Ignoring envy and other inadmissible external effects, such spillovers can in principle be brought 'into relationship with the measuring rod of money', as Pigou (1932) put it, the correct concept, as indicated, being the CV of each person affected. But although the spillover can be measured 'in principle', there are likely to be difficulties 'in practice' of putting reliable figures on them. What can be done in the circumstances is discussed in the section on External Effects. When apparently nothing can be done, the effects may be described in some detail, and entered into the final table of costs and benefits. There is a temptation to go further than this, however, and leave a space opposite such unmeasurable effects for the so-called decision-maker to fill in.

Recourse to this practice is unsatisfactory. A cost-benefit analysis is raised on a single criterion, that of a potential Pareto improvement, which criterion is deemed related to a provision of the virtual constitution. Even if a political decision were made, say, to build a dam, a cost-benefit analysis of the dam that revealed a net loss would be properly regarded as a valid criticism of the political decision—which decision could be defended only by invoking *other* considerations, say equity, or national defence. The determination of the value of a project, or of any part or effect of that project, by the political process is either (economically) arbitrary, or else, if it arises from any other consistent body of principles, is in conflict with the allocative criterion on which a cost-benefit calculation proceeds. To add figures derived on one principle to figures gotten on some other principle produces a sum that carries no coherent interpretation.

The economist, as well as the political decision-making body, should be aware of this. If the decision of the latter is to place the evaluation of the project in the hands of the economist, the economist must perforce base his calculations on a purely economic criterion. By returning some parts of it to be evaluated by the political process, which in the first instance determined to be guided by the purely economic evaluation, is to effect a deception; is to sacrifice meaning on the altar of quantification and to do so in order to save face. If the unmeasurable effect is completely beyond his range of reasonable guesses, so that a decision cannot be reached by the economist on the basis of the measurable data and reasonable guesswork, he serves the public better by confessing the truth: that, with the existing techniques and information, he is unable to discharge his task.

As indicated earlier, however, although the economist is unable to place a valuation on some critical magnitude he should provide the public with whatever information about it that he has (including informed guesses on any aspect of it). Indeed, he should let the public know exactly the sort of question he is trying to answer. What the economist must *not* do in these circumstances is to equate the eventual *political* outcome with the outcome of a *cost-benefit* analysis. As with any sort of (part) political decision, he reserves a right of independent professional criticism.

NOTE B: MORE ACCURATE MEASURES OF ECONOMIC SURPLUS

Chapter 48

THE CONCEPT AND MEASURE OF CONSUMER'S SURPLUS

1. Notwithstanding some ill-considered utterances about consumer's surplus by well-known economists,[1] it is a concept so crucial to allocative economics generally, and in particular to cost-benefit analysis, that there is everything to be said for clarifying both the concept itself, and the relationship between the concept and its measurable proxy, the demand curve.

Marshall's definition of the individual's consumer's surplus, the amount of money a man is willing to pay rather than go without the thing over that which he actually pays, though it has strong intuitive appeal, is not altogether satisfactory: for it implies a constraint on the quantity to be bought. The sum of money the consumer is willing to pay, say, for a licence to buy the good at some given price rather than go without it, depends on how much he is expected to buy. And if, as Marshall implicitly assumed, the amount of the good he is to buy—on paying for this licence—is the same amount as that which he buys at the price *in the absence of* any need for a licence, then he will *not*, generally, pay as much for the licence as he would if, in-

---

1 For instance, Little (1957) stated that it was no more than a 'theoretical toy' (p. 180). According to Samuelson (1963), 'The subject is of historical and doctrinal interest with a limited amount of appeal as a purely mathematical puzzle' (p. 195). This latter remark could be said with some truth of a large number of topics in contemporary economics, but it cannot be accepted as a judgment about consumer's surplus. Without this concept how does the economist justify the free use of roads, bridges, parks, etc., or the operation of industries at outputs for which prices are below marginal costs, or two-part tariffs? Without attempts to measure increments of consumers' surpluses, and rents, cost-benefit analyses would be primitive indeed.

stead, he is allowed to buy as much of the good as he wants. His having to pay for a licence makes him worse off, and if his income effect is positive he would then—at the same price—choose a smaller amount than if he could buy freely without a licence. Consequently, if he is constrained to buy the initial (larger) amount, he will pay less for the licence.[2]

2. Such considerations prompted Hicks' definition (1939) of a *compensating variation* measure of the consumer's surplus. For the privilege of being able to buy the good at the existing price, *in whatever amount he chooses*, the consumer is willing to pay some maximum

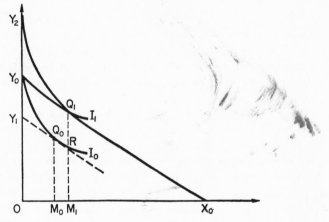

F<small>IGURE</small> VI.2

---

2   Marshall's dissatisfaction, and eventual disillusion, with the concept of consumer's surplus, arose from his utility analysis. Aware that the fall in the price of a good which made the consumer better off had some effect on the amount he would buy, Marshall tried to circumvent the problem by holding the inidvidual's marginal utility of income constant. But this was plausible only for minute changes in the individual's welfare. Moreover, in extending the concept to the market, Marshall's choice of working in terms of cardinal, and interpersonal, utility proved cumbersome and unconvincing.

Once Hicks introduced the more operational distinction between income and substitution effects, it became evident that it was real income, and not the marginal utility of money, that was to be held constant. And despite popular belief to the contrary, these are not alternative methods of expressing the same condition. A constant marginal utility of money does *not* imply constant real income, and vice versa.

sum—his compensating variation. In 1943 Henderson pointed out that the exact measure proposed by Hicks would differ according to whether the consumer had to pay for the opportunity of buying the good at the given price or whether, instead, he was to be paid for abandoning this opportunity. This distinction is illustrated by reference to the indifference curve for a single individual in Figure VI.2.

Along the horizontal axis is measure the good x, to be introduced into the economy at a fixed price given by the budget line $Y_0 X_0$. $O Y_0$ measures his money income over a period during which the prices of all goods other than x remain constant. Prior to the introduction of good x, the individual's money income Y_0 corresponds to a real income indicated by the indifference curve I_0. Once x is introduced at the price given by the budget line $Y_0 X_0$, the individual chooses the point Q_1 on the higher indifference curve I_1, and therefore consumes $O M_1$ of x.

The difference made to the person's real income, $I_1 - I_0$, is unambiguous. Ambiguity arises simply because we are to measure the real gain in terms of money income, as defined, along the vertical axis. Hicks' compensating variation, CV, is equal to $Y_0 Y_1$. For if the consumer is made to pay this sum in order to be permitted to buy x at the price (given by the slope of $Y_0 X_0$), he could just reach Q_0 on his original indifference curve I_0. That is, if he is to be exactly as well off as he was originally before x was introduced, $Y_0 Y_1$ is the maximum sum he can afford to pay for the privilege of buying x at the given price. And if called upon to pay this maximum, the amount of x that he would in fact buy is given here by $O M_0$.

Turning to Henderson's distinction, we now ask a different question: what is the minimum sum the consumer will accept to give up entirely the opportunity of buying the new good x at the market price, given by the slope of $Y_0 X_0$? The answer is a sum equal to $Y_0 Y_2$. For adding this sum to his initial income, $O Y_0$, his total income becomes $O Y_2$, and this income, without any x, is on his indifference curve I_1. He is then just as well off as he would have been if, at his original income $O Y_0$, he was able to buy x at the given price. This measure of consumer's surplus was called by Hicks (1944) the *Equivalent Variation*, EV, inasmuch as, in the absence of x, such a sum provides the consumer with an equivalent improvement in his welfare.

Provided the income effect is positive ('normal'), Q_1 will be to the right of Q_0 on the parallel budget lines. OM_1 will therefore be larger than OM_0, and $Y_0 Y_2$ will be larger than $Y_0 Y_1$. If, instead, the income effect were negative, the ranking would be reversed: Q_1 would be to the left of Q_0, ON_0 would be smaller than OM_0, and $Y_0 Y_2$ would be smaller than $Y_0 Y_1$.[3]

3. More generally, the definition of CV is the sum of money—to be paid to the consumer when the price falls; to be received by him when the price rises—which, following a change in the price, leaves him at his initial level of welfare. The EV, on the other hand, is that sum of money—to be received by the consumer when the price falls; to be paid by him when it rises—which, if he were exempted from the change in price, would yet provide him with the same welfare change. These two measures have been illustrated in Figure VI.2 for the special case of the introduction of a new good x at a given price, rather than for a change in the existing price of x. They are illustrated in Figure VI.3 for the case of a fall in the existing price of x.

Initial money income is again represented by OY_0, initial real income being given by the indifference curve I_1 which is reached by the tangency of the price-line p_1 at Q_1. If the price of x fall to p_2, the tangency of the p_2 price-line at Q_2 raises the consumer's real income from I_1 to I_2. His CV is then equal to $Y_0 Y_1$, this being the maximum sum he could afford to pay for the lower price p_2 without being any worse off. For, if he pays this sum, so reducing his money income to OY_1, the lower price p_2 enables him to reach B on his original I_1 curve. His EV, on the other hand, is equal to $Y_0 Y_2$, this being the minimal sum he will accept to forgo the opportunity to buy what he wants at the lower price p_2. For with this sum his total income would be equal to OY_2, and with this income and the old price p_1 he could just reach indifference curve I_2 at C. This increase in his welfare is exactly equal to that which he could attain with this new price p_2 with his original money income OY_0. Once more, $Y_0 Y_2$ will exceed $Y_0 Y_2$ for a 'normal' good x, as drawn, the reverse being true if x, instead, were an 'inferior' good.

---

3 The reader will note that these relationships hold irrespective of whether marginal utility of real income is diminishing, constant, or increasing—these three possibilities being consistent with any given indifference map of the individual.

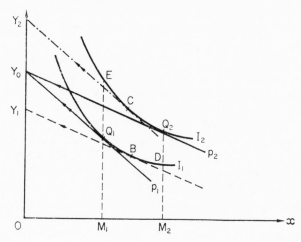

FIGURE VI.3

We can now go through the same exercise for a rise in the price of
x. With income $O Y_0$, we begin with the consumer being faced with
p_2 and, therefore, choosing point Q_2 on indifference curve I_2. A rise
in the price of x to p_1 now induces him to take up the position Q_1
on the I_1 indifference curve. Our definitions would therefore measure
the CV of such a price-rise by $Y_2 Y_0$, this being the minimum sum
that would restore the individual's welfare to its original level I_2
when the price rises to p_1. The EV is now to be measured as equal to
$Y_0 Y_1$, this being the maximum sum the consumer is prepared to
give up if he is exempted from the higher price p_1. For giving up this
sum, and retaining the old price p_2, would enable him to reach I_1
(at B), which is the level of welfare he reaches if he is not exempted
from the rise in price to p_1.

4. These two measures, the CV and the EV are all that are needed
in ordinary circumstances. Solely as a matter of curiosity, however,
we might wish to go back to Figure VI.2 for a precise measure of the
definition put forward by Marshall. This turns out to be a sum equal
to the vertical distance $Q_1 R$, this being the maximum sum the consumer will pay for the privilege of being able to buy x at the given
price *provided* he is constrained to buy $O M_1$ of x—this amount of x
being that which the consumer actually buys when he is permitted

(without having to pay anything for the privilege) to buy freely at the given price. For if he moves along the price line from Y_0 to Q_1, and is then obliged to stay with the quantity OM_1 of x, he must give up Q_1R in order to be at R on his original indifference curve I_0. This measure Q_1R is smaller than Y_0Y_1, as indeed it should be, since the consumer would pay less for the privilege of being able to buy x if he were compelled to buy a particular amount of it (here OM_1) than if, instead, he could choose whatever amount of x he wished.[4]

Thus the Marshallian measure differs from the CV measure only in its having a quantity constraint attached to it. Extending the Marshallian-type measure to a change in price, we can refer to Figure VI.3. For a fall in price from p_1 to p_2, the relevant quantity-constraint is OM_2, and the quantity-constrained CV is therefore measured as Q_2D. A quantity-constrained EV, requiring the consumer to purchase only OM_1 of X—this being the amount he buys at the original price p_1 without receiving any compensation—is measured as Q_1E.[5]

Again, for a rise in price from p_2 to p_1 these measures are reversed. Q_1E becomes the quantity-constrained CV, and Q_2D becomes the quantity-constrained EV.

---

4 This is true (that is the Marshallian measure is smaller than the CV) irrespective of whether x is a 'normal' or an 'inferior' good.

5 It is clear from Figure VI.3 that the quantity-constrained CV measure, Q_2D, is smaller than the unconstrained CV measure, Y_0Y, which is as it should be since he would always pay less for a constrained privilege than for an unconstrained one. For the analogous reason that he would want to receive a larger compensation if he were to be constrained with respect to quantity than if he were not to be so constrained, the quantity-constrained EV measure, EQ_1, is larger than the ordinary EV measure, Y_0Y_2.

Chapter 49

MARGINAL CURVE MEASURES OF CONSUMER'S SURPLUS

1. The two more popular measures of consumer's surplus, CV and EV can be represented on the marginal diagram, Figure VI.4. I_0' is the marginal indifference curve corresponding to indifference curve I_0 in Figure VI.2 of the preceding chapter. In fact, I_0' is the curve of the first derivative of I_0 with respect to x. Similarly, the marginal indifference curve I_1' is the first derivative of the I_1 curve of Figure VI.2. For convenience both marginal indifference curves are represented as straight lines in Figure VI.4. And, since in Figure VI.2, I_1 is indicative of a higher level of welfare than I_0, the assumption of a 'normal' good x requires that marginal indifference curve I_1' be drawn above (or to the right of) I_0'.[1]

If we regard individual welfare as continuously variable the indifference curves are infinitely dense, and so also, therefore, are the marginal indifference curves. For illustrative purposes, however, we

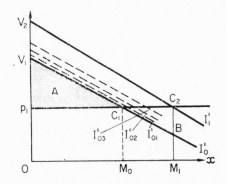

FIGURE VI.4

---

1 If, instead, the income effect on x were negative, the reverse would be true; the I_1' marginal indifference curve would be below the I_0' marginal indifference curve.

could select an arbitrary number of marginal indifference curves, I_{0_1}', I_{0_2}', and so on, as indicated by the broken lines in Figure VI.4.

We shall return to this diagram presently, after taking a closer view of the origin and of the point M_1 by means of an incremental diagram, Figure VI.5. The story opens with no x being available and our consumer having I_0 welfare. The maximum sum he will pay for a single unit of x is shown as the first unit column having height v_1. Let us suppose that he pays this maximum sum, in which case his welfare remains unchanged at level I_0. He is then offered a second unit of x. The maximum he can now afford to pay for this second unit is given by the height of the second column, v_2. Again, we

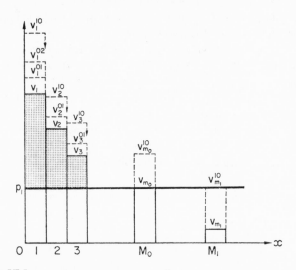

FiGURE VI.5

suppose that he is required to pay this maximum, so retaining his original welfare at I_0, and a third unit of x is offered to him, for which he can pay as much as v_3, the height of the third column. If we continue in this way, he will eventually, after purchasing M_0 units of x, have offered as much as v_{m0} for the M_0^{th} unit of x.

Now, let the price p_1 be set at height v_{m0}. If he buys M_0 units of x on these terms, he will be no better off after buying them than he was before he bought any x. His level of welfare, that is, remains at I_0. The sum of the portions of these solid columns that stick up above the price line (their dotted segments) has now to be interpreted. Since his payment of this sum, in addition to price p_1 per unit, for OM_0 units of x is such that he is no better off than he was originally, without x, this sum is to be regarded as the CV for introducing x at p_1. It is the maximum sum he will be able to pay for the privilege of buying x at p_1 without his being any worse off than he was originally. On the Figure VI.4 diagram, having continuous curves, this CV is represented as the area of the dotted triangle A.

2. Let us now return to our consumer in a more charitable humour, and allow him to buy all the x he wants at the introductory price p_1. His welfare, or real income, increases from I_0 to I_1, and —because his real income effect is assumed positive—he buys more of x; in fact OM_1 of x in Figure VI.4.

Looking at things in the light of the incremental diagram, Figure VI.5, we notice that, because of this increase in real income, the value of the final M_1^{th} unit is now valued at $v_m{}_1^{10}$, equal to price p_1, and not at the smaller value v_{m1}—the maximum he would have paid for the M_1^{th} unit on the first procedure, which retained his welfare at the level I_0. Indeed, because of the increase in the level of his welfare from I_0 to I_1 when he is allowed to buy x freely at p_1 (and ends up buying OM_1 units) the valuation of all preceding units of x are raised; the M_0^{th} unit being valued at $v_m{}_0^{10}$, the third unit being valued at v_3^{10}, and the first unit being valued at v_1^{10}, and so on. The stepped line joining the top of these revised columns in Figure 5, from the first to the M_1^{th} unit, can be represented, however, by the segment V_2C_2 of the continuous marginal indifference curve I_1' in Figure VI.4. Once the consumer has been allowed to buy all he wants of x at the price p_1, and his welfare rises from I_0 to I_1, the area $OV_2C_2M_1$ is the exact measure of what the OM_1 units of x are worth to him.

If the privilege of buying x at p_1 were now withdrawn, he would have to be returned his expenditure on OM_1 units of x, or $Op_3C_2M_1$. But unless he were also paid a sum equal to the area of the triangle $p_1V_2C_2$, he would be worse off than he was with the privilege of buying all he wanted at price p_3; his welfare, that is, would be below I_1. The triangle $p_1V_2C_2$ is, then, the measure of his EV. It is the minimum sum that is needed to make him as well off when the privilege of buying x at p_1 is withdrawn as he was when he enjoyed that privilege.[2]

3. We now return, once more, to Figure VI.5 in order to throw more light on two issues that are somewhat obscure. As mentioned, beginning with welfare at level I_0, the maximum the consumer will pay for the first unit of x is given by the height v_1 of the first solid column. But if, instead of paying this maximal sum, he pays no more than the price p_1, he makes a surplus on this first unit equal to the column segment $p_1 v_1$. As a result his welfare rises, say, to I_{0_1} (greater than I_0), and the maximum he is now prepared to pay for the second, third, and subsequent units of x is—on the assumption of a positive income effect—raised somewhat to v_2^{01} for the second unit, to v_3^{01} for the third unit of x, and so on. Let him now be offered a second unit of x at the same price p_1, and he makes as a surplus on this second unit an amount equal to $p_1 v_2^{01}$. His welfare has risen by another increment to, say, I_{0_2}, and the maximum sum he will pay for successive units also rises. For the third unit he will now pay as much as v_3^{02}, and so on. Proceeding in this way, determining the resulting maximum sum the consumer will pay for each successive unit prior to allowing him to buy it at price p_1, we can trace a locus that has been called (Hicks, 1944), the 'marginal valuation', MV, curve. Its relation to the marginal indifference curves of Figure VI.4 could be shown there, but in order not to clutter up the picture we have reproduced the main features of Figure VI.4 in Figure VI.5, and shown this MV curve as the *broken* line joining V_1 to C_2.

This MV curve is not, however, to be identified with the demand curve. For in order to generate a demand curve for x we trace the path of consumer purchases by gradually *lowering the price* from V_1 to p_1. Although both the MV and the demand curves pass through

---

2 The reader might care to note that the quantity-constrained CV—corresponding to the Marshallian definition of consumer's surplus—is smaller than the Hicksian CV. In Figure VI.4. it can be represented as the dotted triangle A *less* the triangle $C_1 C_2 B$. For the quantity constraint requires of the consumer that, in paying a maximum for the privilege of buying x at p_1, he continue to buy OM_1 units (and not the OM_0 units he would have chosen to buy). Since the marginal indifference curve I'_0 shows the maximum he is prepared to pay for these additional $M_0 M_1$ units of x, and shows that this maximum for each such unit is below the price p_1, his welfare can be maintained—after paying a sum equal to the triangle A—only by refunding him the losses he must sustain on the additional $M_0 M_1$ units, a total loss given by the triangle $C_1 C_2 B$.

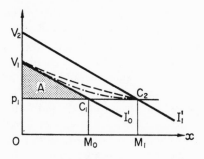

FIGURE VI.6

C_2 when the price is p_1, for all previous quantities of x the MV curve (for a 'normal' good) is above the demand curve, shown as the *dotted* curve joining V_1 to C_2. The reason is simply that, in tracing the locus of the MV curve, the consumer is deemed to buy each successive unit of x, from the first onward, at the actual price p_1. In contrast, the demand curve is generated by having the consumer pay a price that is first equal to OV_1 and, though gradually lowered, remains above p_1 until the final M_1^{th} unit is bought. As a result, the surplus of welfare gained in the purchase of the first, second, third, and subsequent units of x (save for the final M_1^{th} unit) is greater for the MV procedure than for the demand curve procedure. At each unit of x, save the final M_1^{th} unit, the consumer's valuation is, therefore, higher for the MV curve than for the demand curve.

4. In order to broach the second issue, we return to Figure VI.5, and recall that the maximum sum the consumer will pay for the first unit is given by the height v_1 of the first column. If he is permitted to buy this one unit at p_1, his CV for that one unit is equal, as indicated, to the dotted segment of the column above the p_1 line. Suppose we now ask the question: what is the minimum sum he will accept in order to give up the privilege of buying this one unit of x at p_1? Now if this question is asked prior to his having bought any unit of x at a price (such as p_1) below his maximum valuation of a first unit, his welfare will still be at the I_0 level. The minimum sum he would accept to forgo having the one unit of x might then be thought equal to the maximum sum he would pay for it. But whether in fact he has bought this x unit at p_1, and his welfare has risen to the level

335

I_{01} (greater than initial level I_0), or whether he has *not* yet bought this unit of x, and his existing welfare is still at I_0, makes no difference. The minimum sum he will require to forgo the unit he bought at p_1, or the opportunity to buy it at p_1, is in either case the same, and larger, than the maximum sum he would pay to be able to buy a unit at x at p_1. For assume that he has not yet bought any x at p_1, and his welfare is still therefore at I_0, the individual has to ask himself the question: what is the level of welfare I *could* reach if I were permitted to avail myself of the opportunity of buying this units of x at p_1? And the answer, as indicated above, is the level I_{01}, greater than I_0. The sum of money which, therefore, exactly compensates him for *not* being able to attain this I_{0_1} level of welfare (through the purchase of a unit of x at p_1) is equal to the column segment $p_1 v^{01}_1$.

This description of the sum of money, however, corresponds exactly with the definition of the EV—the sum which, if he is exempted from the economic change in question, provides him with the equivalent change in his welfare.[3] More generally, if no constraint is placed on the amount of x the consumer would wish to buy, the EV necessary to induce him to forgo the opportunity of buying x at p_1 is equal to the area of triangle $p_1 V_2 C_2$ in Figure VI.6.

5. Let us summarize these interpretations. The CV for introducing x at price p_1 is given by the dotted triangle A in Figure VI.6. Once x is introduced at that price, the consumer, in the absence of constraint, will buy $O M_1$ units and achieve a welfare level corresponding to indifference curve I_1. In order to persuade him to forgo this opportunity to buy x at p_1, which would take him to I_1 welfare, he must receive a minimum sum equal to the area of the large triangle, $p_1 V_2 C_2$. By definition this is his EV.

If, on the other hand, he has already been given the price p_1, and the economic change consists of withdrawing it entirely, this same minimum sum, equal to triangle $p_1 C_2 V_2$, represents the consumer's

---

3 If, however, the economic change being contemplated is the exact opposite of this; viz. the *withdrawal* of the opportunity of buying a unit of x at p_1 and, as a result, a reduction of the consumer's welfare level from I_{0_1}, the payment of this sum is the appropriate CV for such an economic change. For it is the sum the consumer must receive in order to maintain his existing level of welfare, I_{0_1}, following such a change.

CV, being the sum that must be paid him in order to maintain his existing welfare at I_1. His EV in this circumstance is the smaller triangle A, this being the maximum sum he would pay to be exempt from losing the opportunity to buy at p_1, which payment would in fact reduce his level of welfare to I_0.[4]

Confining ourselves to the CV and EV of introducing a normal good x at price p_1, it is clear that the area between the price and the individual's demand curve, D, is greater than the CV area and less than the EV area; i.e. for 'normal' goods, $CV < D < EV$. It is obvious that the smaller is the income effect the smaller will be the difference between these areas regarded as measures of consumer's surplus. In the limiting case of zero income effect, the three areas coincide.[5]

6. Finally, we can translate the CV and EV measures of Figure VI.3, featuring a fall in the price from p_1 to p_2 onto the marginal diagram of Figure VI.7. At p_1 the consumer is buying OM_1 units. At p_2 he is buying OM_2 units. The marginal indifference curves I_0', I_1', and I_2', are indicated as solid lines, and the demand curve passing through VDH as the dotted-line.

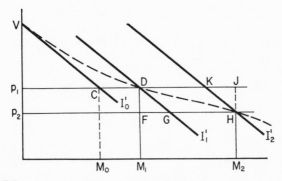

FIGURE VI.7

---

4 It should be self-evident that the maximum sum a consumer will pay to acquire a benefit (his CV) is the same maximum sum he will pay to hold on to it (his EV); that is, to be exempt from its removal once he already has it.
5 If x had a negative income effect we should have $EV < D < CV$. Figure VI.6 would have to be revised by exchanging points M_0 and M_1, C_1 and C_2, V_1 and V_2. The demand curve joining the new V_1 to the new C_2 would then be steeper then either of the two marginal indifference curves. In the extreme, Giffen-good case, the demand curve over a range slopes downward from left to right.

The CV of the fall in the price from p_1 to p_2 is equal to the cost difference for OM_1 units of x, or rectangle p_1p_2FD, *plus* the triangle *DFG*. The EV for that fall in price is equal to the cost-difference for OM_2 units, or rectangle p_1p_2HJ *less* the triangle *HJK*. These measures of CV and EV are, of couse, reversed for a price rise from p_1 to p_2.

The horizontal slice of consumer's surplus under the demand curve, the area p_1p_2HD is an approximation to either of the exact measures, being clearly greater than the CV measure, and smaller than the EV measure, for a price-fall. Again, the smaller the income effect, the closer is the coincidence of the three measures. For a zero income effect the measures coincide. Goods having zero income effect are hard to come by, but for a great many purposes the income-effect involved is small enough for economists to make use of the area under the demand curve as a close approximation of the relevant benefit or loss.

Chapter 50

THE CONCEPT AND MEASURE OF RENT

1. Although the concept of rent, in the specfic sense of a surplus to factor-owners, is not so popular in cost-benefit analyses as the concept of consumers' surplus, it is possible that, with growing awareness of allocation theory and growing refinements in techniques of measurement, it will become increasingly employed. The concept deserves more detailed treatment for another reason: the use of the area above the supply price of a factor is a less reliable proxy for the measurement of rent than is the area below the consumer's demand curve a proxy for his surplus. The reader will appreciate this remark more readily after the concept of rent has been defined.

Textbook definitions that are still in current use can be divided into two types. One conceives of rent as a payment in excess of that necessary to maintain a factor in its current occupation. The other would describe it as the difference between the factor's current earnings and its 'transfer earnings'—the latter term denoting its earnings in the next most highly paid use. As we shall see, the first type of definition is ambiguous because of the quantity constraint. The second type of definition is even more restricted, however, as its validity would require that, in the choice of occupation, men are motivated solely by pecuniary considerations. Indeed, it will transpire that, like consumer's surplus, rent is a measure of change in a person's welfare and, again, like consumer's surplus, can have both a CV and an EV measure.

2. As with the treatment of consumer's surplus, our first recourse will be to the indifference map. Figure VI.8 indicates four quadrants of a diagram in which money income, Y, is again measured vertically, and the good L (which can be thought of as labour services) is measured horizontally. Any horizontal distance to the right of the origin, O, would measure the amount of L acquired by the individual; any horizontal distance to the left of the origin, the amount of L

given up. Similarly, any distance above the origin measures the amount of income acquired, and any distance below it the amount of income given up. As distinct from the consumer goods' situation which is depicted in the North-East quadrant, the factor supplies' situation is here depicted in the North-West quadrant.[1]

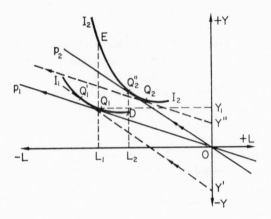

FIGURE VI.8

---

1 This construction has three advantages over the more common leisure-income diagram which is placed in the usual North-East quadrant.

(1) First, the choice among available combinations of two goods, leisure (regarded as a homogeneous good) and money, fails to convey the more general notion of the individual as a demander and a *supplier* of any number of goods and factors, electing to provide a particular combination of them according to market prices. In general, each of the variety of factors the individual can offer requires a different skill and entails a different degree of hardship.

(2) One avoids the artifice of a limit to the amount of the 'good' leisure, say twenty four hours of the day, which artifice has the awkward result that an improvement in welfare is represented along one axis as equivalent to more than twenty-four hours of leisure a day. In the construction of Figure VI.8, the limit to the supply of any factor is governed directly by the shape of the person's indifference curves, and the measure of any welfare change is in terms of the one good, money income.

(3) The indifference map of Figure VI.8, whose curves can be extended to cross the vertical axis, is the correct prior construction to that useful textbook diagram in which a downward-sloping curve from left to right crosses a price-axis, to the right of which the line is interpreted as a demand curve for the good, and to the left of which the line is interpreted as a supply curve of it.

If we construct a price-line p_1 passing through the origin and tangent at Q_1 to the indifference curve I_1, the individual is represented as in his chosen equilibrium position, giving up OL_1 of this particular sort of labour and, in exchange, acquiring OY_1 units of money income. Let the market supply price for this sort of labour rise from p_1 to p_2, and the individual's new equilibrium is given by the combination Q_2 on the I_2 indifference curve. The resulting change from Q_1 to Q_2 may be divided, in the usual Hicksian way, into a pure substitution effect—a movement from Q_1 to Q_1'—and a pure welfare effect—a movement from Q_1' to Q_2. Although the welfare effect can, of course, go either way, it should be noticed that a positive welfare effect—implying a welfare-induced increase in the *demand* for a good or factor—constitutes a reduction in the *supply* of a good or factor. Thus a positive, or 'normal' welfare effect following a rise in the price of a factor acts to reduce the amount put on the market. As we shall see the 'backward-bending' supply curve of the factor owner is the outcome of a strong positive welfare effect overcoming the unambiguous substitution effect.

The increase in the individual's welfare that follows the rise in the price of his labour from p_1 to p_2 can be measured, first as a CV—here, the exact amount of money that has to be taken from him to restore his welfare to its original I_1 level. The measurement of the CV on the vertical axis is, therefore, OY'. It is the maximum sum of money he could give up for the opportunity of selling his labour at the higher price p_2. If he gives up this sum OY', he will have the negative income indicated by Y' and, with price p_2, he can just reach I_1 at Q_1'.

This increase in his welfare can also be measured as an EV—here, the exact amount of money which has to be given to him to ensure that, if the opportunity to sell his labour at p_2 is not extended to him, he is still able to reach the new welfare level as indicated by indifference curve I_2. The EV is, therefore, measured as OY'', along the vertical axis. If he is paid this sum, he will be able to reach I_2 at Q_2'' with the original price p_1. It will be observed that, in the 'normal' case (positive welfare effect), the CV measure of an increase in welfare that follows a rise in the supply price exceeds the EV measure.

Since rent is frequently regarded as a surplus which may be partly or wholly appropriated without having any effect on the supply of factors, it is important to notice that—provided the welfare effects are not zero—wherever the individual has to pay an amount less than, or equal to, his rent (as measured, say, by his CV), the amount of factors he will offer will differ from the original amount. To illustrate, if, after the price has risen to p_2 and he supplies Q_2 of the factor, the CV measure of his rent is equal to OY', as stated. Let him be taxed the full amount of this rent and, with the new price p_2, he will reach Q_1', and supply a larger amount of factors than before.

3. As with consumer's surplus we could also trace out a quantity-constrained CV and EV. This constrained CV, sometimes associated with the Marshallian concept of rent, would be the maximum sum of money the individual would surrender in order to retain p_2 when, at the same time, he were restrained from providing no more than OL_2 of the factor (this being the amount he chose to supply at p_2). This restriction on his choice of quantity, not surprisingly, reduces the sum he is willing to pay for the opportunity of having the higher price p_2 from OY' to Q_2D. Similarly, the constrained EV, the minimum sum he will accept to forgo p_2 when he is compelled to supply the original amount OL_1, is EQ_1 which is larger than the unconstrained EV of OY''. There is obviously nothing 'wrong' in using the quantity-constrained CV and EV. But on grounds of plausibility and convenience they are to be rejected in favour of the CV and EV proper.

4. It is instructive to turn briefly to the case of the supply of a factor in two alternative occupations A and B. Although the individual might choose to work part time in each occupation, owing to institutional arrangements this is not always feasible. We shall therefore confine the analysis to the case of placing his factor L entirely in the A occupation, or entirely in the B.

Figure VI.9 represents a section of a three-dimensional indifference map, with the same vertical axis Y and two horizontal axes, L_a and L_b, crossing at right angles. If we imagine our three-dimensional figure were cut vertically into four equal parts, the figure is the space left after the removal of the vertical quarter in which L_a and L_b are both negative. Our attention is largely restricted to the upper, the positive part, of the diagram.

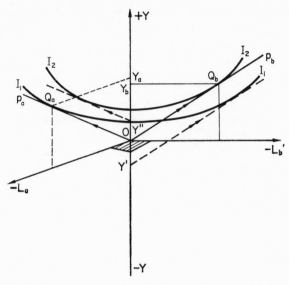

FIGURE VI.9

The rate of pay in A is given by p_a which is higher than p_b. If he chose to work in A at p_a, his earnings, OY_a, would be higher than his earnings, OY_b, in B. Nevertheless, the individual chooses to place his factors entirely in the B occupation, his equilibrium being Q_b on the indifference surface I_2 which is above the indifference surface I_1 on which is found his alternative choice, Q_a. As compared with the equilibrium he could reach in the A occupation, the individual enjoys a positive economic rent which, as an EV, can be measured as OY'—this being the maximum sum he is prepared to pay to remain in B. For after paying as much as OY' he can just reach the I_1 indifference surface—the new, lower, level of welfare which he would reach if he had to move into the A occupation. Conceived as a CV the rent is measured as a sum equal to OY'', this being the minimum sum the individual must be paid in order to induce him to transfer to occupation A. For, after receiving the sum OY'', he will be able, moving along p_a, to reach the I_2 indifference surface—representing his original level of welfare.

It should be manifest that, because of his occupational preference for B, the positive rent from working in B rather than A is accom-

343

panied by a smaller money return. Indeed, the textbook definition of rent, turning on the difference between the factor's current earnings and their transfer earnings, would in this instance be negative for the worker who chooses the B occupation, whereas it is clearly a positive rent on the CV or EV definitions.[2]

---

2 By a *positive* rent in this connection we mean an *increment* in his welfare from being in B rather than in A; an increment of welfare that can be measured either as the EV or as the CV of the move from A to B.

Chapter 51

MARGINAL CURVE MEASURES OF RENT

1. The marginal curves I'_1 and I'_2 in Figure VI.10 correspond to I_1 and I_2 in Figure VI.8, except that, for conventional reasons, they are drawn from left to right. The I'_0 marginal indifference curve in the figure corresponds to some original I_0 curve) (not depicted in Figure VI.8) before any price was offered for the factor L. It is convenient, again, to draw these three curves as straight lines.

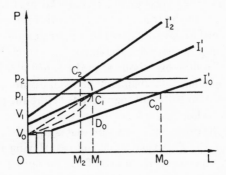

FIGURE VI.10

To fix our ideas we shall suppose L to be labour of a given skill, measured along the horizontal axis in hours per week in a specific industry A, the prices of all other factors and goods being taken as constant.[1]

---

1 We could have used a larger diagram to disclose the nature of the marginal indifference curve I'_0 by taking hourly increments of this labour and—parallel with out treatment of consumer's surplus—constructing successive columns, the heights of which would indicate the individual's valuation of each successive hour offered. Having gone through this process in connection with consumer's surplus in some detail already, we shall not repeat it—though we have drawn in the first three columns under the I'_0 to remind us of the process.

345

When the individual first contemplates employment in A, the I_0' curve is the locus of minimal payments required to induce him to offer there his successive increments of labour. If he receives these minimal payments, and no more, as he moves from left to right along the I_0', he is no better off at any point along it than he is at the beginning, prior to his employment there. The introduction now of an hourly wage, p_1, enables us to represent trianglular areas corresponding to his CV and EV.

2. The individual's CV is a sum of money equal to the area of the larger triangle $V_0C_0p_1$, determined as follows. The area beneath the I_0' curve up to the M_0^{th} unit, equal to $OV_0C_0M_0$, is the minimum sum of money needed to induce him to work the OM_0 hours, whereas the rectangular area, $Op_1C_0M_0$, is what he would be paid for working the OM_0 hours. The *excess* of this rectangular area over that minimum sum, equal to the triangle $V_0C_0p_1$, is therefore the maximum sum he can afford to pay for having the opportunity to sell his labour in A at p_1. For if he pays this maximum sum in exchange for this opportunity of selling his labour at p_1, he is just able—by choosing to work OM_0 hours—to maintain his welfare at the original I_0 level; being then no better off than he was before the p_1 opportunity was presented to him.

His EV, on the other hand, is a sum that is equal to the area of the smaller triangle $V_1p_1C_1$, explained as follows. Having availed himself of the p_1 price to offer OM_1 units of labour and reached the I_1 level of welfare, we put the question: what is the maximum sum he is willing to pay in order not to have to do any work in A.[2] This is equal to the area $OV_1C_1M_1$ under the I_1' curve. However, if he gives up the opportunity to sell his labour at p_1, the total income he forgoes is equal to the rectangular area $Op_1C_1M_1$. And this loss of income exceeds the most that he is willing to pay by the area of the

---

2 Along any marginal indifference curve, a movement *rising upward* (to the right, as drawn in the figure) implies a *giving up* of units, the vertical height therefore measures the *minimum* sums required for successive units offered. A movement *sloping downward* (to the left, as drawn in the figure) implies the *acquiring* of additional units—or the withdrawal of units once supplied. The vertical height therefore measures the *maximum* sums he will pay for additional units.

The same interpretation holds for the consumer's marginal indifference curves, although downward-sloping is, in contradistinction to the above Figure, to the right, and upward-sloping is to the left.

triangle $V_1p_1C_1$. In order, then, to retain this I_1 level of welfare (which he was able to reach with p_1) when p_1 is no longer available to him, he must receive a sum equal to the area of this triangle.[3]

By starting with a supply price equal to V_0 in Figure VI.10, a price at which the individual supplies nothing, and gradually raising the price to p_1, at which price he supplies OM_1 units, we generate the dotted-line supply curve of labour joining V_0 to C_1. For a 'normal' good or factor being offered (one for which *less* is offered as welfare increases), the supply curve will be steeper than the relevant marginal indifference curves. For an 'inferior' good or factor, on the other hand, the supply curve will be flatter than the marginal indifference curves. In the 'normal' case, Hicks' Marginal Valuation curve will also be steeper than the marginal indifference curves. And since, for each successive unit offered, the welfare effect (until the M_1^{th} unit is reached) is greater than that produced in generating the supply curve, the MV curve, indicated by the broken-line curve V_0C_1, will be above the supply curve.

3. We must now face the critical question: how well does the area between the price and the individual's supply price approximate the CV and EV measures of rent? Although the construction of diagrams of this sort can be somewhat arbitrary, it is well known that the supply curve can be much steeper than the marginal indifference curves and, indeed, can be backward-bending—implying a welfare effect that is positive and large relative to the substitution effect. What makes the welfare effect so important in the factor market are the existing economic institutions under which men tend to place all their labour in single occupations. The welfare of each worker, therefore, depends exclusively, or largely, on the level of a single factor price. It is quite possible, in fact as well as in theory, that a further rise in price from p_1 to p_2 would (if he were allowed to choose) result in the worker's choosing to supply OM_2 units, a smaller amount of labour than the OM_1 units he supplies at p_1. The resulting supply

---

3 The quantity-constrained CV, associated with the Marshallian measure, can also be represented in Figure VI.10. Once price p_1 is introduced the amount the individual chooses to supply is OM_1. The most he is willing to pay to obtain this price p_1, while at the same time being constrained to purchase OM_1 units, is a sum equal to the area $V_0D_0C_1p_1$, which is clearly smaller than the unconstrained CV, $V_0C_0p_1$, as indeed it has to be.

curve, passing through $V_0C_1C_2$, though it lies between the CV and EV measures of rent, could be very different from either. This would be bad enough if either measure were acceptable as satisfactory for the purpose in hand. But in a cost-benefit analysis, guided by the criterion of a potential Pareto improvement, it is the CV measure that is required.

Granted 'normal' welfare effects, a project that *raises* the supply price of the factor produces a CV measure of rent that could be significantly *larger* than the area above the supply price. The consequent underestimation of the rent accruing to the factor-owner might, erroneously, preclude an economically feasible project. On the other hand, for a project that *lowers* the supply price of a factor, the area defined by the CV could be significantly *smaller* than the area above the supply curve. The consequent overestimation of the loss of rent resulting from using the area above the supply price as a proxy for the CV measure might then, again, erroneously preclude projects that are economically feasible.[4] How important is this consideration likely to be?

4. As indicated earlier, in modern industry it is the general practice to offer workers a 'package deal'; in its simplest form a wage rate plus a constraint on the number of hours per day, and also on the number of days per week. Such constraints vary from industry to industry, and in occupations within the industry, but this fact makes no difference to the analysis of rent in such circumstances.

Suppose the hours per week in the A industry are set at forty, except in the particular case in which the worker, when offered p_1 per hour, would have in any case chosen to work forty hours, the

---

4 Under the same conditions, the conclusion for changes in the demand price is the opposite of that for the supply price. A project that *raises* the demand price of a good will, in the 'normal' case, have a CV (the minimum sum the consumer will accept as compensation) that is *larger* than the area under the demand curve. If the welfare involved is substantial, the consequent underestimation of the loss could result in a cost-benefit analysis, admitting projects that do not meet the criterion.

On the other hand, for a project that results in a *reduction* of the price of a good to the consumer, the CV is smaller than the area under the demand curve. The consequent overestimate of the gain from using the area under the demand curve as a proxy for the CV might again admit projects that are not economically feasible.

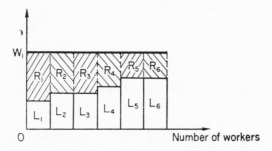

FIGURE VI.11

constraint will be operative. If so, his CV under the forty-hour
constraint will be smaller than it would be without it. Provided it is
positive, however, he will accept the all-or-nothing offer and make
some rent from it. The worker's CV under this constraint—the
maximum sum he will pay in order to have the opportunity to work
the forty-hour week in A at p_1—is the excess of the weekly wage over
the minimum payment he will require. And this minimum weekly
payment he would accept can be represented in Figure VI.11,
as the area of a unit L column with height equal to such minimum
sum. Since the figure ranks the columns in ascending order of height,
column L_1 corresponds to the minimal sum of the first worker;
he would accept a sum lower than all the others and, in consequence,
makes the largest (constrained) CV rent. Letting the total pay for the
forty-hour week be measured as $O W_1$ on the vertical axis, the CV
measure of rent for the first worker is represented by R_1; the shaded
extension of column L_1 to height W_1. Similarly, the areas of R_2, R_3,
R_4, . . . indicate the rents of workers 2, 3, 4, and so on.

Clearly the stepped line got by tracing the tops of the L columns
indicates the beginning of the supply curve of labour for that industry. If we continued adding workers in ascending order of height
we should eventually engage a worker say the nth worker whose L
column was just below, or equal to, the height of the W_1 line. All
workers in the industry, save possibly the nth, will be making a rent.

Where large numbers of workers are involved we may draw a
continuous supply curve to the point of intersection with the weekly-
wage line, the total rent to the workers in this industry being the
area enclosed between the wage line and the supply curve. A length-
ening of the working week, or any other restriction, would be rep-

resented as an upward shifting of this supply curve. The equilibrium number of workers would fall, and the rents of each of the remaining number would be reduced.

We may conclude, tentatively, that notwithstanding the difficulties discussed in connection with the *individual* supply curve, the constraints imposed by industry are such that the area above the supply curve of a particular type of labour to an industry offers a good measure of the rent enjoyed by the number employed. The gain or loss of rent resulting from a rise or fall in the weekly wage can now also be measured in the conventional way.

NOTE C: ALLOCATION, DISTRIBUTION AND EQUITY

Chapter 52
THE CHOICE OF L LAW OR L̄ LAW

1. The effects of the law of liability both on the valuation of the spillovers and on the magnitude of costs of implementing potential improvements have been considered separately in Part III (Chapters 19–21). Each is important in itself, but when added together, as they are in this chapter, they strengthen the argument that the law of liability is a potent factor in determining the economic feasibility of investment projects and the level of optimal outputs. To pursue the argument further, we shall continue to restrict our attention to a mutual-agreement solution in which, provisionally, the only way of dealing with spillovers is taken to be through output-reduction. The conclusions are, however, readily extended to the other ways of dealing with spillovers by mutual agreement.

2. Figure VI.12 is similar to that of Figure III.2 (p. 138) except that two marginal spillover curves have been drawn, $E_L E'_L$ corresponding to the $\bar{L}$ law, and $E_{\bar{L}} E'_{\bar{L}}$—corresponding to the $\bar{L}$ law. BB_1 represents, as before, the excess commercial benefit curve which is here assumed to be invariant to the state of the law.

If the L law prevails, competitive equilibrium is initially at B_1. This L-determined output of x, OB_1, plus its accompanying spillover, determines the welfare level of the victims. Their CV of the spillover produced by the last unit of x—the maximum sum they would collectively, offer for its elimination—is, by reference to the $E_L E'_L$ curve, calculated as equal to the vertical distance $E'_L B_1$. The most the victims will offer to the manufacturer to forgo the production of successive units of x, *less* the associated reduction of excess commercial benefit, continues to be positive until an optimal output

351

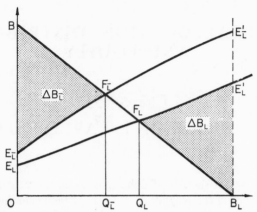

FIGURE VI.12

Q_L is reached. The resulting dotted triangular area, ΔB_L, measures the ESB_L (the potential Pareto improvement) of reducing output under the L law to its optimal. If this area exceeds G_L, the G costs under the L law, then RSB_L, the residual social benefit under the L law, is positive, and the optimal output Q_1 will be established. On the other hand, if G_L exceeds ESB_L, the RSB_L is negative, and output remains at OB_1. In that case the overall net benefit to society of producing this output OB_1 is equal to the triangle BE_LF_L less ΔB_L. This may be positive, zero, or negative. If negative. it would mean that as a result of G_L being larger than ESB_L, and too large, therefore, to justify a reduction of output to Q_L, the production of x will be carried on at a level that, on balance, entails an overall loss to society. Any subsequent inference by the economist that a *reduction* of the competitive equilibrium output OB_1 should not be undertaken, on the grounds that RSB of the movement to the Q_L optimum is negative, is clearly unwarranted. Once we take a step toward realism, and introduce the costs of implementation, G, into the calculation, one has therefore to look again at the overall social gain of producing the good at all—at the *total* conditions, in effect.

If, now, the $\bar{L}$ law prevailed, the spillover being prohibited (in the absence of mutual agreement) the initial output of x, and its spillovers, would be zero. Under the $\bar{L}$ law, therefore, the welfare level of the potential spillover victims will intially be higher than it is under L law. The sum of the minimal payments they are ready to accept for bearing with successive units of spillover, so maintaining their initial welfare, is given by spillover evaluation curve $E_{\bar{L}}E'_{\bar{L}}$ and—assuming they receive no more than the sums indicated by this curve—the optimal output under the $\bar{L}$ law is $OQ_{\bar{L}}$ and the corresponding $ESB_{\bar{L}}$ is the dotted triangular area $B_{\bar{L}}$. If this $ESB_{\bar{L}}$ exceeds the corresponding $G_{\bar{L}}$ necessary for its implementation, the $RSB_{\bar{L}}$ is positive, and the output $Q_{\bar{L}}$ will be reached. If, however, the magnitude of $G_{\bar{L}}$ exceeds $ESB_{\bar{L}}$, the output x will not be produced at all. In producing a zero output there is, of course, neither loss nor gain.

3. Let us consider all the possibilities: first, if the RSB is positive under either law, the optimal output-adjustment always takes place. Under the L law this will be output OQ_L, which is smaller than the output $OQ_{\bar{L}}$ under the $\bar{L}$ law. Second, if the RSB differs according to the law of liability, we have two interesting cases; (a) RSB_L is positive while $RSB_{\bar{L}}$ is negative, in which cases the optimal output OQ_L is reached under the L law, whereas if the $\bar{L}$ prevails, the output produced is zero, and (b), the reverse of this, RSB_L is negative while $RSB_{\bar{L}}$ is positive, in which cases the full output, OB_1, tends to be produced under the L law, whereas, if the $\bar{L}$ prevails, the optimal output $OQ_{\bar{L}}$ is realized.

The (a) case means simply that if $\bar{L}$ law prevails there can be no output of x which is socially desirable. In other words, only in the absence of any production of x can the economy be at an optimal position; any output of x (including the 'optimal' output $Q_{\bar{L}}$) entails a potential Pareto loss. If, however, the L law prevails, and the unchecked commercial output tends to OB_1, the optimal output OQ_L tends to be realized.[1] Case (b) shows that if L law prevails, the competitive output OB_1 appears socially desirable, whereas if $\bar{L}$ law prevails the socially desirable solution, and the one which tends to occur, requires that output $OQ_{\bar{L}}$ be produced.

The third possibility, is that the RSB is negative under either law. No output at all is produced under the $\bar{L}$ law whereas (unless the economist intervenes with an argument about the total conditions) under the L law the competitive output OB_1 is produced.

---

1 Moreover, if the law is changed from $\bar{L}$ to L, then output of x is changed from zero to Q_L, whereas if it is changed from being L to $\bar{L}$, the change in output is merely from Q_L to $Q_{\bar{L}}$.

These three possibilities, (1) each RSB positive under either law, (2) RSB_L positive under L, negative under $\bar{L}$ law (and the reverse for $RSB_{\bar{L}}$) and (3) each RSB negative under either law, have one result in common; that under L law the output of x is always larger than under $\bar{L}$ law, the difference being least for (1) and most for (3). Thus, for (1) the difference is only that between Q_L and $Q_{\bar{L}}$; for (2) it is either (a) that between Q_L and zero, or (b) that between B_1 output and $Q_{\bar{L}}$;[2] while for (3) the difference is between B_1 output and zero output.

This third possibility is the more interesting one. If, owing to G costs being too large, we have a choice of law under which we produce 'all or nothing', we shall be getting 'too much' spillover under the L law and 'too little' under the $\bar{L}$ law. There is no way of knowing in advance, in such an event, which law offers more (or less) social gain. Under the $\bar{L}$, with zero output being the overall optimal outcome, nothing is to be added to social welfare. Under an L law, with OB_1 output being the overall optimal outcome, the potential Pareto improvement of producing OB_1, as compared with producing nothing, is given by area of triangle BE_LF_L less that of triangle ΔB_L, and this, as indicated, can be positive, zero, or negative.[3]

4. Thinking of this all-or-nothing case, we conclude that there are some spillover-generating activities which, under an L law will be completely unhampered, and under an $\bar{L}$ law completely supressed. But, if on allocative grounds alone, we have to choose as between L and $\bar{L}$ law, we cannot determine where the balance of advantage lies without empirical knowledge—provided that mutual agreement about dealing with spillovers is confined to the output changes of

2 The analysis requires a slight modification because of the likelihood that where compensation is received from, or paid to, the potential spillover victims, they are likely to receive more than the absolute minimum they will accept, or pay less than the absolute maximum they can afford. If so, their post-agreement welfare will be greater than it is in the pre-agreement stage under either law and, as a consequence the spillover–valuation curves will be above those in the figure. The optimal outputs resulting will, therefore, be somewhat to the left of Q_L and $Q_{\bar{L}}$ in the Figure.

3 Where (a) $RSB_{\bar{L}}$ is negative and RSB_L is positive, the $\bar{L}$ law yields no social gain, while the L law entails a potential Pareto improvement (after taking account of G_L). Where (b) $RSB_{\bar{L}}$ is positive and RSB_L is negative, the $\bar{L}$ entails a potential Pareto improvement (after taking account of $G_{\bar{L}}$) while under the L law the potential Pareto improvement can be positive, zero, or negative.

method I. If, however, we now consider method II (the use of preventive devices), there appears to be a case on allocative grounds for preferring L̄ law. And we should, indeed, consider the II method for the good reason that preventive devices are generally believed to be a less costly way of dealing with spillovers than reducing output.

Although the three possibilities with respect to L and L̄ law discussed in connection with method I have their counterparts in connection with method II concerning preventive devices—except, of course, that with method II the amount of spillover alone is affected, and not output of x also—there is now a significant and 'dynamic' factor to be reckoned with. Once the burden of spillover-compensation enters into the costs of production (or the costs of using a good), as it does under L̄ law, private industry—searching for the lowest cost method of conforming with the legal requirements—has an interest in discovering preventive devices to avoid comparatively heavy compensatory payments. Wherever industry succeeds, a real economic saving is effected. Under the L law in contrast, there is no similar incentive for industry to investigate and develop as cheap a preventive device as possible. Putting the matter more formally, under L law the entrepreneur, allocating his research funds among alternatives according to equi-marginal principles, will tend to ignore all opportunities for social gains (of replacing welfare-compensatory costs by the lower costs of preventive devices) which might be made by directing research funds into developing improved preventive devices. So long as he is not held accountable for the spillover effects, he concludes, correctly, that directing resources into research to diminish the magnitude of these social afflictions, which necessarily reduce social welfare, serves only to reduce his profit. Under the L̄ law, on the other hand, organized research into ways of reducing spillover costs counts as much, as indeed it should, as research into other ways of reducing costs.

5. Although, as has been stated repeatedly, the rationale of cost-benefit analysis derives solely from the Pareto principle, it is not true that the liberal economist is impervious to a consideration of all other social issues. In particular, taking his values from the community for which he is evaluating the projects in question, he is concerned with the distribution of real income and with the broader

issue of equity. The question of such social considerations entering separately into the final decision and, possibly, qualifying, or conflicting with, the cost-benefit calculation is not being raised here. The question at issue is that of facing a choice he has so far unwittingly evaded in this connection; the choice of basing his cost-benefit evaluations on L law or $\bar{L}$ law. Where the spillovers of a project are large, it can, as suggested, make a crucial difference. The case made out above for habitual recourse to $\bar{L}$ law can be strengthened by some reflection on its implications for welfare distribution and equity.

With respect to welfare distribution, the arguments are tentative but far from negligible. It may be possible to show that the goods which generate significant spillovers earn incomes for, and/or are bought by, groups having higher incomes than average. It may also be possible to show that spillovers such as polutants and traffic noise tend to fall more heavily on poorer neighbourhoods[4]. Inasmuch as environmental quality enters heavily into welfare (though not into GNP) the distribution of welfare may be more regressive than that of 'real' disposable income.

6. Equity is better served by $\bar{L}$ law. In the absence of comprehensive sanctions against trespass on the citizen's amenity, existing institutions lend themselves inadvertently to a process of blackmail in so far as they place the burden of reaching agreement on the person or group whose interests have been damaged Although the disamenities inflicted on innocent parties may be judged with less severity when they are generated as a by-product of the pursuit of profit or pleasure than when, instead, they are generated for the sole purpose of exacting payment from the victim, in either case a Pareto improvement is met by agreement between the parties.

---

4 'Rich' and 'poor' neighbourhoods must be identified before the spillovers appear. If, in fact, spillovers are randomly spread among 'rich' and 'poor' neighbourhoods to start with, and that, as a result the poor began to move into spillover affected areas (in consequence of the decline in property values) and the rich began to move into the unaffected areas, the resulting association between spillover areas and income-groups could not be adduced as evidence for the thesis that spillovers reduce the welfare of the poor more than the rich. In the real world, the existing situation is likely to be the result both of initial discrimination against poorer neighbourhoods and of the subsequent reaction of rich and poor to the spread of spillovers.

The alleged neutrality of the Pareto principle, in respect of the question of who should compensate whom, is to be interpreted only as a matter of complete indifference as between the two alternative ways of giving effect to it. Indeed, the principle, as it were, deliberately opts out of the question. So far as it can be invoked, person N compensating person S to desist is as valid an application of the principle as that of person S compensating person N in order to indulge.

But the two situations may be Pareto symmetric without their being ethically symmetric. The fact that the conflict of interest is mutual does not of itself imply that the sort of settlement effected is a matter of *indifference* to society. Indeed, the neutrality of the Pareto principle is to be conceived simply as a *disregard* of the ethics involved. It is true that if the non-smoker's enjoyment is reduced by the smoker's freedom to smoke, so also is the smoker's enjoyment reduced by having to refrain from smoking to satisfy the non-smoker. Yet smoker and non-smoker are not thereby put on an equal footing. In accordance with the liberal maxim, the freedom of any man, say, to smoke what he wants and where he wants is conceded—but along with the critical proviso that his smoking take place in circumstances which do not reduce the welfare of others. In so far as this critical proviso is not met, the freedom of the smoker to smoke is not symmetric with the freedom desired by the non-smoker. For the non-smoker's desired freedom does not go beyond the breathing of smokeless air. And, unlike the freedom sought by the smoker, it does not reduce the amenity of the other party. The logic of this example is to be extended to the satisfaction a person enjoys as a result of his operating a noisy vehicle, lawn-mower, transistor, a satisfaction that has the incidental effect of destroying the amenity of others. The person who is content to live quietly does not, thereby, damage the welfare of others. In short, the fact that there is a conflict of interest—and an opportunity for mutual benefit—does not imply equal culpability. Unless, therefore, the law is altered so as to provide effective and comprehensive safeguards for the citizen—which is implied by L̄ law—no agreement concluded under the existing L law can be vindicated on ethical grounds.[5]

7. Once the inequity of the L law, in an economy producing adverse spillovers, is acknowledged, reflection suggests that it is more serious than might appear from the consideration alone of a single spillover event. For any Pareto improvement under the L law is one which must begin from the distribution of welfare as determined by reference to the existing amounts of spillover in the economy. Since under L law the initial loss of welfare from those subjected to the spillovers of some new project is estimated as the maximum they would offer to be rid of it—and *not* the larger sum; the minimum they would accept for bearing with it—$\Sigma\, Vi > 0$ is not necessarily met, and there is therefore no assurance that ESB or RSB could be met. Yet the project may qualify under the L law. Since potential victims, under such a law, have no means of limiting in advance, the level to which their welfares may be reduced in consequence of the spillovers yet to be produced along with market goods, their welfare may decline so far as to make life well-nigh intolerable.

Even if negotiation costs fall over time, or if the government appoints an agency to provide the initiative necessary to reach voluntary agreements where possible, the mere fact of the spillovers having grown over time will make any worthwhile Pareto improvement less likely. For the effect of maintaining L law for some time is to permit the growth of spillover-creating industries, and perhaps also to allow some industries to flourish which would not have come into being at all under an $\bar{L}$ law. Eventually, the numbers using the products of such industries, the numbers employed in them, the wealth of the

---

5 Unless there are constant costs over the range of output variation—a not unlikely circumstance—an exogenous change in, say, the demand of a group will, as indicated earlier, affect the welfare of others through changes in goods and factor prices. The attempt to trace welfare changes back to those whose market actions caused them would be too costly a venture to be feasible. The market is justly regarded as an impersonal mechanism. But it is not feasibility alone that differentiates the market-induced welfare changes from those resulting from external effects. Whether an increase, say, in the demand for good x causes its price, and those of related goods, to rise or fall, the resulting distribution of real income may be progressive or regressive. If a judgment were to be made of the market-induced welfare effects it could be made on grounds of distribution only. It could not be made—as it can in the case of external diseconomies—on grounds of equity alone.

owners, and the power and influence of the managers, combine to create a formidable interest that is as difficult to oppose on economic principle as it is difficult to dislodge by political means. For as the magnitude of the spillovers, and of the numbers and wealth of those interested in maintaining them, have grown, the reduction of spillovers back to any initial tolerable level becomes increasingly costly—whether in terms of compensatory payments, preventive devices, or any other method. It becomes, therefore, increasingly unlikely that such a reduction of spillovers will qualify as a Pareto improvement (ESB). Let the L law remain in force long enough, and such a Pareto improvement may become a virtual impossibility. And if, therefore, from such time on all decisions on the spillover problem are referred by the economist to the Pareto principle, there will be nothing to prevent these spillovers increasing without limit, and nothing to prevent the environment sinking ever lower in the scale of amenity. In such circumstances, the case in equity for seeking guidance via the Pareto principle alone is very weak, and the case for establishing L̄ law to redress the existing inequity is very strong.

REFERENCES AND BIBLIOGRAPHY FOR PART VI

Buchanan, J. and Tullock, G. *The Calculus of Consent*. Michigan: University of Michigan Press, 1962.

Dobb, M. *Welfare Economics and the Economics of Socialism*. Cambridge: Cambridge University Press, 1969.

Graaff, J. de V. *Theoretical Welfare Economics*. Cambridge, England, 1957.

Henderson, A. 'Consumers's Surplus and the Compensating Variation', *Review of Economic Studies*, 1941.

Hicks, J. R. *Value and Capital*. Oxford: Clarendon Press, 1939.

—— 'The Four Consumers' Surpluses', *Review of Economic Studies*, 1944.

Hotelling, H. 'The General Welfare in Relation to Problems of Taxation and of Railway and Utility Rates', *Econometrica*, 1938.

Kaldor, N. 'Welfare Propositions in Economics', *Economic Journal*, 1939.

Little, I. M. D. *A Critique of Welfare Economics* (2nd edn.) Oxford: Oxford University Press, 1957.

Marshall, A. *Principles of Economics* (8th edn.). London, Macmillan, 1924.

Mishan, E. J. 'The Recent Debate on Welfare Criteria', *Oxford Economic Papers*, 1965.

—— ' A Reappraisal of the Principles of Resource Allocation', *Economica*, 1957.

Nath, S. *A Reappraisal of Welfare Economics*. London: Routledge & Kegan Paul, 1969.

Pigou, A. C. *The Economics of Welfare* (4th edu.). London: Macmillan, 1932.

Rothenberg, J. *The Measurement of Social Welfare*. New Jersey: Prentice Hall, 1961.

Samuelson, P. A. *Foundations of Economic Analysis* (2nd edn.). Cambridge, Mass.: Harvard University Press, 1963.
Scitovsky, T. 'A Note on Welfare Propositions in Economics', *Review of Economic Studies*, 1941.
Tinbergen, J. *Economic Policy, Principles and Design*. Amsterdam, 1966.

Index